Science and Ethics

The Axiological Contexts of Science

P.I.E. Peter Lang

Bruxelles · Bern · Berlin · Frankfurt am Main · New York · Oxford · Wien

Evandro AGAZZI & Fabio MINAZZI (eds.)

Science and Ethics

The Axiological Contexts of Science

"Philosophy & Politics"
No. 14

Papers presented at the Joint Meeting of the International Academy for Philosophy of Science and the International Academy for Religious Sciences, with the support of the Dipartimento di Filologia Classica e di Scienze Filosofiche dell'Università del Salento, held in Lecce on 17-21 October 2003.

The publication of this volume has received the financial support of the Dipartimento di Filologia Classica e di Scienze Filosofiche dell'Università del Salento, under the Programmma di ricerca cofinanziato del MUR, cofin anno 2005, prot. 2005772593-004, section of Lecce, person in charge, prof F. Minazzi.

© P.I.E. PETER LANG s.a.
Éditions scientifiques internationales
Brussels, 2008
1 avenue Maurice, 1050 Brussels, Belgium
info@peterlang.com; www.peterlang.com

Printed in Germany

ISSN 1376-0920
ISBN 978-90-5201-426-5
D/2008/5678/44

Library of Congress Cataloging-in-Publication Data
Science and ethics : the axiological contexts of science /
Evandro Agazzi & Fabio Minazzi (eds.).
p. cm. — (Philosophy & politics ; no. 14)
«Papers presented at the joint meeting of the International Academy for Philosophy of Science and the International Academy for Religious Sciences, with the support of the Dipartimento di filologia classica e di Scienze filosofiche dell'Università del Salento, held in Lecce on 17-21 October 2003.» — ISBN 978-90-5201-426-5
1. Science—Philosophy—Congresses. I. Agazzi, Evandro. II. Minazzi, Fabio, 1955-   Q174.S24 2008   501—dc22   2008033656

CIP also available from the British Library, GB

Bibliographic information published by "Die Deutsche Bibliothek". "Die Deutsche Bibliothek" lists this publication in the "Deutsche National-bibliografie": detailed bibliographic data is available on the Internet at <http://dnb.ddb.de>.

Table of Contents

SECOND SECTION. SCIENCE, ETHICS AND RELIGION

Les contextes axiologiques de la science

Evandro Agazzi & Fabio Minazzi

Président de l'Académie Internationale de Philosophie des Sciences
Professeur à l'Université del Salento et membre de l'Académie
Internationale de Philosophie des Sciences

Le thème des rapports entre science et valeurs a une longue histoire et a pendant longtemps été conçu comme une question concernant la possibilité, voire la nécessité, de *séparer* la sphère de la science de celle des valeurs. La thèse de la séparation, résumée dans la célèbre notion de *Wertfreiheit* élaborée par Max Weber, semblait d'autant plus justifiée qu'elle avait été défendue dans le contexte épistémologique par un savant qui reconnaissait aux valeurs une place et un rôle de premier ordre dans la réalisation des actions humaines et dans leur étude scientifique. En effet Weber a clairement affirmé qu'il est impossible de comprendre et d'expliquer les actions humaines sans une *référence aux valeurs* qui les inspirent (*Wertbezogenheit*), mais en même temps il affirmait que tout *jugement de valeur* doit être banni de la reconstruction, de la compréhension et de l'explication des actions humaines qui a lieu dans les *sciences* historiques et sociales. Une telle ambivalence n'avait guère le sens d'une ambiguïté parce qu'elle correspondait à une distinction traditionnelle dans l'histoire de la pensée, une distinction qui avait été poussée jusqu'aux limites d'une véritable séparation au sein de la philosophie moderne, celle entre connaissance et action. L'action humaine a ceci de spécifique (par rapport, par exemple, à un processus physique ou à un simple comportement animal), qu'elle est conçue et se réalise en vue de quelque fin consciemment voulue et, parmi les fins qui inspirent ou motivent les actions humaines, il y en a certaines qui sont considérées particulièrement dignes d'être poursuivies et qu'on appelle habituellement *valeurs*. Les valeurs définissent ce que les actions *doivent* ou *ne doivent pas* réaliser et, par conséquent, elles permettent d'exprimer à propos d'une action donnée un *jugement de valeur* qui consiste en déclarer une telle action positive ou négative par rapport à la valeur considérée. On voit donc qu'il existe une différence entre la fin effective qu'un certain individu ou un certain groupe de personnes se proposent de poursuivre (et qu'on peut qualifier comme la « valeur de référence » qui explique leur type d'action) et des éventuelles autres valeurs sur la base desquelles on voudrait exprimer sur cette action un *jugement de valeur* en disant, par exemple, si elle est bonne ou mauvaise. Le scientifique (voilà la thèse de Weber) ne peut pas éviter de faire référence à telle ou telle valeur qu'il estime avoir inspiré les actions humaines qu'il essaie de comprendre et d'expliquer (en cela consiste son travail d'historien ou de sociologue), mais il doit scrupuleusement s'abstenir de prononcer un jugement de valeur sur lesdites actions ou lesdites valeurs, à savoir de les *approuver* ou *désapprouver* puisque s'il le faisait il ferait entrer en jeu *ses propres valeurs* et par cela même son travail perdrait la caractéristique de l'*objectivité* qui est le véritable trait distinctif de la scientificité et, en particulier, celui qui permet de revendiquer la scientificité des sciences humaines face aux sciences naturelles, en dépit des nombreuses différences qui les séparent.

Deux choses résultent facilement de ce qu'on vient de dire : en premier lieu, que les « valeurs » par rapport auxquelles on doit suspendre le jugement sont en pratique les valeurs politiques et éthiques ; en deuxième lieu, que la raison de cette interdiction est la conviction (que Weber affirme explicitement) que lesdites valeurs sont *subjectives* car il n'est pas possible de les fonder et de les défendre selon une méthode strictement rationnelle. Elles sont indispensables à tout être humain pour conduire une vie pleine, consciente, engagée, fournie de sens, et chacun a le droit de lutter pour faire triompher ses propres valeurs, mais en même temps l'homme de science a une sorte de devoir suprême, qu'on pourrait qualifier comme l'impératif de l'honnêteté intellectuelle : ne jamais permettre que ses propres valeurs influencent la présentation et l'interprétation *objective* des faits qu'il étudie, et jamais exploiter les résultats objectifs de sa recherche comme supports dans la défense de ses valeurs personnelles. Nous pourrions dire que l'ancien idéal de l'unicité de la vérité, qui rechasse tout relativisme, et qui s'était affaibli mais aussi reconfirmé dans la notion moderne de l'*objectivité scientifique*, imposait à la science de ne pas se laisser contaminer par ce « polythéisme des valeurs » qui, selon Weber, caractérise les sociétés modernes.

Que dire de cette dichotomie ? Elle présente sans doute des aspects très plausibles dont, d'abord, la distinction entre questions et jugements de fait et questions et jugements de valeur : en effet, la tâche d'établir « comment sont les choses » est différente de la possibilité de prononcer sur cet état de choses n'importe quel jugement positif ou négatif (et même préalable à une telle possibilité). En deuxième lieu, il faut aussi reconnaître que justement dans le domaine des sciences historiques et sociales le risque que les « faits » soient sélectionnés, présentés, interprétés de manière partiale ou partisane est réel et d'autant plus sérieux si l'auteur de la recherche est un intellectuel « engagé » sur le plan politique. Donc la méfiance à l'égard d'une possibilité de faire un véritable travail scientifique *objectif* dans ces domaines exigeait qu'une telle séparation entre jugements de fait et jugements de valeur soit présentée comme règle épistémologique fondamentale par tout auteur intéressé à défendre la scientificité de ces disciplines, ce que Weber a fait.

En dépit de toutes ces bonnes raisons on ne voit pas trop bien comment l'homme de science pourrait être une personne sincèrement engagée au service de certaines valeurs et en même temps soigneuse de ne pas laisser entrer en contact ces valeurs avec le contenu de ce travail de recherche qui constitue en effet la partie prépondérante de son activité, de sa vie concrète et, encore plus, on ne voit pas pourquoi il devrait se condamner à cette sorte de schizophrénie. La réponse à cette question se trouve dans l'esprit complexe qui a caractérisé la civilisation de l'Occident entre la moitié du XIXe et la moitié du XXe siècle, à savoir une fascination « romantique » des idéaux socio-politiques « forts » et opposés (libéralisme, nationalisme, socialisme, communisme, fascisme, nazisme) d'un côté, et de l'autre côté, un culte de la science comme forme suprême (en tant qu'objective et fiable) de la connaissance humaine (positivisme). Or, une des conditions principales pour assurer à la science son caractère de connaissance objective (préalablement à toute détermination de règles strictement méthodologiques) semblait être celle de se présenter comme *désintéressée* et ceci comportait, en premier lieu, que la connaissance scientifique ne soit pas « mise au service » d'intérêts autres que la pure connaissance, avec le risque de manipulation qui s'en suivrait. Mais sur le plan même de la connaissance on devrait essayer de soustraire les affirmations scientifiques au risque d'un attachement ou superprotection qui les concerne : c'est la thèse de Popper, selon laquelle la véritable attitude scientifique consiste, une fois formulée une hypothèse (conjecture) qu'on croit bonne, non pas dans l'effort de trouver des données expérimentales qui la confirment, mais bien de la soumettre aux plus sévères preuves visant à la « falsifier ». Seulement si elle résiste à toutes ces tentatives elle peut être (provisoirement) retenue. Une fois encore, on peut se demander si les scientifiques se comportent réellement dans leur travail selon le style quasi ascétique présenté par Popper, mais cette question n'est pas importante puisque celui de Popper veut être un modèle idéal, ou une « idée régulatrice » dans le sens de Kant, modèle qui est satisfait de manière imparfaite dans la pratique concrète.

La discussion sur la *Wertfreiheit* restait, en fin de compte, assez délimitée au domaine des sciences humaines où elle avait été lancée par Weber car, comme nous l'avons vu, les « valeurs » en question étaient les valeurs politiques et sociales et il semblait évident que, dans les sciences mathématiques et naturelles, cette condition d'indépendance par rapport aux valeurs se réalisait automatiquement puisqu'il n'y a pas de possibilité en elles pour des jugements de valeur, vu que les valeurs concernent uniquement les actions humaines. Toutefois la situation commença graduellement à changer autour de la moitié du XXe siècle, quand la stricte interrelation entre science et technique, devenue inextricable au cours de ce même siècle, présenta de manière éclatante les premiers exemples de *faits* rendus possibles par les technologies les plus avancées, qui posaient des questionnements nouveaux et dramatiques d'ordre éthique, social et politique (que l'on pense à la bombe atomique, aux désastres écologiques, à la pollution de l'environnement, etc.). Il s'agissait de faits contenant au moins beaucoup d'aspects clairement *négatifs* d'après des jugements de valeur et qui apparaissaient comme le produit voulu, ou comme les conséquences non voulues, des technologies modernes qui, partant, en furent considérées *responsables* : comme les technologies sont, à leur tour, en grande partie l'application de connaissances scientifiques particulièrement avancées, l'imputation de responsabilité toucha rapidement la science elle-même.

C'est ainsi que démarra une longue querelle autour de la *neutralité de la science* qui dura une vingtaine d'années et s'épuisa sans parvenir à des résultats suffisamment définis à cause du manque presque complet de convergence sur la signification que les gens engagés dans la dispute donnaient aux concepts fondamentaux, en commençant par celui de « neutralité » et concernant aussi le concept même de science.

Un premier pas dans la direction d'une clarification peut consister dans la distinction de deux significations selon lesquelles on parle habituellement de science. Dans un premier sens, une science (et la science dans son ensemble) est conçue comme un système de connaissances, comme un *savoir* formulé en propositions qui sont acceptées en tant que considérées *vraies* d'après certains critères méthodologiques objectifs. Dans un autre sens, une science est une forme particulière de l'*activité humaine*, une des multiples professions, et la science dans son ensemble est un système très complexe de telles activités. À ce point, si on conçoit la neutralité dans un sens très général, à savoir comme « indépendance » de toute forme de conditionnement, il semble relativement facile d'admettre que la science en tant que *savoir* est et doit rester « neutre » par rapport à tout conditionnement, dans le sens qu'une proposition ou une théorie scientifique doivent être acceptées ou rejetées uniquement parce qu'elles sont considérées vraies (ou fausses) sur la base des critères objectifs et strictement cognitifs que la science en question adopte. Permettre que des considérations morales, politiques, économiques, idéologiques, ou des intérêts de n'importe quelle autre nature puissent induire à accepter une proposition fausse ou à rejeter une proposition vraie signifierait simplement violer la nature spécifique de la connaissance scientifique et, si une telle violation était considérée légitime, on arriverait à priver notre civilisation de cette énorme conquête qu'a été la science. Toutefois, si on considère la science comme un grand système *d'activités humaines* le discours change totalement, car toute action humaine est projetée et réalisée en vue d'un ensemble très articulé de fins, sur la base d'une série assez complexe de motivations et de conditionnements et il serait non seulement naïf de penser que la science puisse faire exception à cette règle, mais bien plus il serait absurde de proposer une telle « neutralité » comme idéal, car une activité humaine vidée de motivations et de finalités, indifférente par rapport à ses conséquences, insensible à l'égard de son contexte social serait en réalité une activité dépourvue de sens, une routine « aliénée » indigne, en particulier, des personnes intellectuellement cultivées qui l'exercent.

On arrive de cette manière à envisager un problème difficile, mais assez clair : comment concilier la neutralité de la science en tant que savoir avec sa non-neutralité en tant qu'activité humaine, ou, si l'on préfère, sa « neutralité cognitive » avec sa « non-neutralité pratique ». Mais voilà que la recherche de solutions pour ce problème déjà difficile a été rendue encore plus difficile à la suite de ce qu'on pourrait appeler un malheureux accident historique qui a quasi imposé une indiscernabilité de pratique et de connaissance. L'histoire peut être résumée de la façon suivante : Popper avait présenté dès le début son principe de falsification comme un critère de démarcation entre science et non-science qui, en particulier, montrait le caractère non scientifique de deux théories en vogue, la psychanalyse et le marxisme. Ensuite il avait plaidé pour une extension de sa méthode de recherche par « conjectures et réfutations » à tout domaine de l'investigation humaine, en qualifiant cette attitude comme « rationalisme critique » qui s'opposait, en particulier, à l'attitude dogmatique des idéologies totalitaires. Après la Seconde Guerre mondiale (c'est-à-dire après la liquidation du fascisme et du nazisme) la cible de ce rationalisme critique restait le marxisme et, tandis que les marxistes « orthodoxes » des pays socialistes continuaient à défendre le marxisme comme théorie « scientifique » de la société, les néo-marxistes occidentaux (notamment les représentants de l'école de Francfort, mais aussi des auteurs comme Althusser et Goldmann en France) adoptaient une stratégie différente. Ils admettaient sans difficulté que le marxisme est une idéologie mais, en même temps, en développant la thèse de Marx et d'Engels selon laquelle les formes de la culture d'une société descendent de sa « structure » de base (consistant en ses formes et rapports de production) et en constituent l'idéologie, faisaient rentrer la science elle-même parmi les composants de l'idéologie. Toute société possède donc, à côté des institutions, des lois, des doctrines philosophiques et des croyances religieuses qui essaient de « légitimer » la position de la classe au pouvoir, aussi la science qui est au service de ses formes de production et aussi bien des standards intellectuels qui se prêtent à défendre la charpente idéologique du pouvoir. Partant on ne peut pas utiliser la science (qui est idéologique en elle-même) pour critiquer l'idéologie ; la prétendue science objective est en réalité la science de la société capitaliste qui doit être démasquée et combattue par tous ceux qui combattent le capitalisme, et ce qu'on dit de la science vaut en général pour toute connaissance : la connaissance est toujours en fonction de la praxis et sa valeur se mesure sur la base des valeurs qui inspirent la praxis (pas sur la base d'une prétendue vérité objective qui n'existe pas).

Pendant qu'en Europe les néo-marxistes diffusaient cette vision, un phénomène analogue se produisait aux États-Unis pour des raisons très différentes, c'est-à-dire à cause de l'influence académique croissante atteinte par la sociologie de la connaissance. Cette discipline, explicitement inaugurée par Mannheim avec un livre publié en Allemagne en 1929 et traduit aux États-Unis en 1956, soutenait que le contexte social détermine profondément soit les formes soit les contenus de notre connaissance, mais il admettait que les mathématiques et les sciences naturelles échappent à ce conditionnement. Avec la publication de *La structure des révolutions scientifiques* de Kuhn en 1962, par contre, une vision « sociologique » des sciences commence à s'affirmer à la suite d'une interprétation de la *dynamique* des théories scientifiques. L'épistémologie analytique issue du Cercle de Vienne ainsi que l'épistémologie popperienne se trouvaient d'accord en soutenant qu'une théorie scientifique T doit être abandonnée si elle entre en conflit avec un fait empirique E qu'elle n'est pas en mesure d'expliquer logiquement ou qui, encore plus, est en contradiction directe avec ses conclusions logiques ; elle est donc remplacée par une autre théorie T' qui doit être capable d'expliquer tous les faits qu'expliquait T et, en plus, aussi E. En cela consiste le progrès de la science. Par des analyses historiques, Kuhn montre que cette prétendue reconstruction logique du changement des théories est loin de correspondre à la réalité concrète : à chaque époque toute science se présente comme une investigation conduite par une *communauté scientifique* bien déterminée qui se définit par un *paradigme* dans lequel entrent des connaissances acceptées, des conceptions particulières concernant ce qu'est un problème scientifique et ce qui ne l'est pas, les méthodes de recherche admissibles, les instruments matériels et conceptuels utilisables et spécialement certaines conceptions et principes de grande généralité qui encadrent la recherche. Pendant qu'une communauté travaille à l'intérieur d'un certain paradigme (science normale), la recherche avance avec des petits changements cumulatifs qu'on peut approximativement interpréter selon le modèle logico-empirique traditionnel, mais cela ne suffit plus quand il s'agit de comprendre les grandes *révolutions* scientifiques. Celles-ci se produisent quand certaines « anomalies », qui résistent aux efforts d'explication selon le paradigme accepté, deviennent de plus en plus nombreuses et significatives et un nouveau paradigme, impliquant en particulier une manière complètement nouvelle de « voir » les choses, prend corps et s'impose à la communauté scientifique. Cette transition constitue une « révolution scientifique » et elle n'a pas les caractéristiques d'un élargissement ou d'une rectification du vieux paradigme d'après des exigences logiques ou empiriques, mais bien celui d'un changement brusque qui ressemble beaucoup à une « conversion » psychologique : les mêmes faits d'auparavant sont vus d'une manière très différente qui a certainement l'avantage de permettre d'expliquer les anomalies précédentes, mais qui est loin de compter, au moins initialement, sur les nombreuses confirmations empiriques et les liaisons logiques dont jouissait le paradigme abandonné. En bref, ce que sont un fait scientifique, une méthode scientifique correcte, un problème scientifique légitime, un résultat empirique ou théorique établi, une théorie scientifique acceptable dépendent des paradigmes adoptés par les communautés scientifiques à l'intérieur desquelles a lieu la recherche en question et n'ont qu'un rapport très vague et faible avec une prétendue « réalité » extérieure qui est soumise à la recherche et même avec les exigences de rigueur logique et exactitude empirique qui semblent constituer le fondement de la rationalité scientifique. Compte tenu des facteurs multiples et en grand partie non explicités et même inconscients qui entrent dans la formation et spécialement dans l'acceptation d'un paradigme de la part d'une communauté scientifique, on peut dire que cette conception de la science de Kuhn – qu'on pourrait appeler « micro-sociologique » parce qu'elle rend la science entièrement dépendante de collectivités restreintes telles que les communautés scientifiques – comporte déjà une profonde influence de facteurs qu'on pourrait qualifier de « extra-cognitifs » sur la constitution de la connaissance scientifique, c'est-à-dire sur la science entendue comme *savoir*.

Le succès rapide de l'aperçu de Kuhn ne fut pas seulement une conséquence de la grande influence académique de la sociologie de la connaissance aux États-Unis à cette époque là, mais aussi d'une crise dont souffrait déjà l'épistémologie logico-empiriste pour des raisons internes, parmi lesquelles il suffirait de mentionner la thèse de l'holisme sémantique de Quine, qui impliquait l'impossibilité de déterminer dans les sciences des faits empiriques indépendants des théories et qui, en particulier, pourraient servir pour comparer des théories rivales ; ou encore la thèse de la sous-détermination empirique des théories, qui empêchait de considérer une théorie comme réellement « prouvée » par n'importe quelle richesse de confirmations empiriques. L'ensemble de ces raisons avait donc préparé le terrain (spécialement à l'intérieur de l'école de Popper) pour une rencontre avec la perspective sociologique de Kuhn qui, en effet, trouva son expression la plus connue dans les thèses de l'anarchisme méthodologique de Feyerabend et ses développements les plus radicaux dans les auteurs de l'« épistémologie sociologique » ainsi officiellement nommée (par exemple, B. Barnes, K. D. Knorr-Cetina, B. Latour et S. Woolgar), qui affirment la dépendance totale de la science pas seulement des micro-sociétés telles que les communautés scientifiques, mais de la structure complexe des sociétés prises au sens large de ce concept.

Mais quelle relation tout ce discours a-t-il avec le problème des rapports entre science et valeurs ? Il s'agit d'une relation assez floue qui pourrait être exprimée comme suit : d'une manière ou d'une autre, la thèse de la neutralité de la science a perdu beaucoup de terrain et bien des auteurs sont disposés à admettre qu'on ne peut pas se passer des valeurs dans la science. Mais malheureusement cette admission est très ambiguë. Par exemple, dans le cadre de la crise de l'épistémologie empiriste déjà mentionnée, plusieurs auteurs ont remarqué que le choix entre deux théories scientifiques capables d'expliquer logiquement les mêmes donnés empiriques n'est pas empêché pour cette raison, mais se fait sur la base d'autres critères tels que la simplicité, l'élégance, la fiabilité, la systématicité interne, la compatibilité avec les informations déjà acquises, la fécondité en prévisions et applications et ainsi de suite. Ces caractéristiques sont appelées souvent *valeurs* et il paraît donc naturel d'affirmer que, vu que les théories scientifiques sont soumises à ces « jugements de valeur » et préférées l'une à l'autre selon lesdits jugements, on doit reconnaître que la référence aux valeurs entre dans la constitution de la connaissance scientifique. Ce qui est critiquable dans cette perspective n'est pas le fait d'avoir explicité la complexité des « raisons » qui peuvent amener à faire le choix entre des théories rivales, mais le fait d'avoir qualifié comme « valeurs » les qualités susmentionnées sans souligner suffisamment que, dans le meilleur des cas, il s'agit de « valeurs épistémiques » qui, en réalité, font partie de la *méthodologie* des sciences, qui en précisent la structure *cognitive*, et ne concernent pas l'*axiologie* des sciences au sens propre. Celle-ci, au contraire, s'occupe des rapports entre la science et les valeurs non épistémiques et non cognitives et, en particulier, de ces valeurs éthiques, sociales et politiques que Weber avait affirmées ne pas devoir influencer l'établissement de la connaissance scientifique objective.

Voilà alors que, à cause de « faits » concrets facilement condamnés comme négatifs du point de vue moral et social (que nous avons déjà mentionnés), un courant de pensée qui a aussi rencontré une audience assez vaste chez l'opinion publique a imputé à la science la responsabilité desdits désastres et a donc affirmé que la science devait être soumise à des jugements de valeur au sens propre et être disciplinée par des restrictions qui en limitent la liberté (les manifestations les plus extrêmes de cette position arrivent à une véritable attitude de anti-science). Dans ce cas, nous assistons donc au renversement total de la thèse de la neutralité de la science, qui arrive facilement à nier sa portée objective et sa valeur cognitive. Face à cette situation, beaucoup de personnes convaincues de la valeur cognitive et culturelle de la science et en même temps sensibles aux problèmes éthiques et sociaux soulevés, se sont efforcées de soutenir l'« innocence » de la science, parfois en séparant nettement science et technologie et en chargeant la responsabilité des faits négatifs sur la seule technique, parfois en distinguant la science (qui est neutre) de l'*usage* de la science (qui peut être bon ou mauvais selon l'intention de ceux qui le pratiquent), parfois en distinguant la science de ses *conséquences* non voulues et imprévisibles, parfois enfin en renfermant science et technologie dans une sorte de tour d'ivoire où les gens travaillent à atteindre des connaissances pures ou efficaces sans aucun objectif extérieur en vue, tandis que, de l'autre côté, agissent les *pouvoirs* sociaux (spécialement économiques, politiques et militaires) qui pilotent et exploitent la recherche scientifique et technologique, et sur lesquels retombe entièrement la responsabilité éthique et sociale.

Entrer dans les détails de ces discussions n'aurait pas un grand intérêt, spécialement parce qu'elles souffrent en général du manque d'une distinction conceptuelle que nous avons déjà faite, celle entre la science entendue comme savoir et entendue comme activité humaine, distinction qui, n'étant pas une séparation, nous invite à trouver la manière de *concilier* le but *spécifique* de l'activité scientifique (qui est l'acquisition d'une connaissance objective et fiable) et la *pluralité de fins* qui influencent (de manière légitime et concrète) cette même activité. La chose devient d'autant plus claire qu'on considère le fait que la science est, particulièrement aujourd'hui, une grande entreprise sociale. De cette prise de conscience résulte en toute clarté la légitimité de jugements éthiques sur la science, puisque l'éthique, ayant comme but spécifique celui de proposer des normes de conduite pour n'importe quelle action humaine, ne peut trouver une exception dans l'activité scientifique (et cela bien au-delà des simples « conséquences » dangereuses des applications technologiques, mais déjà, par exemple, dans la considération des procédures concrètes de la recherche, de ses conditions d'exercice, etc.). Toutefois la chose plus intéressante est autre : si on considère la vie humaine telle qu'elle se réalise dans les contextes sociaux, on voit facilement que les valeurs ne se réduisent pas aux valeurs spécifiquement éthiques ou socio-politiques au sens traditionnel. Il y a toute une pléiade de valeurs qui inspirent, dirigent, motivent les actions des hommes et qui se traduisent dans des conceptions assez bien déterminées du monde, de la nature, de l'histoire, des rapports sociaux, du sens de la vie. Tous ces contextes axiologiques contiennent une partie pour ainsi dire « cognitive » (à savoir une conception de « ce que les choses sont » dans un certain domaine) et confluent dans cette « vision du monde » que chaque personne possède comme encadrement de son existence et qui tend aussi à se généraliser à l'intérieur de chaque société historique. Un fait pareil parle déjà contre cette stratégie pour ainsi dire « protectionniste » qui a largement dominé la mentalité moderne et qui consistait à séparer nettement les domaines pour garantir à chacun son indépendance : séparation cartésienne entre matière et esprit ; séparation entre science et religion ; entre connaissance et morale ; entre morale et politique ; entre liberté individuelle et responsabilité sociale et ainsi de suite. Aujourd'hui nous nous sommes rendu compte que cette approche était fictive et nous sommes en train de regagner le sens de l'unité, de la complexité, de l'interaction, des relations mutuelles et ceci doit, en particulier, concerner notre manière de concevoir et de pratiquer la science. Ceci implique la nécessité de « repenser » la philosophie des sciences elle-même, qui s'est constituée en tant que discipline spécialisée au début du XXe siècle comme épistémologie des sciences : une perspective digne de respect mais partielle. Voilà donc pourquoi un colloque sur le thème « Science et éthique : les contextes axiologiques de la science » a été promu en commun par l'Académie Internationale de Philosophie des Sciences et l'Académie Internationale des Sciences Religieuses, avec l'intention explicite de mettre en dialogue des gens qui ont eu l'occasion de se pencher sur le problème des valeurs à partir d'optiques différentes et, en même temps, ont dû constater que connaissance et valeurs (y compris la connaissance des valeurs) s'entrelaçaient continuellement. Ce volume contient essentiellement les rapports présentés à ce colloque, qui a eu lieu à Lecce en octobre 2004.

Ce volume présente une conférence inaugurale, et une quinzaine de contributions distribuées en deux sections : la première (intitulée *Values in Science*) contient des essais qui traitent le thème général de la dimension axiologique des sciences ; la deuxième (intitulée *Science, Ethics and Religion*) contient des essais concernant plus spécifiquement les rapports entre science, éthique et religion.

Pour son *Discours inaugural* d'ouverture du colloque, le Président émérite de la République Italienne, Monsieur le Sénateur Oscar Luigi Scàlfaro a été invité à développer une réflexion sur le problème de la paix dans le monde contemporain. La décision d'ouvrir un congrès consacré aux rapports entre *Science et Éthique* par l'intervention d'un homme politique éminent était peu usuelle. Toutefois Scàlfaro représente en Italie une figure de grand respect parce qu'il est l'un des pères fondateurs de la République italienne : quand il était encore jeune magistrat, il a participé directement et activement aux travaux de l'*Assemblée Constituante*, d'où est né le texte de la *Constitution italienne*. Dans sa conférence inaugurale, *The Significance and Value of Peace for Contemporary World*, Scàlfaro a soutenu l'idée que dans le monde contemporain il faut reconnaître la nécessité d'introduire un nouveau droit : *le droit à la paix*. À son avis, la proclamation du *droit à la paix* constitue une meilleure tutelle de la personne humaine en ce qui concerne son intégrité articulée. En s'appelant expressément à l'enseignement de la *Constitution italienne* Scàlfaro a illustré le fait que tout ce qui mortifie la personne humaine constitue toujours une agression directe à la paix et il a aussi rappelé qu'en Italie même la genèse de l'État est explicitement subordonnée à la priorité de la personne humaine par rapport à laquelle l'État ne possède aucune supériorité. Au contraire, pour la *Constitution italienne* c'est l'État lui-même qui déclare explicitement reconnaître et défendre l'intégrité de la personne humaine comme un *prius* auquel l'État doit se subordonner. En critiquant le concept d'État éthique – qui a été défendu, de différentes façons, par les diverses dictatures – Scàlfaro a illustré que le *droit à la paix* constitue l'indispensable et stable prémisse pour l'existence et l'affirmation de tous les autres droits : si, en effet, la paix manque, tous les autres droits résultent inévitablement suspendus, violés et rendus vains. En rappelant que dans la *Constitution italienne* la guerre est conçue toujours comme un mal qui doit être ouvertement *répudié*, Scàlfaro a terminé en affirmant que, dans le cadre du monde contemporain il faut travailler concrètement et activement pour la paix, en refusant toujours le recours à la guerre (aussi pour combattre le terrorisme international), en favorisant, en même temps, une politique européenne unitaire, capable d'augmenter le dialogue et la confrontation pacifique entre les différents peuples de la terre.

La première section, *Values in Science*, offre des contributions qui analysent les différentes significations selon lesquelles on peut entendre la « dimension axiologique » de la science, en incluant dans cette dimension aussi bien la considération des « valeurs épistémiques » que celle de valeurs « non cognitives », avec la légitimité d'exprimer les « jugements de valeur » correspondants.

Evandro Agazzi, dans son rapport *Pourquoi une philosophie des sciences ne peut se réduire à une épistémologie des sciences*, considère d'abord la double signification du terme « épistémologie » qui peut signifier parfois « théorie de la connaissance », et parfois « philosophie de la science ». Si la première signification est sans doute la plus traditionnelle, la deuxième est devenue plus hégémonique au cours du XXe siècle. L'ambivalence de ce terme découle de la signification très générale du terme grecque *épistémê* qui désignait ce que nous qualifions aujourd'hui comme « science », mais aussi en générale la « connaissance » ou « savoir », car dans la culture grecque ces trois concepts étaient fondamentalement interchangeables. Sur cette base s'est ensuite superposée une distinction entre une théorie « générale » de la connaissance, indiquée comme « gnoséologie », et une théorie des formes « spéciales » de la connaissance, représentées par les différentes sciences. Toutefois, pendant les trois derniers siècles, surtout suite au développement impétueux des sciences naturelles, s'est presque imposée l'idée que la science naturelle moderne représente la forme la plus authentique de toute connaissance possible et donc constitue le paradigme de la connaissance tout court. Par conséquent la vieille épistémologie arrive à coïncider avec la théorie de la connaissance scientifique. Toutefois, et surtout dans le contexte culturel anglo-américain, le terme *epistemology* a continué à dénoter la théorie générale de la connaissance, tandis que la *philosophy of science* se réfère plus directement aux théories scientifiques. Sur cette base la « philosophie de la science » a acquis une autonomie disciplinaire spécifique, mais elle s'est concentrée uniquement sur les résultats effectivement obtenus dans chaque domaine disciplinaire cultivé par la science. Sur cette base, une évaluation strictement gnoséologique du savoir scientifique s'est développée et a conduit à une considération purement *idéale* des sciences considérées d'après une approche linguistique ou strictement logico-méthodologique qui a absolutisé le savoir scientifique. Mais cette image idéalisée et abstraite de la science est entrée en tension avec la considération des différents contextes historiques et sociaux dans lesquels la science s'est effectivement développée, et la philosophie des sciences plus récente est passée à considérer la science comme un système d'*actions* humaines, de *pratiques* finalisées à la construction d'un savoir utilisable, en considérant les interactions complexes qui s'instaurent toujours avec les différents secteurs d'une société et ses nombreux besoins. En partagent cette nouvelle perspective critique Agazzi montre que l'évaluation correcte de la dimension pratique de la science permet de redonner un espace adéquat aux *jugements de valeur* qui opèrent toujours à l'intérieur de la science, et de dépasser critiquement le dogme de la prétendue *neutralité axiologique* du savoir scientifique. Naturellement, le dépassement de ce dogme doit être achevé en sauvegardant la pleine *valeur cognitive* de la connaissance scientifique qui constitue toujours une forme de *savoir objectif*. C'est pour cette raison qu'il est donc possible de développer une philosophie de la science plus articulée et adéquate, toujours capable d'employer les différents instruments techniques d'analyse élaborés dans chaque champ spécialisé, sans renoncer à développer une meilleure réflexion philosophique sur la connaissance scientifique. Dans cette perspective non seulement la gnoséologie, la logique, la philosophie du langage, mais aussi l'éthique, l'ontologie, la métaphysique, la philosophie de la nature et l'anthropologie philosophique doivent se confronter ponctuellement avec le complexe patrimoine (théorique et technique) élaboré par les sciences, en ayant toujours la capacité d'éclairer la richesse des nombreux problèmes philosophiques qui suivent de ces différentes richesses de secteur.

Javier Echeverría Esponda et Armando Menéndez Viso, dans leur contribution *Axiology of Scientific Activity*, se basent, en premier lieu, sur ce que de nombreux philosophes, sociologues et historiens (comme Frege, Russell, Whitehead) ont affirmé pendant ces dernières décennies, pour délinéer un *framework* non-aristotélicien. Ils affirment qu'il existe de différents genres de valeurs possibles qui conditionnent de nombreux aspects de la science théorique et des activités technologiques. Afin de réaliser une étude de la pratique scientifique (et pas seulement de la connaissance scientifique), les auteurs soulignent qu'ils n'ont pas besoin de s'appuyer sur une particulière théorie de l'action, ni de s'engager dans une définition de l'activité scientifique. Au contraire, ils veulent seulement donner une première, caractérisation sommaire et rudimentaire des actions scientifiques, afin de disposer d'un premier point de départ pour développer un examen de type nouveau. Du point de vue épistémologique, il n'est jamais possible d'étudier des faits sans posséder préalablement une perspective théorique qui nous permet de les caractériser ; à leur avis, il faut procéder de manière analogue dans l'évaluation des actions scientifiques. Pour cette raison, contrairement aux modèles des décisions rationnelles utilisés dans le domaine économique, l'axiologie qu'ils proposent se fonde sur la notion originaire de *satisfaction*, qui est expressément assumée comme terme axiologique primitif. D'autre part, c'est avec l'introduction de ce terme primitif qu'il est possible de parler de l'*objectivité* des décisions scientifiques, même si cette « objectivité » ne doit pas être confondue avec un procédé de mesure capable d'évaluer absolument la valeur d'une décision. Pour les auteurs, une décision doit donc être considérée « objective » quand elle ne dépend pas de l'agent particulier qui la pose. En tout cas, leur perspective les amène à parler de *gradualisme* et de *pluralisme* des valeurs, car on peut aussi employer des références à différentes axiologies pour aboutir à ce résultat : axiologies formelles, objectives, systématiques, empiriques, plurielles, synthétiques, etc. Cette approche permet aux auteurs de délinéer une première matrice de l'évaluation axiologique, même si leur approche critique ne peut pas être présentée, à son tour, comme une discipline scientifique, mais, en revanche, comme une approche éminemment philosophique. Celle-ci, en employant une méthodologie appropriée et une épistémologie adéquate, peut contribuer à augmenter, dans une mesure significative, notre compréhension des technosciences, en nous permettant d'intervenir, en termes positifs et responsables sur leur développement. Cette approche axiologique semble aussi être particulièrement intéressante pour l'étude de l'évolution même des protocoles scientifiques employés soit par la science soit par les différentes technologies.

Fabio Minazzi, dans sa contribution *The Axiological Dimensions of Science*, souligne d'abord que la science elle-même constitue *pour soi* une valeur qui a amplement et positivement influencé les sociétés humaines. En employant les analyses phénoménologiques et transcendentalistes d'origine husserlienne, l'auteur démontre qu'il faut tenir compte des *différents niveaux* de l'agir et de la pensée scientifique, qui permettent ensuite d'élaborer une vision plus critique et plus riche du patrimoine scientifique, et aussi de son impact sur la société contemporaine. Une considération holistique du savoir technoscientifique, *à la* Duhem, permet d'illustrer la complexité des technosciences, en démontrant aussi le caractère spécifique de la vérité scientifique qui, tout en étant une connaissance objective, ne peut plus être configurée comme une connaissance absolue. Cette vision dialectique de la connaissance scientifique ne manque pas d'avoir une notable importance même à l'égard de la dimension axiologique et, plus en général, du monde des valeurs. D'après des indications fournies par des auteurs tels que Geymonat et Preti il faut donc réaliser une nouvelle analyse critique de l'entreprise scientifique, qui respecte d'un côté l'axiologie spécifique qui existe à l'intérieur de la science, et de l'autre côté le rapport que le patrimoine technique et scientifique peut, à son tour, entretenir avec les axiologies qui existent à l'intérieur des différentes sociétés humaines. Dans cette perspective critique et épistémologique la science doit être évaluée comme un programme de recherche essentiellement dynamique, capable d'interagir constructivement avec toute la société, parce qu'elle donne un intéressant et fécond modèle axiologique, fondé sur la criticité et sur l'augmentation de la connaissance, produites par une rectification critique continue du même savoir humain.

Alberto Cordero, dans l'essai *Pluralism, Scientific Values and the Value of Science* propose la considération métaphorique de la science contemporaine comme un plan cartographique composé par une pluralité de cartes partielles, dont des représentations ne résultent pas homogènes les unes par rapport aux autres. Cela constitue peut-être une mauvaise nouvelle pour ceux qui défendent une vision hyper-optimiste de la science, mais pas pour ceux qui défendent une vision sobre du réalisme scientifique et de l'objectivité de la connaissance scientifique. Naturellement, chaque carte nous donne une représentation sélectionnée qui, si d'un côté nous permet de focaliser de nombreux aspects de la réalité, d'un autre côté, néglige d'autres éléments qui ne sont moins importants. Cela engendre, naturellement, de nombreux problèmes et différentes questions à l'égard, en particulier, des valeurs qui se trouvent à l'intérieur de la science, telles que la pertinence de la connaissance scientifique, la nature spécifique du monde dont la science parle, les différentes modalités de la connaissance et même le rôle de ceux qui opèrent à l'intérieur de l'entreprise scientifique. Dans ce contexte problématique, Cordero analyse, en particulier, la connexion qui peut exister entre le pluralisme et le genre spécifique du réalisme suggéré par la métaphore du plan cartographique. Cela lui permet d'illustrer aussi les éléments qui permettent de justifier un point de vue réaliste, surtout afin de revitaliser de manière critique la distinction qui existe entre les ouvertures suggérées par la configuration de la connaissance scientifique et par sa méthodologie (le dénommé « pluralisme intérieur ») et les ouvertures suggérées par le conditionnement exercé sur la science par les forces sociales (le dénommé « pluralisme extérieur »). Cela lui permet enfin de conclure sa réflexion en prenant en considération directe la tendance à accepter la théorisation scientifique sans nécessairement respecter les limites du « politiquement correct ».

Mariano Artigas s'arrête sur le thème *Values in Science* en commençant par une considération critique sur le caractère « non-évaluatif » de la recherche scientifique. On note en effet que même l'attitude non-évaluative de la connaissance scientifique objective peut constituer, en elle-même, une valeur, avec la conséquence que la science neutre ne peut pas se présenter comme absolument indépendante des valeurs, puisqu'on défend les valeurs de l'objectivité et de la recherche de la vérité. D'autre part, à l'intérieur de l'entreprise scientifique existent aussi des valeurs épistémiques qui permettent d'évaluer les différentes théories scientifiques et leur valeur intrinsèque. On ne peut pas néanmoins négliger l'importante distinction, généralement acceptée, entre science pure et science appliquée. En se référant, en particulier, à l'analyse développée par McMullin on peut ainsi caractériser de différents types de valeurs épistémiques comme le pouvoir explicatif d'une théorie, son caractère prédictif, sa précision (soit en ce qui concerne les explications soit en ce qui concerne les prédictions), la variété et l'indépendance des différentes argumentations et aussi le secours mutuel que différentes théories peuvent se donner. Artigas analyse, en particulier, les valeurs institutionnelles qui caractérisent les théories scientifiques, à la façon de Robert Merton, pour évaluer enfin l'impact que le progrès scientifique peut exercer à l'égard des sociétés humaines. Même si on reconnaît que les sciences empiriques sont le résultat combiné de la créativité théorique et de l'interprétation du monde réel, l'auteur partage une position réaliste qui est capable de conjuguer le caractère représentatif des théories scientifiques avec leur spécifique force créatrice.

Dans *The role of Cognitive Values in the Shaping of Scientific Rationality*, Jan Faye discute et souligne le rôle épistémique que les valeurs cognitives jouent dans le débat scientifique. Il reconnaît que, aujourd'hui, la phase « positiviste » est désormais dépassée, phase pendant laquelle on pensait que la science était absolument affranchie de toute contamination axiologique. Faye démontre au contraire l'existence de différents genres de valeurs cognitives présentes au cours l'entreprise scientifique. D'autre part, aujourd'hui il y a des auteurs – comme par exemple van Frassen et Kuhn – qui ne parlent plus de la « vérité » des théories scientifiques, qu'ils ont substituée, respectivement, par les notions d'adaptation empirique et de paradigme. Il faut reconnaître en tout cas que les *valeurs éthiques* jouent un rôle important dans la formulation des buts de la science et cela devient particulièrement évident dans le domaine de la médecine. Toutefois, selon Faye, on peut retrouver cette présence même dans tous les autres domaines de la recherche scientifique. À ce propos, l'auteur mentionne, par exemple, l'appel à l'esthétique fait par des physiciens afin de justifier leur adhésion à une théorie physique plutôt qu'une autre. En considérant la controverse entre Niels Bohr et Albert Einstein à l'égard de la physique quantique, Faye démontre analytiquement que leur discussion s'enracine dans un désaccord à propos de valeurs cognitives et métaphysiques, et ne naissait donc pas des faits empiriques. Il faut dès lors reconnaître que « la rationalité de la science n'est pas fournie par Dieu » et, au contraire, qu'elle surgit d'une série d'obligations épistémiques et méthodologiques liées aux différentes croyances partagées par les savants. Par conséquent, ces valeurs cognitives ne sont jamais non-modifiables parce qu'elles se lient aux différents contextes, historiquement modifiables, de la praxis scientifique.

Dans son essai *The Places of Values in Science*, Paul Weingartner distingue quatre différents niveaux d'analyse puisque la dimension axiologique se manifeste d'une façon plutôt différenciée. Il faut donc considérer d'abord le niveau concernant les buts de la science, finalisés à obtenir la vérité. À ce niveau, la science se configure comme une activité contrôlable qui atteint une validité approximative toujours corrigible. Il faut considérer, ensuite, les règles de la méthodologie scientifique au sujet desquelles on peut formuler des normes générales et des normes spécifiques pour chaque domaine scientifique. Ces normes établissent des règles de conduite que les savants doivent respecter : si elles sont violées, c'est le but de la recherche scientifique qui est violé, même si la connaissance produite par la recherche scientifique est toujours rectifiable et corrigible. De plus, les « faits » dont la science s'occupe sont toujours insérés et lus à l'intérieur d'une explication téléologique précise qui pose des valeurs à la lumière desquelles ils sont évalués et interprétés en tant que « faits » singuliers. Des disciplines différentes se réfèrent toujours à des normes téléologiques différentes. C'est pour cette raison que, en quatrième lieu, il faut aussi considérer les justifications argumentées des normes et des valeurs méthodologiques employées par les différentes disciplines et par les différentes théories. Grâce à cette considération de l'axiologie dans le domaine de la recherche scientifique, l'auteur offre donc une perspective qui permet de mieux comprendre la complexité spécifique du problème lié au rapport entre l'éthique et la connaissance scientifique.

Dans l'essai *Science and Technoscience : Values and their Measurement*, Ramón Queraltó envisage le problème de la complexité de la science contemporaine en soulignant le fait que, aujourd'hui, il faut parler expressément de « technosciences » car l'entreprise scientifique concerne de plus en plus strictement la dimension de la recherche théorique et celle de ses applications pratiques qui ont un important impact sur la société. Dans cette perspective « systémique », la technique ne peut plus être conçue comme « science appliquée », en particulier parce que, comme de nombreux spécialistes l'ont souligné, le profil de la connaissance scientifique est devenu de plus en plus complexe et articulé. Dans ce contexte précis, l'auteur porte sa réflexion sur la possibilité de mesurer les valeurs scientifiques et, en vue de ce but, il suggère un critère qui devrait permettre de comparer les différents systèmes de valeurs présentes et opérantes dans les technosciences. Queraltó est toutefois conscient que chaque valeur impliquée dans une action des technosciences ne possède pas le même « poids » et la même « importance ». Il faut donc distinguer le rôle de ces différentes valeurs qui peuvent développer des fonctions différentes. Dans cette perspective on rappelle que la vérité scientifique est toujours relative à l'égard d'un certain contexte de référence. Toutefois, cette « relativité » n'implique aucun « relativisme », parce que la connaissance scientifique s'instaure toujours dans un contexte précis et délimité, dans lequel elle exerce son action directe et revêt aussi une valeur déterminée. L'essai se termine en soulignant que les choix des valeurs qui opèrent dans la science impliquent toujours une approche systémique car l'ensemble des

25

technosciences constitue une totalité ouverte, jamais fermée et définie de manière absolue.

La deuxième section, *Science, Ethics and Religion*, contient des contributions qui portent directement sur les deux sphères à l'intérieur desquelles se manifeste de manière plus aiguë le débat actuel et les tensions entre ceux qui voudraient défendre à tout prix la science contre les « interférences » de la morale et de la religion et ceux qui voudraient les mettre en rapport, sans danger d'intromission ou interférence. En particulier, dans les essais compris dans la partie finale de cette section, et dont les auteurs sont des théologiens, la religion n'est pas considérée comme porteuse de valeurs strictement religieuses, mais plutôt comme une aide pour une dimension axiologique en générale et contribuant à la concrétisation de la perspective éthique.

Hervé Barreau dans sa contribution *Ethics in Face of Science and in Face of Research* s'adonne à une défense de l'éthique à l'égard de la science et même de la recherche scientifique ; tout en distinguant expressément le niveau de la connaissance scientifique de celui de la recherche et de l'entreprise scientifique, il sent toutefois la nécessité de souligner l'importance indispensable de la dimension éthique. La dimension éthique se lie d'une façon différente à la science théorique et à la recherche scientifique, toutefois elle constitue toujours un point de référence impératif. Dans cette perspective, Barreau prend en considération directe essentiellement le domaine des recherches biologiques et souligne que les programmes de recherche scientifiques ne sont pas soumis en général à des limitations précises données par l'éthique. Par contre, il faut élaborer une éthique précise pour la recherche, une véritable bio-éthique, qui soit capable d'indiquer les parcours autorisés de la recherche scientifique, en les diversifiant par rapport à ceux qui sont jugés éthiquement non-souhaitables. Selon Barreau, même en considérant le rôle que la science et la technologie ont tenu au cours du XXe siècle, il n'est pas possible d'envisager le XXIe siècle sans introduire des limitations précises d'ordre bioéthique à la recherche scientifique. Et pour cette raison, il clôt sa contribution en souhaitant une complète renaissance de l'éthique même à l'égard de la science.

Peter Kemp, dans sa contribution *Les valeurs éthiques dans les sciences médicales*, reconnaît deux raisons fondamentales pour introduire la considération de valeurs éthiques dans la pratique médicale : l'une est commune à tout usage des sciences et des techniques, quand celui-ci doit se confronter à des décisions et à des choix pour lesquels la science ne nous offre pas de critères ; l'autre dépend du fait que, dans la pratique médicale, on a directement affaire à la personne humaine. L'auteur conçoit la valeur comme signifiant une qualité de vie qui est jugée bonne dans le sens où elle mérite d'être vécue et qui est renforcée par la dimension communautaire. Historiquement, le concept de valeur n'existait pas dans la philosophie classique et il est devenu central dans l'éthique de Kant où il exprime la coprésence de l'être et du devoir-être. Mais dans l'éthique actuelle, ce concept a perdu son rôle central, à cause de la signification subjectiviste qu'on lui a attribuée et du fait qu'on a renoncé à reconnaître l'existence d'une hiérarchie des valeurs. Venant spécifiquement à l'éthique médicale, Kemp reconnaît en elle la présence de quatre valeurs fondamentales : le respect de la dignité humaine, la reconnaissance de l'autonomie du patient et du sujet d'expérimentation médicale (consentement informé et libre), le souci pour l'intégrité vulnérable du patient, l'appel à la solidarité et à la justice.

La contribution de Valentin A. Bazhanov, *Proof as an Ethical Procedure,* est au contraire consacrée à une étude des démonstrations et des argumentations (surtout dans le domaine logique et mathématique) comme procédures éthiques considérées d'un point de vue psychologique. Dans cet essai, l'argumentation est donc présentée comme un processus de persuasion expressément dirigé à la communauté scientifique, plutôt que comme un moyen pour la recherche de la vérité. L'argumentation se configure donc comme un instrument qui permet enfin d'assumer la responsabilité d'une thèse partagée, souvent obtenue à travers une intuition à laquelle se lie un « rayonnement » de sa validité. Les mots-clefs et les concepts qui permettent ce « rayonnement » d'une vérité scientifique partagée sont l'argumentation, la persuasion, les épreuves, la responsabilité, la communauté scientifique, les « insight ».

Craig Dilworth envisage *The Vicious Circle Principle and the Biological Basic of Morals.* Le principe du cercle vicieux (VCP) affirme, en synthèse, qu'une situation de besoin, produite par un certain changement de l'environnement, conduit à l'actuation de quelque innovation technologique qui ensuite est largement employée et permet d'amorcer, à son tour, un développement qui ne se limite pas à satisfaire aux nécessités initiales, mais incite aussi une croissance de la population qui, à son tour, détermine une nouvelle situation de nécessité : le cercle se pose ainsi à nouveau et inaugure un nouveau processus de croissance qui déterminera un développement aboutissant à une nouvelle situation problématique et ainsi de suite. En employant ce principe du cercle vicieux on peut non seulement expliquer l'histoire humaine, des origines de la présence humaine sur terre à la révolution industrielle du XIXe siècle, mais on peut aussi donner une nouvelle interprétation de la morale elle-même en démontrant ses liens avec le développement biologique de l'humanité. À cet égard, après avoir ponctuellement rappelé et défini quelque concept de la biologie contemporaine (comme gène, génotype, génome, caryotype, etc.), Dilworth souligne qu'il existe de différents niveaux biologiques qui doivent toujours être considérés pour mieux comprendre les différentes modalités de la sélection naturelle et de la lutte pour la survie, au cours de l'évolution des espèces, en devant nécessairement distinguer, par exemple, la lutte pour la survie qui se vérifie à l'*intérieur* des différentes espèces (pour la conquête des femmes ou bien pour le contrôle du territoire ou pour les deux objectifs ensemble), et la lutte pour la survie qui s'instaure parmi *des espèces différentes* généralement pour la conquête de la nourriture et, en sous-ordre, pour le contrôle du territoire. Ces considérations permettent à l'auteur de souligner le différent niveau qui existe entre gènes et caryotypes, en démontrant que même la morale humaine renvoie à l'existence des caryotypes. Avec la conséquence que notre moralité dépendrait et serait augmentée par ce qui se révèle biologiquement le meilleur et le plus vital pour les espèces humaines. C'est surtout cette conclusion qui montre donc toutes les limites du principe du cercle vicieux et de sa foi dans l'expansion illimitée qui peut être correcte et avantageuse seulement dans certaines circonstances où il est possible de coloniser de nouveaux territoires. Au contraire, quand ces conditions résultent absentes, même le principe devient dangereux et désavantageux.

Dans son étude très articulée et documentée, *Creation Belief and Natural Science : a Systematic Theological Approach*, Otto Hermann Pesch introduit la discussion du thème qui l'intéresse plus particulièrement, à savoir celui des relations entre la doctrine judéo-chrétienne de la création et les théories de l'évolution, par un discours plus général concernant les rapports entre science et foi religieuse. Sa reconstruction historique détaillée de ces rapports l'amène à rejeter aussi bien la thèse de l'incompatibilité des deux approches à la compréhension de la réalité que la thèse d'une pure et simple compatibilité sans de réels points de rencontre. Selon la conception qu'il propose, les deux approches ne doivent absolument pas renoncer à leurs perspectives et attitudes intellectuelles spécifiques et cela implique, en particulier, que la théologie affirme sans hésitation certaines thèses fondamentales, c'est-à-dire la création divine du monde et de l'homme, qui ne se confond pas avec le problème des « origines » temporelles, mais souligne la « contingence » de la création ; le fait que cette création exprime l'amour de Dieu à l'égard de monde et de l'homme ; la thèse que l'homme constitue en effet le « couronnement de la création » mais, en même temps, fait partie de la Nature ; la thèse que cette position, soulignée par le fait que l'homme et lui seul est doué de liberté, implique une responsabilité dans l'exercice de son droit d'administrer le monde naturel. Ceci dit, le problème théologique fondamental est celui de comprendre et de défendre l'unicité de l'être humain, unicité qui est centrée sur la caractéristique de la liberté personnelle. Cette caractéristique est en même temps un fait théologiquement fondamental, scientifiquement constatable mais scientifiquement inexplicable. L'importance de la liberté pour la théologie dépend du fait que la foi religieuse est un acte libre, de libre acceptation d'une parole, qui trouve ses racines dans l'expérience religieuse. Celle-ci doit être reconnue comme étant une forme de connaissance, sans pourtant être assimilable à la connaissance telle que les sciences la conçoivent. Mais ici justement se trouve le point de contact : les sciences peuvent nous faire connaître les étapes à travers lesquelles a eu lieu cette « préparation » de l'être humain, mais seulement le concept de création nous permet d'entendre comme don gratuit et imprévisible de Dieu la création (au sens complet) de l'homme comme être simultanément libre et rendu participant à la vie divine.

La contribution de Vassilis Saroglou, *Religion and Psychology of Values : « Universals » and Changes*, est consacrée à une étude systématique et métathéorique des valeurs qui se trouvent à l'intérieur des différentes religions et ce, à travers l'utilisation du modèle théorique élaboré par Schwarz. Selon ce modèle, on établit une hiérarchie de dix méta-valeurs fondamentales : le pouvoir, la réalisation, l'hédonisme, la stimulation, l'autonomie, l'universalisme, la bienveillance, la tradition, le conformisme et la sécurité. Cette structure, obtenue à partir d'une recherche scientifique ponctuelle, est employée pour construire un modèle universel de référence, déterminé par l'étude des différentes relations qui peuvent subsister parmi les différentes méta-valeurs. En se fondant toujours sur les résultats obtenus par Saroglou, il est donc possible de comparer les différentes traditions religieuses – en particulier, les religions chrétienne, musulmane et hébraïque – en se référant aux méta-valeurs, en tenant compte aussi de la corrélation qui existe entre les différentes religiosités et les valeurs présentes dans les différents pays méditerranéens et dans les pays de l'Europe occidentale. Sur cette base, en même temps empirique et théorique, Saroglou développe de nombreuses considérations, pour conclure que les valeurs religieuses, dans les différentes sociétés et dans les différents contextes, constituent une dimension universelle qui, tout en assumant des nuances et des accents différentes, présente un certain degré de stabilité qui déroule une précise et inéliminable fonction soit dans le développement économique d'une société, soit dans la spiritualité contemporaine.

Jean-Marie Van Cangh dédie sa contribution à une considération spécifique du lien qui existe entre *Evangelical Values and the Foundations of Science*. Sa contribution s'articule autour de deux différentes sections : dans la première, on analyse en détail la narration biblique concernant la création de l'homme et de la femme, et aussi la création d'un cosmos indépendant. À la lumière de cette ponctuelle analyse textuelle, Van Cangh démontre que la narration biblique a encouragé implicitement le développement de la science, parce que la terre et la création ont été confiées à l'homme par la divinité, en vue d'en être dominées et transformées. Dans la deuxième section, l'auteur prend en directe considération le discours des béatitudes qui se trouve dans l'*Évangile*. Dans ce cas aussi une analyse textuelle précise se développe afin de souligner la valeur révolutionnaire de ce célèbre discours de la montagne. L'auteur, d'accord avec Albert Jacquart, souligne le fait que la valeur éthique révolutionnaire du discours sur les béatitudes constitue une référence nécessaire non seulement pour les savants croyants, mais aussi pour les savants agnostiques. En ce sens, les valeurs évangéliques ne fondent pas l'agir scientifique en tant que tel, mais elles constituent la référence incontournable pour tous les hommes, y compris les hommes de science.

Stuart George Hall, dans sa contribution *Value and Truth in the Fathers. Is there a Patristic Axiology?*, illustre la possible présence d'une axiologie patristique au cours des quatre premiers siècles de l'histoire de l'Église. L'auteur fait noter qu'on peut discuter le problème des valeurs dans le domaine des vertus théologales, à partir d'un *background* philosophique souvent inexprimé et inconscient (à cet égard, il suffit de penser à la figure singulière de Marcion du Pont). Clément d'Alexandrie examine les implications morales du problème de la foi en se référant au néoplatonisme de Justin, et, par la suite, en adaptant des éléments de la logique aristotélicienne et stoïcienne aux Saintes Écritures, dans le but d'introduire une étroite relation entre connaissance et foi. La lecture parallèle du livre VII et du livre VIII des *Confessions* d'Augustin d'Hippone manifeste la source néoplatonicienne de sa théorie de l'illumination, mais, en même temps, comble la lacune du platonisme par la vertu évangélique de l'amour, pris comme objet de l'aspiration humaine vers Dieu. Le Credo de Nicée-Constantinople se développe à partir de la tradition platonicienne et néo-platonicienne à l'égard du discours sur l'Être, mais il introduit le concept de *philanthropia*, d'amour pour l'humanité, qui révèle l'espoir du salut.

La réalisation du colloque dont ce volume contient la plupart des contributions a été possible grâce au soutien généreux de la Province de Lecce et à la collaboration scientifique du Département de Philologie Classique et de Sciences Philosophiques de la Faculté de Lettres et Philosophie de l'Université del Salento. La clairvoyance de la Province de Lecce et, en particulier, de son Président, Lorenzo Ria, a été d'une importance capitale pour la promotion d'un type d'initiative culturelle à l'égard duquel les pouvoirs politiques, dans le monde entier, se montrent de moins en moins sensibles. Le choix de Lecce comme siège du symposium avait été motivé, d'ailleurs, par la considération de la vocation historique de la terre du Salento qui, au cours des siècles, a été un point de contact privilégié entre l'Orient et l'Occident : une véritable porte ouverte vers de nombreuses et différentes traditions de pensée, quelque chose qu'aujourd'hui on souhaite renouveler dans la conscience qu'une culture morale, qui se trouve vraiment au niveau des connaissances scientifiques contemporaines, ne peut pas renoncer à un dialogue critique avec les différents traditions mondiales de la pensée. C'est donc avec une gratitude particulière que nous remercions – au nom des deux Académies sœurs (l'Académie Internationale de Philosophie des Sciences et l'Académie Internationale des Sciences Religieuses qui ont pu réaliser en cette occasion une réunion commune très fructueuse) – les autorités politiques et académiques de Lecce susmentionnées.

Significance and Value of Peace for Contemporary World

Oscar Luigi SCÀLFARO

Emeritus President of Italian Republic

1. The Question of Peace

Permit me, first of all, to thank the organizers of the symposium, the authorities present, all the speakers and, in particular, Professor Fabio Minazzi, the organizer of this initiative, for inviting me to Salento and the enchanting city of Lecce. I also wish to thank all of the students present who have made no small effort to attend an event like this, which testifies to the existence, here in the deep south and among the vital intellectual forces of Salento's academic world, of a rare and valuable sensibility, both civil and cultural. This, at least to my mind, constitutes a good and positive sign of a reflection and a teaching that comprehends the importance of closely relating the most serious, complex, severe and difficult philosophical-scientific thought with a pervasive civil sensibility that has always enlivened and animated the most important and significant pages of our cultural history. And this is all the more true because Salento, by its geographical position and its historical vocation, projects itself naturally into the heart of the Mediterranean, forming an ideal bridge between West and East, so conferring on this whole initiative a further value by fostering international dialogue and debate with the participation – as evinced by the program of work – of scholars, philosophers and intellectuals from numerous countries around the world. This dialogue, conducted in this hospitable land, strikes me as a good omen not only for your work, but also for that valuable civil sensibility that is increasingly developing among the different populations of the world, responsive to the construction of a new civil coexistence on our whole planet.

I also have to confess that presenting an introductory address to such a demanding and complex convention as one devoted to the relationship between Science and Ethics is far from simple or immediate. For this reason I wish once more to thank you for the invitation you have extended to me, but I also thank you for the subject entrusted to me – *the significance and the value of peace in the contemporary world* – with which, with a courageous choice, perhaps somewhat unusual and new, you have chosen to open the work of a scientific and philosophical convention and directly given a voice to political reflection. In truth we might recall that there also exists a *political science* that should never lose sight of ethics and the consequent and truly vital, problem of responsibility (civil and moral) which most directly affects day-to-day political action. From this more general point of view, the theme entrusted to me is related to a subject which is both classic and truly terrible: that of the relationship between peace and war.

Naturally there exist certain rules that, even when we are dealing with such a harsh and grievous question, enable us to outline the exact ethical perimeter. And more: there also exist global manifestations in which we also participated recently – and which, in a certain sense, are not completely finished – that showed that this important page of ethics has been forgotten today, at least by some significant components of the global civilized society, which have not only chosen war, but also preferred not to confront and discuss the question of peace, though warned against it by millions of people.

2. The Institutional Role of Parliament

But, more generally, the subject of war is also the subject of peace, and for this reason I would now like to reflect with you on some crucial issues, expounding thoughts that I have long advanced, even in the most acute moments of the world crisis, in particular when the Italian Parliament was called on at least to discuss – certainly not to decide – issues of global war and peace. Besides, at present, while no longer holding any direct institutional position of responsibility and in fact deliberately choosing to remain in the background, I still feel a civil and moral duty to discuss certain questions openly, above all in relation to the direct responsibility that I have had over the years and in which I am engaged in Parliament.

I harbour, and long have, an enormous respect for the Italian Parliament, partly because at the *Constituent Assembly* I voted fully consciously (and also enthusiastically) for the birth of a *parliamentary democratic republic*, whose summit is represented precisely by Parliament. And Parliament, as is well known, elects the Head of State. True, as will be justly observed, it acts together with the representatives of the regions, but there is no doubt that the majority of the electors of the

President of the Republic are in Parliament. In addition, Parliament always passes a vote of confidence in the Government, and it is again Parliament that can cause a Government to fall by withholding its confidence. Again: it is Parliament that decides whether to go to war, at least according to our *Constitution*, and when it decides this it then transmits its vote to the Head of State, who has the institutional task of declaring war. Moreover, currently in Parliament there are pending some bills that, in this respect, actually seek to introduce a fundamental amendment, by providing, for example, that in an emergency or in cases of special urgency it should be the Government alone that decides whether the nation should go to war. Nevertheless, in considering this proposal, I wonder: do there ever exist declarations of war expressed in a state of serenity? Or, to give another example, can they ever be expressed with that serenity which will allow one to hold over a problem that is not urgent to the resumption of parliament in autumn? What if – to take an extreme case – it was possible to declare war while waiting for the end of the Christmas period? Isn't it instead true, as history teaches, including the recent history of Italy, that every war has always been declared in conditions of international emergency and of particular urgency?

If this bill should pass, then to declare war the decision of a Government would suffice. It would then communicate it to the President of the Republic, whose function would merely be confined to issuing the declaration of war. It is clear that, in the light of this bill, we would find ourselves faced with a complete distortion the provisions of our Constitution. Certainly this bill has still to be debated and tabled in Parliament; all the same, it presents a rather problematic and highly questionable measure, because, if it is passed, the President of the Council of Ministers no longer has to have the confidence of Parliament but can instead ask, if it is so desired, for a vote on his whole platform. But if Parliament should not give him a majority, then the government would be obliged to resign and the President of the Republic would immediately have to decree the dissolution of Parliament. Note carefully: this bill does not affirm that the President of the Republic *can* dissolve Parliament. Instead it affirms that the Head of State *must* dissolve Parliament. In this perspective the President of the Republic is, in short, reduced simply to a rubber stamp.

We will see, however, if this bill will be presented and eventually deliberated. Nevertheless, I chose to make a preliminary reference to it so as to stress the true prerogatives of the Italian Parliament, in the present state of affairs, expressly established by the Constitution. At present, in fact, there still exists a *Constitution*, which I voted for sincerely believing in it. So during the seven years of my Presidency I adhered closely to what is expressly laid down in the *Constitution* and the consequent defense of the majority in Parliament. In fact, as long as Parliament lives under the nightmare of dissolution, it then ends up becoming a Parliament open to blackmail, and no longer enjoys full freedom and full responsibility.

3. The Right to Peace

But to return now, more directly, to the subject of the value of peace for the contemporary world, I hope I may be permitted to recall that recently, at a precise moment of particularly acute political and moral tension, at a certain point I was questioned about my thoughts on the war on Iraq. Now, in such a delicate conjuncture – without carefully considering whether my words might perhaps influence the political forces in some way, positively or negatively, but only on the basis of my own particular and wholly personal *sense of responsibility* – I stood up in Parliament and declared openly that, faced with the possibility of war against Iraq, my judgment was decidedly opposed and strongly unfavorable. I also stated that my firm *no to war* was a determined *no*, which had no alternative of any kind or sort. In short: mine was and is an *absolute no.*

Why? Because this *no* to war follows in turn from another principle: *that war constitutes a violent no to peace.* Better still: war constitutes an open and flagrant aggression *against the right to peace.* You have understood correctly: I spoke expressly of *the right to peace* because I am convinced that at present, besides all the sacrosanct rights that are normally defended in our civilization (what scholars in general also indicate as the rights of the first, of the second and of the third generation), in my opinion there definitely has to be added a new right: *the right to peace.* A truly fundamental right, because only by this means can we respect and fulfil all the other rights (the right to work, to freedom of movement, freedom of speech, the right not to die of hunger, the right to justice, etc.), which are correctly proclaimed and defended against every possible abuse of power and against every attempt to diminish them. In this context the right to peace is a condition that is an authentic *sine qua non* for the fulfilment of all the other rights: how can one demand work, freedom and justice in the midst of war? Only peace creates the civil and social conditions for the fulfilment of all other rights. For this reason, beside the rights that our Western culture has traditionally expressed historically, today we must have the courage to insert, with extreme clarity, also the affirmation of this new right: *the right to peace.*

I repeat: a right to peace, without qualifications, restrictions or other fanciful limitations. The right to peace is a fundamental right that must be protected and guaranteed not only as an indispensable premise for the fulfilment of all other civil rights, but also as an effective and positive reality. Peace is a good, a right, which cannot be denied and that has to be protected as a precious and indispensable good for a civilized life capable of truly being such. Without peace there is no civilized life worthy of this name. Without peace the very value of human life, more generally, is irremediably degraded and placed in a dramatic situation of serious crisis. Peace is the foundation and protection of life: life without peace is an ordeal and a continuous risk, because only peace can ensure that individuals will enjoy an orderly and serene development, an existence within which they will be able to fulfil themselves in all their capacities and within the framework of their own freedom.

On the topic of the decisive importance of this *right to peace* and of the inevitable nexus that its proclamation must necessarily find in the political sensibility of our contemporaries, permit me to refer to a European commitment, still on the path to fulfilment. Recently we have witnessed authentic choruses of praise for the highly praiseworthy work that has been achieved by the European convention to outline the famous European treaty, which has finally entered its final phase of drafting. As is well known, this treaty is divided substantially into two parts: in the first place into a section concerning the institutions of the European Union (with an analytic statement of its purposes and multiplicity of objectives) and in the second place into a section containing a declaration of the rights of European citizens. Now, the responses to this important work have been prevalently, almost exclusively, laudatory. Naturally I myself appreciate all the work performed by this commission, as well as the effort devoted to drafting this important document. Nevertheless, I hope I will also be permitted to express publicly a personal disappointment of my own. Those who possess a certain sensibility for legal studies and legal culture need only observe that in reading the universal declaration of the rights of man proclaimed in 1948, we can clearly perceive that it also constitutes the expression of an international assembly like that of the United Nations, representing the whole world. We feel this, because the preamble of this universal declaration possesses, undoubtedly, a soul and a specific force, that emerges overwhelmingly at the point where it proclaims that *all human beings are born free and equal in dignity and in rights*. Moreover, this first article also terminates with a remarkable word with which it qualifies the relations of fraternity that should always inspire human relationships. Remember that this international assembly did not constitute in any way an ecclesiastical body based on the proclamation of a religious dogma drawn from the well-known theological virtues of "faith, hope and charity". Instead it constituted a political, secular and human assembly, which spoke of *human* rights and *human* values. Now it is precisely this human assembly that speaks explicitly of *fraternity*.

Note that fraternity constitutes a far stronger and more binding dimension than that embodied in solidarity or in shared responsibility or, again, in mere cooperation. Why? Because brotherhood indicates a blood tie, and it is truly remarkable to proclaim the existence of a blood tie between all people on earth. For this reason, on reading the articles of this universal proclamation of human rights, we note and perceive, with extreme clarity, the force that underpins their emblematic proclamation. So you can comprehend my personal disappointment, my regret when I hear it said that in the world there are some thirty "wars being waged" and yet in the document elaborated by the European commission there is not a single article that affirms, without uncertainties and ambiguities, that "*every human being has a right to peace*".

4. The Italian *Constitution* and the Role of the Human Person

Instead *the right to peace* constitutes – and this must be proclaimed energetically – a fundamental, vital right, rooted in the very *dignity* of the human person. Note: it is a right that it must be added coherently to all the other rights and that, as a result, must be added, with full entitlement, to that list of rights that more generally affect the right to life, the right to the dignity of the human person, the right to freedom, the right to work, the right to education, the right to freedom of movement, etc.

We open the text of the Italian *Constitution* and we see immediately that the first eleven articles have a comprehensive title that speaks, explicitly, of *fundamental principles*, which furnish an immediate presentation of the human person, who truly appears as the triumphal figure in this *Constitution* of ours, because the first article, speaks expressly of a democratic Republic *founded upon work*. In this way, the article immediately expresses all that is highest in the intelligence, in the will, but also in the muscles, in physical toil itself and in the effort of daily work, factors that are all perceived as directed towards the fullest enhancement of the person. Or rather, in these articles it is actual the human person that is presented to us with immediacy and concreteness as the authentic permanent center of gravity of our *Constitution*, because *work* itself is presented as the true and authentic foundation of the Italian Republic.

Moreover, we need only remember those specific, symptomatic, incisive, and highly distinctive words, which appear in the text of the

Constitution and which in my opinion possess a quite outstanding ethical, semantic, civil and evocative force. Reading them immediately takes me back to the precise historical moment of the vote on all these constitutional articles, a vote carried out in that unrepeatable and very special atmosphere immediately after the war in the *Constituent Assembly*. Just listen to the wording of the second article: "The Republic recognizes and guarantees the inviolable rights of man, both as an individual and in the social formations in which his personality is developed". It *recognizes and guarantees*: the Republic is the State, founded on work, within which sovereignty belongs to the people, who exert it in the forms and within the limits laid down by the *Constitution* itself. Here we have a truly wonderful sentence, because it presents a singular *virtuous civil circuit* within which everything gravitates around the person and around his dignity, as it is manifested in his daily work.

This is not all: article 11 affirms – in my opinion in a truly splendid way – that, "Italy repudiates war as an instrument of offence to the freedom of other peoples and as a means of solving international controversies". *Repudiates*: can you feel the incredible force of this word? It does not speak of the Republic but Italy: it amounts to the same thing, but to affirm explicitly that "*Italy repudiates war*" possesses a wholly distinctive force, because it means that a whole people, unanimously, is saying no to war. Which is deeply in profound civil, political and cultural accord with that firm, radical condemnation of dictatorships of all kinds, a condemnation linked with the affirmation of the human person as the generator of the Italian state.

Therefore our *Constitution* holds that the person generates the State, which is born and lives with a precise task: that of serving and protecting the person. In all these fundamental articles there emerges a truly innovative and highly significant purpose, which is at once civil, political and cultural. This eleventh article therefore embodies this harmonic virtuous circle, by rejecting war definitively and without appeal, as well as all those various questionable theories that at a certain point have actually succeeded in constructing arguments of a right in favor of war, arguments in which, in reality, the "right" no longer existed. Why? Because in a dictatorship the person loses all dignity, his whole personality, which is destroyed, annihilated and crushed, so that he no longer counts for anything, in keeping with Mussolini's famous slogan of 1925: "Everything in the State, nothing against the State, nothing outside the State". These theories maintained that the person possesses no primary rights, only reflected rights, because the entitlement to primary rights is the exclusive prerogative of the State. Note that by saying "of the State" it is understood that only the State can bestow these rights, as it can also suspend them: it can suspend some of them, or revoke them and then bestow them again, acting on its own unquestioned judgment, since it is the holder of these rights. Here we have what is called the *ethical State*, as it is described in the philosophy of law. But when we are faced with these theories concerning the ethical and totalitarian State, a basic question arises. What is the origin of the State? Does the origin perhaps lie in a group of people who declare: "We are the State", meaning self-investiture, as happens in every dictatorship? Instead, by saying "the State recognizes" we almost seem to foresee the genesis of the state that arises in its constitutional, institutional and administrative structure. And at the moment when it arises, as its first action it bows down to the person that brought it into the world and recognizes what was there before it was born, because the person is a *prius* while the State is not a *prius*. This is a far cry from the superior ethical values of the State!

5. Italy Repudiates War as Evil

Article 11 of the *Constitution* also rests on the basis of these funda-mental principles. I would have been very pleased to see this article incorporated in those principles that are to be the foundation of the constitutional life of Europe. I would have judged very favorably the proclamation of this principle: "Europe repudiates war". In truth today I still feel some hope of seeing this principle proclaimed in the European constitutional charter, but I have to acknowledge that this hope is truly rather weak. Besides, if we do not wish to use this expression, "Europe repudiates", because this term "repudiates" is highly distinctive and could almost indicate a certain "over-assertiveness" on the part of the Italians, for goodness' sake, let us use any other term, provided it af-firms the same concept of a firm rejection of war. In my opinion, on this topic it is necessary to rouse European public opinion, if necessary even with recourse to petitions, public appeals and other forms of activism, so as to open a serious and public debate on the subject. For my part, *before* meeting with the European Commission, but when its general bearings were already quite clear, I spoke directly to the Italian vice-president, formerly President of the Council of Ministers, namely the Hon. Giuliano Amato, a man indisputably of high legal and also politi-cal qualifications. I asked him: "Giuliano, do you feel it will prove possible to insert this remarkable exhortation to repudiate war into the European text?" Remember that this assertion does not add anything new to international law, because international law, as such, when it deals with the question of war only admits legitimate self-defense. So, to use Dante's words, would it ever be possible, by the *contradizione che nol consente*, to state a contradictory "right to aggression"? Besides, even if it were ever possible to speak of a "right to aggression", I am moved to ask: does this perhaps mean that we could even have a "right to kill", a "right to rob", a "right to murder", a "right to kidnap"? I would like to get a clear idea of this truly paradoxical situation, since the term "aggression" immediately involves a violation and an obvious wrong done to the rights of other people and so can never be reconciled, in any way, to the sphere of right.

Remember, moreover, that when the *Constituent Assembly* embraced this formula – absolutely exceptional – used in the eleventh article of the *Constitution*, it also very emphatically stressed at the same time *legitimate defense alone*. This topic clearly suggests other subjects. In particular, it means that legitimate defense, to be such, entails, on the international plane, the same conditions that this right also places on legitimate self-defense among individuals. The first condition is that there is already an *act of aggression being committed*. For now we shall omit, however, these considerations and observe that to be able to say *no to war and yes to peace* – because *yes to peace* certainly constitutes something more than just *no to war*, because it constitutes a *yes to life, a yes to mankind*, a *yes to freedom*, a *yes to the possibility of living in freedom in the midst of the freedom of others* – we must have one idea clear in our minds: that *war is evil*, that *war is always evil*.

Personally I travel a lot and, at least as long as the good Lord has the kindness to leave me health and a mind undimmed, I will always try to do so, because at these multiple encounters I always force myself to explain and make the Italians realize wherein lie the riches of a constitutional document like ours. For this reason, whenever I state forcefully that war is evil and that it fails to solve anything, I also find myself being presented with some objections. What's more, at some public debates I have been directly admonished. On one occasion, for example, I was asked this precise question: "But do you really think that we could have got rid of the evil of Hitler or Mussolini without a war?" Personally I can answer this question positively: I think we could have. To my mind, this question is in fact wrongly placed, because it examines the problem when it has reached its final stage, the stage of rottenness.

To my mind the question calls for a different approach. At a time when we are living in freedom, in democracy and in respect for human rights, there may also exist, within this precise situation, some *symptoms* which alert us to the fact that these very rights may be attacked and impaired. In an interview I also gave this example: the *Constitution* is made of a remarkable kind of wood and of the finest quality and strength, that is not damaged by the passing of time. Nevertheless, if at a certain point some worm bores its way into this wood and damage it from within, the time will eventually arrive when as soon as someone rests a hand on the wood it will penetrate inside it. Why? Because the worms have hollowed out the wood from inside: outside it seems to be intact, but all the wood inside has been reduced to dust and it is hollow. When this happens the least pressure is sufficient to make the outer surface give way. I have not chosen this example entirely by chance because it actually happens that in the estate of the Quirinal which overlooks the sea at Castel Porziano, there used to be some singular constructions in wood built a long time before, and if you rested your hand on one of them it would penetrate easily inside the wood, because it had been completely hollowed out by processionary caterpillars. It was not even possible to dismantle this structure and partially restore it, because there is a danger that the damage could spread further into the whole structure, so seriously jeopardizing the stability of the whole. To prevent this all the wood had to be burnt. But if someone had realized in time that this process of erosion had begun then it would have been possible to save the wood. How many symptoms were there that the wood had begun to be damaged? In the same way we have to ask ourselves: how many symptoms were there that revealed that Mussolini when in power was planning a situation that would end in dictatorship? That he was travelling along a road that would lead him to reject democracy and the parliamentary rules of the day? When did a similar process of systematic erosion of democracy and human rights begin in Germany with Hitler? At that time how many people felt they had a duty to take risks for the immense gift of freedom and how many instead believed that silence and fence-sitting were preferable, led by a concern to avoid trouble and protect their own private peace and quiet? In the last analysis, those who reasoned in this way believed that the values of freedom and human rights did not deserve to be paid for at a price that might even have involved not only the loss of their peace and quiet, but also the supreme value of the loss of their lives. Then, at least to my mind, it is useless to raise the question only when we are actually faced with the final and devastating state of these degenerated social processes, when the sole remaining remedy is the extreme one of starting a fire, because there is no longer anything else to be done.

6. Everything that Mortifies the Human Person Constitutes an Attack on Peace

Consequently the *no to war* affirms, without possible compromises, that war is evil. I will also add immediately that, while respecting Article 11 of the *Constitution*, we can also resort to arms for the sake of legitimate defense. As I told the *Constituent Assembly*, I voted this article with great conviction; but this repudiation of war does not in the least conflict with the legitimate defense of a territory and of a nation. Bear in mind that legitimate self-defense may even be a duty. It is, in particular, when a part of the state, for example in a border area, is attacked for any reason or when its rights are in some way impaired. In this case Government and Parliament have the duty and not just the right to intervene to protect the rights of the citizens living in these zones of the state. Why? Because these citizens have a right to safety. A right to safety that – if we think about it for a moment – is closely bound up with the right to peace, which is fundamental. Note well: in this case, too, the recourse to arms constitutes an evil, but it is a *necessary evil*, an unavoidable evil, an evil involved in the defense certain fundamental rights.

Will we ever succeed in educating ourselves to accept these ideas? We will succeed if we really want to emerge from a situation that has already caused incalculable tragedies and untold sufferings in recent centuries. In this respect we need only think of the 20th century and its immense tragedies and the untold sufferings that were a part of it. This means we have to appraise, with extreme precision, exactly what constitutes an attack on peace. Now I would say that *everything that mortifies the human person constitutes an attack on peace.* If there exists a true, essential and constituent difference between a dictatorial regime and a democratic regime, we have to say that it is rooted in the different degrees of consideration they give to the person. When people's rights are crushed – they lack the right to vote, the right to association, they are forced to belong to a sole party, they lack the right to speak their thoughts publicly and freely, etc. – then the individual is obviously under attack. When this annihilation of the person occurs, democracy certainly no longer exists. There is no doubt that democracy is a term that can be highly controversial. Nevertheless I would say, synthetically, that *democracy constitutes the enhancement of the rights of the person.*

I speak of "enhancement", pointing out that the fact that the rights are written certainly constitutes a considerable achievement: only the existence of this written document permits citizens to take full cognizance of their rights and enables them to protest if they are denied. But I should also add that precisely the specific space of true politics is also rooted on this ground, meaning politics with a capital letter, which operates precisely in the passage from rights proclaimed to rights lived. This constitutes, in reality, a continuous and even troubled but truly decisive development. It is in this precise context and in this specific space that we have to confirm that the symptoms of any gap between the abstract reality of rights and their concrete fulfilment can be perceived as authentic attacks on peace.

7. War Always Involves Lies

This is not all: in the light of what has been said above it is also necessary to point out that the denial of truth also constitutes an aggression. In the past we have frequently been able to verify the presence of this aggression. Communism, for example, consecrated large spaces, truly incredible spaces, to the *no to truth*. But we can also ask ourselves: how should we place the situation that has arisen in international affairs, when, it was repeatedly stated by the American president Bush, with force and determination, that there definitely existed undeniable proof which justified the Americans in affirming that Iraq possessed weapons of mass destruction? This is something have we all lived through quite recently and which we are still living through today. We all know that those whom the United Nations appointed to carry out inspections to discover these weapons of mass destruction in Iraq said they found nothing. And recently they specifically requested to be allowed six months longer to complete their investigations, which had failed to find any trace of these weapons of mass destruction. What's more, now American forces themselves have spent a long time in Iraqi territory and have still failed to find anything. Italian radio – not television – in a recent broadcast actually quoted a British Minister as saying that the fact that to date no trace of these weapons of mass destruction has been found in Iraq does not mean that these weapons don't actually exist. Naturally this argument might even be put forward more or less brilliantly and cogently. Nevertheless, speaking as a magistrate, permit me to observe that if we place ourselves on this level then we can say anything and the opposite of anything. If as a magistrate I had reasoned in this way, I would have been dismissed from the service because with this kind of logic everyone would be a law unto himself. Just think, for example, of the situation of a person who accused someone else of being a murderer:

You're a murderer.

"But at least tell who I'm supposed to have killed", the defendant would object.

No, you're a murderer and there's nothing more to be said.

I do feel there's nothing more to be said. As a magistrate I have become accustomed to reasoning in a rather different way, because I always have to stick to the *facts*, which can and must be checked, verified and documented.

However these arguments are not two thousand years old, they go back just a few weeks. When we state that there exists a bloodthirsty dictator who tyrannizes over the people of Iraq no one in the least disputes this fact. Just as no one disputes the fact that Saddam has been one of the worst and most bloodthirsty dictators. All the same, we can also ask some questions and make some observations. We can ask, for example: how long has Saddam been a bloodthirsty dictator? Naturally ever since he started killing thousands of people. But why is he being charged with this crime only today, so many years later? Or was there perhaps a period when Saddam was self-evidently a bloodthirsty dictator and was there then another period when a veil of silence was on the whole drawn over the fact that he was a bloodthirsty dictator? I should also add that when I was a magistrate the defendant that I had to deal with was never intermittently a defendant, but was always the defendant until the end of the trial, when he would be either acquitted or sentenced. On this plane of reflection there naturally emerges the ethical dimension: we cannot use one measure of judgment because at a certain point it proves useful, while at another time it is no help and therefore we forget about it. So we can ask ourselves whether Bin Laden was always an enemy or whether for many years he wasn't actually a friend. Certainly: we can easily have some friends and then change them, however it is also necessary to add that there always exists a minimum of human and intellectual rigour. When this rigour disappears our arguments are no longer ethical but simply risk becoming rubbish or opportunism and the most blatant cynicism.

But can we really bring civilization to a people – a people that has lost much of it or that never had it – by starting with a *lie*? The *no to truth* actually constitutes one of the gravest and most serious social crimes, precisely as the negation of justice constitutes an attack on peace, and also the denial of equitable conditions of life or the denial of equal dignity to people can only increase an objectively conflict-ridden situation, wholly opposed to peace. In this respect I would also like to refer to a historically macroscopic fact that, when I was Head of State, I used to speak of on endless occasions: will we ever give serious consideration to the devastating effect on the human spirit of the glaring contrasts between excessive affluence and true poverty? Poverty wreaks terrible havoc with the dignity of the human person and ends up nullifying many human rights, even though they may be recognized in the abstract. So we should clearly realize our precise responsibility, when at a certain moment on one side there is the arrogance of power, while on the other side there are literally people abandoned to the blackest and most absolute poverty, without any help forthcoming. This is the very opposite of solidarity and brotherhood! Whenever this happens we observe the open *wound* inflicted on these feelings. To my mind, when these scandals occur we have to assert, with force and determination, that peace and the right to peace constitute the protection of the whole set of the rights of the person, what we call and affirm constitutes *human rights*.

8. Human Rights and the Death Sentence in the World

Besides, we need only reflect on the historical case of the death sentence. In our recent European civil history the penal code – not just the military code but also the civil code – explicitly provided for the death sentence. In general, the classic case that invoked the death sentence was that of murder deliberately committed during an armed robbery. After the downfall of fascism and the birth of democracy, in Italy the death sentence was finally removed from the civil code. Nevertheless, it should also be added that it would not be wholly correct to affirm that the death sentence was finally abolished when "democracy was born", because, in actual fact, there still exist today some peoples that claim, justly, to be civilized and democratic and that include the possibility of inflicting the death sentence in their penal codes for specific offences. We need only think of the many states of the United States in which the death sentence still exists and where the executioner's work has still not finished his work. Those who, because of their civil commitment or in the line of duty, have had the opportunity of approaching a person under sentence of death know the full significance of the dramatic moment of the passing of the death sentence. A person sentenced to capital punishment, with a his hopes intimately and directly bound up with life, naturally always thinks that it is impossible that he will really be exterminated and annihilated and therefore, from the day following the sentence, he awakes and begins continually to nurse the hope that sooner or later he will finally be reprieved. Then there comes a morning when he is informed that within just a few hours he is to be put to death.

Then we perceive how this man, at this point, seems already to have made a distant leap: he seems to have entered another dimension, so true it is that much has even been written about what happened to those people who, at the very moment when they were to be put to death (by hanging or shooting), for some reason were finally reprieved at the last moment. This "return" to the world was not always serene and peaceful. At times it even caused profound traumas, because the condemned man had already suffered a previous trauma of "departure", leaving life and the world behind him. It is necessary to ponder on these experiences and on the tragic dynamic of these sentences so as to fully understand all their horror and tragedy.

In this respect I wish to remember that I personally had the opportunity to discuss the death sentence serenely with Jan Xe Ming – who, at least until a few months ago, was number one in China, which is a country, we should always remember, of 1.3 billion human beings. Our conversation took place within the customary framework of international relations which, naturally, always need to be appraised with great calm and attention. Certainly it is out of the question to think one has become like an old friend of the head of a foreign state as the result of a conversation lasting just a few minutes. One may even gain this impression, but it is only a fine and rather misleading thought. One reason is the by now irreplaceable use of English, which, as you know, does not use forms of courtesy in direct speech: speakers simply address each other as "you". So this may help foster this illusory impression of closeness. All the same, we should never draw some hasty conclusions, because then we end up falling into self deception. Nevertheless, it is also true that at times there can spring up a more cordial and human strain of conversation, as well as a relationship of deeper trust, as when one succeeds in looking into another's eyes with a certain depth, feeling a certain harmony.

Well, at one of these meetings that I had with Jan Xe Ming I remember that I discussed the death sentence as part of a rather courteous and indeed friendly conversation (of course I did not speak in the improbable role of an "attorney general", accusing the Chinese with practicing the death sentence). I recalled that we ourselves, for a certain period, had contemplated the death sentence in our criminal code and how at a certain point we finally abolished it altogether. In this respect I also wish to recall that as Head of State I had the honor of signing the law with which the death sentence was abolished in our military criminal code. I remember, finally, that when I was a young student and our professors explained this military rule to us, it seemed to be logical enough and wholly comprehensible, because when a soldier flees from the enemy, he is escaping from the possibility of death at the front (life imprisonment is obviously not an option at the front). Parallel with this specific action of flight, a conviction to life imprisonment seems to almost coincide with winning a prize, because in this case the soldier's life would be safe. So only the death penalty seemed appropriate to the crime committed by escaping from the danger of death, which was faced by all the other soldiers who did not fail to do their duty. Only subsequently did we realize that the death sentence is always an evil, because we never have the right to deprive a human being of life.

Be that as it may, when I spoke of this with Jan Xe Ming, he told me something that was very true. He observed that the Chinese people would not have understood a decision to abolish the death penalty; or rather they would have thought that from then on criminals would feel authorized to do whatever they liked. Since our conversation was taking place on a cordial human plane, wholly serene, I refrained from adding other arguments against the death penalty (such as its final and irre-versible character, together with the fallibility of human judgments) because by insisting I would have committed a grave discourtesy, as if I wanted at all costs to put him in a difficult position. In particular I refrained from pointing out that the Chinese carry out an average of some 1,500-2,000 executions a year. Naturally the issue is not merely quantitative, because the population of China is well over a billion, and just one case of capital punishment is sufficient to set its seal on a country. I might, however, have asked what how effective these numer-ous cases of capital punishment were, given the very high number of executions registered in China every year. How effective was the death sentence in China if it led to so many executions? This objection is certainly the most simple, but also the most difficult to answer. True, it could be answered that the number of felonies in China is relatively small, precisely because of the death penalty. It is not, however, my intention here to discuss this problem in detail: my purpose is to direct your attention to the fact that in the present world there exist some civilized peoples and other peoples who refuse to respect this civiliza-tion. Nevertheless, even among the civilized peoples there are states that still retain the roots of non-civilization and that maintain them also with an aggravating circumstance in the way in which they inflict the death penalty. Because, when a person is sentenced to death and the sentence is applied shortly after, this a grave fact in itself. But it is even more serious when several years may pass between the sentence and its execution. Remember that the years do not pass with the condemned person being informed that for a precise lapse of time the sentence has been suspended. No, this is not what happens, because instead the years pass with the criminal knowing that every day that dawns may bring the execution which follows from a sentence that has already been handed down. The result is that the condemned person lives through this period in continuous and agonized expectation of the precise instant when he will finally be told that the sentence will be executed by the state. This is why we read that at times a person has been awaiting execution for ten or twelve years or more. As you can imagine, this is an utterly terrible and unacceptable situation. Personally I do not understand how a person can support such a devastating psychological situation for years on end, and I dare not even think imagine the effects of this anguished waiting. Moreover, these dramatic situations create those highly singular human divisions, with one person is found on one side and the other on the other side, with the result that their reciprocal collocation is radically different.

9. The Struggle Against Terrorism and its Prerequisites

But let us now return to our principal subject. When I pointed out that the European statutes ignore this right to peace, I did not deny that in these statutes and in their comprehensive articulation there appears to be a series of rights that may also move in this wished-for direction of the repudiation of war and the affirmation of the right to peace. Certainly we cannot overlook the fact that *Constitutions* always, by their very nature, tend to indicate potentially ideal situations, which are never perfect realized in the world. Besides, if we were to achieve the complete and perfect fulfilment of the first eleven articles of our *Constitution*, it would certainly help in the attainment of peace, justice, freedom, full respect of others, etc. (Remember that I am neglecting the twelfth article of the *Fundamental Principles of the Constitution*, because it concerns the Italian flag, which for us is clearly all that is most sacred. However the flag expresses, but it does not constitute, a right and it does not constitute even an assertion of a right. At most it is the symbol of all these rights, the symbol of this people, the symbol of this our homeland).

But the subject of peace that I am required to talk about also entailed consideration of the problems bound up with *respect for the rules*. It is needless to add that this second subject is of considerable breadth, because there exist the rules of normal democratic life, of administrative life and constitutional rules, or rules concerning, more directly, the specific realities that we experience. I will dwell a little one on this subject. After 11 September, President Bush declared he intended to wage war on terrorism. At that time I did not approve of this position and said so at the first discussions that took place on the same day that Bush made this declaration of war on terrorism. I allowed myself to observe – and I still persist in the same opinion today – that if the expression used by Bush, "to make war", was used in a general sense, in the sense that we should fight and oppose terrorism, then certainly I had no misgivings. Besides, for four years I was the Minister of the Interior when terrorism was raging in Italy, at a highly dramatic time, and so I know well what fighting terrorism means. But I also know that if instead we use the term "war", in the traditional sense – meaning one state attacking another – then, at least in my opinion, he was definitely heading down the wrong path right from the start. Why? Because in this sense a war involves a people and a whole people is never guilty. To show that a people is guilty some incredible tests are necessary. Can we really claim that the Italian people who on 10 June 1940 went into a public square to praise the Duce and acclaim Mussolini (who stated that the declaration of war had already been delivered to the ambassadors of

49

France and Britain), were really responsible for the war? Can we maintain it in all conscience, with legal, logical, serious arguments?

9.1. International Solidarity

Starting in part from my experience as Minister of the Interior I can claim with good reason that certain diseases are always the same, independently of the fact that they affect millions of people or only ten or fifteen individuals. The disease does not change because of the numbers of the persons involved. The first element of struggle is supplied by *solidarity*. How can we fail to remember that when the towers in New York were attacked, expressions of solidarity flowed in from nearly all the world? Remember that in those very days there was a meeting between Bush and Premier Putin, representing Russia. Do you remember that meeting? Do you remember that people dressed in local costumes also took part? This solidarity towards the Americans sprang naturally from the hearts of the different peoples of the world, who in those days were really clasped the Americans in an ideal embrace. Even those who were far from New York then felt the need to express their sympathy for the American people tangibly. Those days also led to a meeting between Bush and Jan Xe Ming. This meeting happened in the days following 11 September. The Chinese people, so far away, also felt the need to meet Bush directly. Then it was truly a human meeting, because each felt that in those towers and in those thousands of people massacred all of us were injured because the whole of humanity had been injured, mankind, the person in his dignity. Therefore, in the struggle against terrorism the first and fundamental element was precisely solidarity. But how was this solidarity expressed? Was it expressed perhaps by saying, "We will go and fight this or that people?" Or was it expressed by acting in such a way that the alliance between the different peoples was transformed into an effective operative instrument, for greater coordination and communication of all the information that each can possibly collect so as to better understand terrorism and fight against it? Acting so that each country makes available to the all the other countries all the information and all the knowledge it possesses, so as to fight international terrorism with greater knowledge and better coordination? Anyone who is responsible for the forces of law and order knows full well just what it means to share all the available information, including much that may strike us as useless or of little significance. In fact what to us may seem uninteresting can actually help another organization to sound the alarm by ensuring significant measures to better understand terrorism and so combat it. This solidarity is of fundamental importance in working successfully to concentrate different forces on a single, common strategic objective. Certainly on the international plane one can also realize a movement of thousands of people, comparable to the movement of an army that moves to attack specific points, to seek to drive out terrorists and to succeed in identifying some secret alliances that screen or assist the various terrorists. But this international collaboration in the struggle against terrorism is quite different from a traditional war, conducted against a state.

Besides, precisely now – just when Bush has now declared that the war in Iraq has ended – the Americans are actually having to accept terrible human losses, since the number of their young soldiers killed in Iraq *after* the cessation of hostilities is clearly higher than the number of the soldiers killed in combat. But is there anyone who is willing to maintain that the Iraqi soldiers who died in battle were terrorists? Or has perhaps someone discovered that all these soldiers were terrorists? In reality they were only soldiers and officers who went to do their duty to because their homeland, their government, called on them to defend their country. Bush's attempt to superimpose the phenomenon of terrorism on a whole state or a whole people is a complete failure to respect the international rules. Authentic respect for the rules would have involved sharing his knowledge and truly working together and in unison, without acts of selfishness or disloyal competition between the various states. If one state has specific information, it may decide to carry out a mission so as to make a good showing, but in this case it only seeks its own advantage at the price of wrecking the solidarity with its allies.

I remember that when I was Interior Minister, at Ministerial Council Meetings, I always used to repeat the same argument, with the intention of promoting a series of agreements between all of the states of Europe that were really willing to create a unified front to fight terrorism. In this way I contracted a series of international agreements that enabled the various member countries of the European Community to act in close liaison. When I first went to Brussels or Strasbourg, I can't remember which it was, I attended a meeting with all my colleagues from other countries in the European Community who had my same responsibility, and immediately pointed out that no state could win this battle against terrorism alone. And what was even more serious, that no one would ever lose it alone: if even one state was defeated in the battle against terrorism, then the others would also succumb. For this reason we all had to act together, very carefully and warily, constantly coordinating our common efforts and the aims of our struggle. For this same reason, rather than discussing the issues simultaneously with all my European colleagues, I instead began to meet and discuss them individually with each of my different colleagues. In this way I succeeded in contracting agreements with each European state and, subsequently, also with the more accessible states on the Mediterranean front in Africa and finally also in the Middle East.

9.2. Understanding the Causes of Terrorism

I still remember the threats that rained in when we signed an agreement with Israel and I also recall the threats from the Arab world, even though we had also signed agreements for extensive alliances with this Arab world, which deserves respect and which is also important in maintaining a peace front. At the time my sphere of action against terrorism enabled me substantially to discover, to prevent and to strike. For this precise reason, when I went to the Council of Ministers – the president was Craxi (with whom I had an excellent relationship, for which I am grateful) – I also remembered that it was necessary to study the causes of this disease represented by terrorism. Those who are in the front line, like the Interior Minister, cannot confine themselves to preventing and striking at terrorism; they also have to study its causes and try to get to the roots of it. From this point of view, American policy as adopted and pursued by Bush reveals a complete failure to respect the rules. And I can also see a parallel failure in the study of the causes of international terrorism. This is because it is essential to study their causes if we are to have the courage to question ourselves. Faced with international terrorism America must inevitably question itself, above all if we consider that it possesses a tradition of respect for the truth that does it honor. Above all, when it had the courage to admit that anthrax had been found in American territory which had been manufactured in the USA itself.

We must also bear in mind – as has been confirmed and explained also by our own air force pilots – that the twin towers of the New York Trade Center attacked by the terrorists, when approached at a certain height, were narrower than two pencils. So if the pilots succeeded in making direct hits on them, this means the pilots must have been exceptionally skilful. But where had they been trained to fly airliners with this precision? Had they trained in a terrorist country, a rogue state, or in a free and democratic country? So will we have the courage to question ourselves and study these problems thoroughly?

10.   War Is Always Evil

These are the questions and problems that lead us to say: take warning, because war is always evil. Recently I was invited to a discussion and I began by saying that I had actually been invited rather like a period piece. In fact I was introduced as having been invited because they appreciated "listening to someone from the period", meaning a person who had been a member of the *Constituent Assembly*, when the *Constitution* was voted. In particular I was asked how much time we spent deliberating Article 11. Now, if you actually read the proceedings of the constituent assembly, you will find that there are scores of pages of discussion devoted to most articles. But in the case of Article 11, you will find only a few pages, five or six. Why? Because no one presented any particular objections. This term "repudiates" – which to my mind is truly splendid because it leaves no room for any doubt – was proposed by the commission because different terminologies were being used, but the concept was always the same: the rejection of war. If there were a few moments of debate, it only centerd on international law, considering that the article in question confronts a prophetic subject, because it affirms that Italy "agrees to limitations of sovereignty where they are necessary to allow for a legal system of peace and justice between nations, provided the principle of reciprocity is guaranteed; it promotes and encourages international organizations furthering such ends".

As can be seen, with this article Italy is pledged to work for the creation of international institutions, such as the United Nations and the Security Council, for the aims of peace and justice between nations. On this basis, the discussion and the vote, held on 24 February 1947, was very brief and concise. Why there was so little discussion? Because in February 1947 less than two years had passed since May 1945, when Second World War ended in Europe. We still had no idea how many people had died in that Second World War and perhaps we still cannot really tell even today. Then, for the first time more civilians had been killed than soldiers. Cities were destroyed, railways blown up, bridges and roads were largely impassable. We were faced with an authentic disaster. Does this mean, asked one of those who were present at that assembly, that to be firm in our repudiation of the war we need to have lost thousands or hundreds of thousands of deaths? Is it necessary for a nation to be destroyed? Whole cities devastated?

11. The Need for a Unified European Policy

What has saddened me is to see that those who discussed these measures for Europe did not close all doors to war, because they believed there might even a probability that war can solve certain problems. In reality, this has never been true and will never be true. If I may be allowed to remember the following episode, which happened to me many years ago, when, for a weekend, I visited Alto Adige, at a time when there existed enormous pressure for these territories to be handed over to Austria. Someone who saw me may have thought I was been born in the 18th century, but I assure you that I was born in 1918 and was therefore born at a time when six hundred thousand people died in war. Those young people born in 1918, at school – the and not only at school, but also in the family and in the whole of society – were taught and admonished thousands of times over of the cost to Italy of the First World War, which was meant to represent the definitive conclusion of the Italian Risorgimento, with the conquest of Trento and Trieste. Not for nothing when we were still at primary school, did they explain the historical importance of this conquest, even though they did it in such a way that some of my classmates actually believed that Trento and Trieste were next door to one another and very close to us.

When it was finally explained that this was not actually the case, it was confirmed that with the conquest of these two territories finally Italy "was complete" within its definitive boundaries, and that the sacrifice of all those who fell in this First World War had made it possible to permanently complete the Italian national territory. But some twenty years later, by which time I was an adult, these territorial gains were again in jeopardy. Or rather, Trieste was not in jeopardy, while Trento was loudly demanding annexation by Austria. So what was the use of the earlier sacrifice of our six hundred thousand Italian soldiers? Besides, can we forget that on 10 June 1940 we then declared war against France, when it already faced defeat?

Fortunately there were these authentic prophets of Europe – I am thinking of De Gasperi, Adenauer and Schuman – who affirmed an important principle, all too often forgotten: only a *political Europe* will be fit and able to say a definitive no to war. Of course the Europe of the unified market and the Europe of the single currency are also important, but this economic Europe does not fully possess the intrinsic strength that can only stem from its political unity. You will all certainly remember the tragic situation that we lived through not long ago, when war finally resurfaced directly in Europe. No one would ever have believed it possible that war could return to Europe after the devastation wrought by Second World War. At their meetings, how often did the Foreign Ministers of the various member countries of Europe order a ceasefire in Kosovo and all the other regions where war was raging? They did so repeatedly, but it was of completely ineffectual, it was as if they had not even spoken. And remember this: it was not that they lacked authority, but they lacked a strong, unified *political* voice. To truly build Europe, it is essential to have this strong, common *political* voice. Only the political unity of Europe will succeed in laying the most enduring and effective foundations to ensure we speak with an authoritative voice that will be heeded in the international context, capable of contributing effectively to world peace. Without this common political unity in the world context, the voice of the Europe will always be too weak and ineffective.

So, at least to my mind, our condemnation of war as a false and illusory method of solving international differences must be radical and coherent, while it is equally necessary to fully recognize the right to legitimate self-defense against any aggression.

12. The Duty of Dialogue and Peace

Though I may perhaps have made heavy demands on your patience, please allow me to sum up these observations. Recently a journalist asked me, the inevitable question: what can we oppose war with? *Dialogue*. Because if we are convinced that war is evil, then only dialogue will enable us to understand the reasons of others. If man is a rational creature then he should use reason, not his muscles. But if man, when he is in the right, uses his muscles and his fists, then he descends well below his own humanity. The same thing happens with war, whose affirmation and whose proclamation coincide simply and equally radically with the inability to engage in dialogue. If someone asked provocatively, "But do you want to engage in dialogue even with Bin Laden?", I would answer that in truth I was not the one who engaged in dialogue with Bin some Laden some years back. And besides, can't the same people who were able to engage in dialogue with Bin some Laden some years ago do the same now?

I remember that when I had governmental responsibilities, each year we confirmed a comprehensive no to dialogue with China because China failed to respect human rights. Then, when the China applied to enter world markets as part of the business community, everyone forgot about human rights. Because when it entered the market, China came not only to sell but to buy. Today the Economic Minister raises various objections, but it should also be added that when a precise economic interest exists, then other objections are rapidly brushed aside, because economic reasons alone prevail. But respect for human rights will win only if we believe completely in dialogue and debate between people. But if it is to win it is essential not to harbour any uncertainty about the value of dialogue and debate.

I would also like to draw a second indication that, moreover, is closely bound up with great and immense political figure of Alcide De Gasperi, who taught us these concepts, disseminated them around the world and always wanted to fulfil them as far as possible. Bearing in mind what we were told by the Metropolitan Archbishop of Lecce, Monsignor Cosmo Francesco Ruppi (when he spoke to us about this day, with its celebrations for John Paul II's twenty-fifth year of papal service), I would like to take a cue from this news to stress the way this pontiff has always proclaimed peace to the world and has defended peace not as the head of a religion but as a man who has authority over humanity and who, as such, defends people of every color, of every faith, and even those without any faith. In this defense of peace by the pope, everyone feels interpreted by this man, who does not defend Christians or Christianity alone, or Muslims and Islam alone.

This defense of peace by Pope John Paul II struck me as remarkable, possessing a universal value. This is because the pontiff represents one who said, "I give you peace, I give you my peace", but not as the world gives it. This is the man who, when he announced his agenda, said only: "I give you a new commandment". It is not new in the sense that it had never been proclaimed before, but in the sense that it affirmed a vital teaching, that it possessed a vital force for the continuous renewal of the world: "Love one another", with a special crescendo: "This love is how everyone will know you". Wonderful! We also recognize those who are friends of peace. And others will also recognize us if we are friends. But in the evangelical message there is then a final crescendo, an authentic high note, with Jesus saying: "Love your enemies". What did he say? "Love your enemies". If in the course of your life you never meet any enemies, then the question is simple and faith can be uncomplicated. But the question becomes much more challenging and difficult if instead we encounter enemies with whom we have to attempt the path of dialogue and peace.

This teaching recalls us to another duty. To the duty of remembering that this our *Constitution* – which today, as often at other times, all too often, is being subjected to attacks – was paid for with great bloodshed and many tears by people who fought and pledged to give us a different Italy: free, democratic and republican. Now, this *Constitution* certainly has as its guardians the Head of State, Parliament, Government, and the Constitutional Court. Nevertheless, its first protection lies in all Italian citizens who believe in this *Constitution* and who keep watch with open eyes, because they know and love it. Here, too, it is a case of love, because our *Constitution* embodies certain fundamental values. So I am prompted to close these observations with a greeting that Francis of Assisi always addressed to all: *"The Lord give you peace"*.

FIRST SECTION

VALUES IN SCIENCE

Pourquoi une philosophie des sciences ne peut se réduire à une épistémologie des sciences

Evandro AGAZZI

Università di Genova

1. La double signification du terme « épistémologie »

Une certaine difficulté dans la manière de concevoir la philosophie des sciences dépend d'une circonstance purement linguistique, à savoir du fait que, en certaines langues et notamment en français, le terme « épistémologie » signifie parfois « théorie de la connaissance » et parfois « philosophie des sciences ». La première signification est plus ancienne et se retrouve, par exemple, dans le titre d'un ouvrage classique comme *Épistémologie* de van Steenberghen (qui est un traité de théorie de la connaissance dans le sillon de la tradition thomiste) ou dans une expression devenue elle-aussi classique comme l'« épistémologie génétique » de Piaget (qui est une théorie des étapes de la constitution des structures cognitives humaines basée sur des recherches de psychologie expérimentale). Toutefois, la signification de ce terme est devenue de plus en plus, dans les publications des années récentes, celle de 'philosophie des sciences'. Cette ambivalence s'explique d'ailleurs par le fait que le terme grec *èpistémê*, qui en constitue l'étymologie, est traduit habituellement par « science », mais aussi par « connaissance » ou « savoir », ce qui est dans une certaine mesure légitime puisque dans le contexte de la pensée grecque les trois termes étaient pratiquement synonymes. Au sein de la culture occidentale moderne, toutefois, le terme « science » a été rapidement employé pour dénoter les sciences naturelles et les mathématiques, à savoir des formes et systèmes de connaissance spécifiques et plus parfaits que la connaissance de sens commun ou celle qu'on obtient dans d'autres domaines disciplinaires. De cette manière on pouvait penser à une sorte de distinction entre une théorie « générale » de la connaissance (que les langues néo-latines ont appelée habituellement « gnoséologie ») et une théorie de cette forme

« spéciale » de la connaissance qu'est la science (et pour cette deuxième théorie le terme « épistémologie » se présente comme tout à fait naturel). Toutefois cette partition semble exprimer une convention plutôt qu'une claire distinction conceptuelle et en effet la confluence de ces deux significations a été encouragée par le fait que la science naturelle moderne s'est vite imposée comme une sorte de paradigme du savoir tout-court (spécialement avec Kant), et cela a eu comme conséquence que les conditions de la connaissance « scientifique » ont été présentées comme conditions de la connaissance authentique *en général*. Par conséquent, certains philosophes ont été de l'avis que la philosophie de la science est en réalité la forme moderne de la théorie de la connaissance. En adoptant ce point de vue on pourrait donc dire que la vieille gnoséologie ou épistémologie a évolué sans solution de continuité dans l'étude de la connaissance scientifique en gardant légitimement sa dénomination d'« épistémologie ».

On pourrait analyser d'autres raisons du déclin de la théorie générale de la connaissance, liées spécialement au fait que, après la saison de l'idéalisme, on a perdu l'habitude de considérer la connaissance comme une « forme » ou « activité » de l'esprit et on s'est concentré, en philosophie, sur les procédures et méthodes qui sont censées produire une connaissance et qui sont représentées essentiellement par les sciences. Toutefois nous ne voulons pas ignorer qu'une pareille identification de théorie de la connaissance et théorie des sciences n'est guère universellement adoptée dans le monde philosophique. En particulier, dans le contexte culturel anglo-américain contemporain *epistemology* continue à dénoter la théorie de la connaissance (selon la terminologie introduite par J. F. Ferrier en 1854) et ne se confond pas avec la *philosophy of science*, en dépit de la haute considération dont jouit la science dans ce même contexte.

2. L'optique gnoséologique de la philosophie des sciences

La distinction entre théorie de la connaissance et philosophie des sciences qui, comme on vient de le voir, a été admise par plusieurs philosophes contemporains n'a pas empêché que la philosophie des sciences, à partir du moment où elle s'est constituée comme discipline philosophique spécialisée (à savoir, dès le début du XXe siècle) se soit caractérisée largement comme une étude concernant la portée cognitive et les modalités cognitives de la science, c'est-à-dire, selon une perspective qui considérait la science essentiellement comme un *savoir*, se rattachant par cela à l'identification « science = savoir » qui a dominé la culture occidentale. Pour les anciens méritait le nom de science (*épistémê*) un savoir plein et bien fondé, c'est-à-dire consistant en propositions vraies, jouissant des caractéristiques de l'universalité et nécessité, doué d'une certitude qui lui venait du fait de se fonder déductivement sur des principes ontologiques évidents, d'après un modèle de connaissance axiomatiquement articulée et garantie par l'intuition intellectuelle et la rigueur logique. Kant n'avait pas modifié cette conception de la science, se limitant à trouver le fondement du savoir non plus dans l'intuition intellectuelle de principes ontologiques mais dans l'action législatrice des formes pures *a priori* de nos pouvoirs cognitifs, s'appliquant aux donnés des sens. Les « objets » de notre connaissance n'étaient plus que des « phénomènes », mais on pouvait atteindre à leur sujet un *savoir* authentique et bien fondé. Pour les philosophes des sciences contemporains le problème n'est plus celui de proposer un modèle général de savoir dont les sciences pourraient être de bons exemples. Ils présupposent que les sciences sont les formes les plus réussies du savoir et, sans se préoccuper de rechercher des fondements ontologiques ou des conditions de validité dans les formes de nos pouvoirs cognitifs qui les garantissent, sans même prétendre que ce savoir soit doué de certitude, universalité et nécessité, ils *analysent* les structures de ce savoir, en employant des analyses méthodologiques, logiques, linguistiques. Nous pouvons donc conclure que la philosophie des sciences, dans ses premières manifestations, se présentait comme une sorte de « théorie de la connaissance partielle appliquée » dans le sens suivant. Dans la théorie de la connaissance traditionnelle on peut distinguer deux domaines : l'un concernant l'étude des procédures, des « mécanismes » cognitifs qui permettent au sujet de connaître les choses ; l'autre concernant les résultats de ce connaître, c'est-à-dire le savoir. La philosophie des sciences ne s'occupait pas du premier domaine, mais seulement du deuxième (voilà pourquoi nous disons qu'elle était une théorie de la connaissance partielle) et, de plus, elle se voulait une théorie du savoir « appliquée », c'est-à-dire consciemment limitée à l'étude du savoir scientifique. Pour ces raisons nous pouvons affirmer que la philosophie des sciences s'est constituée à l'intérieur d'une *optique gnoséologique* : en l'appelant « épistémologie » on soulignait implicitement que son intérêt se limitait à étudier l'aspect gnoséologique (c'est-à-dire « épistémologique » au sens traditionnel) de la science. Partant, la philosophie des sciences a été conçue pendant une longue période comme une *épistémologie des sciences*.

3. Le dépassement de l'optique strictement gnoséologique

L'approche que nous venons de décrire conférait à la philosophie des sciences certains traits de la théorie traditionnelle de la connaissance, à savoir les caractéristiques d'une investigation abstraite. La vieille gnoséologie (ou 'épistémologie') étudiait des entités abstraites telles que la sensation, la perception, la mémoire, la fantaisie, l'abstraction, le jugement, l'argumentation. La nouvelle épistémologie s'occupait d'un objet également abstrait : « la science » qui était conçu comme la juxtaposition de deux « types idéaux », celui des « sciences formelles » et celui des « sciences empiriques ». L'idéalisation se manifestait d'abord dans le fait que les sciences étaient réduites à des *constructions linguistiques* et, en deuxième lieu, dans le fait que la « constitution » et la « légitimation » de ces constructions étaient déterminées d'après des simples *critères méthodologiques* : pour les sciences formelles le critère de constitution était l'axiomatisation formelle (conçue selon l'approche formaliste de la nouvelle méthode axiomatique) et le critère de légitimation se réduisait essentiellement à la cohérence ou non-contradiction. Pour les sciences empiriques les critères de constitution étaient la présence de termes « observationnels » et les « généralisations empiriques » et le critère de légitimation consistait dans le « contrôle empirique » des généralisations obtenu moyennant une procédure « hypothético-déductive ». Nous ne sommes pas intéressés ici à considérer les lourdes présuppositions d'*empirisme radical* qui caractérisaient une telle philosophie des sciences ; nous voulons simplement souligner que des facteurs tels que l'expérience, la déduction logique, la cohérence, l'analyse conceptuelle et linguistique étaient considérés comme les uniques aspects pertinents, pour étudier une « science » idéalisée en dehors de toute considération historique véritable. En effet, quand on parlait de science au sein de ces études on se référait vaguement à une mathématique idéale construite d'après les règles de la méthode axiomatique et à une science empirique vaguement identifiable à la physique classique. Les rares références que ces auteurs faisaient de temps en temps à quelque exemple tiré de l'histoire des sciences étaient très élémentaires et sommaires et se prêtaient facilement à des interprétations opposées.

La situation a graduellement changé dès qu'on a commencé à apprécier les effets de la contextualisation historique et sociale de la science, une mise en contexte qui ne se limite pas à influencer les approches intellectuelles et les cadres conceptuels de la recherche scientifique, mais qui pèse beaucoup sur l'acceptation et l'abandon des théories scientifiques. À ce moment on s'est rendu compte que la simple analyse logico-linguistique ne suffit pas à nous faire comprendre l'aspect *dynamique* de la science et que, partant, la vision de celle-ci comme un savoir uniquement fondé sur le jeu réciproque d'évidence empirique et cohérence logique ne capture pas sa nature véritable. Malheureusement beaucoup d'auteurs ont tiré des conséquences excessives de cette prise de conscience et, au lieu de reconnaître le rôle nécessaire que jouent ces facteurs *à l'intérieur d'un contexte socio-historique déterminé*, ont affirmé que les sciences ne constituent pas une forme de *savoir* plus rigoureux et fondé que n'importe quelle autre forme de prétendue connaissance. Il ne nous intéresse pas de critiquer ici ces positions car nous voulons examiner maintenant quelles sont certaines « dimensions » de la science qui se sont imposées à l'attention des philosophes des sciences et qui ne se réduisent pas à sa dimension cognitive.

4. La dimension pratique de la science

Le point central de la nouvelle perspective consistait dans le fait de considérer la science essentiellement comme un système d'*actions* humaines, de *pratiques* visant sans doute à construire un savoir, mais en même temps rentrant dans un réseau complexe d'interactions avec d'autres activités et pratiques humaines au niveau social. Il s'agissait, d'un côté, d'une conception moins « intellectualiste » de la science dans le sens que, tout en admettant que l'intention de connaître y demeure centrale, on reconnaissait que les instruments de cette connaissance ne sont pas déposés dans une sorte de « raison scientifique pure », mais résultent d'un système très complexe d'idées générales, de catégories, de méthodes, de styles de vie et de communication qui enveloppent l'activité scientifique à l'intérieur d'une société donnée à une époque donnée. Jusqu'ici il s'agissait, en fin de compte, d'appliquer à la connaissance scientifique (qui en était restée pour ainsi dire exonérée) les réflexions critiques développées au sein de la sociologie de la connaissance, éventuellement renforcées par les considérations des pragmatistes américains concernant la liaison étroite entre connaissance et action et leur conception de la connaissance comme étant fondamentalement une 'solution de problèmes'. Si nous nous limitons à ce genre de considérations nous devons conclure que la nouvelle perspective avait produit un élargissement intéressant de l'épistémologie des sciences, mais il s'agissait toujours d'épistémologie. La véritable raison de nouveauté ne réside donc pas dans une modification de l'approche épistémologique, mais bien dans le fait que, à partir du moment où on considère la science aussi bien comme un système d'actions et de pratiques, il faut utiliser, si on veut la comprendre, des approches et des types de réflexion qui dépassent la simple analyse d'un certain type de savoir.

Ce changement de perspective à propos de la science implique des conséquences nécessaires sur la philosophie de la science. Si la science n'est pas uniquement (et peut être même pas principalement) un savoir, les outils *philosophiques* pour la comprendre ne pourront pas se réduire à ceux de la théorie de la connaissance : la philosophie de la science ne pourra se limiter à être une « épistémologie spécialisée », mais elle devra inclure les approches d'autres branches de la philosophie qui s'occupent des actions humaines, telles que l'éthique, la philosophie politique et sociale, la philosophie du droit. En général, cela reviendra à donner un espace adéquat à toute une série de *jugements de valeur* concernant l'activité scientifique, ses finalités, ses procédures, ses conditions, ses conséquences. Ces jugements sont bien différents de ces jugements de valeur *cognitifs* qui, de toute manière, ont toujours été présents dans l'épistémologie des sciences et utilisés pour décider de l'acceptation de propositions, hypothèses et théories (par exemple, exactitude, rigueur, cohérence logique, adéquation empirique, simplicité, généralité). Ils sont différents parce qu'ils s'exercent « en dehors » du savoir scientifique.

Mais justement pour cette raison la nouveauté qu'on vient de mentionner semble contredire une sorte d'impératif méthodologique qui a été largement partagé jusqu'à la moitié du XXe siècle, celui de la *neutralité axiologique* de la science, qu'on pourrait synthétiser en disant que le savoir scientifique doit être protégé de toute interférence venant « du dehors » et qui risquerait (au nom de quelque « valeur » supposée supérieure) de compromettre la *valeur cognitive* de ce savoir. En réalité un tel impératif maintient sa légitimité s'il est correctement entendu comme prescription de ne pas admettre des critères de valeur non-cognitifs pour évaluer la valeur cognitive d'une affirmation ou d'une théorie scientifique. Toutefois cela n'empêche guère que la science, se déroulant en tant qu'*activité humaine* dans un contexte chargé de valeurs et de jugements de valeur (qui orientent, dirigent et inspirent la gamme très vaste et complexe des activités humaines), soit aussi soumise à plusieurs considérations de valeur. Cela revient à reconnaître qu'une axiologie des sciences, loin d'être un élément perturbateur et de confusion comme beaucoup le pensaient encore il y a quelque dizaine d'années, constitue une partie très significative d'une philosophie des sciences.

5. Une philosophie des sciences à plein titre

Ce que nous venons de dire à propos des réflexions axiologiques sur les sciences n'est qu'une partie d'un discours plus général : une philosophie des sciences ne doit pas renoncer à soumettre les sciences à n'importe quel type d'investigation philosophique, en adoptant les instruments de n'importe quelle branche spécialisée de la philosophie qui puisse résulter pertinente pour l'étude de tel ou tel autre problème. Donc, non seulement la gnoséologie, la logique, la philosophie du langage, mais aussi l'éthique, l'ontologie, la métaphysique, la philosophie de la nature, l'anthropologie philosophique et ainsi de suite peuvent et doivent se confronter aux sciences. Et cela tout simplement parce que les sciences sont, avec leur contenu de savoir et avec le réseau de leurs activités de recherche et leurs applications technologiques, une partie prépondérante de la *réalité* de notre temps : elles influencent notre manière de penser, notre vision du monde, notre image de nous-mêmes, nos conditions de vie, nos habitudes, nos goûts et nos choix et pour cette raison elles ne peuvent se soustraire à une prise de conscience critique telle que nous permet une réflexion philosophique. Si, comme Hegel le disait un jour, la philosophie est notre temps appréhendé à travers la pensée, on doit reconnaître qu'une philosophie qui se veut contemporaine ne peut éviter une réflexion sur les sciences, pas dans le sens limité de se consacrer à une épistémologie des sciences, mais dans le sens plus plein de faire jaillir des sciences toute la richesse de problèmes philosophiques qu'elles renferment.

Axiology of Scientific Activity

From A Formal Point of View

Javier Echeverría EZPONDA & Armando Menéndez VISO

Instituto de Filosofía, CSIC, Madrid (Spain)

Philosophers of science, as well as scientists themselves, have traditionally tended to keep values away from their disciplines. The proud positivism proclaimed and praised the neutrality of sciences since the 19th century. As it is well known, things changed after Second World War. Robert K. Merton spoke about the *ethos* of science in the 1940s. But it was in the 1960s, when some philosophers of science began to battle against neo-positivism by asserting the presence of values inside sciences. In the 1970s, Thomas S. Kuhn stated a new question:

> What, I ask to begin with, are the characteristics of a good scientific theory? Among a number of quite usual answers I select five, not because they are exhaustive, but because they are individually important and collectively sufficiently varied to indicate what is at stake. First, a theory should be accurate [...]. Second, a theory should be consistent [...]. Third, it should have broad scope [...]. Fourth, and closely related, it should be simple [...]. Fifth – a somewhat less standard item, but one of special importance to actual scientific decisions – a theory should be fruitful of new research findings [...]. These five characteristics – accuracy, consistency, scope, simplicity, and fruitfulness – are all standard criteria for evaluating the adequacy of a theory. [...] Together with others of much the same sort, they provide *the* shared basis for theory choice.[1]

He assumed that there are values in science, specifically cognitive ones – as Putnam and Laudan later called them.[2] These values do not

---

[1] Kuhn, Thomas S.: 1977, "Objectivity, Vale Judgement, and Theory Choice", in *The Essential Tension. Selected Studies in Scientific Tradition and Change*, Chicago and London, The University of Chicago Press, p. 321-322.

[2] Hempel and Levi had previously pointed out the existence of *epistemic* or *scientific* values. See Hempel, C.: 1960, "Inductive inconsistencies", *Synthese* 12, p. 439-469; Levi, I.: 1967, *Gambling with Truth*, New York, Knopf; and Levi, I.: 1980, *The Enterprise of Knowledge*, Cambridge, MIT Press.

determine scientists' decisions between alternative theories, but they are absolutely essential for a theory to be seriously considered.

The presence of values *inside* sciences and their role on scientific activity has been a major question among philosophers of science in the last forty years. Laudan, Giere, Longino, Rescher, Putnam, Agazzi and Boudon are among the main contributors to the collapse of the dogma of axiological neutrality of science. Sociological, ethical and gender perspectives play an important role in the prominent debate about values and the status of sciences. But they are not the only ones. In the last few years, our research team have been developing its work, trying to analyse and explain the wide variety of value systems related with scientific activities – which are seen, thus, as value-guided actions.

There is no doubt that sciences intervene in the world and change it. According to what philosophers, sociologists and historians of science of the 20th century have told us, scientific activity involves ethical, social and, of course, epistemical elections, which are seldom necessary consequences of empirical or theoretical constrictions. Therefore, widely accepted criteria must exist, which avoid arbitrary decisions – for, even though there are some, it is evident that the success of technosciences is not a matter of fortune. The major target of this paper is to supply a roughly formalized, analytical and empirical axiological portrait of scientific activity, which will be useful to study the processes of evaluation having place inside sciences and technologies.

1. A Non-Aristotelian Framework

How to define values? The Western mind is deeply determined by Aristotelian ontological framework. In his *Categoriae*, Aristotle starts with *what is said* (*légesthai*), both words and things, distinguishing two major types:

> Forms of speech are either simple or composite. Examples of the latter are such expressions as "the man runs", "the man wins"; of the former "man", "ox", "runs", "wins".[3]

The second ones – i.e., things that can be said independently, without being combined with other terms – composed the well known Aristotelian board of categories, later reassumed in his *Metaphysics*.

---

[3] *Cat.*, 1, 16-20. Translated by E. M. Edghill, in W. D. Ross (ed.): 1928, *The Works of Aristotle Translated into English*, Humphrey Milford, London, Oxford University Press.

Expressions which are in no way composite signify substance, quantity, quality, relation, place, time, position, state, action, or affection.[4]

One can easily realise that it is hard to find a proper place for values in that board. They are not substances, of course. They could be qualities,[5] or even relations, with many thinkers insisting in their relational nature.[6] Values are also tightly linked with action, but one should not confound them both – although evaluation processes should be seen from the viewpoint of a real theory of action. But the actual use of axiological terms push towards considering them sheer entities: we talk about values as if they were "expressions which are in no way composite". In other words, the usual Aristotelian language trends to make values into mere things, removing their inherent, conceptual tension.

Yet there are some alternatives to classical categories. The ways in which mathematicians usually define concepts and notions have revealed themselves as particularly fruitful options. In his article "Function and Concept",[7] Frege translated into logical terms the mathematical notion of function. Every function can be distinguished through its own form – in this case, $2\cdot(\ )^3+(\ )$. This formal expression, however, means nothing. To acquire some meaning, it must be applied on something. In other words, mathematical functions as such are unsaturated. They get a value only by being complemented by a relevant argument, i.e., when they are applied to a particular object. Function, argument and value are the three basic, "ontological" notions in Frege's view.

What kind of things can be taken as arguments for a mathematical function? First of all, numbers; but not only them. Frege defined functions for objects in general, giving birth to the concept of *propositional function*, then profusely used by Russell and Whitehead in their 1903 *Principia Mathematica*, and later by manifold logicians.

> Statements in general, just like equations or inequalities or expressions in Analysis, can be imagined to be split up into two parts; one complete in itself, and the other in need of supplementation, or "unsaturated". Thus, e.g., we split up the sentence "Caesar conquered Gaul" into "Caesar" and "conquered Gaul". The second part is "unsaturated" – it contains an empty place; only when this place is filled up with a proper name, or with an expression that replaces a proper name, does a complete sense appear. Here too I give

---

4   *Cat.*, 1b, 25-27.
5   So believes Max Scheler.
6   That is the point of view of Ehrenfels or Ortega y Gasset.
7   Frege, Gottlob: 1891, *Funktion und Begriff*, Hermann Pohle, Jena, p. 7-8; *Function and Object*, translation by Peter Geach in McGuiness, Brian (ed.): 1984, *Gottlob Frege. Collected Papers on Mathematics, Logic, and Philosophy*, Glasgow, Basil Blackwell.

the name "function" to what is meant by this "unsaturated" part. In this case the argument is "Caesar".

We see that here we have undertaken to extend the application of the term in the other direction, viz. as regards what can occur as an argument. Not merely numbers, but objects in general, are now admissible; and here persons must assuredly be counted as objects. The two truth-values have already been introduced as possible values of a function; we must go further and admit objects without restriction as values of functions.[8]

This breaks the Aristotelian framework. Instead of paraphrasing the sentence into "Caesar was the conqueror of Gaul" and then splitting it up into subject ("Caesar"), copula ("was") and predicate ("the conqueror of Gaul"), Frege considered the whole action of the statement as a *function* – later named *propositional*. This leads to a new *logical paradigm*, which entails at least the following implications:

– Definitions of logical concepts are merely *formal*:

When we have thus admitted objects without restriction as arguments and values of functions, the question arises what it is that we are here calling an object. I regard a regular definition as impossible, since we have here something too simple to admit of logical analysis. It is only possible to indicate what is meant. Here I can only say briefly: An object is anything that is not a function, so that an expression for it does not contain any empty place.[9]

– Consequently, true or false sentences do not need to have the form 'S is P'; i.e., the primary notions are no longer the *object* and the *properties* (or *predicates*) it *has*, but *formal expressions* that can be *satisfied*.

– It is not necessary to start from determined ontological or epistemological assumptions in order to organise objects and concepts in genera and species.

The Fregean logical framework is, then, a good starting point to build a, in some extent, formal axiology of sciences. Nevertheless, we are not going to follow him literally, but only as a basic source of inspiration.

In Frege's view, values are objects:

We give the name "the value of a function for an argument" to the result of completing the function with the argument. Thus, e. g., 3 is the value of the function $2 \cdot x^3 + x$ for the argument 1, since we have: $2 \cdot 1^3 + 1 = 3$.[10]

---

[8] Frege, *op. cit.*, 17; p. 147.

[9] Frege, *op. cit.*, 18; p. 147.

[10] Frege, *op. cit.*, 8; p. 141.

Yet we are going to speak of "value-functions" or just "values", meaning unsaturated expressions capable of being completed by an argument, which properly yields the *concrete value* of the value-function.

Thus, we can distinguish two alternative concepts of values: values conceived as members of a kind of entities that *exist* – e.g., precision, freedom, honesty, and so, which are said *to be* values – and values *possessed* or *satisfied* by a particular object, agent or action – which can be judged to be precise, free, honest, and so, without being considered itself as a value.[11] We will even do without the Fregean notion of "object", using "variable" in its place.

2. Evaluation of Scientific Actions

If we are to study scientific practice, and not only scientific knowledge, we need a kind of action theory – if only elementary and *par provision*.[12] Of course, we are not seeking to define here what scientific action *is*: we only intend to give a rough characterisation of scientific actions, just as an explicit start point. Since, as philosophy of science tell us, it is impossible to reach the facts without a previous theory about them, that purpose seems to be more a claim of honesty than a pretentious aim – even so, it will divert us from our route for a little while.

Actions and values are the two basic notions of our axiology of science. Values are unsaturated functions, while actions are saturated ones. A scientific action could be described as follows:

An agent X_1 does (X_2) X_3 to X_4 with X_5 in X_6, under X_7 conditions, with the end X_8, following X_9, obtaining the X_{10} outcome, with the implication X_{11}, at the risk of X_{12}.

X_1 could be a person, but also a machine, a group, a university, a corporation, a Ministry and so on. That is why we prefer to speak of *agent* better than *subject*. Besides avoiding the philosophical connotations of the latter word (agents do not *underlay* to actions, but they project and execute them), the term *agent* leaves room for something other than human individuals.

X_2 indicates the action itself. One should put in its place the relevant verb which describes the particular action that takes place; e.g., measure, cut, combine, observe, and the like.

---

[11] More on this in Menéndez, Armando: 2002, "Valores, ¿ser o tener?", in *Argumentos de razón práctica*, 5, p. 223-238.

[12] See Echeverría, Javier: 2002, *Ciencia y valores*, Barcelona, Destino.

X_3 means what grammarians call direct object, and X_4 stands for the indirect one. X_6 designates the locus and X_7 refers to the circumstances of action.

X_8 represents the objective, end or aim of the agent, while X_9 indicates the rule or set of rules, according to which the action is carried out.

X_{10} stands for the result of a particular scientific action. It is precisely in the results of scientific actions where knowledge lies – in data, graphs, measurements, successful experiments, proofs, laws, theories, and so on. Insofar as philosophers of science have traditionally focused on scientific knowledge, they have disregarded other components of scientific actions, and even actions themselves. Despite the major interest of scientific knowledge, a true philosophy of scientific activity should consider scientific outcomes an element among others in scientific actions.

Along with results, scientific actions could entail manifold subsequent implications, once they are already executed. These implications derive from "last" results, but also from agents, intermediate phases, instruments or circumstances. We should take into account not only the "highlights" of science, but also the forgotten reminders of scientific activity. This is what X_{11} intends to represent.

Finally, scientific actions could involve risks for their agents, objects, instruments or their environment. All these risks are designated by X_{12}.

Thus, we can formally represent a scientific action, X, through the following expression: $X=<X_1, X_2, X_3, X_4, X_5, X_6, X_7, X_8, X_9, X_{10}, X_{11}, X_{12}>$, where X_i stands for each component. More broadly: $X=<X_i>$, with $i: 1,…, n$. Of course, each X_i could be subdivided into l different subcomponents (agents, instruments, circumstances, etc.) when it is the case. Needless to say, not every action should have every component.

In sum, *scientific facts are always results of scientific actions*. That is why we should characterise scientific actions before thinking about scientific facts. In other words: praxiology and axiology are previous to epistemology, which does not mean that the two first terms are the grounds for the latter.

Anyway, neither actions, nor their outcomes can be considered properly *scientific* without first being evaluated. Facts, calculations, observations, experiments, measurements or proofs are accepted as scientific ones only after a whole process of – as we like to call it – *axiological sifting.*[13] The following paragraphs are devoted to this central idea.

a. Satisfaction

Everything that slips through the sieve must *satisfy* certain conditions or values. Unlike the rational decision model of economics, our axiology will be based on the notion of *satisfaction*. This can be considered a *primitive axiological term*. Tarski, perhaps the one held mainly responsible for the later success of the notion, explained its meaning as follows:

> We can then significantly say of every single object that it does or does not satisfy the given function. In order to explain the sense of this phrase we consider the following scheme:
>
> *for all a, a satisfies the sentential function x if and only if p*
>
> and substitute in this scheme for "*p*" the given sentential function (after first replacing the free variable occurring in it by "*a*") and for "*x*" some individual name of this function. Within colloquial language we can in this way obtain, for example, the following formulation:
>
> *for every a, we have a satisfies the sentential function "x is white" if and only if a is white*
>
> (and from this conclude, in particular, that snow satisfies the function "*x* is white").[14]

But it was H. A. Simon who introduced this notion in opposition to *maximization,*[15] and Giere the first philosopher of science in assuming Simon's proposal. Unfortunately, Giere was interested only in decisions and elections among theories:

> Once one begins to think of scientists as decision makers, one realizes that the typical scientist makes dozens of decisions of all sorts every days. From this perspective a decision to *accept* a model as providing a roughly correct picture of some part of the world has to be a rare event. Nevertheless, because this type of decision is so important in science, and because it has re-

---

[13] This idea of sifting, as well as its formalization under the shape of mathematical matrices is due, in a great extent, to José Francisco Álvarez, member of our research team and professor at UNED.

[14] Tarski, Alfred: 1956, "Concept of Truth in Formalized Languages", in *Logic, Semantics, Metamathematics. Papers from 1923 to 1938*, Oxford at the Clarendon Press, p. 189-190.

[15] Simon, H. A.: 1945, *Administrative Behavior*, Free Press, New York.

ceived so much attention by all students of scientific life, I shall concentrate on it here.[16]

Our axiology is to give account of this type of decisions, but it pretends as well to explain "smaller" ones, as choice of instruments, consideration of data series and initial conditions, contrast of experimental results, and the like. All these processes entail evaluations of possible alternatives and decisions according to these evaluations. Scientists are continuously balancing and choosing. With this article, we are trying to argue that their decisions are not taken by maximization of utility functions, but by gradual satisfaction of different evaluation criteria.

Giere assumes that their own interests, aims and values guide decisions of agents. As Giere points out, "it is interesting to note that not even *normative* decision theory dictates how the agent should evaluate specific outcomes. Rather, it imposes only general constraints, like linear ordering, on the agent's relative evaluation of outcomes. Thus, even normative decision theory, basically takes the agent's own values as given".[17] If values are to be considered elements of the evaluation process, a theory that does not give account of them cannot offer a satisfactory explanation of scientific choices – and, therefore, of scientific actions. In Giere's words:

> Scientists, as a matter of empirical fact, are not Bayesian agents. Reconstructions of actual scientific episodes along Bayesian lines can at most show that a Bayesian agent would have reached similar conclusions to those in fact reached by actual scientists. Any such reconstruction provides no explanation of what actually happened. For that we need another account.[18]

Giere found that account in Simon's work. According to the model of "bounded rationality" of the latter, agents are seldom capable of having a coherent, complete set of preferences and usually operate in a few given scenarios with restricted options. However, they can distinguish whether an option is satisfactory or not. They act more as *satisfizers* than *maximizers*.[19] Which means, amongst other things, that there is no always a unique right choice, since many possibilities could satisfy the required conditions. A satisfaction-based decision theory can be determinist in some cases, but most of the times it won't.

---

[16] Giere, Ronald N.: 1988, *Explaining Science. A Cognitive Approach*, The University of Chicago Press, Chicago and London, p. 142.

[17] Giere, *op. cit.*, p. 143.

[18] Giere, *op. cit.*, p. 157.

[19] See Simon, *op. cit.* and: 1982, *Models of Bounded Rationality*, MIT Press, Cambridge.

An axiological function is characterized by the kind of empirical models that satisfy it. This is to say that an axiological screen is not defined by *the* decision it allows to make, but by the whole range of choices capable of passing through its filter. From this point of view, valuation processes are rather recursive discarding ones (i.e., properly a *sifting*), than calculations seeking to achieve this or that rational optimum.

b. Objectivity

The notion of satisfaction allows us to talk about a certain objectivity in scientific decisions, although this is not, of course, the kind of objectivity that allows us to speak of *absolute best* ends or means. Once again, we refer here to the whole scientific activity, not only to its outcomes. The objectivity of the model, if there is such a thing at all, should be found in every step of the path that leads to results.

A decision is objective when it does not depend on the particular agent that makes it. What is objective in a decision? Above all, that it is made or not. Within a *maximizing* traditional model of rational choice, objectivity comes from this fact, i.e., from the uniqueness of the best election – when possible. Within the sifting model, in turn, objectivity arises from the sieve itself. It is not that there is a best filter – maybe there is, but this must be discussed at a higher, different level –, but, given a particular one, it always sifts the same, no matter which agent uses it: agents are interchangeable. In our axiological model, an agent is just another element of the process, not a privileged one. Objectivity, then, acquires here the shape of *inter-subjectivity*.

How is this so? The first step in decision-making is always a rough sifting, through which possible choices that do not satisfy certain minimum prerequisites are discarded. These prerequisites are not fixed by the agent alone, but along with the action itself, the object, the circumstances, the theoretical context, the historical moment, the possible future implications – each X_i of the particular action. There are, thus, *minimum benchmarks* (or maximum ones, when the matter in question is a negative one) defined by the axiological functions that compose the filter. Axiological thresholds, when useful and used in fact, are not subjective.

Let's hear Putnam on this topic:

> When a theory conflicts with what has previously supposed to be fact, we sometimes give up the theory and we sometimes give up the supposed fact, and as Quine famously put it […], the decision is a matter of trade-offs that are "where rational, pragmatic" – and that means (although Quine, of course, doesn't say so) a matter of informal judgements of coherence, plau-

sibility, simplicity, and the like. Nor is it the case that when two theories conflict, scientists wait until the observational data decide between them, as Popperian philosophy of science demands it should.[20]

This objective, first process of discarding is probably the most "rational" and effective way of tackling the manifold everyday scientific decisions – and surely the way in which scientists, just as all of us do, usually decide:

> You would not claim that scientists test every falsifiable theory if as many crazy theories crossed your desk as they cross mine![21]

Sometimes that minimum or maximum threshold can be defined numerically – as actually happens in exams, recruitment processes, choices between measurements, and so on. But in many occasions they cannot – like in considering fruitfulness, simplicity, beauty or absurdity. Objectivity (i.e., the independence of every particular subject) is not the same as exact arithmetical definition.

c. Gradualism

Nevertheless, if not always along a metrical scale, the axiological sifting should produce some kind of order. There is a minimum threshold for a particular action to be considered as relevant. But, once this threshold is trespassed, the axiological function (or value, in a less precise terminology) can be satisfied in different degrees. There is a sort of *graduality principle* for the evaluation of scientific actions.

Functions can be *qualitative* (like "white", "beautiful", "true" and the like), when they arise from the definition of a class of equivalence (reflexive, symmetric, and transitive) and can be represented numerically by 1 (if they are satisfied) or 0 (if not); *comparative*, when they give rise to ordinal scales and magnitudes; *quantitative*, when they are comparative and additionable; or *metrical*, when they are quantitative and capable of undergoing the other three arithmetic operations. Value-functions can be found of each of these types that define different gradual scales. We'll have, then, expressions like $v_j(x_{ij}) > v_j(y_{ij})$.

---

[20] Putnam, Hilary: 2002, "The Philosophers of Science's Evasion of Values", in *The Collapse of the Fact/Value Dichotomy and Other Essays*, Cambridge, Mass., and London, Harvard University Press, p. 142.

[21] Bronowski to Popper, quoted by Putnam, H.: 2002, "The Philosophers of Science's Evasion of Values", in *The Collapse of the Fact/Value Dichotomy and Other Essays*, Cambridge, Mass., and London, Harvard University Press.

d. System

A scientific action can very seldom be evaluated through a unique value-function. Usually, a filter consists of many of them. Furthermore, this plurality is not an amorphous lot, formed by sheer addition. Value-functions are not independent of each other. Those what compound a particular sieve, present special relations between them; in other words, they constitute a *system*.

The notion of system opposes here to neo-positivist atomism. When we evaluate only a single element of a scientific action, or we evaluate this action using just a few value-functions, our evaluation will result biased for sure. Thus, e.g., to evaluate the precision of an instrument, one should take into account another value-functions (or values), like its reliability, its strength or its efficiency. In their everyday work, like in other spheres of human activity, scientists (ore scientific agents in general) do not effect *absolute* valuations, but *relative* ones; relative to all elements of action: other agents, instruments, the historical moment and, of course, to previous theories and their like scientific results.

Systems of values (or of value-functions, more precisely) could be analysed into two different directions: an horizontal one, separating values by their "functional shape" into epistemic, technical, economic, military, environmental, political, social, legal [...] and giving rise to multiple sub-systems, or a vertical one, distinguishing nuclear and orbital values. We obtain, thus, a rough outline of the *structure* of scientific activity. A value-function of the sub-system V_i is a *nuclear* one if its satisfaction is necessarily required so that the evaluated element is not rejected, i.e., to let the evaluating process continue. *Orbital* values are those that are not nuclear. Nuclear value-functions are, then, in close relation with the idea of sifting.

e. Pluralism

Our proposal could be considered pluralistic in two respects. First, because, if elements of action are plural, so can its values. And, second, because each element of an action can be valued differently, depending on the sieve (i.e., on the concrete characteristic we are evaluating), and, what is more important, depending on the singular moment in which the sifting is made. Since core set of values can change through time, we should accept multiple consecutive evaluation systems. That opens the possibility of a *dynamics* of evaluation, which complements and limits the usual *statics* often proposed by scientists themselves (e.g., by Kuhn, despite its revolutions – or maybe because of them).

Our pluralism is not only ontological, or epistemological, but *teleological* too. Among the various components of scientific activity, ends are not an exception: they are also plural. This is particularly evident in war times, when power joins the assembly of notable ends, and occupies its chair along with truth and knowledge; or within industrial research, where so often profit seems to be above all other possible ends, although it is not the only one.[22]

3. Matrices of Evaluation

Let's try to formalise what has been said until now. A sample matrix of valuation could present a shape like this:

		X_1	X_2	X_3	...	X_n
V_1	v_{11}	g_{111}	g_{112}	g_{113}	...	g_{11n}
	v_{12}	g_{121}	g_{122}	g_{123}	...	g_{12n}
V_2		g_{201}	g_{202}	g_{203}	...	g_{20n}
V_3		g_{301}	g_{302}	g_{303}	...	g_{30n}
V_4	v_{41}	g_{411}	g_{412}	g_{413}	...	g_{41n}
...	...	...	...	...	...	...
V_m	v_{mp}	g_{mp1}	g_{mp2}	g_{mp3}	...	g_{mpn}

The elements of the matrix are:

- The set of the elements of an action, $X=<X_i>$, including time.
- The set of sub-systems of values, $V=<V_{jkj}>$, which could be nuclear and orbital.
- The particular values within each sub-system V_j, $v_{jk} \in V_j$, with their respective pondering.
- Different degrees of satisfaction, g_{ijk}, of a value v_{jk} by a component x_i, $v_{jk}(x_i)=g_{ijk}$.

In a matrix like that, we can find sub-matrices of the following kinds, already defined:

- Qualitative
- Ordinal
- Quantitative

---

[22] Maybe the reader is now thinking that, in some way, it is difficult to distinguish between values and ends. Certainly this could be a matter of deep discussion, but unfortunately (or not) we have hear no place to proceed with it. We just say that values are defined also (not only) by ends.

– Metrical

We can operate only with matrices of the last kind.

The determination of the particular values that constitute the core and the whole of the matrix is empirical. Nonetheless, the matrix shape allows us to obtain the following formal definitions:

– *Positive evaluation*: for an evaluation to be considered positive, it must satisfy the two following necessary (though not sufficient) conditions: $m_{ijk} < v_{ij}(x_k)$ and $\neg v_{ij}(x_k) < M_{ijk}$, where m_{ijk} stands for the minimum satisfaction threshold of value v_{ij} and M_{ijk} represents the maximum satisfaction threshold of the opposite value, $\neg v_{ij}$.

– *Better action*: an action $x = \{x_k\}$ is axiologically better than an action $x' = \{x'_l\}$, $x \dashv x'$, with respect to the sub-system of values V_i, if and only if: $\forall j \, \forall v_{ij} \in V_i, \, v_{ij}(x_k) \geq v_{ij}(x'_l)$.

– *Pondered better action*: an action $x = \{x_k\}$ is axiologically better than an action $x' = \{x'_l\}$, $x \dashv x'$, with respect to the sub-system of values V_i, if and only if: $\Sigma_{i,j} p_{ij} \, v_{ij}(x_k) \geq \Sigma_{i,j} p_{ij} \, v_{ij}(x'_l)$, where p_{ij} are the pondering factors assigned to each value, v_{ij}.

– *Best action*: $\exists_{i,N,O} x_k$, $\forall i \, \forall v_{iN} \in V_N, \, v_{iN}(x_k) \geq m_{iN}$ and $\forall i \, \forall v_{iO} \in V_O$, $v_{iO}(x_k) \geq m_{iO}$, where V_N and V_O are, respectively, the sets of nuclear and orbital values, and m_{iN}, m_{iO} are minimum thresholds which depend on each value and could be modified during the evaluation process.

– *Scientific acceptability*: the action x is scientifically acceptable if $\exists j, \, m_{ij}, \, M_{ij}, \, m_{ij} \leq \Sigma_{i,j} p_{ij} \, v_{ij}(x_k(t))$ and $\Sigma_{i,j} p_{ij} \, \neg v_{ij}(x_k(t)) < M_{ij}$, where t stands for time.

The problem is that this kind of matrices and properties does not provide rules for its interpretation. They are only auxiliary tools for decision-makers. They just tell us what cannot be (that's why the sieve metaphor seems to be particularly appropriated), instead of giving us positive answers about what to do.

4. Conclusions

Axiology materialises into the protocols actually used in research centers, companies and universities to evaluate projects, results and individuals – and, consequently, to discard or admit them. These protocols are often more decisive than any other factors for the course of sciences and technologies. However, in spite of this use, axiology in general is not normative, even though it could provide normative systems just by defining closed sub-systems of values and establishing thresholds for them. Why? Because there are no protocols for the protocols or, in other words, because there is no upper level above value functions where we can find necessary knowledge about them.[23]

In its widest respect, our proposal does not entail any algorithm or a board of decision rules. Actually this can be considered as a main implication of the precedent lines: scientific activities are not to be explained, much less predicted, by sheer algorithmic formulas. What is offered here is not a scientific, necessary theory about scientific activity, but just a second-order analysis, a *meta-scientific* work, absolutely dependent of the possible, relevant empirical or scientific findings and the social, historical, political, &c. context.

The above presented formalisation avoids reductionism of any nature, at the same time that it allows partial approaches of all kinds – sociological, historical, psychological, epistemological, and so on. Our axiological point of view gives room to knowledge, truth or coherence, as well as to social constrains, traditions, self-interests, profit or common good. The facts affecting scientific activity are a multitude and all of them must be considered, even though they must be properly pondered in each occasion.

Axiology, thus, is just a part of the philosophy of science, together with epistemology and methodology. It is a part that connects this philosophy with sociology, history, ethics and other different science and technology studies; but also a part that clarifies the limits and the scope of those sub-disciplines.

Finally, let us remark that what has been said so far is the result of a work in progress, liable to further critics. In any case, it is a first step in a path to clarification of the contemporary technoscientific activity.

References

Agazzi, E., (1996), *El bien, el mal y la ciencia*, Madrid, Tecnos.

Boudon, R., (2001), *The Origin of Values. Sociology and Philosophy of Beliefs*, New Brunswick, N.J., Transaction Publ.

Echeverría, Javier, (2002), *Ciencia y valores*, Barcelona, Destino.

Frege, Gottlob, (1891), *Funktion und Begriff*, Hermann Pohle, Jena; *Function and Object*, translation by Peter Geach in McGuiness, Brian (ed.): 1984, *Gottlob Frege. Collected Papers on Mathematics, Logic, and Philosophy*, Glasgow, Basil Blackwell.

---

[23] Laudan has said something similar a couple of years ago in his 1984, *Science and Values. The Aims of Science and Their Role in Scientific Debate*, Berkeley, University of California Press. Unlike him, however, we are not saying that axiology itself is *above* methodology or epistemology, but *beside* them.

Kuhn, Thomas S., (1977), *The Essential Tension. Selected Studies in Scientific Tradition and Change*, Chicago and London, The University of Chicago Press.

Laudan, Larry, (1984), *Science and Values. The Aims of Science and Their Role in Scientific Debate*, Berkeley, University of California Press.

Putnam, Hilary, (2002), *The Collapse of the Fact/Value Dichotomy and Other Essays*, Cambridge, Mass., and London, Harvard University Press.

Putnam, Hilary, (1988), *Reason, Truth and History*, London, Cambridge University Press.

Simon, H. A., (1945), *Administrative Behavior*, New York, Free Press.

Tarski, Alfred, (1956), *Logic, Semantics, Metamathematics. Papers from 1923 to 1938*, Clarendon Press, Oxford.

The Axiological Dimension of Science

Fabio MINAZZI

Università del Salento

> The philosophy of science itself cannot be epistemology – even if it has its lowest level, and therefore its object in this. Like all philosophy, it has as its object the forms and the conditions of a civilization: in this case, the civilization of the sciences.
>
> Giulio Preti, *Pluralità delle scienze e unità eidetica del mondo* [1965].

1. Does Science Constitute a Value?

Science is *wertfrei:* it does not evaluate. In fact the *epoché* of any evaluation is essential to the scientific attitude. But life is imbued with values; and the world of life is a world of values. Here lies the limitation – in truth a self – limitation – of science, so that Term I of the pair [i.e. the first term of the dialectical pair "humanistic culture/scientific culture" – *ed.*] cannot be reduced without any residue to science itself. This is the strongest argument of the polemical attack which the supporters of literary culture make on scientific culture: that it is not only *free from* values but *blind to values*. This is the point from which should start the attempt, which has been repeated for centuries, to lower science to mere technics (or rather technology): a subordinate, instrumental activity, which bends "matter" to the ends of the "spirit". This vision draws not only on the stupidest and most obscene forms of spirituality and idealism, but also on even subtler, more expert forms, some even apparently "scientistic", such as historical-dialectical materialism and certain forms of pragmatism.[1]

---

[1] See Preti [1968], p. 59, italics in the text. On the work and thought of Preti I may refer the reader to Minazzi [1994a] and [2004].

So wrote Giulio Preti in *Retorica e logica*, towards the end of the 1960s, grasping a theoretically decisive point concerning the full defense of the authentically cognitive and theoretical nature of scientific knowledge, and opposing its every arbitrary reduction to the level of technology, by considering it as a merely instrumental and subordinate activity. The cultural debate of the period turned principally on the analysis of the problem of the discussion (and the conflict) between the "two cultures" of the humanities and science, a subject raised by the publication, in 1959, of a widely read volume by C. P. Snow, soon translated into various languages and in Italy presented with a Preface by Ludovico Geymonat (who then devoted one of his most eminent works to the historic theme of the confrontation between the two cultures).[2]

We should also point out that this full and open defense of the cognitive value of science necessarily entailed raising, contextually, certain issues capable of illustrating the problematic character of this same defense. If in fact one is to present, *à la* Weber, science as definitely *wertfrei*, then immediately, contextually, there also arises the problem of establishing the precise, specific "vaule" of this *wertfrei* knowledge. Science supposedly constructs value-free pictures of the world, but then, one may legitimately ask, what is its precise value? A cognitive value? So does knowledge, even *wertfrei* knowledge, not constitute, per se, a *value*? Does Weber himself perhaps see the value of scientific knowledge itself as rooted precisely in the fact that it constitutes a knowledge that *does not possess* values? But, in reality, can there ever really exist a knowledge which is truly *value-free*? Be that as it may, even a possible and paradoxical positive answer to this question cannot conceal the inevitable axiological contamination regarding scientific knowledge. Without mentioning the fact that it would really be highly singular to deprive science itself, precisely as knowledge, of its own specific valorial and axiological significance. In this case we would in fact be faced with the paradoxical situation that knowledge, as such, is supposedly lacking, by its very nature, in any authentic and autonomous value.

At least in the decades down to the nineteen-sixties, the Weberian conception of scientific knowledge was fairly widespread: the specific value of science was thus seen as consisting precisely in its being ex-

---

[2] See Snow [1959], available in Italian in the translation by Adriano Carugo published by Feltrinelli in 1964 with a significant preface by Ludovico Geymonat, who then devoted to the subject of the two cultures one of his most important and significant works, the monumental *Storia del pensiero filosofico e scientifico* (see Geymonat [1970-76]. It is regrettable that in the recent Italian reissue, published by Marsilio in 2005, of Carugo's translation of Snow's volume no longer contained the preface by Geymonat.

empt from the contamination of values. But subsequently, in the course of the last three decades of the past century, this conception, though for conflicting theoretical and practical reasons, has gradually come to appear more problematic and debatable. The point has now been reached where, in the culture that grew up following the protest movements of 1968, it has actually been inverted into a completely antithetical position, which sees science as connoted by complex axiologies, so transforming it from a form of objective knowledge, capable of enabling us to know the world seriously and "neutrally", into a form of *political ideology* by means of which a specific group use science, among other means, to enforce their own vision of the world. The upshot was that some people even began talking about a "bourgeois science" which had to be opposed by a "proletarian science": a dangerous ideological drift that actually persuaded some people to even reject mathematical logic as an "imperialistic" discipline, which would have to be countered by a mythical revolutionary "dialectic logic"[...] Be that as it may, with this ideological reversal, science, from being *wertfrei* and objective knowledge, was transformed into an ideological assumption that dismissed, without any residues or critically significant margins, all possible objective implications.

Nevertheless, even though culture has fluctuated between these two opposite poles, it is, however, legitimate to ask ourselves today whether these two antithetical and paradoxical visions of scientific knowledge are such (that is to say opposed and antinomic) precisely because their intrinsic schematicity leads them to delineate a highly reductive and extremely schematic vision of both scientific knowledge and of its complex interactions with the historical world and modern society. It seems, in fact, that the problem of the axiological implications of scientific knowledge – which always develops within a specific, historically configured society – cannot be confronted adequately in a schematic or reductive manner, because if we are to analyze these problems we need to carry out a highly articulated analysis, one capable of accounting for the multiple aspects of the questions that we are seeking to deal with. This is because scientific knowledge and its production are rooted in a stratified social reality that may therefore produce different images of the human knowledge itself. Nor, finally, can we neglect the fact that science itself, precisely as the eidetic form of a civilization like the modern, has historically contributed, directly and variously, to the progressive and laborious construction of a new world, the world of modern civilization, whose children we all are, for better or worse, willingly or unwillingly.

Besides, it is impossible to deny another intrinsic threefold observation. *Firstly* we can observe that science, in itself, as a decisive element of modern civilization, constitutes *a world* and, therefore, also *a value.* Science has had a truly extraordinary impact on the history of humanity, not only in technical terms but also in the way it affects our vision of reality. As a professional historian like Herbert Butterfield has pointed out, the birth of modern science introduced a wholly innovative point of no return into the history of humanity, which has contributed to change the lives of millions of men and women all over the planet, far more decisively than thousands of years of pre-scientific culture ever did.[3]

From this point of view, science has introduced a radical break-through that bears no comparison with either the multiple religious reforms (including those of modernity) or with the revival of the classics of the Graeco-Roman world which began with the Renaissance. The novelty of the scientific enterprise – a novelty both theoretical and technological – truly constituted an epochal point of no return, by means of which humanity, in some three centuries of development of technical-scientific knowledge, has changed the world and its own life more than it was ever capable of doing in the four thousand years of pre-scientific life. To say it with Russell: "One hundred and fifty years of science have proved more explosive than five thousand years of pre-scientific culture". The upshot is that today it is more difficult and nearly impossi-ble to ignore the complex and articulated body of knowledge continually produced by the increasingly impetuous development of science and technology.

Secondly, if we evaluate science as such, it is difficult to avoid the impression that the scientific enterprise, far from being *wertfrei* in the traditional Weberian sense of the term, possesses within itself certain precise axiological values, in the name of which science itself appears as the driving force of a new world and of a new civilization. If anything, this specific point of view leads to a new and decisive problem, that which seeks to analyze with precision the exact impact that the new knowledge and the new possibilities of humanity's technical-practical intervention in material reality may have on the traditional axiologies. In other words: if science, with its knowledge and its technical-practical solutions presents us with new theoretical and operative scenarios, we then have to ask ourselves how we should relate to these new scenarios with our traditional values. If the new knowledge and the new technolo-gies enable us to make new choices and carry out new operations, we have to ask ourselves whether the traditional values developed by humanity within the ambit of the pre-scientific society are completely

---

[3]   Cf. Butterflield [1958]; this thesis had been presented earlier also by Bertrand Russell [1931] (the quotation which follows in the text is taken from the Introduction to his book) and was also shared by Geymonat [1970-76], Vol. II, p. 7-27.

adequate to respond to the new possibilities and the new challenges presented by the development of the techno-sciences. From this specific point of view, *knowledge* and *human freedom* are closely interwoven and always connected: the expansion of knowledge makes possible actions previously inconceivable. On the other hand, this new freedom of action also raises new moral problems, which we have to be able to answer with the elaboration of a new axiology wholly adequate to the new knowledge and to the new operative possibilities. This presents itself as the authentic and innovative challenge of the present time. An ambitious and fascinating challenge. To solve it we cannot simply turn back to the past: we have to be capable of developing our own, new, autonomous and creative thought, fully adequate to the new challenges that technical-scientific knowledge now presents to humanity. It should also be pointed out that science itself, if it is to develop and grow in depth, requires the full defense and contextual protection of some precise axiological assumptions. To offer a few examples, these should include the possibility of more open criticism, tolerance for conflicting and discordant opinions, the systematic opening up of its institutional structures, the publicity of its results and the right to public and intersubjective verification of its results, by which *the civilization* of modern and contemporary science has been shaped, at least potentially.

And then, *thirdly*, we have to add – so further complicating the problem – that the ever more impetuous development of scientific knowledge and the multiplicity of technological innovations today confronts us with an increasingly complex and stratified situation, by virtue of which the interaction between science and technology is so strong (and increasingly highly structured) that, strictly speaking, we should speak more correctly not of technics but of technology and of the presence, in our contemporary world, of the "techno-sciences", as well as of the existence of a specific, and more highly articulated, "technical-scientific patrimony". The first of these terms, techno-sciences, stresses the integration, increasingly close, vital and indispensable, between the development of theoretical science proper and the dimension of technology that has come to pervade the world of the science. This has reached the point where today, in many fields, it is really highly problematic to seek to separate clearly the dimension of theoretical science from its more specifically technological dimension.

With the reference to the "technical-scientific patrimony" I wished to stress the increasingly complex articulation which the techno-sciences have produced, forming a complex "patrimony" (to use Ludovico Geymonat's expression) or a complex "capital" (to quote Pierre Duhem) of knowledge and technologies, within which we can identify different "curves of level" indicating the different degrees of sophistication and varying axiomatic rigour of the various theoretical disciplines and the multiplicity of technological devices. And at the same time we cannot forget the peculiar and continuous osmosis that has historically been created between these different "levels" of development of the multiple components of the technical-scientific world. It is precisely within this intricate labyrinth of complex interactions that we then have to deal, at least in my judgment, with the problem of the axiological dimension of contemporary scientific knowledge.

2. Interest and Fertility of a Phenomenological Approach

In unravelling this complicated question, it may perhaps to be of interest to start by bearing in mind a fertile indication (methodological and philosophical) which comes, comprehensively, from the tradition of the Kantian critical rationalism, from the phenomenology of Edmund Husserl and also from the reflections of an Italian thinker all too often neglected, Antonio Banfi.[4] Thanks to the lesson of Kantian rationalism and to that of phenomenology, we have to be aware that it is necessary to distinguish between the different prospective-material planes within which our problem can be appropriately dealt with. At the same time, we also need to bear in mind the necessity of not confusing different philosophical levels of analysis, while also taking ensuring critically that we are able to pass from phenomenological description to the analytical and formal construction of the different fundamental concepts in each specific field. In order to carry out such a complex analysis, of which the present paper will only be able to indicate the main points, providing no more than a "plan of work", we can also draw on a valuable pointer of Banfi's. He observes that in order to analyze the moral problem it is necessary to distinguish at least three different levels of reflection: the plane of pragmatic reflection, the plane of moral philosophy and, last but not least, the plane of the philosophy of morality. Partly in the light of this indication of Banfi's, it is easy to understand how this prospective approach not only draws on the articulated tradition of the European critical rationalism, but also to present its specific lineage from the great and classical Kantian lesson of transcendentalism, also duly influenced by all the complex and highly articulated developments in the thought of modernity. Naturally, it is not now possible to follow, in all its theoretical, historical and historiographical implications, this rich and complex tradition of thought, For a programmatic theoretical analysis of it, however, I may be permitted to refer to my other recent contributions,

---

[4]   Cf. Husserl [1928] and Banfi [1959], in particular Vol. II, p. 371-81 and p. 499-69.

which should also be associated with other contributions, particularly some by Evandro Agazzi and Ludovico Geymonat.[5]

At any rate, at least from our present point of view, it is urgent to stress that also in the case of the comprehension of the problem of the axiological dimension of scientific knowledge, it is indispensable to achieve a precise identification of the different planes by which we can carry out a possible philosophical analysis. This means it is necessary to distinguish at least three different analytic-philosophical planes within which an adequate understanding of the reality of modern science itself can develop. As precisely suggested by such an acute student of Banfi as was Giulio Preti,[6] whom we have quoted above, science can be considered from at least three different point of view:

a) in the first place as a form of knowledge. In the history of modernity this form of knowledge has also sought to impose itself as the only possible form. This has given rise to a multiplicity of problems, also specifically related to science itself. It is significant that the epistemological and philosophical debate of the last three centuries has been dominated by the question of establishing, once and for all, the true and correct method of scientific research. This is due to the presumption (or Cartesian syndrome)[7] that once we have established the precise nature of the scientific method, it would then be possible to apply it mechanically to any aspect of reality and so produce certain and reliable knowledge. This dream, which runs from the *Discours de la méthode* (1637) of Descartes down to *Against Method* (1975), *inclusive*, of Feyerabend, already in itself constitutes a symptomatic misunderstanding of the complex and articulated reality of scientific procedure. A misunderstanding that, note, is not found at all in the pages of a recognized father of modern science like Galileo Galilei[8] – we need only think of the observations precisely developed in *The Assayer* (1623) – but it is clearly present in the followers of the classics and has, at the very least, been a feature of much of the spread of scientific thought in the course of modernity. At any rate, at least from the philosophical point of view, this first possible interpretation of science, as a form of knowledge, constitutes a traditional object of gnosiology;

b) but science also constitutes a form of "culture" or "civilization", by means of which humanity establishes a specific relationship with the

---

[5]   Cf. at least Minazzi [2004b] and [2006], to be supplemented by the preceding contributions by Agazzi [1992] and Geymonat [1977] and [1985] (then [2005]).

[6]   Cf. Preti [1989], p. 56-7.

[7]   Cf. Pera [1991]., p. 3-17.

[8]   For an analysis of these aspects I may be permitted to refer the reader to Minazzi [1994b] as well as Geymonat [1956].

world within which it conducts its life. In this specific sense, science, as the "civilization of science", has forged the modern world, so giving rise to an increasingly pervasive and hegemonic historical-social reality. From this specific point of view, science can then be the object of the Philosophy of Culture, which studies and investigates the precise configuration of this modern civilization. Moreover, this social and civil reality may be, in its turn, the object of other multiple critical analyses: for example, of sociological analyses (with regard to the social structure of the scientific world, its institutes, its dynamics, the specific configuration of the different scientific "communities", the problem of succession in the governance of these structures, the problem of the training of new recruits etc.), of economic analyses in relation to the socio-economic dynamic of the society, but also in the specific economic significance of its configuration, without mentioning the interactions that may exist between the sphere of the economy and the approaches adopted in the different programs of scientific research, etc.), of historical analysis (concerning the history of the scientific community, its vicissitudes, transformations, the way it structures itself in "institutions" capable of protecting certain scientific research traditions, etc.), of legal, ethical or aesthetic and analysis, and many other kinds.

c) science can also be considered *in itself*, in its real historical-theoretical status, as a privileged object of the philosophy of science, which studies the structure of scientific theories, its languages, its methods, its comprehensive configuration, its strategies (theoretical and technical). From this third point of view, science, considered as such, in its relative autonomy, constitutes the specific object of philosophical analysis, or rather of the philosophy of science, or also of epistemology. In fact these two expressions, "philosophy of science" and "epistemology", can be understood as almost synonymous, yet, from the theoretical point of view they can also indicate different levels of analysis of science as such.

In fact, from this specific theoretical point of view, within this third level – represented by science considered as such – we can again distinguish different levels of inquiry, by exploring the level of an exclusively *methodological* examination of science, or by investigating the nature of the scientific method, the different configurations of the various methodological approaches that are progressively codified in the different fields of scientific inquiry (from physics to biology, from medicine to chemistry, etc.). Nor is this yet all, because from this first methodological level we can then rise to a systematic analysis of *scientific language*, examining directly, specifically and autonomously the *logical conditions* of the scientificity of science in general. This gives rise to a particular approach to science, which develops a "logic of science" or of "epistemology" properly speaking.

Naturally this second level of possible philosophical analysis of science as such presupposes in its turn, as its *materia subjecta*, the first methodological level, even though this new epistemological level significantly changes the point of view from which science is studied. Finally we can then rise to a third and different point of view, which we can indicate as that specific to the "philosophy of science" as such, in which science, as reality in itself, is no longer considered in relation to the logical conditions of scientificity, but rather in relation to knowledge as such, to its conditions, its limits and its intrinsic value, considering science *in general* in relationship to civilization and to humanity itself. Also in this third case this specifically philosophical consideration of science presupposes the epistemological level as its *materia subjecta*, starting from which it raises itself to a different and more general consideration of science as such. Nor is this all, because we can also observe how these different considerations of the scientific enterprise all relate to a typically circular structure of philosophical reflection, with the result that every level of analysis refers and is related, at the same time, to all the others, within the framework of an extremely articulated and flexible conception of philosophical analysis. In this respect, Giulio Preti observes:

> Ruytinx rightly says: "La philosophie est une *métaréflexion dont le niveau est toujours susceptible d'être déplacé*". True: philosophy is a meta-reflection, and for this reason it does not have a locus of its own. With regard to science, epistemology is philosophy; but with the development of a scientific epistemology, the locus of philosophy moves to a higher level, that of meta-epistemology. Do we want to call it "metaphysics"? We're free to do so: but it has nothing to do with the theory of ideas, the demonstrations of the existence of God or the *Ethica more geometrico demonstrata*.
>
> The philosophy of science itself cannot be epistemology – even if it has its lowest level, and hence its object, in this. As always in the case of philosophy, it has as its object the forms and the conditions of a civilization: in this case, the *civilization of the sciences*.[9]

So philosophy advances [...] like a crab, through a succession of meta-reflections. Precisely within this specific and complex web of problematic interconnections it is therefore necessary to analyze the problem of the axiological dimension of science. This approach, however one chooses to judge it, enables us to avoid a very common preliminary error: that of claiming to be able to exhaust, dogmatically and a

---

[9] Cf. Preti [1976], Vol. I, p. 512, italics in the text. For the quotation from Ruytinx cf. Ruytinx [1962], note 2 on p. 339.

priori, the complex phenomenon of contemporary science by reducing it, without residues, to a single (and truly mythical) plane of privileged analysis. Or rather: this transcendentalist-phenomenological approach, typical of and specific to the tradition of European critical rationalism, also enables us to stress the complexity of the phenomenon that we have chosen to study, as well as the need to equip ourselves adequately, so as to be able to develop a multipolar approach to science. Excluding, for a start, all dogmatic reductionism, as well as the pretension to be able to relate science to some individual element that can then be hypostatized on an absolute plane (whether epistemic or philosophical).

By contrast, this approach makes it possible to constantly stress the need to develop an intrinsically malleable and flexible analysis. The reciprocal and continuous interconnection between the different planes of analysis and the parallel observation that a discipline can be considered in its relative autonomy, or as the *materia subjecta* of another discipline, or yet again as the eidetic perspective of a specific problem, enables us to delineate a far more articulated analysis with a far wider scope, set within the framework of an intrinsically "circular" reflection, which makes it possible to underline the dynamic articulation of the problem in question. Also because, as Geymonat[10] rightly insisted on a number of occasions, science can never be adequately comprehended without an analytic study of its real history. A history that is not entirely logical and which has to be borne in mind in all its complexity, precisely in order to understand the character, at times paradoxically zigzagging, of its historical evolution.

3. Criticity as the Axiologic Specific of the Civilization of the Sciences

If we bear in mind the problematic picture referred to above in § 2, and it we place ourselves on the second level of analysis identified – that which considers science as a form of modern civilization – we can then ask ourselves what are the specific axiological elements of this innovative civilization of the sciences. In other words, we can ask what are the precise axiological values present within the model of civilization foreshadowed by science.[11]

---

[10] Cf. Geymonat [1960].

[11] The plural of the term may be used to stress the multiplicity of the scientific disciplines by means of which the human stock of knowledge has been increased, while the singular can be used to stress the edectic moment of scientific knowledge, though without having the dogmatic pretension to being able to reduce science to a single method.

A first value can naturally be identified in the presence and the consequent full scientific and cultural exploitation of rationality. By definition, science constitutes, in fact, the fruit of human reason, a reason with which humanity, though *con fatica grande* (or "very laboriously"),[12] as Galileo reminds us in his *Dialogue Concerning the Two Principal World Systems*, seeks to understand the laws of the physical world.

In effect, the role of reason within the scientific cognitive process cannot be in the least diminished, while recognizing the role played by the experimentation. Nevertheless, also the experimental dimension is always directly bound up with the heuristic role performed by rationality, which enables different theories to be configured and "tested". Though the Baconian image of science is widespread; yet from Galileo to Einstein, nearly all the most eminent militant scientists have always emphasized the decisive role played by reason in delineating the various scientific theories, precisely because rationality constitutes the most authentic and decisive fulcrum for the critical increase of knowledge. Einstein, to give just one emblematic example, in his famous *Autobiographical Notes*, assimilates scientific knowledge to a sort of "intellectual possession" of the extra-personal world.[13]

Naturally, while an established and qualified tradition of scientists is unanimous in stressing the irreplaceable role of human rationality in the construction of the scientific patrimony, there also exist various and even conflicting conceptions of this same rationality, which nevertheless agree in considering that human reason can perform a guiding function in the conquest of knowledge. On this methodological plane, special consideration is due above all to the view defended and variously illustrated by a 17th-century poet like John Milton, in his *Areopagitica*, in which we read expressly that "reason is but choosing".[14] With the result that "where there is much desire to learn, there of necessity will be much arguing, much writing, many opinions; for opinion in good men is but knowledge in the making". So, we read: *"In good men opinion is but knowledge in the making"*. But it is "knowledge in the making" only "in good men".

As a consequence, humanity is "good" precisely because it is willing to change its opinion and knowledge represents something that is essentially dynamic. This perceptive configuration of human rationality and of the knowledge peculiar to humanity as intrinsically flexible and

---

12 Galileo [1632], VII, p. 289.
13 Cf. the *Autobiographical Notes* published in Schlipp [1949].
14 Milton [1644], p. 40, while the quotation which follows immediately in the text is on p. 74.

dynamic clearly illustrates the deepest nature of scientific knowledge. A knowledge which has, therefore, always to be *reasoned* and which, at the same time, must be susceptible of continually being corrected, rectified and replaced by a deeper knowledge of reality. Here we can quote the words of an author like John Stuart Mill, in his no less well-known essay of 1858 *On Liberty*, in which he states:

> If even the Newtonian philosophy were not permitted to be questioned, mankind could not feel as complete assurance of its truth as they now do. The beliefs which we have most warrant for have no safeguard to rest on but a standing invitation to the whole world to prove them unfounded. If the challenge is not accepted, or is accepted and the attempt fails, we are far enough from certainty still, but we have done the best that the existing state of human reason admits of: we have neglected nothing that could give the truth chance of reaching us; if the lists are kept open, we may hope that, if there be a better truth, it will be found when the human mind is capable of receiving it; and in the meantime we may rely on having attained such approach to truth as is possible in our own day. This is the amount of certainty attainable by a fallible being, and this the sole way of attaining it.[15]

In this sense the "foundations" of scientific knowledge then constitute a challenge: the challenge to be able to find a better argument to defend a specific theoretical explanation. This foundation, as inferred from Mill's words, does not, however, possess any more absolute, metaphysical or dogmatic foundation, because everyone is invited to devise a "better" theory than those that form part of the cognitive patrimony of humanity. Note that in this epistemic perspective a theory is only thought of as "better" and never as metaphysically "exhaustive" of reality: that is to say as capable of explaining, once and for all, the true nature of reality. Out of this grows the dynamic and propulsive element of science itself, which makes its appeal to human reason precisely because it identifies in the reason of humanity a critical tool by which all knowledge can be always and constantly improved. This is in accordance with an epistemic model that coincides openly with that practiced in the field of technology, in which each technical product can only be assessed by comparison with other analogous technical products, in order to then judge which is "best". And just as no technical product is "absolutely" and finally the unsurpassable technical solution to a specific problem, the same is also true of scientific theories, which are never unduly absolutized and transformed into taboos or dogmas. Faced with every result – whether theoretical or practical – human reason can always claim its right to criticism, so as to identify theories or technical

---

[15] Mill [1858], p. 81.

inventions that are "better" than those previously devised by human intelligence.

Moreover, this dynamic and critical configuration of scientific knowledge constitutes an image that does not in the least reduce science to a wholly relative and transient reality, resulting in a comprehensively sceptical outcome. The sceptical outcome constitutes a reversal which is the mirror image of dogmatism and, by its intrinsic nature, it is no less dogmatic than every absolutist solution. In fact every theory that turns out to be "better" than a previous one always possesses a (relative) objective content of authentic knowledge, with respect to which we have to compare all the other alternative and possibly conflicting theories. In other words, the knowledge developed by science, though never absolute knowledge (like that dear to traditional metaphysics) constitutes, nevertheless, an objective knowledge, capable of revealing, *cognitively*, some "strands of truth" about reality, yet without ever giving us an absolute vision of the reality that it studies.

It follows that the axiological model intrinsic to the deepest dynamics of scientific knowledge, which is fully constituent of the scientific enterprise itself, can then be identified in *criticity*. In fact it is critical knowledge that increases human knowledge continually. As a result criticity can be conceived as an axiological constituent element not only of the scientific enterprise but also of the scientific civilization itself. Seen in this perspective, criticity calls for the construction of an open society capable of protecting, as its maximum good, precisely the increase of this critical spirit. This was explained clearly by Immanuel Kant in the first edition of the *Kritik der reinen Vernunft*:

> Man hört hin und wieder Klagen über Seichtigkeit der Denkungsart unserer Zeit und den Verfall gründlicher Wissenschaft. Allein ich sehe nicht, dass die, deren Grund gut gelegt ist, als Mathematik, Naturlehre etc. diesen Vorwirf im mindesten verdienen, sondern vielmehr den alten Ruhm der Gründlichkeit behaupten, in der letzteren aber sogar übertreffen. Eben derselbe Geist würde sich nun auch in anderen Arten von Erkenntnis wirksan beweisen, wäre nur allerest vor die Berichtigung ihrer Prinzipien gesorgt worden. In Ermangelung derselben sind Gleichgültigkeit und Zweifel, und, endlich, strenge Kritik, vielmehr Beweise einer *grüdlichen* Denkungsard. Unser Zeitalter ist das eigentliche Zeitalter der *Kritik*, der sich alles unterwerfen muss. *Religion*, durch ihre *Heiligkeit*, und *Gesetzgebung*, durch ihre *Majestät*, wollen sich gemeiniglich derselben entziehen. Aber alsdenn erregen sie gerechten Verdacht wider sich, und können auf unverstellte Achtung nicht Ansprich machen, die die Vernunft nur demjernigen bewilligt, was ihre freie und öffentliche Prüfung hat aushalten können.[16]

---

[16] Kant [1781], p. 10, spacing in the text.

The age of criticism that Kant appeals to constitutes an authentic axiological model of reference. Not only on the scientific plane, obviously, but also on the civil and the political planes. So true is this, that Kant himself points out that religion and legislation cannot escape from the requirements of criticity by appealing to *sanctity* and *majesty* respectively: so even sanctity and majesty must submit to a confrontation with human reason and subject themselves to critical analysis. Criticity constitutes a rigorous and profound mode of thinking, the only one to which we can appeal in maintaining, arguing and defending any thesis. Consequently, this open, rationalist approach has to permeate the whole of human society, which, precisely in order to protect this critical spirit, must necessarily be an open and tolerant society. Open and tolerant towards the needs of criticity. To put it extremely concisely, if the core of scientific knowledge consists of criticity, it follows that a human society should be so constructed as to ensure the fullest respect for an education in criticism and enhanced opportunities to develop critical comparisons between different positions. The open and tolerant society therefore appears as the result of the founding axiological value of science itself.

4. Knowledge and Freedom: the Two Axiological Faces of Modernity

As we have noted, an increase in human knowledge can be achieved only through the systematic use of the critical reason, through the investigation of arguments and the establishment of increasingly rigorously criticism. But, as can also be deduced from the earlier, brief quotation from Milton, this criticity – which therefore constitutes, the truest Archimedean and constituent fulcrum of scientific knowledge – can be properly increased only by "good men". In other words, it calls for people authentically determined to increase human knowledge critically. This shows us that the problem of human rationality is only one face of the medal, which is immediately connected with another side of the problem: that of the human will, which takes us, even more decisively, into a practical-moral dimension, meaning into the specific and undisputed realm of axiology. The human reason, even if conceived in its maximum criticity possible, is not rooted in a void, but can be developed and increased only by *flesh and blood* humanity, which lives within a specific society, historically configured.

Consequently, the value of rational criticicity must necessarily be referred, by its intrinsic nature, to an extra-rational dimension, that of morality and good will. This point, which would seem at first sight to deviate from the study of our problem, instead constitutes an extremely

The Axiological Dimension of Science

valuable prescription, one that helps us to arrive at the heart of this analysis of the axiology of scientific civilization. This was again emphasized by Immanuel Kant who, to explain the precise nature of the century of the Enlightenment – which he saw as coinciding with the age of criticism – expressed the following, very famous definition of the Enlightenment:

> *Aufklärung ist der Ausgang des Menschen aus seiner selbst verschuldeten Unmündigkeit.* Unmündigkeit ist das unvermögen sich seines Verstandes ohne Leitung eines anderen zu bedienen. *Selbstverschuldet* ist diese Unmündigkeit, wenn die Ursache derselben nicht am Mangel des Verstandes, sondern der Entschliessung und des Muthes liegt sich seiner ohne Leitung eines anderen zu bedienen. *Sapere aude!* Habe Muth dich *deines eigenen* Verstandes zu bedienen! Ist alzo der Wahlspruch der Aufklärung.[17]

With this definition of the Enlightenment, Kant enables us to understand that the appeal to the criticity of reason is by itself insufficient, unless this same criticity is rooted, in its turn, in the concrete ability of the human will to act according to the indications that emerge from the workings of human rationality. This may seem almost a "vicious circle", but in reality it is not, because Kant understood that human reason (human, note, and not absolute) cannot live and be expressed outside a humanity of flesh and blood who desire to apply and follow it. The "tutelage" of humanity is not due only to a possible deficit of rationality, but also (and above all) to the lack of ability to follow, by force of our own will power, the dictates of reason.

With the result that *reason* and *will* represent two realities that cannot be disjoined. Naturally they are, however, two different realities that always have to be duly supplemented: rationality needs to be supplemented by criticity, which has to induce us to analyze, always with adequate rigour, our own statements. On the other hand, also the human will, by itself, can indicate very little, unless we add a fundamental qualification directed to working for good and on the basis of the indications that emerge from critical rationality itself. Besides, the human will may be either a "good" will, or a "bad" will. Consequently the two different qualifications determine, in their turn, two approaches, which are not in the least opposed, for a correct evaluation of rationality itself. But, in "good men" there is no doubt that human rationality becomes an instrument for pursuing positive and just ends.

If we translate Kant's observation into a consideration of more general and universal scope, it is easy to realize how Kant, with his programmatic indication, identified the two sides of a single medal, that of

---

[17] Cf. Immanuel Kant [1784], Vol. VIII, p. 35, spacing in the text.

modernity. In fact the increase in knowledge, a specific result of the deepening of critical rationality, then has to be connected, in its turn, with a parallel increase in human freedom. In this way knowledge and freedom exist in a closely dynamic interconnection: the increase of knowledge determines the possibility of new actions which, in their turn, call for an expansion of human responsibility. On the other hand, greater freedom is also required so as to increase the critical cognitive spirit which constitutes the most authentic fulcrum for the increase of human knowledge. This is why, in the history of modernity the increase of knowledge and the construction of increasingly free, open and de-mocratic societies, capable of better protecting the fundamental human rights (and the freedom that is its consequence) have often developed, *generally speaking*, in parallel. It is precisely because freedom and knowledge represent, in the last analysis, the two faces of modernity. Without the development of knowledge there is no development of freedom.

On the other hand, the expansion of freedom cannot help but benefit scientific research itself, which always presupposes greater freedom to develop its free critical investigations in different directions. Moreover, this dynamic interaction between knowledge and freedom is never conducted in the abstract void of an ideology, but always in close con-tact with the concrete and diversified patrimonies (civil and cognitive) of freedom and knowledge truly achieved by humanity in the course of its real history. For this reason, those who defend the possibility of a critical investigation of human knowledge at the same time must neces-sarily defend a progressive and fuller expansion of human freedom. Here lies the point: freedom and knowledge are the two faces of moder-nity, of that modernity by which the civilization of science of the mod-ern world has been historically constructed.

References

Agazzi Evandro, (1992), *Il bene, il male, la scienza*, Milan, Rusconi, translated into English *Right, Wrong and Science. The Ethical Dimensions of the Techno-Scientific Enterprise*, edited by Craig Dilworth, Amsterdam-New York, Rodopi, 2004.

Banfi Antonio, (1959), *La ricerca della realtà*, Florence, Sansoni, 2 vols.

Butterfield Herbert, (1958), *The Origins of Modern Science*, London, G. Bell and Sons Ltd.

Einstein Albert, (1949), *Autobiographisches* cf. Schlipp (1949), p. 2-95 (origi-nal text in German and English translation).

Galilei Galileo, (1632), *Dialogo sopra i due massimi sistemi del mondo*, Florence, Giovan Battista Landini, work cited in the reissue published in the

Edizione Nazionale, edited by Antonio Favaro, Florence, G. Barbera, 1968, 20 vols., Vol. VII.

Geymonat Ludovico, (1956), *Galileo Galilei*, Torino, Einaudi, 10 ed. ivi 1980, text translated from the Italian with additional notes and appendix by Stillman Drake, *Foreword* by Professor Giorgio de Santillana: *Galileo Galilei: A biography and inquiry into his philosophy of science*, New York-Toronto-London, Mc Graw-Hill Book Company, 1965.

Geymonat Ludovico, (1960), *Filosofia e filosofia della scienza*, Milan, Feltrinelli.

Geymonat Ludovico, (1970-1976), *Storia del pensiero filosofico e scientifico*, Milan, Garzanti, 7 vols.

Geymonat Ludovico, (1977), *Scienza e realismo*, Milan, Feltrinelli.

Geymonat Ludovico, (2005) [1985], *Lineamenti di filosofia della scienza*, Milan, Mondadori.

Husserl Edmund, (1928), *Logische Untersuchungen*, Halle, Max Niemeyer, 2 vols, in 3 tomes.

Kant Immanuel, (1781), *Kritik der reinen Vernunft*, Johann Friedrich Hartknoc, Riga, reissued in I. Kant, *Critica della ragione pura*, German text on facing pages, Introduction, translation and apparatus by Costantino Esposito, Milan, Bompiani, 2004.

Kant Immanuel, (1784), *Beantwortung der Frage: Was ist Aufklärung* in Kant's Werke, Berlin und Leipzig, Walter de Gruyter & C., 1923, Band VIII, p. 33-42.

Mill John Stuart, (1859), *On Liberty*, West Strand, London, John W. Parker and Son, new edition, *On Liberty*, edited with an Introduction by Gertrude Himmelfarb, Harmondsworth, Middlesex, England, Penguin Books Ltd, 1985.

Milton John, (1644), *Areopagitica* in J. Milton, *Areopagitica*, introduction, translation, notes and apparatus by Mariano Gatti and Hilary Gatti, English text on facing pages, Milan, Rusconi, 1998.

Minazzi Fabio, (1994a), *L'onesto mestiere del filosofare*, Milan, Franco Angeli.

Minazzi Fabio, (1994b), *Galileo "filosofo geometra"*, Milan, Rusconi.

Minazzi Fabio, (2004a), *Il cacodémone neoilluminsita*, Milan, Franco Angeli.

Minazzi Fabio, (2004b), *Teleologia della conoscenza ed escatologia della speranza per un nuovo illuminismo critico*, Naples, La Città del Sole.

Minazzi Fabio, (2006), *L'épistémologie comme herméneutique de la raison*, Naples-Paris, La Città del Sole-Librairie Philosophique J. Vrin.

Pera Marcello, (1991), *Scienza e retorica*, Rome-Bari, Laterza.

Preti Giulio, (1968), *Retorica e logica*, Turin, Einaudi, 1968.

Preti Giulio, (1976), *Saggi filosofici*, *Presentazione* di Mario Dal Pra, Florence, "La Nuova Italia" Editrice, 2 vols.

Preti Giulio, (1989), *Lezioni di filosofia della scienza (1965-1966)*, a cura di Fabio Minazzi, Milan, Franco Angeli.

Russell Bertrand, (1931), *The Scientific Outlook*, London, George Allen & Unwin Ltd.

Ruytinx Jacques, (1962), *La Problématique philosophique de l'unité de la science*, Paris, Société d'Édition "Les Belles Lettres".

Snow Charles Percy, (1959), *The Two Cultures: And a Second Look. An expanded version of the two cultures and the scientific revolution*, Cambridge, Cambridge University Press.

Schlipp Paul Arthur, (1949), *Albert Einstein Philosopher-Scientist*, edited by Paul Arthur Schlipp, "Library of Living Philosophers", Illinois, Tudor, Evanston, 1949.

Pluralism, Scientific Values, and the Value of Science

Alberto CORDERO

The Graduate School CUNY & Queens College
City University of New York

Truth and the Map Metaphor

Anti-objectivist critiques of science fuss about theory dependence, scientific truth and the ineliminable presence of conventionalist elements in all human representations. Sensible realists respond by pointing to the truth and objectivity of *good maps*. Good maps, they urge, show how a strong sense of truth and objectivity can be made compatible with significant levels of theory dependence and conventionalism.[1] In particular, a map can provide a truthful representation of stuff in the world yet function in accordance with conventions (about coastal lines, rivers, cities, and so forth), cartographic projections (cylindrical, Mercator, etc.), goals (a map may focus on physical aspects, as opposed to political, zoological, or other kind of aspects), and socio-cultural contingencies (specific symbols employed, geographical orientation and so forth). No grand authentication is needed in order to decide whether a given map succeeds as a provider of proper (i.e. relevant and true enough) representations of its intended domain. Also, maps are in an important sense always "partial": a sensible map-makers doesn't seek to represent anything "completely"; nor could he do so if he wished to. Maps are abstract, every map corresponds to a particular perspective of representational interests. What a given map specifically seeks to describe (what it includes and leaves out, its scale and level of accuracy) is something primarily determined by its intended use. No matter what it tries to portray, a map will be *good* only to the extent that the relevant information it provides is accurate within previously specified standards. A good map tells relevant truths about its intended domain, even if maps are variously limited in this regard. One limitation concerns the selectiv-

---

[1]   Toulmin (1953), Giere (1997), Sismondo & Chrisman (2001), Kitcher (2001).

ity of aspects regarding the domain of relevant interests, while another has to do with the intended level of accurate discrimination (1 m, 100 m, 1 km, etc.) which can never be perfect in actual maps. Yet another, with the range of correct representation (for example, just the coastal line of a given territory, 100 km into the land, etc., depending on both the map's intended use and the state of relevant knowledge at the time). In addition, appropriate reading of a map requires knowledge of all the conventions that were employed in its construction. All these restrictions functions as limitations. Yet, arguably *it is precisely through their judicious implementation that maps manage to achieve their descriptive goals* (how else but by specifying some coarse-grained range of reliable partial depiction could appropriately isomorphic representations be achieved in cartography?).

One map-related notion of obvious interest to realists is truth accumulation. On the whole, cartographic lineages display *descriptive progress*, especially in terms of accuracy and range of correct representation. Take, for example, the depiction of the Amazon River, its tributaries, and the region's topography, in maps from the 16th century on. Of course, talk of "progress" presupposes the applicability of such valuative notions as *good* and *bad*, *better* and *worse*, which are notoriously troublesome when considered in the abstract. Applied to maps, however, rankings are helped by the existence of an objective standard, namely, conformity to the relevant aspects of the territory in question, as determined by the specific uses intended for the map. The map metaphor attracts the realist precisely because it does not burden the notions of truth and progress with extravagant philosophical baggage. Indeed cartography invites a version of scientific realism which, though comparatively modest, seems powerful enough to save all the sensible realist intuitions. It is a realism in which theory construction is compared to map making in certain specific respects, particularly the following four:

a. Theory development aims at improving our description and understanding of aspects of the world we find significant, as determined by current interests and knowledge. Typically, the study of any empirical domain allows in principle for a multitude of perspectives. Different sets of interests generally give salience to different aspects of the world.

b. What a theory or model means to depict depends upon the theory's intended perspective, the scales and ranges targeted, the resources available to the scientists articulating it, and so forth.

c. A given theoretical representation is correct only to the extent that the descriptions it supplies of its intended domain are correct in the relevant way.

d. How to best describe and understand a given part or aspect of the world hinges greatly on the current *state of knowledge*. The latter may sometimes encourage approaching the items of a given domain reductionistically – as being "secondary" relative to the fundamental entities and processes of a larger field. Alternatively, current knowledge may encourage looking at some items non-reductionistically relative to other scientific fields. Then again, current knowledge may invite a multi-level approach.

Finally, some *negative analogies* need to be noted as well. First, there is the fact that assessing scientific representations generally requires more than just "logic and observation". Here matters are not nearly as straightforward as in the case of geographical maps. Declaring part of a theoretical narrative beyond reasonable doubt requires prior acceptance of important realist theses, particularly about the actual epistemic achievements of abduction. In particular, a realist will insist that theoretical science has plenty of credible enough and stable enough descriptions of "the unobservable" in numerous areas – as credible and stable as the best empirical claims we have about the ordinary level. The realist, then, is not *grounding* his position on the accuracy and objectivity of maps, but rather using cartographic success to illustrate the compatibility of constructivist constraints with *epistemic goals*. Secondly, the kind of fruitful unification projects often found in the sciences is something rare in cartography. Scientific theorizing is propelled in part by a tendency to relate and even unify previously independent representations. While this aspect of science is often exaggerated, impressive partial unifications are certainly on view in the natural sciences.[2] A third negative analogy has to do with the workings of *internal constraints* on scientific agendas: scientific theorizing is not as freely pluralistic as in cartography, for several reasons. Let us briefly consider some of the most important.

Internal Pluralism

World phenomena generally allow for more than one correct analysis. A virus, for example, can be variously looked at by scientists as a physical system, a biological entity, or a sociological object, to mention some possibilities. Interestingly, however, within the mature sciences pluralism is generally a moderate affair, limited to rather few clearly legitimate sources, conspicuously the following three:

---

2 Consider, for example, the way possibility structures of previously separate fields keep getting embedded into increasingly comprehensive networks in physics.

a. One is the internally perceived incompleteness of scientific knowledge. This source is particularly strong at the deepest foundational frontiers, where present knowledge generally has little constraining rational force on the imagination. At this level the interesting questions are often quite open – such as whether all physical systems are ultimately quantum-mechanical, whether the world is deterministic, and whether the most distinctive features of the human mind have relevant Darwinian histories. Scientific conceptual explorations are not nearly as fluid as this at less fundamental levels of theorizing.

b. Pluralism also prospers in domains where several fruitful explanatory perspectives coexist. Two disciplines may deal with a given domain and actually sustain strong inter-theoretic relationships yet focus on different levels of understanding. For example, genetics and molecular physics connect at numerous levels, but in some areas of genetics the main interest is in phenomena that operate at morphological levels not very relevantly connected to the level of physico-chemical structures. A textbook example of this is provided by the explanation of the paring and separation of gene-related traits in crossing-over processes, which in general biology appeals to just the rough overall shape of chromosomes (without any reference to their molecular constitution).

c. Finally, a very important reason for encouraging pluralist incursions against current views is our general fallibility and our all-too-human tendency to stick to received perspectives. Established scientific theories easily turn into dogma unless their actual (less than perfect) epistemic foundations are not forgotten – hence the internal appropriateness of encouraging challenges from as many alternative points of view as practicable.

The above sources characterize a form of open-mindedness that is both fuelled and constrained primarily by the epistemic state of current science. I'll call it "internal scientific pluralism". Its underlying contrast with "external" influences works well in disciplines with strong track records of scientific success and cumulative growth. Ostensibly, in such disciplines the formulation of questions, the discussion of issues, the acceptance of ambiguity, the practice of tolerance, and the formulation of research agendas operate in a context that is both attentive to prior learning and scientific reasons. Within this environment, pluralist explorations spring from an awareness of the epistemic limitations of current science rather than other considerations. Indeed it seems fair to claim that the more mature branches of contemporary natural science now have available levels of philosophical autonomy unprecedented in the history of thought.

This aspect of modern science has been the subject of much attention since the 1960s. Prominent among such efforts are works on the power and scope of internal scientific rationality by such figures as Dudley Shapere, Ernan McMullin, and the early Mary Hesse.[3] Particularly relevant here are, I think, Shapere's studies of how, in the major modern conceptual revisions, notwithstanding the existence of external social pressures, questions about theory acceptance, rejection or suspension of belief *could* have been tackled exclusively on the basis of knowledge and scientific evidence available at the time, ultimately on the basis of *reasons* as opposed to just socio-political "causes".[4] Hypotheses still lacking hard scientific support can be, and have been, forced in (as in Galileo's official "rejection" of the idea that the Earth moves around the Sun), but they do not convince.

All these pluralist openings are strongly tied to epistemic interests generated at the interior of the scientific activity, nourished by reason and knowledge. As with map making, however, science too connects with a much larger sphere of interests. Society entertains projects in all sorts of directions; scientific interests compete with the wider interests prevailing at the time in the larger milieu. Projects of the greatest epistemic interest are often at odds with current social priorities, particularly in the case of projects requiring extensive external funding. For example, although the Hubble telescope is highly valued by astronomers, scientists and many lay people, the United States Congress would now seem determined to abandon it, because of doubts among politicians about the interest and value of its prospective yields for ordinary people (as opposed to scientists and their supporters).[5] At any rate, the epistemic values of science have never been equally cherished by all human beings. Increasingly, in the case of publicly sponsored research, it seems only fair that science should serve the interests and values of the society that pays for it. It is generally difficult to state the exact interests and values of a society like ours, but some agreements seem to be in place. In reasonably serious democratic societies one expects the selection and support of publicly-funded activities to be the outcome of responsible discussion, with due consideration to such inputs as representative expert recommendations from the relevant scientific disciplines, the cost and viability of submitted projects, their expected impact on society, and so on.[6]

---

[3]   See, for example, Shapere (1974, 1991), McMullin (1978, 1981), and Hesse (1965).

[4]   Shapere (1974) provides a good illustration of this "internalist" approach.

[5]   As of this writing (December, 2003).

[6]   One engaging model of this is Philip Kitcher's conception of "well-ordered science" (2001).

Not all science is publicly-funded, however. A growing proportion of important research activity now issues from the private sector. Regarding this part of science the social restrictions may be expected to be more modest, but by no means absent. One obvious area of legitimate social interest concerns quality supervision of products and services destined for public consumption. Another concerns basic humanity. Researchers cannot be permitted to use people in any way they wish. But, what exactly should not be permitted? Some people would have social control reaching wide and deep into scientific practice, a topic which brings into view a much more variegated – and unruly – level of pluralism.

The Good Life

Pluralism about the *good life* is central to the project of "liberal democratic societies", in which people are left free to figure out for themselves as much as possible what makes life good. Some values get to be widely recognized as "important" – freedom, solidarity, truth and truth-seeking, sensual pleasure, social progress, to name a few. Not all these are valued equally, however. Nor are all values valued by everybody. "High" values may well be irreducibly diverse, conflicting and often impossible to harmonize, so that sometimes when they come into conflict there may be no rational resolution to hope for. Most relevantly for present purposes, not everyone thinks of the pursuit of truth as an intrinsically noble activity. Some people, albeit mostly from "academic circles", even deny there are objective truths of any kind to be had.[7] The point is that science operates within a social milieu that is both strongly committed to axiological pluralism about the good life and correspondingly tolerant to very many life projects. How to deal with conflict is not a simple issue, of course – especially in our growing "cultures of complaint".[8]

For present purposes the key topic is individual *freedom to try to learn about the world*. What sensible moral considerations, if any, may constrain that freedom? We widely agree, for starters, that nobody has a right to conduct experiments with human beings without their prior, well-informed and explicit free consent. So, let us accept that there is no overriding right to pursue knowledge for its own sake, regardless of the

---

[7] Such is the slogan of, for example, the so-called "radical constructivists", for whom all scientific debates, including the most ostentatiously rational, are but deceptive extensions of wider struggles that are ultimately political.

[8] Societies that encourage people to complain as much as possible about as much as they can get away with. See, for example, Hughes (1994).

means resorted to. What further restrictions does it make sense to impose on scientific practice?

Many of us think moral constraints on scientific activity should be as modest as possible, but opinions vary as to how to interpret this. Some socially concerned intellectuals worry about the human impact of research dealing with socially sensitive topics. Thus, for example, Richard Lewontin, Philip Kitcher and the late J.S. Gould, have variously warned us against certain lines of research they consider morally problematic in the context of present social realities. These thinkers primarily have in mind some psycho-biological research, which – they fear – is virtually guaranteed to interfere negatively with the freedom of members of certain human groups to develop and exercise their skill and to define and choose their own life project. And so, in their view, scientists engaged in such research lines deserve moral opprobrium. One field these critics have especially set their sight on is Darwinist research on whether some specific human groups differ in inheritable psychological dispositions and skills – for example, explorations into the possibility that men may be *naturally* more gifted than women for disciplines like mathematics. The noted critics find such investigations inappropriate, especially because – as they see it – the targeted groups have endured much negative discrimination in recent times. The outrage here is not new. Ever since the loud publication of E.O. Wilson's *Sociobiology* in 1975, many concerned scientists and thinkers have been busy exposing projects of this sort as both flawed and socially pernicious.

So, should we morally condemn a line of inquiry if we think it likely to hurt already disadvantaged groups or decent "forms of human life"? Lewontin *et al.* say "yes". Kitcher (2001) in particular believes it is simply false that knowledge, however painful, is always a good thing to have – a society, he stresses, can simultaneously value knowledge yet, at the same time, ignore the results of certain investigations, even refuse to advance that line, if there they have reason to think that doing so may undermine ongoing forms of life. The key thought here is that even the rumor that scientists suspect that a certain group of human beings are somehow "naturally" deficient in some valued area could be horribly consequential to that group. Put this way, who can disagree that there is a moral difficulty here.

Inquiry and Morality

The interesting issue is how to determine when a topic is so potentially disturbing that scientifically probing into it, *however carefully*, ought to be morally discouraged in social contexts like those now prevailing. I'll concentrate on the kind of research Gould, Lewontin and

Kitcher have been exposing as particularly censurable since the late 1970s.

Consider the Darwinist project of discovering whether men and women differ in "natural skills" in mathematics. Critics point that such investigations are morally problematic because, given the current broader social context, the investigations are likely to result into hasty actions against beneficial policies currently in place. Admittedly the Darwinist project at hand *might*, in some scenarios, interfere with the rights women so painfully secured during the last century to develop their talents and to define and freely choose life projects for themselves. A crucial question is how much conflict between careful science and ongoing social agendas is acceptable. In the specific (yet, I suggest, representative) Darwinist line under consideration the grounds for a general condemnation seem weak. The only arguments in sight appear to be ones of the wrong consequentialist sort.

According to the critics, investigations into possible differences in valued skills between genders, races or classes tend to have adverse effects on people who are already disadvantaged. A recent argument by Philip Kitcher both clarifies and generalizes this charge to cover a whole genre of scientific projects. In a parallel work (Cordero 2004) I have tried to show that Kitcher's argument fails because several of its key premises fail to convince. The reasons why they fail have to do with relevant facts about the role of inquiry in fallibilist contexts, the texture of belief in contemporary natural science, and the wider moral benefits of scientific research.

In contemporary science explanations and correlations are embedded in thick conceptual and theoretical causal networks. Even the simplest assertion about, say, some "fossilized bone" involves massive arrays of theoretical connections – with knowledge about the biology, chemistry and physics of fossilization; with geological knowledge about the place where the piece was found, ultimately with a good proportion of the whole of natural science. Pseudo-scientific disciplines are very different (think, for instance, of creationist accounts of the age of fossils). Bringing this to bear on bio-psychological research, the basic theoretical texture is provided by Darwinian theory, and so the consequentialist import of its working hypotheses will be mediated by the specific way Darwinian theory structures natural possibilities. The key point is that the very texture of Darwinist approaches to human nature prevents them from properly leading to claims about *what anyone ought to do* or *how anyone should be treated*. While traditional views about human nature are both strongly teleological and loaded with imperatives, this is not true of their Darwinist counterparts; the latter purport to explain some distinctly human psychological and social tendencies as traits forged by natural selection in the context of our pleistocene evolution. As such, the warranted instrumental use of Darwinist psychology is limited to probabilistic viability assessments for possible human projects.

Let us try to imagine, then, the disturbing findings that may ensue from scientifically serious Darwinian projects. What exactly would follow from, say, an authentication of the idea that "men are *naturally* better at mathematics than women"? Whatever may follow, it could not amount to a straightforward challenge to any individual person's life project. At the most, a Darwinian claim might help individuals estimate the initial "natural" likelihood of possible life projects. This is generally something worth learning about, as it provides the sort of instrumental probability estimation one routinely finds valuable in practical affairs. The point is that Darwinian biology, and for that matter the contemporary natural sciences, are silent about the moral import of moving along or against natural tendencies. About options of the latter sort the only "warning" we can get from serious science is that moving against natural tendencies will normally require investing some extra resources. Once a goal has been selected, it may be argued, the next reasonable step would be to take maximal advantage of whatever natural tendencies happen to be available. Such as it is, the Darwinist approach seeks to provide no more than a "best current map" of the possibility and probability structures regarding differential aspects of our biologically-rooted nature, only now with important sectors of the distinctly human sphere tentatively brought into the map's range.

Still, as suggested, some critics from the liberal camp emphasize the consequentialist import of lingering histories of unfair discrimination against groups of people who were already disadvantaged to begin with. Wouldn't even rumors that some scientists are seriously thinking that boys may be generally more gifted than girls for mathematics lead to an effective lowering of the latter's opportunities and self-esteem? One obvious reply is that society can take reasonably adequate precautions against such possible outcomes and attend to the needs of potential victims through legislation and public funding. Kitcher (2001) expresses skepticism about the plausibility of such programs. But why? As a point of fact, boys have long been suspected of being "naturally" more gifted than girls for analytic thinking. Yet, especially since the 1950s, measures have been taken to prevent such suspicions from doing too much harm. And, though imperfect, the measures in place have succeeded to a significant degree. Real opportunities for women have broadly expanded over the last century and continue to do so rather vigorously.

There is something else worth stressing: as already said, contemporary scientific research yields more than isolated "assertions". This is key, particularly when the assertions amount to "bad news". For instance, studies of cancer and genetics do more than advance diagnosis – typically, such studies also direct attention to possible ways of combating the disease; research can always get morally out of hand in all sorts of ways, but regulation sees to that menace increasingly well. The point is that one major characteristic of contemporary natural science is that its hypotheses are embedded in theoretical networks that are structurally rich in terms of conceptual and causal links. Well-constructed hypotheses not only tell what some part of the world is like, but also cast light on how subsequent research might (sometimes even should) proceed. This is overwhelmingly true in the case of investigations into evolutionary lineages, genomes, oncogenes, and indeed every significant piece of research in the natural sciences today. Because of the theoretical structure of the scientific claims involved, bad news about oncogenes regularly come accompanied by pragmatic guidance, and through it also by realistic hope for affected people in the long run. In Darwinian psychology this pragmatic aspect is furthered by the circumstance that variations in inherited skills are generally open to the combined equalizing impact of environmental stimuli and Baldwin effects.[9]

Scientific Maps, Dignity and the Bounds of Pluralism

Now, how does all this apply to explorations involving Darwinian nativist hypotheses? Suppose that at some point in the future, strongly compelling evidence made it difficult to deny that a given group of people are comparatively lacking in some valued respect. What then? Is there reason to think that this scientific finding would lack the texture of disturbing findings in other parts of science (like, say, cancer research)? If Darwinists ever managed to convince us that (say) women are, on average, less naturally gifted than men for mathematics, would this finding be unlikely to function as a springboard for subsequent research into desirable equalizers, and the like? Given the texture and context of the case that would have to have been made, it seems inescapable that the Darwinists' claim would be pretty rich. If so, in conjunction with prevailing egalitarian ideals, there is reason to expect that the totality of the suggested discovery would also cast light on how to search for correctives – educational and eventually even molecular-biological ones – to be made available to all those who might be interested in them. The point is that the feared consequentialist grounds for condemning nativist

---

[9]   See, for example, Dennett (1995), Chapter 3.

inquiries like the one just highlighted fail because the relevant arguments resort to premises that are independently defused, first by the character of Darwinian theory, and then also by the rich theoretical network embodied by contemporary scientific conjectures. The larger point, I suggest, is that Darwinian nativist inquiries cannot be so easily presumed to upset currently thriving "projects of human life". Despite all of the consequentialist finger-wagging against them, no clearly uncontrollable unfair consequences from such inquiries for anybody seem convincingly discernible.

And so, at least in the particular genre of nativist cases considered, leftist anxiety would seem misplaced. This, however, does not quite meet the critics' "higher-level point", which I take to be about the possibility and resolution of conflict between life projects. Here the clash is between the "internally driven" life project of a handful of scientists on the one hand, and certain "moral views" prevailing in wider sectors of the society on the other. The issue here is the possibility of conflict between non-converging projects of human fulfillment. Attributing unfairness at this level is not a simple matter, partly because the whole thing is strongly tied to whatever view of life is used as starting point, which is not clearly the same for all human beings. At this more general level of discussion the Darwinist case at hand exemplifies, I think, the possibility of serious confrontation between the pluralist demands generated within one form of life (in the present case, epistemically-driven science and philosophy), and demands generated and adhered to jointly in wider sectors of society.

"Non Plus Ultra", public advocates shout loud to the wreckless explorer approaching the Columns of Hercules, reminding him of the abyss that awaits him and his helpless crew if he persists in his unconscionable search. But what if this explorer has compelling reason to believe that no such abyss exists; and furthermore, after trying to reason with the public advocates, he sees no way to get his views across. In the specific case reviewed, (a) the Darwinist explorer's honest and deeply felt point is that the social impact of his research is not at all as the critics fear, whereas (b) the honest and deeply felt point of a larger human group is that the explorer's research constitutes enough of an effrontery to deserve moral opprobrium. What is the Darwinist to do?

I cannot attempt such a massive question, of course. However, I would like to end with an observation about reasonable limits on research from a particular contemporary perspective – that of the kind of scientific realism with which I began, only now combined with Millean liberalism. A realist of the noted sort, let us recall, tries to integrate naturalism, fallibilism, and the thesis of map-like partiality regarding both scientific representations and theoretical progress. In turn, the realism-friendly aspect of the Millean liberal project I take as central is the ideal of the thoughtful human being who seeks, and sometimes achieves, some measure of truth about the world and some refinement of thought. Let us think of a person trying to live by these ideals, i.e. by reason, sound democracy, and the best "scientific maps" within reach.

To this person, democracy is incompatible with anything like the "tyranny of the majority". The pluralism that matters is the pluralism of people who seek to approach all views with an open mind but also clarity as to both the evidential support and limitations of their views. This is a realist-liberal perspective, in which the fact that present social realities leave a lot to be desired is something of paramount concern, yet not something that can be easily turned into a reason for condemning research lines simply because they probe into potentially disturbing topics in some "politically incorrect" manner. As a naturalist realist, this imagined person tries to base his decisions on the best knowledge available, which may sometimes clash with the "deepest desires of the age". This is a liberal perspective in which irreducible social conflict is a serious possibility. This is also a realist perspective in which truth and cognitive progress are not mere illusions. So, when, having arisen, conflict proves immune to negotiation, the liberal-realist would seem to have no option but to rise to the challenge, sometimes with great courage.

References

Cordero, Alberto, (2004), "Contemporary Nativism, Scientific Texture, and the Moral Limits of Free Inquiry"; 2005 in *Philosophy of Science* (Vol. 72).

Dennett, Daniel, (1995), *Darwin's Dangerous Idea*. New York, Simon & Schuster.

Giere, Ronald N., (1997), *Understanding Scientific Reasoning*, 4th edition. Orlando, Fl, Harcourt Brace & Co.

Gould, Steven J., (1980), "Sociobiology and the Theory of Natural Selection"; in Ruse, M., *Philosophy of Biology*, London, Macmillan (1989).

Gould, Steven J., (1981), *The Mismeasure of Man*, New York, W.W. Norton & Co.

Hesse, Mary B., (1965), *Forces and Fields*, Totowa, N.J., Littlefield, Adams.

Hughes, Robert, (1994), *Culture of Complaint: The Fraying of America*, New York, Warner Books.

Kitcher, Philip, (2001), *Science, Truth, and Democracy*, New York, Oxford UP.

Lewontin, R.C., (1975), "Genetic Aspects of Intelligence", *Annual Review of Genetics* 9, p. 387-405.

McMullin, Ernan, (1978), *Newton on Matter and Activity*, Notre Dame, in University of Notre Dame Press.

McMullin, Ernan, (1981), "Is Philosophy Relevant to Cosmology?"; *American Philosophical Quarterly*, 18, p. 177-189.

Shapere, Dudley, (1974), *Galileo: A Philosophical Study*, Chicago, Ill, University of Chicago Press.

Shapere, Dudley, (1991), "The Universe of Modern Science and its Philosophical Exploration"; in E. Agazzi & A. Cordero (eds.), *Philosophy and the Origin and Evolution of the Universe*, Dordrecht, Kluwer Academic Publishers, p. 87-202.

Sismondo, Sergio Nicholas & Chrisman, (2001), "Deflationary Metaphysics and the Natures of Maps"; *Philosophy of Science*, 68, p. 38-S49.

Toulmin, Stephen, (1953), *Philosophy of Science*, New York, Harper and Row.

Values in Science

Mariano ARTIGAS

I have found in the Internet some 4,110 pages containing the exact phrase "science and values". Number one is the Homepage of Science and Values at the University of Pittsburgh, where you are informed about a Summer Seminar discussing questions about "types of values, the ideal of value free science, the underdetermination of theory by facts, the nature of norms, value pluralism and objectivity". This is a good collection of philosophical issues. We are also informed that, "In addition to the general philosophical issues we will focus on a series of cases studies on agriculture, cognitive science, mental illness, archeology and ecology. At a time when science is on center stage in the media delivering us prescriptions and proscriptions for living a healthier life, saving the planet, or succeeding economically and politically, and the government and the courts are relying increasingly on scientific experts in making policy and judgments; responsible, reflective citizens need to be equipped to navigate through the entangled straits of fact and value".[1]

My aim here is more modest. I would like to comment on the fact that the development of modern empirical science has contributed, in a great extent, to spreading a whole set of values that are inherent to the practice of science.

We can consider empirical science as a human activity directed towards a twofold goal, namely to obtain a knowledge of nature that may permit a controlled dominion over the natural world. In order to achieve this goal we must formulate hypothesis and submit them to empirical testing: this is the general method of science. The use of this method furnished us with a body of knowledge, i.e. a set of statements and theories. In each one of these three levels we can discover a whole set of values that have an ethical character and are present in the scientific activity, independently of the ethical commitments of the individual scientists.

---

[1]   http://www.pitt.edu/~pkmach/valuesci.htm (read on 14 October 2003).

I am going to consider two questions. Firstly, which values are essentially linked to the scientific enterprise, and secondly the impact of scientific progress upon them.[2]

Why Scientific Values

First of all, I must face a preliminary question. Why should we admit ethical values within science? After all, isn't the value-freedom of empirical science one of its main traits, that make it objective, i.e. independent of subjective judgement about values?

It is apparently easy to answer this objection when we realize that objectivity itself can be considered a value. Nevertheless, we may ask why we should appreciate objectivity at all. The answer is anything but trivial. In fact, objectivity seems to be closely linked to the analytic perspective that tries to rationalize everything, leaving aside the most cherished features of human life and creating a kind of rational space where there is no place for feelings and personal evaluations. Many people insist today that we should control objective science, and not let it invade the ambit of human values.

In this context, we can think of Monod's naturalism, which represents the human being as a merely chance product of blind natural forces, as if this were the logical result of a "postulate of objectivity" essential to the natural sciences. Monod asserts that empirical science is the only source of truth, and presents this as the result of an "ethical" choice.[3] However, the very fact that Monod acknowledges scientific objectivity as a value and presents it as the result of an ethical choice, shows that there is something more in empirical science than meets the eye. The ethical character of this presupposition shows that, besides the ambit of empirical science, there are other ambits where knowledge-claims and evaluations are possible.

I would add that these ambits include knowledge-claims that are more fundamental than those of empirical science, as they provide the basis for the evaluation of the entire scientific enterprise. If we recognize scientific objectivity as an important value in itself, then we are dealing with the *search for truth* as an *ethical value*, and this is hardly compatible with the perspective that considers empirical science to be "the *only* authentic source of truth", as Monod puts it.

---

[2]   I have developed this argument in more detail in Mariano Artigas, *The Mind of the Universe*, Philadelphia & London, 2000, Templeton Foundation Press, p. 251-342.

[3]   Jacques Monod, *Chance and Necessity. An Essay on the Natural Philosophy of Modern Biology*, New York, Knopf, 1971, p. 21, 169 and 176.

One of the main reasons in favor of thinking of empirical science as value-free is that this seems to be the only way to protect the autonomy of the scientific enterprise. The distinction between pure and applied science serves to reinforce the non-commitment of pure science to any kind of meta-scientific values; indeed, pure science seems completely committed to its own goals and procedures, and only applied science or technology would be related to extra-scientific values. For example, Imre Lakatos says:

> *In my view, science, as such, has no social responsibility.* In my view it is society that has a responsibility – that of maintaining the apolitical, detached scientific tradition and allowing science to search for truth in the way determined purely by its inner life.[4]

Nevertheless, Lakatos refers to the "search for truth" as an essential characteristic of science that must be respected and even favored by society. Therefore, he acknowledges the search for truth as an ethical value. Also, everyone would agree that scientists must not forget how their results can be used. Lakatos adds:

> Of course scientists, as citizens, have responsibility, like all other citizens, to see that science is *applied* to the right social and political ends. This is a different, independent question.[5]

As a matter of fact, pure and applied science are so closely intertwined in our days that, according to a widespread opinion, instead of insisting on the distinction between pure and applied science, we should rather speak of a single reality called "technoscience".

I am ready to admit the increasing dependence of pure science on external goals and also on technology. Nevertheless, I think that the distinction between pure and applied science continues to be valid. The main reason is that empirical science is, above all, a human activity guided by the search for true knowledge of the natural world.

The search for truth is a very important value, and commitment to objectivity in the use of argument, as required by the search for truth, is another important value. These values are a part of science itself, as empirical science would be meaningless without them. They are implicit values that act as ethical presuppositions of the entire scientific enterprise.

---

[4] Imre Lakatos, *The Social Responsibility of Science*, in John Worral and Gregory Currie, editors: Imre Lakatos, *Mathematics, Science and Epistemology, Philosophical Papers*, Cambridge, Cambridge University Press, 1978, Vol. 2, p. 258.

[5] *Ibid.*

Which Values?

We already have a clue for determining the values inherent to the scientific enterprise. Empirical science includes some ethical values: at least, those related to its goals. These values work as implicit presuppositions that can be ignored in routine scientific work. Their analysis and evaluation is a meta-scientific task.

We can also add those values associated to the general method of empirical science, namely those related to the public character of the experiments and theoretical tools involved in the construction and evaluation of theories.

I would admit the existence, within science, of an entire whole of values that are inherently related to the goals and methods of the scientific enterprise. I would say that natural science carries within itself a double set of values: *constitutive* values, which refer to its general goals, namely, the search for truth (*epistemic* values) and for a controlled dominion over nature (*pragmatic* values), and *institutional* values, which refer to the social aspect of science and are closely related to the general method used in natural science. I am going to comment on some particular values of each kind.

Epistemic Values

Epistemic values are the values used as criteria to decide the acceptability of scientific theories. In a 1973 paper, Thomas Kuhn tried to answer the critics of his posing theory-choice as dependent on the collective judgement of scientists.[6] Kuhn tells us that he does not mean, as his critics suppose, that there are no objective criteria that help to choose between competing theories; in fact, he takes for granted that everyone knows which these criteria are. In order to avoid misunderstandings, in the first part of his paper Kuhn formulates and explains these criteria, which correspond to the characteristics of a good scientific theory. From a number of them, he selects five, namely *accuracy*, *consistency*, *scope*, *simplicity*, and *fruitfulness*. He adds:

> I am suggesting, of course, that the criteria of choice with which I began function not as rules, which determine choice, but as values, which influence it.[7]

---

[6] Thomas S. Kuhn, *Objectivity, Value Judgment, and Theory Choice*, in Thomas S. Kuhn, *The Essential Tension*, Chicago and London, The University of Chicago Press, 1977, p. 320-39.

[7] *Ibid.*, p. 331.

Scientists committed to the same values, according to Kuhn, may make different choices, as there is some ambiguity in the application of values.

Dealing with this kind of value, Ernan McMullin highlights that the rationality of science "is learned by experience".[8] This means that we have learnt, and continue to learn, to appreciate these values through the practice of empirical science. For example, one of the steps that led to the birth of modern empirical science as a self-sustained enterprise was due to the relevance that Kepler attributed to a small difference between observed data and theoretical prediction in the motion of the planet Mars, at a moment when the degree of accuracy of such concordance was not considered as relevant as Kepler considered it. McMullin rightly sees in this point a convergence between the historical and the logical perspectives. I would add that this point is most important for my argument, as it clearly shows the feedback of scientific progress on scientific values. The experience acquired in the development of science teaches us which values are relevant for the evaluation of theories and how they can be applied.

McMullin underlines that *predictive accuracy* is the desideratum that scientists would usually list first. He also comments on *internal coherence*, *external consistency*, *unifying power*, and *fertility*, as key epistemic values.

I use to highlight *five epistemic values* that are used in scientific practice, as I think that they contain, in some way, all kinds of epistemic value usually mentioned. These are: *explanatory power, predictive power, accuracy* of both explanations and predictions, *variety of independent proofs*, and *mutual support* of different theories.

It is not necessary here to enter into more details. I would only add that, if we accept that the scientific enterprise has a realistic meaning, and even more if we accept that this realism is not limited to a regulative ideal but includes our attaining specific pieces of true knowledge, then the cognitive value of science in general and the particular epistemic values acquire meaning. This coincides with the position of Alasdair MacIntyre, who concludes that, because of its realism, natural science is a moral task.[9] This is a very important assertion, which is justified by the appeal to the commitment of science to realism. It is the search for truth,

---

[8]   Ernan McMullin, *The Goals of Natural Science*, in Imre Hronszky, Márta Fehér and Balázs Dajka, editors, *Scientific Knowledge Socialized*, Dordrecht, Kluwer, 1988, p. 50.

[9]   Alasdair MacIntyre, *Objectivity in Morality and Objectivity in Science*, in H. Tristram Engelhardt, Jr. and Daniel Callahan, editors, *Morals, Science and Sociality*, Hastings-on-Hudson, New York, The Hastings Center, 1978, p. 21-39.

considered as an internal good of science, which is at stake here: and the search for truth has obvious moral connotations.

MacIntyre's reference to history as a justification of realism is also important. We can perceive here an echo, from a different point of view, of Kuhn and McMullin saying that we learn to appreciate scientific values through the actual development of science, which coincides with my emphasis on the feedback of scientific progress on the ethical presuppositions of science.

Pragmatic and Institutional Values

It is especially easy to acknowledge the existence of an ethical value in science when we consider its application to the welfare of the human being. This value can be identified with service to mankind, which is achieved through technology. I am not going to argue in this line. I am going to concentrate on *institutional values*.

Institutional values refer to scientific work so far as it is institutionalized as a communal enterprise and, as such, implies an entire set of values which should be pursued by the members of the scientific community.

This kind of value has no independent source separate from that of the constitutive values, namely the general aims of science. All kinds of scientific value stem from the same source, as they are instrumental to achieving the general aims of science or, at least, requirements that are necessarily linked to them. However, institutional values also contain the requirements derived from the communal character of the scientific enterprise.

This can be easily perceived if we recall the institutional values enumerated by Robert Merton in his 1942 paper "The Normative Structure of Science", where we find out an analysis of the values contained in empirical science considered as a social institution.[10] Using his vocabulary, he analyzes the following four values: *universalism*, *communism*, *disinterestedness*, and *organized skepticism*. *Universalism* means that truth-claims must be independent from the race, nationality, religion, class, and personal qualities of their protagonists, so that they are to be subjected to "pre-established impersonal criteria". Merton relates universalism to the impersonal character of science, and also to democracy, as he sees the open democratic society as being characterized by "impersonal criteria of accomplishment and not fixation of status". An

---

[10]   Robert K. Merton, *The Sociology of Science. Theoretical and Empirical Investigations*, Chicago and London, The University of Chicago Press, 1973, chapter 13, p. 266-278.

expression of universalism is that careers be open to talents, regardless of reasons other than lack of competence. *Communism* refers to the "sense of common ownership of goods", so that "the substantive findings of science are a product of social collaboration and are assigned to the community". *Disinterestedness* does not mean altruism. It rather refers, like the other norms, to patterns of institutional control. Indeed, scientific research involves the verifiability of results by fellow experts. Merton asserts that "the activities of scientists are subject to rigorous policing, to a degree perhaps unparalleled in any other field of activity". Disinterestedness is based on the public and testable character of science. It is related to "absence of fraud"; in empirical science, "spurious claims appear to be negligible and ineffective". Scientists usually are not involved in a direct relationship with a lay clientele; rather, they are subject to a control exercised by qualified compeers. Finally, *organized skepticism* "is both a methodological and an institutional mandate" which includes "the temporary suspension of judgement" and "the detached scrutiny of beliefs in terms of empirical and logical criteria".

The Impact of Scientific Progress

This is enough for my present purpose. I wish to highlight that the historical development of the scientific enterprise has contributed, in a great extent, to spread the values I have mentioned, and others related to them. I would even say that scientific progress has been, and continues to be, a major source of ethical progress, as it goes hand by hand with the spreading of the values necessarily connected with science. In this line, I would say that our scientific civilization carries within it an important set of values.

Someone could object that those values are not properly ethical, as their ethical character depends on the personal meaning that each individual attaches to them. This is, of course, partly right. Nevertheless I would say that, from an objective point of view, the spreading of the values connected to the scientific enterprise is a fact that imposes and facilitates a kind of behavior that goes hand by hand with ethics. One can do good things for a bad purpose, but the action in itself continues to be right even though the lack of good intention makes it objectionable from the ethical point of view.

I would like to refer especially to the *pursuit of truth*. In the beginning of the encyclical *Fides et Ratio*,[11] John Paul II says (No. 5) that he is going to focus on philosophy and explains the reason saying that, "at the present time in particular, the search for ultimate truth seems often to

---

[11] John Paul II, letter encyclical *Fides et ratio*, 4 September 1998.

be neglected". How have we arrived at this darkening? The situation is paradoxical. A great progress in many ambits of the human knowledge has occurred; the Pope mentions "anthropology, logic, the natural sciences, history, linguistics and so forth – the whole universe of knowledge has been involved in one way or another". Nevertheless, the great variety of positive results have had as a consequence that the direction towards a unifying truth has been forgotten, so that pragmatic criteria prevail and the technical effectiveness is used like a pattern of behavior. Thus it has happened that "rather than make use of the human capacity to know the truth, modern philosophy has preferred to accentuate the ways in which this capacity is limited and conditioned".

This diagnosis is valid for the philosophy of science in our time. On the one hand, everybody is convinced that sciences progress in a spectacular way, but on the other hand no consensus exists about the very existence of scientific truth.

Scientific realism affirms that scientific truth exists and that we can reach it. It must face difficulties that can be reduced to two main points. On the one hand, science consists of our constructions that are not simple photographs of reality. Especially in mathematical physics very abstract models are formulated that, frequently, do not have a clear correspondence with reality. On the other hand, due to purely logical reasons, we cannot verify our hypotheses in a definitive way, therefore they must remain always open to further criticism and eventual change.

I have been maintaining, for years, a kind of scientific realism according to which in empirical science we can reach a true knowledge, with a truth that is always contextual and therefore partial, but, at the same time, is an authentic truth. Scientific truth is always "contextual" because it must be interpreted within the conceptual and experimental context that we use in each theory. Being contextual, it is also "partial", and it does not exhaust all that can be said about the object we study. But, at the same time, it can be an "authentic" truth in the classical sense of correspondence with reality. Of course, as there are many different types of scientific constructs, there will also be different modes of correspondence with reality. Thus, in order to establish such a correspondence we will have to pay attention, of course, to the concepts and data used in every case.[12]

In this line, we can speak of a feedback of scientific realism upon our image of the human being. Scientific progress helps us to know better and better our own capabilities, as it enlarges in a great way the reach of

---

[12] See this proposal in my: *Filosofía de la ciencia experimental. La objetividad y la verdad en las ciencias*, 3rd ed., Pamplona, Eunsa, 1999.

our knowledge. Actually, what the various methods used in empirical science have in common is a peculiar combination of theory and empirical control, which requires a subject capable of combining both aspects. Moreover, this combination cannot be considered a merely external aggregation of two different elements; both aspects, the rational and the empirical, are closely intertwined from the very beginning and in every step of the working of science.

In fact, the development of epistemology clearly shows the failure of strong versions of empiricism or conventionalism, to say nothing of idealism, as these positions cannot account even for the more elementary achievements of empirical science.

Empirical science is the combined result of creativity and interpretation. Progress implies opening new roads by using our creative capacity, which carries us far beyond the data which are available at any moment in time. And we evaluate our creations by using theoretical arguments and empirical tests which include high doses of interpretation.

It is evident that we are natural beings, and this fact accounts for the empirical and pragmatic features of the scientific enterprise. But scientific progress shows that we transcend the natural world. Indeed, we are able to represent it as an object. Besides, we build up idealized models that serve not only to represent specific features of the world, but also to conjecture the existence of new unobserved features. We can use arguments in order to test the adequacy of our models. And, as a consequence of our use of those abilities, we make an enormous progress in our scientific work. All this clearly shows that, even if we are natural beings, we also transcend the natural level.

I would end by pointing out that the feedback of scientific progress on the epistemological presuppositions of science shows that, even though we are a part of nature, nevertheless we transcend it. Scientific creativity is a proof of our singularity. It shows that we possess dimensions which transcend the natural ambit and can be labeled as spiritual. The very existence and progress of the natural sciences is one of the best arguments that show our spiritual character. But, at the same time, the success of the scientific method shows that our spiritual dimensions related to creativity and argument are intertwined with our material dimensions, so that we are a single being constituted by both aspects. Therefore, the existence of human spiritual dimensions which are intertwined with material conditions may be considered a plain fact which is corroborated by the explanation of the existence and progress of empirical science.

The Role of Cognitive Values in the Shaping of Scientific Rationality

Jan FAYE

University of Copenhagen, Denmark

Introduction

It is not so long ago that philosophers and scientists thought of science as an objective and value-free enterprise. But since the heyday of positivism, it has become obvious that values, norms, and standards have an indispensable role to play in science. You may even say that these values are the real issues of the philosophy of science. Whatever they are, these values constrain science at an ontological, a cognitive, a methodological, and a semantic level for the purpose of making science a rational pursuit of knowledge. Philosophy of science is in place when one discusses what makes science possible both as a theoretical and a practical discipline.

It is useful to distinguish between the external and internal values of science. On the one hand, the external values are somehow imposed on science from the outside in the sense that they are not inherent in the scientific practise or necessarily for science to be a rational enterprise. They are the demands that society puts on science that its results should be publicly relevant and technologically useful and be to the benefit of mankind. On the other hand, the internal values are immanently situated in the scientific practise and discourse. Scientists take them for granted as they carry on with their research because these values shape the rationality of science. But it is also clear that external values to a certain extent and in certain fields form some of the internal values. Medicine is a typical example of a scientific practise where internal values and external values merge into the same goal.

Some philosophers, e.g. social constructivists, may argue that there are no internal values of science. Values are always of social origin and determined by social demands, and it does not make sense to distinguish between values imposed from outside and values imposed from within. I find this an unreasonable claim. Indeed, values of science are formed and supported in part by individuals, but they are also upheld by the scientific community where they, together with particular theories, form the shared basis of a group of researchers. We therefore see that individual scientists may disagree about which values one ought to sustain. A scientist may diverge from the majority of colleagues concerning some cognitive values, or one group of scientists may deviate from another with respect to their norms and standards. Cognitive values are indirectly established in students through learning, training, and tradition, as they labour to grasp the factual content of the scientific theories. Norms and standards are tacitly presupposed most of the time. They constitute an intimate part of the scientist's rationality, and when scientists disagree, they very seldom realize that it may not be about factual matter, as they believe, but that it is these tacit values which are at stake. This does not mean, however, that these values are arbitrary and that one cannot give reasonable arguments for their constitutive role of scientific rationality.

I. The Kinds of Cognitive Values of Science

In the scientific practise we find all sorts of internal values that both guide and constrain our actions and reasoning. Some of them are important in specifying the aims of science; others are significant in stating the methodological prescriptions that may allow scientists to pursue those aims in the most rational fashion. The goals of science set the standards towards which the scientific practise should aim its activities. We do science with the purpose of acquiring new kinds of propositional knowledge, and therefore the values that guide science towards this aim are those we associate with calling something knowledge.

Truth is often taken as the definitive goal of science because true beliefs are what partly characterise propositional knowledge. Science goes with truth. If scientific statements were not true, they would be worthless as expressions of knowledge and as guidance to technological successes. Thus truth is considered to be the main *epistemic value of science*. This is also how most scientists look upon theories of their field. They believe that theories express what they and their colleagues take to be true about the objective world.

As long as we are talking about ordinary knowledge, it seems to be correct to say that we possess true beliefs and that these constitute the aim of our cognitive activities. But we know that some philosophers have expressed doubt about truth as a totally indispensable standard of scientific inquiry. An epistemic anti-realist, like Bas van Fraassen, has replaced the notion of truth with that of empirical adequacy. He argues that our epistemic commitments go with observational support and not with truth.[1] Scientific theories may or may not be true, what is important is that they are empirically adequate in the sense that they are true with respect to observation. Instrumentalists go even further in their denial of truth as an indispensable epistemic value. For them it is enough if theories are able to organize our observations in a coherent and thought-economical way in order to for us to make empirical predictions. In fact instrumentalist may deny that theories can be ascribed any form of truth. Thus, simplicity, thought-economics and predictability becomes the most important epistemic standards.

In the standard theory of knowledge, it is also a requirement that true beliefs should be justified, i.e., that they can be said to be rationally held. But where a belief may be true by chance, and therefore in addition has to be justified in order to count as knowledge, a belief is empirically adequate only if it is justified with respect to our observation. The claim that a belief must be justified expresses a *methodological value* and the fulfilment of the standards of justification is what makes our beliefs justified. Moreover, any justificatory procedure normally counts as a reliable method in the sense that by following it there is a high chance of getting closer to truth than to falsehood. So being a method of science the procedure must fulfil some standard of reliability, and a scientist would act epistemically responsible in cases where he pursues truth in accordance with these standards. We can just think of the requirements of variation, control, and accuracy posed on the collection of data.

It is well known that Thomas S. Kuhn questioned the traditional notion of scientific rationality by saying that methodological values and standards change when the scientific community discards a paradigm and replaces it with another. Moreover, Kuhn believed that alternative paradigms are incommensurable. Many philosophers have therefore accused him of denying scientific rationality. Indeed, it is correct that Kuhn rejected that truth could have any important role to play as a guide to scientific rationality and the choice of theories. In this he seems to have had an attitude to empirical adequacy much like van Fraassen's (before the latter gave the concept real consideration). A scientific theory or a paradigm must agree with observations, but apart from this it does not have to fulfil the epistemic value of being true. Rather a paradigm should deliver material for normal science and puzzle-solving.

---

[1] Van Fraassen (1980).

Although Kuhn believed that scientific standards are paradigm-dependent, he nevertheless suggested that there might be some methodological values which are paradigm-independent and can be used as guidance for theory choice.[2] Such transparadigmatic values are accuracy, consistency, perceptiveness, simplicity, and fruitfulness. 1) The consequences of a theory have to fit closely to those observations and experiments which the theory is supposed to describe. 2) A theory has to be internally consistent but also externally consistent with respect to other relevant theories. 3) The consequences of a theory have to reach much further than to those observations according to which it was posed to describe at the first hand. 4) A theory must be simple and be able to unite phenomena which would appear otherwise separated. And 5) a theory must be able to predict new phenomena which nobody knew anything about previously. But Kuhn also emphasized that neither the importance nor the weight of them was something agreed on among scientists because different paradigms may satisfy each differently and in various degrees.

Sometimes, however, other kinds of epistemic goals are being substituted for truth, empirical adequacy or simplicity. But there is no reason to think that truth or empirical adequacy as epistemic values can be replaced by or reduced to any other kind of value. Truth is not reducible to, say, political correctness, nor do political ideals reduce to true beliefs. *Political values* are not part of science at all if one takes truth to be the ultimate goal of science. Nevertheless, political norms are sometimes claimed to play an explicit function in the formulation of the aim of science. Marxists, for instance, think that the purpose of economics and sociology are to save the working class from poverty and economical exploitation. In this case the truth of a theory is twisted by political purposes. Most modern societies also spend a lot of money on science. In return these societies want science to pursue goals which help improve the need and the health of their citizens. But these external demands are clearly not part of the scientific practice itself.

Ethical values may also take part in the formulation of the aims of science. Medicine is a clear example of a science in which ethical values play a significant role in selecting what is considered to be acceptable research projects. The goal of pharmaceutical research is not merely truth but also the curing of illnesses and a general improvement of people's health. You can even say that the practical success of bringing a disease to an end is often more important in medicine than having a correct theory concerning the aetiology of disease itself. Indeed, truth and recovery very often go hand in hand, but one should not be misled

---

[2]   See Kuhn's paper "Objectivity, Value Judgment, and Theory Choice" in his (1977).

by this fact to think that the latter can be fulfilled only in the case of the former.

Among scientists one sometimes finds an explicit claim that truth and beauty go hand in hand. An elegant mathematical theory must be true due to the beauty of nature, and since mathematics is nature's own language, it must reflect all the beauty we find in nature. Scientists like Albert Einstein, Herman Weyl, Paul Dirac and Steven Weinberg have all expressed strong belief in a close connection between scientific truth and aesthetics. Dirac, for instance, maintained that "a theory with mathematical beauty is more likely to be correct than an ugly one that fits some experimental data".[3] More scientists would say that *aesthetic values* guide their research in the sense that they prefer an elegant theory rather than a clumsy one. This indicates that the aesthetic values of a theory are taken as evidence of its being true even though truth and beauty may not be considered identical. Such records should indeed be taken serious. Aesthetic properties may, as a matter of fact, sometimes be taken into account in both theory formation and theory choice. But it only makes sense if one has to select between, perhaps temporarily, empirically underdetermined alternatives. A scientist may prefer his own theory on aesthetic grounds in case its empirical success is identical with alternative theories with a similar or identical success. Having worked very hard with his own theory, he would try to vindicate it for other reasons.

I agree, however, with McAllister's conclusion when he denies that there is any connection between *scientific success* and the use of aesthetic criteria. "Contrary to Dirac, Einstein and others, I see little evidence that aesthetic properties correlated with high degrees of empirical adequacy in theories have yet been identified in any branch of science. If they had, the empirical benefit of choosing theories on particular aesthetic criteria would be far more obvious".[4] Nor is there any argument that connects *truth* and beauty. What is considered to be the aesthetic criteria varies according to the ruling taste. At one point in history, philosophers and physicists considered the circular movement to be the true and perfect motion; thus the circle described the movement of the bodies of heaven. Nevertheless, Kepler had to give up on this idea because of new empirical evidence. So the characteristics which scientists at one time regard as belonging to the aesthetic cannon are rejected at another time. The beauties are never always beauty and therefore never necessarily true. As McAllister points out, scientists' aesthetic taste is inductively induced through their professional training and the

---

[3]   Kragh (1990), p. 284.
[4]   McAllister (1996), p. 102.

taste of the scientific community varies depending on its theories and experience. Like art, like science. What is taken to be aesthetically attractive differs not only through different epochs but also between different scientific disciplines. In contrast, truth and empirical adequacy are cognitive norms that are independent of the taste of beauty. They last longer and make up the rational basis of the scientific practise.

Scientists, indeed, do not aim at truth as such. They need theories to be able to grasp what is true. Truth must be explicated in terms of theories to become a target of empirical investigation. A scientific theory yields the explicit explanation of what is taken to be the truth. But every scientific explanation rests on theoretical interpretations, and theoretical interpretations do not provide the "natural" and only understanding of our experience. Hence theoretical claims go beyond what can be empirically settled. Any theoretical interpretation must take its departure in a set of *metaphysical values* that shape our global worldview. Such values are assumptions which state how the foundation of a scientific theory ought to be and which ontological requirements it must meet. They are tacitly present in the given research practise in the sense that they constraint the scientific theories without their validity being discussed. They form the ultimate basis of what a scientist would regard as a possible theory. Values of this sort are associated with commitments to realism and objectivity; in particular, how reality should be understood. We may feel committed to mechanical descriptions, physicalistic descriptions, naturalistic descriptions, or some other form of description. For instance, a physicist may prefer deterministic theories instead of indeterministic theories, mechanical theories instead of non-mechanical theories, or action-at-a-distance theories instead of field theories.

II. Methodological Prescriptions

The Danish physicist Niels Bohr made important contributions to the development of atomic physics, and later he and Einstein were involved in discussions about the interpretation of quantum phenomena. Here I shall show that much of this debate was a debate about values and not about facts. As we shall see, Bohr believed that quantum mechanics was methodologically sound because it was developed based on what he regarded as acceptable values and he therefore thought that determinism had to yield for indeterminism.

Bohr presented his core model of the atomic structure in 1913. The model could explain the spectroscopic lines of the hydrogen atom and ascribed to the atom some strange non-classical features due to Planck's quantum of action. The discrete atomic spectrum is caused by electrons jumping between well-defined stationary energy states, at the same time it was impossible for these electrons to occupy the empty space between the stationary states. The model is called semi-classical since it still presented stationary states as classical orbits around the atomic nucleus.

Bohr's model gave a successful description of the spectral properties of hydrogen atom but it was incomplete when applied on atoms of any higher atomic number. Bohr eventually realized that his model, and Sommerfeld's modification of it, was only a first step in the direction of a coherent theory, and that a future theory possibly would require an even more radical deviation from classical notions than his earlier ideas.[5] Helping him in the search for such a new theory, he thought that it was necessary to find some general methodological requirements which might serve him or other physicists as guidance in the formulation of a better theory. He advocated what he called the correspondence rule according to which the prediction of the behaviour of a free electron based on classical theory and on the new theory should be numerically the same. In the beginning Bohr thought of the correspondence argument as a purely formal argument, which requested only the existence of syntactic or structural features between the two theories, but already in the 1920s he realized that a new theory should be subjected to intelligibility or semantic constraints as well. Before we can put questions to quantum phenomena and provide answers, there has to be many things about common sense, the experimental apparatus, and physical knowledge as such, which we cannot doubt in the actual situation of inquiry. A theory must be meaningful and relevant with respect to what we know and in general assume to be true. As a consequence, he believed that the use of classical concepts, developed by classical physics to describe our experience and experimental practise, was necessary for any appropriate understanding of quantum phenomena.

In her recent book, the Italian philosopher and historian of science Michela Massimi (2005) gives us a painstaking description of the development from the success of the Bohr-Sommerfeld model of atomic structure to its failure to cope with the anomalous Zeeman Effect and many other spectroscopic phenomena. Massimi follows their struggles to understand the spectroscopic data within the atomic core model. It was not until Pauli suggested that some of these data could be interpreted such that in an atom two electrons with the same quantum numbers were impossible that it became obvious that the core model was in severe crisis. The immediate consequence was the abandonment of the atomic core model. Instead a young American physicist Ralph Kronig considers s, one of the two angular momenta, l and $s = \frac{1}{2}$, as an intrinsic

---

[5]   Some of Bohr's reflections are mentioned in Faye (1991), p. 113-119.

angular momentum due to a rotation of the individual electron about its axis. This interpretation was first really accepted nine months later in 1925 when George Uhlenbeck and Samuel Goudsmit published a similar conclusion. But Pauli's proposal meant a lethal blow to the core model; but also "Bohr's correspondence principle was left out: how to reconcile the classical periodic motions presupposed by the correspondence principle with the classically non-describable *Zweideutigkeit* of the electron's angular momentum?"[6]

Although the exclusion rule and the introduction of spin broke with the attempt of explaining the structure of the basic elements along the lines of the correspondence argument (as Pauli pointed out in a letter to Bohr) Bohr continued to think of it as an important methodological principle in the attempt to establish a coherent quantum theory. In fact, he repeatedly expressed the opinion that Heisenberg's matrix mechanics came to light under the guidance of this very principle. In his Faraday Lectures from 1932, for instance, Bohr emphasizes: "A fundamental step towards the establishing of a proper *quantum mechanics* was taken in 1925 by Heisenberg who showed how to replace the ordinary kinematical concepts, in the spirit of the correspondence argument, by symbols referring to the elementary processes and the probability of their occurrence".[7] Bohr acknowledged, however, that the correspondence argument failed too in those cases where particular non-classical concepts have to be introduced into the description of atoms. But he still thought that the correspondence argument was indispensable for both structural and semantic reasons in constructing a proper quantum theory as a generalized theory from classical mechanics.

Indeed spin is a quantum property of the electrons which cannot be understood as a classical angular momentum. Needless to say, Bohr fully understood that. But he didn't think that this discovery ruled out the use of the correspondence rule as guidance to finding a satisfactory quantum theory. Allow me to give a lengthy quotation from Bohr's paper "The Causality Problem in Atomic Physics" (1938):

> Indeed, as adequate as the quantum postulates are in the phenomenological description of the atomic reactions, as indispensable are the basic concepts of mechanics and electrodynamics for the specification of atomic structures and for the definition of fundamental properties of the agencies with which they react. Far from being a temporary compromise in this dilemma, the recourse to essentially statistical considerations is our only conceivable means of arriving at a generalization of the customary way of description sufficiently wide to account for the features of individuality expressed by the

---

[6]   Massimi (2005), p. 73.
[7]   Bohr (1998), p. 48.

quantum postulates and reducing to classical theory in the limiting case where all actions involved in the analysis of the phenomena are large compared with a single quantum. In the search for the formulation of such a generalization, our only guide has just been the so-called correspondence argument, which gives expression for the exigency of upholding the use of classical concepts to the largest possible extent compatible with the quantum postulates.[8]

This shows that, according to Bohr, quantum mechanics, as formulated by Heisenberg, was a rational generalization of classical mechanics when the quantum of action and the spin property were taken into account.

My purpose for bringing Bohr's statement to our attention is a further point which Massimi makes in her book. She accepts Kuhn's claim that there was a "revolutionary transition from the old quantum theory to the new quantum theory around 1921-1925".[9] This revolution came about as a result of a crisis of the old quantum theory between 1922 and 1925. Kuhn also thought that the old quantum theory could not be called a full-blown theory but rather a set of algorithms to solve problems and paradoxes. Massimi uses this revolutionary transition as an argument against Friedman's suggestion that a rational continuity of revolutionary transitions originated from a well-established fact that, at a later time, is elevated to the constitutive a priori principle of a new theory. Her reason is that in the case of the Pauli rule there was no such well-established fact, nor was the rule as a "phenomenological" law elevated to the status of a constitutive principle of the new quantum mechanical framework. But what if there was no revolution between 1922 and 1925? If Kuhn and she are wrong, it seems that she has no argument against Friedman.

This depends very much on how we characterize a scientific revolution: how can an event of this sort be identified? Kuhn presented something like a definition of a scientific revolution. It is a historical change of incommensurable paradigms. The defining feature of a revolution in scientific thoughts, according to Kuhn, is discontinuities and gaps between these thoughts which make them incommensurable. In his *The Structure of Scientific Revolutions* the concept of incommensurability covered meaning variance, epistemic standards, and psychological attitudes. He therefore made the famous remark about a change of paradigm that the world does not change, but that the scientists afterwards work in a different world. Later he attempted to articulate incommensurability in terms of the untranslatability of lexical taxonomies.

---

[8] Bohr (1998), p. 96.

[9] Massimi (2005), p. 73.

But Massimi does not have this definition of a scientific revolution at hand. Rather than reading lexical taxonomies as constitutive, as Kuhn did as a philosopher of science, she argues that it makes much more sense to understand lexical taxonomies as having a regulative task. As she says: "a mild Kantian reading of lexical taxonomies allows us to reformulate the new-world problem in a way that does not license incommensurability, and, on the other side, vindicates Kuhn's 'post-Darwinian Kantianism'".[10] I think her reading reconciles Kuhn as a philosopher with Kuhn as a historian, but at the same time deprives her from talking about scientific revolutions. Indeed, this may explain why Kuhn stuck to his concept of incommensurability.

Massimi's analysis of the conceptual changes along these lines squares well with the fact that there was no incommensurability between the atomic core model and the spin model, and therefore no revolution in Kuhn's sense. It seems as if Massimi has an unarticulated view on scientific revolutions. She continues to talk about revolutions, but she also talks about demonstrative induction in which non-classical concept are derived from some relevant theoretical assumptions of old quantum mechanics and spectroscopic anomalies: "The electron's *Zweideutigkeit* was not plucked out of the air as a bold conjecture. It rather followed from spectroscopic anomalies with the help of theoretical assumptions (a)-(f), i.e., it came out in a non-ampliative way from the interplay between the old quantum mechanics and anomalous phenomena".[11] A historiographic term like "revolution" is not a natural kind term, so I wonder how this quotation reports a revolution. At least I imagine that the lexical taxonomy of historiography should not be interpreted as constitutive.

The historiographic term "revolution" is taken from political history. Its present meaning signifies a change of power which happens against the constitution through the violent actions on the part of the people. Such events are often very rapid and short termed. But we also think of revolution more broadly when we talk about the Glorious Revolution, the Industrial Revolution and a scientific revolution, and Lenin even thought of the Permanent Revolution. So it cannot be the length of time that defines a revolution. But how do we then distinguish a revolution from an evolution? Just how normative these notions are, is clearly testified by the fact that Kuhn, the historian of science, didn't see Copernicus' introduction of the heliocentric system as a revolution where other historians have considered it to be the scientific revolution par excellence. The important thing is, if we think of a scientific revolution

---

[10] Massimi (2005), p. 97.

[11] Massimi (2005), p. 106.

analogous to a political revolution, that one should require that there be a total replacement of a whole conceptual system rather than a mere generalization of a conceptual system in terms of change and addition of concepts in the direction of increased richness and precision. This, I think, leaves us with very few, if any, scientific revolutions.

Moreover, I think that Massimi's reconstruction of the development of the atomic core model into the spin model as a demonstrative induction comes close to how the major partisans themselves realized the development during those years. Her reasons for dismissing the correspondence principle are not convincing. Being the most dominating figure from the creation of the first atomic theory in 1913 to the interpretation of the second theory in 1927 Bohr did not consider the transition from the Bohr-Sommerfeld model to the Heisenberg matrix mechanics as a revolution. His methodological prescriptions in terms of correspondence rule were very different from what Kuhn's retrospectively observed as a philosopher. Where Kuhn saw revolutions and incommensurability, Bohr (and Heisenberg) looked for rational generalizations and commensurability. Where Kuhn saw himself as a post-Darwinian Kantian, we may characterize Bohr as a Darwinian Kantian. Were Bohr and his younger disciple wrong? I think that Friedman's view is closer to Bohr's; it also seems more evolutionary than revolutionary. Planck's discovery of the discontinuity of the black body spectrum was considered by Bohr as a well-established empirical fact which was elevated to a constitutive (*a priori*) principle in his model of the atom. This semi-classical model applied to the hydrogen atom, and not much else. From then on, a continuous struggle began of enlarging the model to deal with atoms with higher numbers and to reach a proper theory which could explain the dynamics of elementary particles. One may therefore argue that the period between 1913 and 1925 was one long process of conceptual adaptations which involved a collection of the most brilliant physicists at that time. This process only partly ended in 1925 when Heisenberg established a proper *theory* of quantum mechanics in which the quantum of action still formed the constitutive a priori principle.

Thus I believe it is correct to say that the correspondence rule with its syntactic and semantic constraints formed a major role of shaping the rationality of theory construction of quantum mechanics, and because the principle of correspondence stayed intact as a methodological prescription during the critical years there was no scientific revolution when atomic physics moved from Bohr's atomic core model to Heisenberg's new quantum mechanics.

III.   The Bohr-Einstein Debate

It is well known that Albert Einstein was not the least happy with quantum mechanics, and that he had some intense discussions with Bohr during the 1930s. In my opinion the discussions arose because these prominent physicists were divided with respect to their fundamental cognitive and metaphysical values. They did not themselves realize the foundation of their disagreement; instead of having an open methodological discussion about cognitive and metaphysical values, they buried their intellectual conflicts in physical considerations which might have helped them to understand each opinion but instead hid the real issue.

Gerald Holton was among the first who focused explicitly on individual presuppositions in the process of theory formation; he calls them themata and sets up a theoretical framework to analyse them.[12] Themata are concerned with metaphysical, epistemological, methodological, ethical or aesthetic issues. Most of these issues are clearly different kind of values as they have been described above. In his study of Einstein's thematic guidelines to theory construction, Holton isolates a number of motivating issues on which the investigator makes some presuppositions or takes a stand: formal rather than materialistic explanations; unity and unification, logical parsimony and necessity; symmetry; simplicity; causality and determinism; completeness, continuity; and constancy and invariance. In addition one could also mention: value-definiteness; locality; separability; and the objectivity of theoretical descriptions. Other scientists may hold opposing themata. Niels Bohr did not hesitate to accept theories motivated by discontinuity, indeterminacy, value-indefiniteness, superposition, non-separability and entanglement, and intrinsic probabilities. Moreover, Bohr preferred physicalistic rather than formal explanation; he regarded the classical concepts to be essential for any unambiguous communication of experimental results in physics, and he denied objectivity in the sense that the theoretical description represents the state of the system as it really is.[13]

As mentioned before, Bohr developed his sets of norms and standards as a reaction to the discovery of the quantum of action when he recognized that this feature, in the same way as the invariance of the velocity of light with respect to the special theory of relativity, should be given a constitutive role in a new theory of atomic physics. But because the introduction of the quantum of action as the foundation of a future theory led to radical deviations from the ontology of classical mechanics, the physicists needed some methodological standards which could

---

[12]   Holton (1973).

[13]   See Faye (1991), p. 197-210.

guide them safely through to the new theory. This was the prescriptions of correspondence. The theory which came out in the other end was non-classical, and it did not fit easily with the norms of classical physicists. Bohr accepted that quantum mechanics did not allow ascription of conjugate variables to an atomic object at one and the same time because it did make sense to attribute a property to an atomic object which could not in principle be measured. As he once said:

> The emphasis on permanent recordings under well-defined experimental conditions as the basis for a consistent interpretation of the quantal formalism corresponds to the presupposition, implicit in the classical account, that every step of the causal sequence of events in principle allows verification.[14]

Hence Bohr looked at the quantum formalism to be complete and consistent; he also believed that it did not give us a true picture of reality.

Some philosophers, myself included, see Bohr as a realist about systems but an antirealist about states. In many places Bohr refers to the mathematical formalism of quantum mechanics as the mathematical *symbolism*, and he talks about *symbolic operators*. Concerning the aim of science Bohr says: "In our description of nature the purpose is not to disclose the real essence of phenomena, but only to track down as far as possible relations between the manifold aspects of our experience".[15] Furthermore he stated that "within the frame of the quantum mechanical formalism, according to which no well defined use of the concept of 'state' can be made as referring to the object separate from the body with which it has been in contact, until *the external conditions involved in the definition of this concept* are unambiguously fixed by a further suitable control of the auxiliary body"[16] – in other words, it makes no sense to say that a quantum system has a definite kinematical or dynamical state prior to any measurement. Hence we can only ascribe a certain state to a system given those circumstances where we epistemically have access to their realization. Based one these and other considerations, I still think it makes good sense to argue that Bohr was a realist with respect to atomic systems but antirealist with respect to their states.

Thus, Bohr was an entity realist who believed that the aim of science is not to provide true theories which explain quantum phenomena, but theories which are empirically adequate and useful for regimenting and describing our experimental experience. The value of science is unambiguous communication about the experimental phenomena in question. Bohr had

---

[14] Bohr (1963), p. 6.
[15] Bohr (1929 [1985]), p. 18.
[16] Bohr (1938b [1998]), p. 102, my emphasis.

no scruples of accepting a description of physical objects which contain discontinuity, indeterminism, value-indefiniteness and entanglement if this was what it takes to set up such an unambiguous communication.

Einstein came to quantum mechanics with a very different experience. He had discovered the theories of relativity in 1905 and 1915, and in the following years he was constantly working on a uniting theory of gravitational and electromagnetic fields. Einstein really believed that the aim of science was to give us true theories of physical nature. Although he contributed as earlier as 1905 to the atomic physics with the explanation of the photoelectric effect, the discontinuity of this description was something he never gave serious thought as a formative principle. Because the object of relativity was continuous fields, Einstein automatically took the notion of continuity in space and time to be the norm in terms of which any coherent theory of quantum should be constructed. Therefore he wanted to show that quantum mechanics was only a limiting case of a theory which remains to be discovered but which was based on a field concept.[17] Before then he had hoped to prove that quantum mechanical formalism was inconsistent. This happened at the Solvay conference in 1927 and 1930 in discussion with Bohr. In 1930 Bohr made his famous touché when he used the theory of relativity against Einstein's objections. But when Einstein finally agreed to the fact that quantum mechanics was consistent, he then attempted to show that the theory was incomplete. This happened with the publication of the paper of Einstein, Podolsky, and Rosen.

Besides consistency, completeness is another methodological value which we would like our theories to hold because this means that they do not leave anything out that might have led to new knowledge. In their common paper Einstein, Podolsky, and Rosen argued that a physical theory is complete only if "every element of the physical reality has a counterpart in the physical theory" and we may find out whether it has "if, without in any way disturbing a system, we can predict with certainty (i.e. with probability equal to unity) the value of a physical quantity".[18] They then constructed a thought experiment by which they hoped to show that it was possible in principle to find such states. Today, we also know that they didn't succeed as demonstrated by the experimental attempts to prove Bell's theorems.

But what was Bohr's reaction? He realized, perhaps surprisingly, in his contribution to the volume on Einstein in *The Library of Living Philosophers* that it was a question of rationality. He said: "The apparent contradiction in fact discloses only an essential inadequacy of the customary

---

[17]   See Pais (1982), p. 460 ff.

[18]   Einstein, Podolsky, and Rosen (1935).

viewpoint of natural philosophy for a *rational* account of physical phenomena of the type with which we are concerned in quantum mechanics".[19] Shaping a new form of physical rationality required a new criterion of reality. Bohr regarded the causal account of the physical phenomena to be the rational account of the same phenomena. This account constitutes the criterion of reality. But since the application of that criterion is severely restricted because of "the necessity of a final renunciation of the classical *ideal* of causality", it follows that we are forced to accept "a radical revision of our attitude towards the problem of physical reality".[20]

Both Bohr and Einstein shared the same Kantian idea that the subsumption of physical phenomena under as causal description is what makes nature intelligible. But Einstein was fond of the classical ideal of causality according to which physical processes take place in a continuous manner between different states with well-defined values. So he believed that a physical description of a physical system which obeys the classical ideal of causality is objective in the sense that the description represents the system as it really is. Bohr, however, did not feel obliged to sanction any of these commitments. Based on his idea about complementary description, he gave up the idea that a quantum system is in a definite dynamic state except when measured. Therefore, he believed that quantum mechanical formalism does not represent the truth, the real truth, and nothing but the truth. Science should pursue something more humanely important – unambiguous description.

Conclusion

Today we have to recognize that science is saturated by epistemic values, methodological prescriptions and metaphysical principles in order to make it intelligible, rational, and objective. The rationality of science is not given by God. It is installed by us in the form of an epistemic and a methodological obligation towards the treatment of beliefs and the possession of knowledge. Adjusted to our cognitive faculties and constantly imposed on our belief-processing system we are entitled to hold that these cognitive norms guarantee that science is rational. The norms are not eternal but changeable depending on the context of the scientific practise. More often than not they are invisible for the working scientists, since they form an integral part of the scientific enterprise. It is only as long as we dissect the scientific practise of belief acquisition that we may be able to discover their role. I think, however, that a good place to look for them is in the rise of quantum mechanics and in the

---

[19] Faye (1991), p. 178, my emphasis.
[20] *Ibid.*

debate between Bohr and Einstein on its interpretation, not because similar cognitive values are not shaping scientific rationality elsewhere, but because they surface in the debate whenever a new revolutionary paradigm is about to take over the scene. In some sense it makes science less sacrosanct. However, it also makes science more interesting.

References

Bohr, N., (1985), *Atomic Theory and the Description of Nature. The Philosophical Writings of Niels Bohr*, Vol. 1, Woodbridge, Conn., Ox Bow Press.

Bohr, N., (1963), *Essays 1958-1962 on Atomic Physics and Human Knowledge*, London, J. Wiley & Sons.

Bohr, N., (1998), *Causality and Complementarity. The Philosophical Writings of Niels Bohr*, Vol. 4. edited by Jan Faye and Henry Folse. Woodbridge, Conn., Ox Bow Press.

Einstein, A., Podolsky, B., and Rosen A., (1935), "Can Quantum-Mechanical Description of Physical Theory be Considered Complete" in *Physical Review*, 47, p. 777-780.

Faye, J., (1991), *Niels Bohr: His Heritage and Legacy. An Antirealist View on Quantum Mechanics*, Dordrecht, Kluwer Academic Publisher.

Faye, J., (2003), *Rethinking Science*, Ashgate.

Holton, G., (1973), *Thematic Origins of Scientific thought: Kepler to Einstein*. Cambridge, Harvard University Press, Rev. ed, 1988.

Kragh, H.S., (1990), *Dirac: A Scientific Biography*, Cambridge, Cambridge University Press.

Kuhn, T.S., (1977), *The Essential Tension. Selected Studies in Scientific tradition and Change*, Chicago, University of Chicago Press.

Massimi, M., (2005), *Pauli's Exclusion Principle. The Origin and Validation of a Scientific Principle*, Cambridge, Cambridge University Press.

McAllister, J.M., (1996), *Beauty and Revolutions in Science*, Itacha, N.Y., Cornell University Press.

Pais, A., (1982), *Subtle is the Lord. The Science and the Life of Albert Einstein*, Oxford, Oxford University Press.

Van Fraassen, B., (1980), *The Scientific Image*, Oxford, Claredon Press.

The Places of Values in Science

Paul WEINGARTNER

Values may play different roles in the sciences. However, there are four places where values play a very important role in the sciences. These are the following places:

1. In considerations about the aim of science. If we agree with the old Greek answer that the aim of science is truth, then scientific activity as a search for truth confirms that this aim is a high value.

2. In the methodology of science in general and in the methodology of a specific discipline. The methodological rules and norms have been established in order to reach the goal of scientific activity; if they are violated then the goal cannot (or cannot easily) be reached.

3. In all cases where facts are explained with the help of values and aims in the sense of motives. This happens very frequently in the historical sciences but also in psychology, the social sciences, education and political science.

4. In all cases where value judgements receive an explanation or a justification like in ethics, education and in all the new branches of ethics like bioethics, medical ethics, etc.

I. The Aim of Science

If we speak of the aim of science then we mean the aim or goal of a kind of activity of mankind which is called scientific research. Not the results of this research are meant, since these *are* goals themselves, while the research activity *has* an aim (goal).

The Greek answer to the question what is the aim of science was very direct and short: Truth. And it is a correct answer for the following reason:

> The task of science is to find out what is (the facts about the world and the universe). But instead of saying that something is a fact or something *is so* we may say that a sentence, representing it, is true: "What do you mean by there being such a thing as Truth? You mean that something is SO".[1] There-

---

[1]   Peirce (1958) 2.135.

fore the task of science is to find out the true sentences (representing facts), or "to find out the truth".

On a closer look however we have to add some differentiation and specification. Because as Boole says:

> the estimation of a theory is not simply determined by its truth. It also depends upon the importance of its subject, and the extent of its applications.[2]

(a) It is not enough to search for singular truths even if a lot of singular data are necessary to test and confirm or criticize certain hypotheses and to stimulate finding new hypotheses. On the other hand the task of science includes to search for universal truths.

(b) However it is not enough to search for universal truths since mere tautologies and trivialities, although they might be universal like $x = x$, are not the aim of science.

The search in sciences is not for mere tautologies or for uninteresting singular truths but for comprehensive truth expressed by law statements. Thus scientific knowledge requires informative truth or informative approximate truth since we are rather sure not to have arrived at the final truth.

(c) Further: for scientific knowledge one has to require the thesis: if the person a knows scientifically that p, then p is testable or confirmable true (or approximate true). In other words: for getting an adequate concept of scientific knowledge one would not allow to say that a knows that p if in fact p is neither testable nor confirmable (for a or at least for a scientific community who can inform a). In addition one has to realize that the actual situation in scientific research is often such that we cannot have testable or confirmable truth as a necessary condition for scientific knowledge but only testable or confirmable approximate truth.[3]

---

[2] Boole (1951), p. 2 (preface).

[3] According to a very straightforward and adequate idea of Popper a theory A is a better approximation to the truth (or to the true theory) than a theory B if A has more true and less false consequences than B. It was shown by Tichy and Miller in 1974 that this idea or its respective definition leads to difficulties in the sense that two not completely true theories cannot stand in such a relation (of the one being a better approximation than the other) to each other. However it was shown by Schurz and Weingartner that Popper's idea can be rehabilitated by "restricting" the consequence class of the theories to the class of most informative consequence elements and filtering out redundancies (with the help of a relevance criterion). It can be proved that thereby no information is lost. Cf. Schurz/Weingartner (1987) and Weingartner (2000), ch. 9.

(d) Further: since the aim of science can efficiently be reached by scientific activity governed by methodological rules, these rules have to be also confirmed, revised and improved. But such methodological rules are norms and they are better called valid or invalid and not true or false.[4] Therefore we have to incorporate also rules or norms into the aim of science. From this consideration it follows that the aim of science and of scientific research is not only to find out what is the case but also what ought to be the case with respect to important goals of mankind. And it is important to notice that not only the inclusion of ethics requires that but already the scientific investigation of, and reflection on, the methodological norms of scientific research within every scientific discipline.

Summarizing (a) – (d) above we may say that the aim of science in the sense of a goal of scientific activity is testable and confirmable, informative and comprehensive truth (approximate truth) or validity (approximate validity).

It is a historical fact and it has been a historical experience of mankind that informative, testable and confirmable truths were the result of scientific research activity; and in most cases of scientific research activity which was done by a scientific community who acted according to methodological rules. Today scientific research activity shared by a community of scientists and governed by methodological rules is a necessary condition for reaching informative, testable truth (or approximate truth) and scientific knowledge. As Hempel says, scientific research, if it is rational "will have to specify certain goals of scientific inquiry as well as some methodological principles observed in their pursuit; finally, it will have to exhibit the instrumental rationality of the principles in relation to the goals".[5]

This leads us directly to chapter 2 about the rules (norms) of scientific methodology.

II. Rules (Norms) of Scientific Methodology

In order that scientific research activity proceeds more efficiently to reach the goals of truth and approximate truth it has to be ruled by rules and norms of methodology. Or to put it into a true conditional: if scientific research activity is not ruled by methodological rules, it does not lead efficiently to informative and testable truth and approximate truth. These rules and norms are also subject to scientific test, criticism and

---

[4] For the difference between rules (norms) and true or false statements see chapter 4 of
    Weingartner (2000).
[5] Hempel (1979), p. 58.

confirmation in order to be revised and improved permanently. A test for the validity of such a rule or norm consists mainly in an empirically testable *modus tollens* argument of the following form: if the scientific activity or research activity does not proceed according to this or that rule, it either does not lead to truth or approximate truth (for instance, it leads to false statements), or it does not reach this goal efficiently. In this sense every scientific discipline has also the task of establishing and testing the methodological norms which are specific for that discipline.

Such rules can be twofold: (1) general ones applied in all or most research activities. (2) Special ones applied in one discipline (say physics or psychology) or in a smaller group of disciplines (say social sciences). The general rules may be subdivided again into those (1a) which, if violated violate the first goal: truth (validity) or approximate truth (approximate validity); and into those (1b) which, if violated prevent scientific research from proceeding more efficiently to the first goal. Again (1a) can be further divided into those rules (1aa) which if violated violate the first goal (truth, validity) as such and those (1ab) which if violated violate the aspect of *informative* and *contentful* truth (validity).[6]

II.1. General Rules of Methodology

Examples for general rules of the type (1a) and (1aa) are: base your hypothesis (thesis) on all scientific information available. New hypothesis (theories) should include the correct results of the old (the forerunner) hypothesis (theory) as special cases. If such rules are violated then almost certainly false statements will enter, thus a violation of such rules violates the first goal.

Examples of general rules of the type of (1b): try to create hypothesis which make new predictions (in the widest reasonable sense of the word)[7] and which make suggestions for new kinds of tests. Take the scientific tradition into account. Violating such rules prevents scientific research from proceeding more efficiently to its goal and from observing the aspect of testability and confirmability.

Examples for general rules of the type (1ab): explain the particular with the help of the universal. Explain the concrete with the help of the abstract. If these rules are violated the particular and concrete is ex-

---

[6] For a detailed discussion of general and special methodological rules see Weingartner (1980).

[7] Not only predictions in astronomy and natural science are meant here. A historical hypothesis may suggest ("predict") a place to find new historical sources or it may suggest to investigate the works of a historical person not yet considered for the explanation of a certain epoch. Cf. the qualitative conditions for a theory being nearer to the truth than another in Popper's (1963) ch. 10, p. 231 ff.

plained again with the particular and concrete; i.e. there are no universal statements (laws, hypothesis) in the explanation. And this again means that the explanans does not contain enough *contentful* and *informative* truth which violates the goal with respect to the underlined properties.

The last two rules have been proposed already by Greek philosophy whose ideal was: to describe and explain the visible, observable, concrete, particular, changing, material world by non-visible, non-observable, abstract, universal, non-changing and immaterial principles.

Before I shall give some examples of special rules I want to point out that every rule has to be handled with some caution: concerning (1a) there are situations where all the information available in a certain field can hardly be interpreted consistently; and further that the new theory may contain new concepts such that it is inaccurate to speak of "special cases" (even if some of the doctrines of "incommensurability" are bold exaggerations). Concerning (1b) one has to avoid to ask for such new predictions or tests which trivially satisfy the respective hypothesis. Don't forget that reinterpretation of tradition belongs mainly to the history of science even if one can learn from it. Concerning (1ab) we have to remember that strict universal laws are not always available and statistical laws are genuine laws too.[8] And further that searching for abstract laws does not mean rejecting application and concrete tests.

II.2. Special Rules of Methodology

Do not transfer laws from the finite to the infinite. Since many of the laws in mathematics are different for the finite and the infinite domain a violation of this rule leads usually to false results. But one should not forget interesting relations between the two domains (for example: Compactness Theorem and results of Model Theory).

All physical laws should be invariant against coordinate transformations. A violation of this norm would first of all destroy our understanding of a physical law since space-time invariance is the oldest and probably most important invariance concerning physical laws. Besides this it would weaken the requirement for content high degree of information and explanatory power. However, one should be cautious not to transmit this kind of invariance to historical or social laws, where one cannot have space-time invariance.

Try to interpret the phenomena in such a way that they have always a continuous dependence upon their causes. This rule which has the general principle of continuity and infinitesimal structure (of all relations in the real world) as its basis (at least for Leibniz) was successful

---

[8]   Cf. my (1998).

for about 300 years. It leads to the interpretation of motion by laws (differential equations) of motion.

The principle of continuity as a general one in all domains was refuted by Quantum Theory and therefore the methodological norm was shown to be invalid by the "ought-can" principle. But it is still valid and applied in a wide range of research areas.

Specify the independent variable and the dependent variable on one hand and control the contaminating variables on the other. This rule is applied in experimental tests in psychology and the social sciences. If it is violated (assuming that variables have been defined for the experimental test) then the general rule of methodology: "Try to confirm your hypothesis by seriously testing and criticizing them" is violated too and this means a serious danger for falsity to enter.

All fundamental (formal) ethical laws should be invariant with respect to transformations in value scales (value systems). This rule was defended by Thomas Aquinas where he explains his formal basic principle for ethics: "The good should be done, the bad should be avoided". This one is an example for being invariant with respect to different value systems. The invariance principle is analogous to the one of physics (replace space time coordinates by value coordinates). A violation would destroy our understanding of most general (formal) ethical laws.

Summarizing this chapter I want to stress once more that scientific research of all the scientific disciplines can only proceed in a rational way if it obeys methodological rules which connect the scientific research activity with intrinsic goals and values of science, i.e. with informative and testable (approximate) truth and validity. These rules themselves are confirmable and have their justification as necessary means for the goal: if they are violated the goal is violated or weakened, too. But these rules can also be criticized and revised. One important example was the successful rule of looking for continuous dependencies (based on a general principle of continuity) which was restricted by Quantum Theory.

III. Facts Explained by Motives and Aims

III.1. Example of a Teleological Explanation: Facts Explained by Motives and Aims

Example: Queen Elizabeth I's (a) aim (Z) was not to offend either the Anglican Church nor the Roman Catholic Church (Z (p, a, f)) in respect to certain circumstances f. These circumstances f are described by the historian Maitland.[9] Elizabeth, when she had to proclaim her title, was "confronted with the alternatives either of acknowledging with the late Mary (who became Queen after Henry VIII) the ecclesiastical supremacy of the Pope or of voiding the Marian statutes and breaking with Rome as her father had done – a decision for either alternative being fraught with grave perils, because the alignment of political and military forces both at home and abroad which favored each alternative was unsettled. Maitland therefore argued that in order to avoid committing herself to either alternative for the moment, Elizabeth employed an ambiguous formulation in the proclamation of her title – a formulation which could be made compatible with any decision she might eventually make".[10]

Queen Elizabeth believed that – given the field (of circumstances) f – a necessary condition for not offending either the Anglican Church nor the Roman Catholic Church was to employ an ambiguous formulation in the proclamation of her title (q) and she believed also that she is able to do that: aB (q is a necessary condition for p in $f \wedge a$ is able to bring it about that q). The ambiguity of the formulation consisted in putting "etc." in the title instead of continuing with "only supreme head on Earth of the Church of England called Anglicana Ecclesia" (or the like as her father). Further Elizabeth preferred p (i.e. not to offend either of the churches) to q (i.e. to not being ambiguous or in other words to give a clear and unabbreviated formulation which is definite in one way or other) in respect to (the circumstances) f.

This example can be brought into the following valid teleological argument:

(1) If p is a goal (Z) for x in the field f and x believes (B) that q is a necessary condition for p in f and that he (x) is able to bring it about that q and x prefers (P) to non-q in the field f then x acts (A) in such a way that q obtains.

(2) p is a goal for (the person) a (instance of 'x') in f, a believes that q is a necessary condition for p in f and that he (a) is able to bring it about that q and further a prefers p to non-q in f.

(3) Therefore: a acts in such a way that q (obtains).

That the above argument is logically valid is easily seen by the fact that it is an instance of *modus ponens* + universal instantiation. It is also easily seen that the argument is teleological in the following sense: the conclusion expresses a fact while the premises contain a value statement

---

[9]   Maitland (1911), Elizabethan Gleanings.

[10]   Cf. Nagel (1971), p. 552. Nagel discusses the example as a case of historical explanation.

in the sense that something is said to be a goal (a relatively highest value) with respect to necessary means for reaching that goal. That means that the argument explains facts with the help of values, i.e. with the help of aims and goals.

The example of Queen Elizabeth may be generalized by the following argument: always (or in most cases) if a politician has to announce something publicly and if – according to his beliefs (his estimation) – using an unambiguous language would offend at least one of the influential groups of people, and if he prefers to use an ambiguous language over such an offence then the politician uses an ambiguous language. Also here the conclusion i.e. that the politician uses an ambiguous language expresses a fact which is explained by the premises which consist of both factual statements and value statements: that the politician announces something publicly and that he has certain beliefs and estimations are factual statements. The value statement is hidden, sometimes it is even not mentioned but presupposed: the politician prefers to use an ambiguous language over an offence against influential people. His aim is not to offend or even to please people.

III.2. What Is a Teleological Explanation?

From the example in 3.1 it can be grasped what the characteristics of a teleological explanation are. To determine it more completely we are offering the following description.

A teleological argument is an argument whose premises contain value predicates or value operators (at least one) essentially whereas the conclusion does not contain a value predicate or value operator. Statements which contain value predicates or value operators essentially are called "value statements" (or "value judgements"). Used as an explanation a teleological argument uses value statements as the explanatory statements and statements without values as the explained statements. Turned into a jargon it "explains facts with the help of values". This is connected with a programme not too clearly formulated by Dilthey and Spranger for explanation of states of affairs (in the "Geisteswissenschaften"), "die in einen Sinnzusammenhang eingeordnet werden sollen" (i.e. which should be subordinated under a hierarchy of aims). If I am not mistaken von Wight's Practical Syllogism was understood by him as a solution in the direction of this program, at least in his book *Explanation and Understanding*.

Already from this description it is clear that inferences in which the conclusion is a norm (a normative sentence or an imperative) do not fall under teleological arguments as they are understood here. The former may be called value explanations or value justifications (insofar as the conclusion is explained or justified with the help of the premises) the latter may be called explanations or justifications of norms (by the same reason as above). The fact that these types of inferences are not always clearly distinguished is responsible for a number of confusions in different comments on the so-called "Practical Inference".

III.3. What Is a Value Statement?

A value statement is a statement which contains a value predicate or value operator essentially.[11] To begin with examples a value predicate occurs essentially in the following statements: this ring is valuable, Lying is bad, Knowledge is better than error, Action A is good for person B in the circumstances C.

A value operator occurs essentially in the following statements: that John came was nice, that Jack pretended to know was dishonest. In general: if a value predicate or value operator occurs in an atomic statement it occurs essentially. With compound statements the matter is more complicated. The most straightforward device is this: if a value predicate or operator occurs (essentially) in any atomic part of the compound statement then it occurs essentially in the compound statement too. So "action A is morally good" is a value statement (since it is atomic and it contains a value predicate) and by the device given above the following compound statement is a value statement too: only if an action A is committed by pure duty then it is morally good. To put it in different words: if any atomic part of a compound statement (where compound means that it is built up by atomic statements with the help of propositional connectives: negation, disjunction, conjunction, implication, equivalence, and quantifiers) is a value statement then so is the compound (whole) statement.

This straightforward device leads to some paradoxes. However they can be avoided with a relevance criterion (relevance filter) put on Classical Logic which restricts the consequence class to non-redundant and most informative consequence elements.[12]

In the following four further groups of cases the compound statement is a value statement, i.e. a statement in which the value predicate or value operator occurs essentially, if the atomic part is already a value statement: (1) adding modal operators ("it is necessary that the judge be

---

[11] For a more detailed definition see Weingartner (1983).

[12] This is however not the place to go into details. The mentioned relevance criterion which has a very widespread field of application in avoiding paradoxes was originally proposed in Schurz/Weingartner (1987) and is described in its essentials in Weingartner (1997) and (2000) ch. 9.

just", "it is possible that …", "it is contingent that …") does not lead from a value statement to a non-value statement. The same holds: (2) for action operators ("the person *a* acts in such a way that his action is to the benefit of his children"), (3) for the operator "knows that …" (if "knows" is taken in the strong sense with the consequence: "knows that $p \to p$") and (4) for value operators ("it is good that the judge is just") together with their iterations. In each case the statement following the that-clause is a value statement and since the mentioned operators do not change it into a non-value statement the compound (whole) statement is a value statement too.

III.4. Value-like Statements

A value-like statement is one which contains a value predicate or value operator, but inessentially. To begin with examples a value predicate occurs inessentially in the following statements: Amin says, that he is not guilty (for the people killed in his country), the minister believes that his decision was good, the politician wants that his action is for the benefit of all.

The examples show already the three important groups of cases where the compound statement is only value-like (the value predicate or value operator occurs inessentially) though the atomic part of it is a value statement: (1) *speech-act-operators* like "says that", "writes that", "questions that", etc. (2) *epistemic operators* like "believes that", "claims that", "doubts that", "is of the opinion that", etc. (with the exception of a strong concept of "knows that" as mentioned above), (3) *volitive operators* like "regrets that", "wants that", "wishes that", "intends that", "hates that", "loves that", etc.

III.5. Teleological Explanations in Biology

There seem to be several examples of explanations in biology which can be classified as teleological explanations in the sense described here. One of the suggesting examples is the so-called evolutionarily stable strategies (ESS) in Sociobiology.[13] An ESS represents a strategy which is balanced w.r.t. certain parameters like expectation values for offspring, for food, for winning the battle. If the ESS is interpreted as a goal of a population of animals then many activities of the population and of its individuals are explainable with the help of it. In this case the explanation is a teleological argument (explanation).

---

[13] Cf. Maynard-Smith (1982) and Wickler/Seibt (1987), p. 57 ff.

IV. Reasoned Justification of Value Statements and of Norms

In teleological arguments value judgements are used in the premises, i.e. as justifying or explaining sentences w.r.t. the conclusion. In such arguments they are used to explain or to justify statements in the conclusion which are factual statements and no value judgements. On the other hand in cases of justifying or explaining value judgements there are value judgements occurring in both, in the premises and in the conclusion. Similarly in cases of justifying or explaining norms: in such arguments norms occur in both, premises and conclusion. Scientific disciplines which use only teleological explanations, i.e. which explain facts with the help of values (motives, aims, goals) I am calling here *teleological disciplines*. On the other hand, disciplines which use also (in addition) arguments to justify or explain value judgements or norms, i.e. which justify or explain value judgements (norms) with the help of other value judgements (norms) I am calling here *value disciplines* or *normative disciplines* respectively. According to this demarcation the historical disciplines are teleological disciplines but not value disciplines and not normative disciplines; while ethics is both a value discipline and a normative discipline. It seems to me that the science of literature including comparative literature is a value discipline but not a normative discipline, whereas education seems to be both a value discipline and a normative discipline.

IV.1. Examples for Reasoned Justification of Value Statements

IV.1.1. Mother Child Separation

Argument: (1) if a separation of mother and child for more than 3 weeks happens during the first year of child's life then the child will show anti-social behaviour in its later development. (2) There was such a separation happening to child *A*. (3) Child *A* showed anti-social behaviour later in his (her) development.

That (3) is a value statement is perhaps not so easy to see. But on a closer look we can uncover its value-ladenness. In "normal" societies "anti-social behaviour" will have negative connotation in the sense that some of the goals (which are values) of education have not been achieved by this child. Also both premises are value laden. It is clear and well confirmed that mother-child separation (for more than 3 weeks) especially in the first year is against the (justified) desires of the child and is a violation of one of its basic values; where *basic value* can be defined as something (some state of affairs) which is necessary for child's survival or for his (her) health.[14] According to these remarks all the three statements of the above argument are value statements. Further the above argument is logically valid, it has a simple *modus ponens* structure plus universal instantiation. Therefore the argument is a reasoned justification of conclusion (3) by the premises (1) and (2).

IV.1.2. Value of Literary Work of Art

Argument: (1) if a literary work of art is admired by all (most of all) later generations then it has such a multiplicity of values and such a rich and comprehensive esthetical value such that at least one of its structures pleases every later period to a high degree. (2) If a literary work of art has such a multiplicity of values and such a rich and comprehensive esthetical value such that at least one of its structures pleases every later period to a high degree then it is of *classical value*. (3) The literary works of art of Homer and of Shakespeare are such that they are admired by all (most of all) later generations. (4) Therefore: the literary works of art of Homer and Shakespeare are of *classical value*.

Also here a closer consideration will show that all the three premises and the conclusion are value statements (value judgements). The values at stake here are *esthetical values*. They are explicitly claimed in premises (1) and (2) but more hidden in premise (3): to be admired as a work of art means to have esthetical value.[15]

IV.2. Reasoned Justification of Norms

Concerning the norms (and rules) of methodology there is reasoned justification of norms in every mature scientific discipline. Since every mature scientific discipline develops its own methodology consisting of a set of rules and guide lines for the scientific research activities (recall chapter 2). There are however also scientific disciplines which contain reasoned justification of norms which do not belong to the methodological norms. Consider the following two examples:

IV.2.1. (1) If the conservation of life on earth is a high value then every atomic war ought to be avoided. (2) The conservation of life on

---

[14] It is assumed here that the child has no real substitute for his mother, like a wet-nurse or something similar.

[15] It should be emphasized that there are many different kinds of values which are not ethical or moral values. This means also that different scientific disciplines which do not presuppose or include ethics or morality may deal with values in different respects. The ethical or moral rules for the respective scientists however hold for every scientist and are therefore independently of whether some scientific discipline deals with values, like history, or comparative literature.

earth is a high value. (3) Therefore: every atomic war ought to be avoided.

IV.2.2. (1) If a person commits murder he (she) ought to be imprisoned for at least ... years. (2) Person A committed murder. (3) Therefore: person A ought to be imprisoned for at least ... years.

In IV.2.1. the first premise is a mixed sentence consisting of a value statement as its antecedent and a norm as its consequent. The justified conclusion is a norm (normative sentence).

Example IV.2.2. is a case of the application of criminal law. The first premise is also a mixed sentence consisting of a statement about the *facts of the case* (as the antecedent) and the norm concerning punishment (as the consequent). The antecedent is not just a simple descriptive statement since the states of affairs happening (the murdering) are not identical with the *facts of the case*. Rather the states of affairs happening have to be subsumed under and "translated" into the respective *facts of the case* (after hearing accuser, public prosecutor, defending counsel and witnesses).

The important thing to be observed here is that the judge gives a reasoned justification of his judgement (*sentence*) with the help of (a paragraph of) the criminal law (premise (1)) plus the *facts of the case* (premise (2)). The respective scientific discipline in which such arguments for reasoned justification of norms are studied is jurisprudence. This discipline has also the difficult task to discuss the justification and revision of the laws (norms) of criminal law itself. Because without these laws as premises the judge cannot give a reasoned justification of his judgement (sentence).[16]

References

Boole, G., (1951), *The Mathematical Analysis of Logic*, Oxford, Blackwell.

Hempel, C. G., (1979), *Aspects of Scientific Explanation*, London.

Maitland, F. W., (1911), *Elizabethan Gleanings*, "Collected Papers", London, 1911, p. 157-165.

Maynard-Smith, J., (1982), *Evolution and the Theory of Games*, Cambridge, Cambridge UP.

Nagel, E., (1971), *The Structure of Science*, London.

Peirce, C. S., (1958), *Collected Papers*, C. Hartshorne, P. Weiss, A. Burks (ed.), Cambridge, Mass.

Popper, K. R., (1963), *Conjectures and Refutations*, London, Routledge and Kegan Paul.

---

[16] For an excellent discussion on the testability of norms of criminal law cf. Savigny (1967).

Von Savigny, E., (1967), *Die Überprüfbarkeit der Strafrechtssätze*, Freiburg, Alber.

Schurz, G., Weingartner, P., (1987), *Verisimilitude Defined by Relevant Consequence-Elements. A new Reconstruction of Popper's Original Idea*, in Th. Kuipers (ed.), *What is Closer-to-the-Truth?*, Amsterdam, Rodopi, p. 47-77.

Weingartner, P., (1980), *Normative Characteristics of Scientific Activity*, in R. Hilpinen (ed.), *Rationality in Science. Studies in the Foundations of Science and Ethics*, Dordrecht, Reidel, p. 209-230.

Weingartner, P., (1983), *Definition of Value-Judgment*, in E. Agazzi (ed.), *La Responsabilité de la Science*. [Proceedings of the Conference of the Académie Internationale de Philosophie des Sciences (Forli 1982)] Special Issue of *Epistemologia 6* (1983), p. 79-86.

Weingartner, P., (1997), *Reasons for Filtering Classical Logic*, in D. Batens *et al.* (eds.), *Frontiers in Paraconsistent Logics. Proceedings of the First World Congress on Paraconsistency, Gent 1997*, London, Research Studies Press, p. 315-327.

Weingartner, P., (1998), *Are Statistical Laws Genuine Laws? A Concern of Poincaré and Boltzmann*, "Philosophia Scientia" 1998-1999, 3 (2), p. 215-236.

Weingartner, P., (2000), *Basic Questions on Truth* (Series *Episteme* 24), Dordrecht, Kluwer.

Wickler, W., Seibt, U., (1987), *Das Prinzip Eigennutz*, München.

Science and Technoscience

Values and their Measurement

Ramón QUERALTÓ

University of Sevilla (Spain)

I. Values in Science

The influence of technological means in scientific research is perhaps one of the most relevant facts in the development of Science nowadays. In many branches of Science, technology has come to be a strict condition of the possibility of the scientific process. This fact has the consequence that the concept of Science is evolving to be considered as *technoscience*, which designates an important change in the nature of scientific work. For all intents and purposes, the current technoscience can be described as a system of human actions based on scientific knowledge and directed towards the transformation of reality with the goal of achieving benefits for humankind.

This fact carries a myriad of consequences. The first to consider is of a pragmatic nature. Technoscience emphasizes the importance of the pragmatic aspect of scientific knowledge. This emphasis is especially relevant today, when compared to other historical periods. From a historical viewpoint, it is right to assert that the practical uses of Science originate, broadly speaking, along a second phase of the global elaboration of scientific knowledge, after obtaining the cognitive results that solve epistemological queries mainly, and not pragmatic uses. In this sense, for example, technology was normally conceived as applied science for a long time, that is, it was thought necessary to firstly get scientific knowledge as such, and afterwards its pragmatic uses were searched for. Nowadays this situation has changed notably, because technology is no longer conceived as applied science" but rather as a

155

condition of the possibility of scientific research,[1] because of the influence of technology on science.[2] Precisely, the current interdependence between science and technology is expressed by the term technoscience.[3] Moreover, to put the emphasis on the pragmatic aspects of scientific knowledge can be considered a convergent fact with the so called "pragmatic turn" in todays philosophy, that is to say, with the promotion of the pragmatic concerns to a first rank in philosophical reflections. Consequently, it is hardly surprising that the notion of technoscience has a definite place in the scientific and philosophical thought nowadays.

Secondly, many important scholars have conceived the philosophy of science as a philosophy of scientific action or a philosophy of scientific work. A result of this has been the increase in the number of philosophical features to be considered in Science. In this way, other new factors have been incorporated to the traditional ideas of logical, methodological and epistemological concerns, to include matters of a political, social, ethical and economic nature. The analysis of these new dimensions must be considered completely necessary for the correct understanding of the complexities facing Science today.

Thirdly, as an effect derived from these consequences, the analysis of every kind of value included in the elaboration of scientific knowledge has become a central issue in the philosophy of science as technoscience. This effect should hardly come as a surprise, given that if Science is conceived as a system of human actions derived from scientific knowledge, then the axiological dimensions, which are always included in human actions, must be taken into account for a proper understanding of scientific work.

Without a doubt, one of the most important sets of values to be considered will be ethical, yet these are not the only values to be contemplated. Because of the pragmatic notion of value, when examining from this new perspective, namely, value as a guideline for solving problems, this entails values such as social and environmental concerns, for example, and others which have been previously mentioned. This is a crucial

---

[1]   R. Queraltó, Technology as a New Condition of the Possibility of Scientific Knowledge, in H. Lenk and M. Maring (eds.), *Advances and Problems in the Philosophy of Technology*, Münster-London, Lit Verlag, 2001 (Technikphilosophie, b. 5); p. 205 ff.

[2]   Cf. J. Agassi, Between Science and Technology", *Philosophy of Science*, 47 (1980), p. 82 ff., I. Niiniluoto, Aproximation in Applied Science", *Poznan Studies in the Philosophy of the Sciences and the Humanities*, 42, (1995), p. 127 ff., E. Agazzi, *Il bene, il male e la scienza*, Milano, Rusconi, 1992, p. 72 ff.

[3]   Cf. J. Echeverría, *La revolución tecnocientífica.* Madrid, Fondo de Cultura Económica, 2003, p. 61 ff.

point in order to rightly understand all what follows. From a pragmatic point of view, which is indispensable for envisaging technoscience, the concept of value is no longer the traditional idea according to which value is something worthy of putting in practice because of its intrinsic ontological qualities, but rather value obtains its axiological meaning as far as it is an efficient means for overcoming and for solving some concrete problems. On that account, the idea of specific efficacy is fully connected with the notion of value, and this is the key content of the pragmatic conception of value. Hence the fact that the central criterion of the technological rationality is just that of operative efficacy.[4] So, from a general axiological point of view, every scientific action would involve a set of values which could be expressed in the following way:

$$Sv_i$$

Now, this situation raises a fundamental problem to be considered in the light of the philosophy of science. More specifically, one must take into account the problem of value assessment, whose main focus is to establish a reasonable preference, a rational choice, from amongst several different plans of actions which are all directed towards achieving the same ends. The value assessment has two specific features. First of all, it must be global, that is to say, the assessment refers to the major set of values included in a specific scientific action, but it will not refer only to epistemological values, for example. Secondly, as far as the assessment falls into the category of scientific activity, it must include some kind of measurement of value, which implies a sort of quantification of value itself. Obviously, it is at this point where the controversy emerges.

The reasons are not hard to point out. From the received view of axiology, value, as such, has been considered as something which is qualitative and foreign to any type of measurement. Now, however, it seems necessary to broaden this accepted view to some extent, if we have to carry out a general assessment of technoscientific actions.

To begin with it is necessary to consider that the scientific-pragmatic value, as long as it is conceived as a guideline for solving problems, receives its axiological meaning not only because it is based on an ideal and metaphysical realm, nor because it is valuable intrinsically, but rather it should be considered because it is an efficient means for solving any problematic situation that may arise during the process of the

---

[4]   Cf. R. Queraltó, "Does Technology construct Scientific Reality?", in C. Mitcham (ed.), *Philosophy of Technology in Spanish Speaking Countries*, Dordrecht, Kluwer Academic Pub., 1993, p. 167 ff.; "Hypothèse, objectivité et rationalité technique", *Philosophia Scientiae*, Vol. I, Cahier Spécial, 1996, p. 187 ff.; *Ética, tecnología y valores en la sociedad global*, Madrid, Tecnos, 2003, p. 73 ff.

elaboration of scientific knowledge. This opens a possible way for addressing the question raised before.

In general, it can be asserted that a certain value (or set thereof) in a specific scientific action appears with more or less intensity than in another action (principle of graduality),[5] both being directed towards the same objectives. In other words, we can speak in terms of more than" or less than" when referring to the values concerned. For example, it is common nowadays to analyse the degree of undesirable cultural impact of a technoscientific action, by establishing some measurements concerning the larger or lesser intensity of such an impact. This is the well-known case of the technology transfer to traditional societies whose social structure is very different from that of other societies which have easily used this technology before. Similarly, it is also a current situation to examine the impact on human privacy in the case of many digital technologies. Here the impact is also assessed in terms of more or less. In such situations, those technoscientific actions whose influence is lower are the preferred ones. An important consequence arising at this point is that the assessment inspired by the "more than/less than" criterion can be determinant in order to decide the course of the technoscientific investigation. That is the decisive relevance of the value assessment for the elaboration of scientific knowledge today.

Of course, this "more than or less than" cannot be measured with the precision of traditional properties such as velocity or electric charge, but undoubtedly we can establish a global quantitative comparison, although without any specific numerical result. So, in the value assessment we could write

$$Sv (A) > Sv (A') \text{ or } Sv (A) < Sv (A')$$

A and A would represent two alternative procedures or actions. The possibility of establishing this comparison by means of the partially quantitative criterion "more than/less than" implies an important consequence: the capability of justifying a reasonable choice, that is to say, a rationally well founded choice, within the process of elaboration of scientific knowledge. In what follows, I shall refer to this criterion as MLC, "more/less criterion".

Broadly speaking, this manner of assessment can be applied to values of all sorts, throughout the elaboration of scientific work.[6] So, things

---

[5] On this graduality, cf. J. Echeverría, *Ciencia y valores,* Barcelona, Destino, 2002, p. 95 ff., U. Moulines: *Exploraciones metacientíficas*, Madrid, Alianza, 1982, p. 32 ff.

[6] Cf. J. Echeverría, Axiología y Ontología: los valores de la ciencia como funciones no saturadas", in *Argumentos de Razón Técnica* (Spanish Journal on Science, Technology and Society, and Philosophy of Technology), 5 (2002), p. 21 ff.

such as the environmental impact in reference to different technoscientific actions can be measured, and consequently, one can opt for one action or another. We could also assess a rational preference in reference to ethical values such as human freedom and other related issues. This last case presents itself, for instance, with respect to the many problems connected to genetic engineering.

We have said before, however, that the assessment in technoscience ought to be global. On that account, the standard situation would normally refer to a set of values which have to be previously bounded. More concretely, for establishing the before mentioned comparison it is necessary to reach an agreement on the specific system of values to be assessed, which operates as the middle term of the comparison. For this reason, a second rule now arises, having to do with value assessment, namely, the bounding rule of values (BR), along side MLC criterion. Usually in technoscientific practice there is no chronological order between them, but rather things occur simultaneously. Indeed, MLC and BR are logical conditions of the possibility of every value assessment.

The aim of this bounding rule is obvious. On the one hand, it provides a necessary means for establishing the reasonable intersubjectivity along the process of value assessment, that is to say, it is a very convenient instrument for the discussion amongst the different assessing agents. It is thus a normal procedure to carry out the value assessment by taking into account the diverse points of view of the social groups concerned. So, the bounding rule is indispensable for designating the common terms of the discussion; otherwise the assessment would be impossible. On the other hand, the bounding rule tries to avoid an endless discussion in the process of the assessment. Undoubtedly, this situation could be originated if there is not any common axiological language regarding the values to be considered.

Nevertheless, the technoscientific praxis is even more complicated. In effect, because many times a set of values can be in conflict with another set of values, that is to say, one finds some opposition between two – or more – axiological systems, at least in respect to some specific values. In such cases, the assessment comparison would be the following:

Sv (A) > S'v' (A') or

Sv (A) < S'v' (A')

Here, the question is immediately begged: what should be the criterion for opting for either S or S? A possible response would be to search the assessment comparison by means of other more comprehensive values than the initial ones implied. This new system of values would operate as an axiological metasystem (MS) of the former systems. By applying this metasystem in the manner of MLC we would be able to establish a reasonable preference (rationally founded) about S and S. But, here an objection comes up, because this procedure could lead to a process *ad infinitum*, that is to say, the situation could be reproduced in respect of the metasystem MS, and therefore the process would be repeated endlessly.

For this reason, it is fully convenient to provide some rational instrument for avoiding this unended quest. In this case, the rule has to be more qualitative than in the former case, for the sole purpose of breaking the vicious circle mentioned above. But it does not mean that this rule has to be only qualitative, as will be seen in the following. Let me call to this rule a rule of prudence (PR), which consists of taking into account other prior technoscientific actions that have been already accomplished, and to compare their results in regard to their fulfilment of the same values or similar values to the ones under consideration. The term "prudence" is justified here because to take into consideration the results of prior assessments constitutes a sort of practical "wisdom", which is connection with the classical philosophical concept of "phrónesis". The advantage of this procedure is obvious, namely that the degree of fulfilment of values is already well known, and therefore it will be easier to make the prudent comparison. In other words, the middle term of the comparison will have been previously bounded, and consequently it will be possible to establish a form of more than/less than, applying MLC again. Moreover, in so doing, we are not going outside of the former conditions of the value assessment. In this way, PR, BR and MLC, are three key points of the value assessment.

As can be seen, value assessment encompasses qualitative and quantitative traits, in general, which are not hard to justify given the point of departure, that is to say, the conception of scientific knowledge as a kind of human action, or rather, a very special variety of it.

II. The Measurement of Values

But, it is necessary to pay attention now to another important trait. It is that every value implied by a technoscientific action does not possess the same weight. The question refers to the fact that it is always necessary to consider a specific appraisal of values according to the kind of knowledge or action that we are assessing. In our case, it deals with technoscientific knowledge or actions. For this reason it is very convenient now to introduce some particular reflections in this respect.

There are basic values that are distinguishing marks of scientific procedure as such. These values are worthy of a special analysis because without them – or at least a minimum fulfilment of them – we could not speak about Science properly. Can these values be subjected to a value assessment as described before? What aspects have to be now taken into account because of their relevance for Science?

Undoubtedly, a set of these is the set of epistemological values, especially the value of truth in scientific knowledge. Because of its centrality in Science, the analysis of this value could be considered a key procedure for studying those basic values that distinguish scientific knowledge specifically.

From a pragmatic technoscientific view, it is important to remark two features of the concept of truth. First, the relative trait of truth, which is not to be understood as relativism at all, but rather as *relativeness*. Under this term we want to point out that the content of scientific truth always refers to a specific problem or to a particular object. It does not deal with truth in the sense of an absolute truth, but rather with an epistemic content that solves a precise problem according to the strict conditions under which it has been raised. Accordingly, this epistemic content is true in relation to the epistemological conditions defined initially. In this respect, and only in this respect, we say that scientific truth is "relative to" something. For example, Popper, in his defense of quantum mechanics, asserted that if the quantum scientific problems were probabilistic, then it was unreasonable to demand a greater degree of exactness in the mathematical results of the theory, and therefore it was not right to argue incompleteness in quantum mechanics because it would be an epistemological fallacy.[7]

Secondly, it is also convenient to remark the trait of truth as sufficient truth. To sum up, this means that an epistemic result will be true whether or not it fulfils the basic initial conditions of testing that have been established for the problem under consideration. A set of them is, for example, the set of empirical conditions. So, it is possible to affirm that a scientific statement is valid regarding such a problem to a *sufficient* extent if it overcomes these conditions. It is due to the fact that every kind of knowledge carries out a specific epistemological reduction of reality. Scientific knowledge does it too. This process consists of two phases: first, it demarcates the realm of objects to be considered, and second, it delimits the outlook from which these objects will be investigated. Then, it establishes a precise methodology in order to develop the cognitive aims according to the previous epistemological reduction. In this manner, we obtain a specific selection of the traits to be taken into account. This process of selection is here denominated epistemological

---

[7]   Cf. K.R. Popper, *Quantum Theory and the Schism in Physics,* From the Postscript to the Logic of Scientific Discovery, London, Hutchinson, 1982.

reduction. Sufficiency of truth, in turn, means that the epistemic result of our investigation satisfies those initial conditions of testing, that is to say, the truth of this epistemic content is sufficient in respect of those initial conditions. In other words, truth will be sufficient according to the epistemological structure of the problem raised. For example, a scientific statement will be considered valid if it overcomes the empirical conditions of testing and other possible requirements that should have been initially demanded. In this way, the epistemic content is said to be sufficient regarding all these conditions and requirements.

Now, it is also feasible to raise a value assessment in respect to these two traits. As far relativeness is concerned – not relativism, we must insist – it is possible to assess an epistemological proposal by taking into account whether it refers fully to a greater or smaller number of objects than other proposals, according to the initial conditions. Even more, the best situation will be that in which the proposal can include not only the initial objects and problems, but also other new objects which emerged throughout the research process. In both cases MLC and also BR can be applied, and in this way, to conclude that the result of this assessment shows that a theory (T) encompasses a greater field of objects and problems than another one (T'). If X and Y are the fields of reference respectively, it is then possible to write

BR (T) = X

BR (T') = Y

$$\overline{}$$

X > Y

This result can suggest a possible preference in the choice between two theories, which is the main objective of the value assessment. Moreover, it adds an important advantage, because it does not mean that the theory obtaining lower results, in this case T, must be rejected completely. Rather it implies that this theory has not been the preferred or chosen one. In turn, it means that this theory can be taken into account later, if the conditions of scientific research require it, for instance, in regarding other problems. This situation contributes to the increase of the global set of scientific ideas and perhaps to establish a sort of "stock" of knowledge to be used later.

Similarly, it is possible to proceed with the trait of epistemological sufficiency. This trait refers to the basic fulfilment of the testing conditions, that is to say, it concerns the conditions *sine qua non* that a statement is compelled to fulfil in order to be considered a true statement. But this degree of fulfilment is not the only one, because such a statement can also fulfil other testing conditions which were not initially required, or simply it can be positively tested many more times than another proposal. What we try to say is that the trait of epistemological sufficiency requires an unavoidable borderline (a minimum), undoubtedly, but this does not mean that it entails a maximum necessarily. This last idea should be understood at two levels. There is no limit, either regarding the number of testing conditions or the number of proofs of these conditions.

Things being such, it seems clear that it is also possible to conceive some inequations of the more/less kind in respect to epistemological sufficiency, that is to say, to recur to the MLC criterion again. The result of this assessment leads to establish degrees of epistemological sufficiency. It is not hard to accept this notion because it formally connects with the received view in philosophy of science, for instance when we speak of degrees of corroboration, etc. So, Z and W being the epistemological sufficiency of T and of T respectively, we could write

$$Z (T) > W (T) \text{ or } Z (T) < W (T)$$

As is well known at this point, the result of this value assessment will be useful for pointing out some reasonable preference between two theories, for example. In the same manner as before this fact does not imply necessarily the full rejection of the lower theory in the assessment, especially because in this case it fulfils the requirement of the minimum (borderline) mentioned before. Otherwise, this theory had not been subjected to the value assessment.

However, in this brief summary on value assessment a last question arises: how should we proceed in the case that the result of the assessment about relativeness and epistemological sufficiency are the same, or at least very similar? How can we establish the reasonable preference that the value assessment is searching for?

In such cases the preference will be established by the assessment of other values belonging to the problem under consideration. These values may be new epistemological values or not, but they always have to be included in the system of values bounded by the BR rule. From a technoscientific point of view, this procedure is fully coherent, because we note at the beginning that technoscience consists of a system of actions which encompasses a set of very different values. So, we can then assess values such as methodological values (logical simplicity), instrumental values (more or less accuracy of technological means), social values (more or less human profit), economic values (more or less researching cost), etc.

Finally, the preference will be established by a global assessment on the set of values concerning the investigation. This is in agreement with the systemic character of modern technoscience. It consists of a system of actions based on scientific knowledge, therefore it embraces many different elements which are interconnected amongst themselves. Consequently, a correct value assessment must refer to the totality of values chosen by the bounding rule BR.

Nevertheless, it is always necessary to remember that the task of value assessment in technoscience has to conceive that totality as an open totality. The reason for this axiological potentiality is twofold. First, because many new values can appear throughout the research process. If these values were not included initially and if they are necessary for justifying reasonable preferences, then they must be also considered. Second, the set of values is open because the boundaries of technoscientific research are often increased in order to be successful respecting the initial aims. These two situations are very common in practice, especially in the case of social aims.

This means that value assessment is always a never-ending task, in the same way that the pursuit of scientific knowledge is too.

References

Van Boxsel, J., (1994), "Constructive Technology Assessment: A New Approach", in G. Aichholzer and G. Schienstock (eds.), *Technology Policy: Towards an Integration of Social and Ecological Concerns*, Berlin-New York, De Gruyter.

Crane, J., (1987), "Risk Assessment as Social Research", in P. Durbin (ed.), *Technology and Responsibility*, Dordrecht, Reidel.

Echeverria, J., (2002), *Ciencia y Valores*, Barcelona, Destino.

Echeverria, J., (2002), "Axiología y Ontología: Los valores de la ciencia como funciones no saturadas", in *Argumentos de Razón Técnica* (Spanish Journal on Science, Technology and Society, and Philosophy of Technology), 5, p. 21 ff.

Echeverria, J., (2003), *La revolución tecnocientífica*, Madrid, Fondo de Cultura Económica.

Giere, R., (1991), "Knowledge, Values and Technological Decisions: A Decision Theoretic Approach", in D.G. Mayo and R.D. Hollander (eds.), *Acceptable Evidence: Science and Values in Risk Management*, Oxford, Oxford University Press.

Hottois, G. (ed.), (1988), *Évaluer la technique: aspects éthiques de la philosophie de la technique*, Paris, Vrin.

Laudan, L. (ed.), (1984), *The Nature of Technological Knowledge,* Dordrecht, Reidel.

Lenk, H., (1982), *Zur Sozialphilosophie der Technik*, Frankfurt, Suhrkamp.

Lenk, H. and Maring, M. (eds.), (2001), *Advances and Problems in the Philosophy of Technology*, Münster-London, LIT Verlag, (Technnik philosophie, band 5).

Longino, H., (1990), *Science as Social Knowledge: Values and Objectivity in Scientific Inquiry*, Princeton, Princeton University Press.

Menéndez, A., (2002), "Valores: ser o tener?", *Argumentos de Razón Técnica* (Spanish Journal on Science, Technology and Society, and Philosophy of Technology), 5, p. 223 ff.

Mitcham, C. (ed.), (1993), *Philosophy of Technology in Spanish Speaking Countries*, Dordrecht, Kluwer Academic.

Porter, A.L. *et al.*, (1980), *A Guidebook for Technology Assessment and Impact Analysis*, New York, North Holland.

Queraltó, R., (1993), "Does Technology Construct' Scientific Reality?", in C. Mitcham (ed.).

Queraltó, R., (1996), "Hypothèse, objectivité et rationalité technique", in *Philosophia Scientiae*, I, Cahier Spécial 1, p. 187 ff.

Queraltó, R., (2002), *Razionalità tecnica e mondo futuro. Una eredità per il terzo millennio*, Milano, Franco Angeli.

Queraltó, R., (2003), *Ética, tecnología y valores en la sociedad global*, Madrid, Tecnos.

Rip, A., Misa, T., Schot, J. (eds.), (1995), *Managing Technology in Society: the Approach of Constructive Technology Assessment*, London, Pinter.

Shrader-Frechette, K., (1985), *Risk Analysis and Scientific Method*, Dordrecht, Reidel.

Winner, L., (1995), "Technology Assessment and Reflexive Social Learning", in A. Rip, T. Misa, J. Schot.

SECOND SECTION

SCIENCE, ETHICS AND RELIGION

Ethics in Face of Science and in Face of Research

Hervé BARREAU

CNRS-Strasbourg-Nancy

We have chosen to distinguish between science and research in their relationship with ethics, since the debate hinges on different issues for one and for the other. Science, for its part, is not to be subordinated to ethics given that what is definitively established as true according to the rules of scientific validity does not in itself depend upon any ethical demands; it simply gives expression to what is universally accepted within the context of a scientific discussion. In the case of research, however, it is possible to talk in terms of subordination to ethics given that research aims at objectives and employs means that enter within the framework of ethical demands which govern all forms of human activity. No activity – even for the purposes of science – has the right to violate the dignity of human beings. Prior to examining this form of subordination, however, we shall see that the exposition of science, involving the demonstration of what is scientifically established, is also subject to important ethical criteria which do not govern good in itself but truth. It is not always easy to determine what is truly scientifically established, yet it is our duty, from an epistemological point of view, to distinguish science from the ideology that most often accompanies it and may contribute not only to its success but also to its stagnation.

Ethics of Science Considered as Valid Knowledge

The ethical nature of science where the latter is considered as valid knowledge is quite habitual. Even those people who refuse to subordinate moral ethics to science and therefore to attribute supreme value to the latter, readily underline the moral demands required for the correct application of science, those which are capable of ensuring its progress and success. Consequently, all forms of lying and cheating are banned. It is forbidden to falsify experimental results in order to make them comply with the hypothesis that we would like to confirm. We are required to acknowledge the rights of intellectual property and refrain from appropriating the results of other researchers. In the case of their "ideas", strictly speaking, it is difficult to trace the limits of property. For an idea, as soon as it has been expressed, belongs to anyone capable of understanding and appropriating it in an original manner. Nobody – or hardly anybody – has until now accused Einstein of having borrowed Poincaré's idea of the "principle of relativity" which he applied to electromagnetism and the entire field of physics in a manner of his own, thus enabling him to superbly extend to general relativity. It is precisely because younger minds adopt the ideas of their elders that they are able to attain new results which the latter are generally incapable of achieving since they are too attached to old-school scientific heritage and less inclined to engage in scientific "revolutions".

There is thus a purely intellectual aspect to scientific research which enters into the category of the ethics of science in the strict sense of the term. It is that which concerns the attribution of inventions and discoveries; we know that it sometimes takes a while to settle controversial issues such as the priority of the publication of the invention of infinitesimal calculus, which is to be attributed to Leibniz, or the absence of plagiary that the latter is claimed to be guilty of with regard to the – albeit earlier – work of Newton. Disputes over priority are practically inevitable and all we can expect of the quarrelling parties is to show proof of good faith. However, before being taken beyond what are its limits in all ages, science must be properly acquired and interpreted. Yet it is precisely within this domain of acquired science that scientists are confronted with the obligation of not making any changes. If we modify the state of knowledge acquired it will then not only be impossible to improve upon it but we are also doing harm to an acquisition into which a great deal of hard work has been invested. Yet this form of modification is all the easier when dealing with a domain that is of greater complexity. Those who might be tempted to modify mathematics or physics are rapidly shown up to be impostors. Even if they do not modify anything and simply advance rash theories, the latter are very quickly forgotten about if they simply fail to produce any new results. Within these relatively simple domains, any disputes – even if they are sometimes justified and interesting – will inevitably subside. This is not the case, however, within the far more complicated domains explored by the social sciences and even the life sciences.

In the case of the social sciences we sometimes imagine that we have sufficient safeguards thanks to the historical and sociological data available in our archives. Yet science is never just an accumulation of empirical data. It needs a theoretical framework which make it possible to organise and classify such data. Is it possible to attribute a general validity to this framework? Should this not be the case, we would have to forego all scientific ambition. Nonetheless, it is extremely difficult to claim to be able to establish explanatory laws for any given human society, irrespective of its degree of economic, social or cultural development. The solution generally consists in determining the precise historical-social conditions within which the theoretical framework may claim validity. It has to be admitted that this task is sometimes rather difficult given the mimicry of the social players and the phenomena of contagion that occurs amongst them within the ideological realm. Let us take the example of Marxism: we may consider that it had been refuted by the end of 19th century by way of the very fact that the most industrially developed nations had not opted for the path of the proletarian revolution in order to settle their economical-social problems. This did not prevent attempts being made to introduce Marxism first in Russia and then in China; some even dreamt of introducing it within all countries enjoying industrial development – in other words, the whole world. It is striking to note that those who wished to renounce this unjustified extension – and who were themselves sometimes highly attracted to fundamental Marxist ideas – found it difficult to be taken seriously, at least until the fall of the Soviet empire. They had to call upon moral courage in order to put forward and gain adherence for arguments that ran counter to improper and simplified generalisations when, on political grounds, these generalisations were very widely accepted.

Are we not today witnessing something similar with regard to the science of the evolution of the living species? It cannot be contested that Darwin came up with an important idea when he demonstrated – and backed up with examples – that the species were dependent upon the environment in which they lived and that many of them had been eliminated due to their failure to adapt to this environment. We know that the Darwinian theory goes much further: by selection, the environment is claimed to be responsible for the apparition of new species given that it saves and even advantages the early representatives of these species, which had appeared in the course of accidental mutations, since these representatives find themselves better adapted to the conditions of this environment than the others. Such a theory of transformism could be considered as scientific as long as the theories of heredity were not themselves scientific. The theory became more difficult to defend when Weisman demonstrated that reproductive cells (*germen*) were separated from ordinary cells (*soma*). This is the period from which neo-Darwinism dates whose programme involves the adjustment of Darwinian ideas to the discoveries of genetics. Today, although these discoveries have attained great accuracy it is impossible to make them contribute towards a coherent theory. Whatever is done, the secret of genes –

namely the active role they play in the constitution of a species – remains well guarded. In face of the mounting difficulties a certain number of biologists believe that the neo-Darwinian programme is a hopeless one. Yet this is not how the theory of evolution is generally presented to the public, pupils and students. It is maintained that neo-Darwinism can continue to be enriched without being brought into question. The fact that major dissension has appeared amongst neo-Darwinians themselves – some of whom refuse to attribute as much importance to the environment as Darwin did – has been overlooked. Authors like Marco Schützenberger who have demonstrated that neo-Darwinism can no longer claim to be scientific – even if no other strictly scientific theory is available to replace it – are few and far between. In face of this situation it is more than justified to believe that both in the biological domain of the evolution of the species and the social domain of the history of the human race it is essential to call upon philosophical choices in order to guarantee a high degree of theoretic unity. It would thus be honest to take act. In this way, it would be demonstrated that epistemology does not only have a speculative function as a critic of scientific knowledge but that by correctly assuming this function it consequently has an ethical function. For we are not entitled to attribute scientific validity to that which is void of any such validity and here the demand for truth shows up in all its force. We must be able to distinguish between that which is truly scientific and that which cannot be labelled as such, even if some hypothesis – henceforth insufficient – at one stage contributed to the progress of learning. No considerations of prestige should prevail in face of this demand for truth in scientific matters.

The Ethics of Research Considered as a Legitimate Trial

Research is by definition an attempt to grasp a reality that is not clearly represented by knowledge already acquired. We can therefore see that such research is based on the supposition that the epistemological task concerning the validity of the knowledge available has already been correctly carried out. Naturally, however, no attempt is made to call upon philosophers to confirm such a supposition. We consider that the experts of a discipline have already correctly accomplished their task while we may in fact be improperly extending their scope of competence given that a specialist who contributed to the progress of a discipline was generally only able to do so by considering it under a specific angle. It is thus to be recommended that specialists discuss together as to the usefulness of carrying out a particular piece of research – and the necessity of such discussion can undoubtedly never be sufficiently underlined. In this respect it is striking that a slogan came into use that scandalized non-scientists. It read as follows: "Anything unscientifical is unethical". If what is meant by this is that it is science that determines the validity of moral standards, then the slogan is truly scandalous. Once again, ethics goes far beyond the science to which it applies. Yet it would appear that this phrase is to be understood in a different manner and namely as follows: amongst all projects of research that claim to be of scientific interest, only those which do not usurp such a claim – in other words, those projects which can be reasonably expected to enhance the scope or reliability of scientific knowledge – should be chosen. Should a project appear to specialists to be utopian or fanciful, the experts should be entitled to set it aside. Giving free rein to pure fantasy and passion – which may be invested in other fields at their risk and peril – stands in stark contradiction with the objective of science defined as the quest for truth as validated by unquestionable criteria.

The only projects of scientific research that we should therefore accept are those that carry a definite interest for science. This represents a prerequisite. Yet is this in itself sufficient? Most certainly not. For there are certain projects that would be interesting to carry out for the advancement of science yet present such considerable danger for mankind that they should be proscribed. This is the case today of human reproductive cloning which has been rejected by all competent authorities in the field of scientific and medical research. We know, however, that these same authorities have not issued the same bans with regard to what is termed as therapeutic cloning. Even if such cloning involves the destruction of numerous embryos (or oocytes) just like the aforementioned practice, it must be admitted that the issue raised is different and yet raises grave ethical questions which have nothing to do with the technical-scientific achievement – which, as we have learnt since March 2003, was unable to be carried out amongst rhesus monkeys which are so close to the *Homo*. For, as we already stated, any form of cloning involves the destruction of a considerable number of embryos based on the presumption that one or more cloned embryos could at least develop. In the case of animal embryos, the issue failed to arouse any moral twinges of conscience. In the case of human embryos, however, the debate is quite different. May we consider human embryos as material for research? Some will say that the supernumerary embryos produced by the techniques of medically assisted procreation will in any case be destroyed if they are no longer the subject of any parental project. Could they not at least be placed at the service of scientific and medical research development? This is the main argument put forward in favor of their use, from an ethical point of view. Yet it is precisely the origin of such embryos that is not ethically innocent. The creation of a considerable number of embryos *in vitro* which are logically subject to diagnosis prior to being implanted in order to become foetuses is actually a form of eugenics that would have been considered scandalous fifty years ago. This form of mastery over life represents a grave danger for mankind whereby we become accustomed to selecting subjects that are worthy or not of human life in such a way that, in the name of this mastery, mankind may be subjected to the politico-medical projects described by Aldous Huxley in *The brave new world*, the mere mention of which – even failing their actual realisation – is enough to make one tremble. Consequently, by making use of supernumerary embryos, whose production is not considered legitimate by many moralists, in order to designate them for the production of "stem cells" which might be useful for the treatment of certain illnesses we are bestowing upon them a form of *a posteriori* legitimacy which presents enormous ethical risks. Is this not a step towards creating human embryos solely for the aims of medical and/or scientific research? Officially such suggestions are refuted, yet might we not be lead in the future to gradually accept what is banned today by dint of a remnant of respect for a "potential human being"? In view of the total metaphysical agnosticism in which our liberal societies delight, there is cause, in this respect, to exercise precaution. When we do not wish to understand the nature of what we are manipulating and yet we are aware of the effect that such manipulation has on the respect accorded to the human embryo which has become the slave to reckless projects whose success is far from being guaranteed, we would be better advised to abstain.

Does that mean that we should condemn any tentative to obtain "stem cells" which is said to be the objective of such manipulations? Naturally not. However it is known that such cells can be extracted from bone marrow and the umbilical cord. These techniques may admittedly be more difficult to carry out yet at least they avoid the ethical questions raised by the all too easy recourse to human embryos and should thus be encouraged from an ethical point of view. Whatever the case, the justification of the end does not signify the justification of the means; when the latter is more than questionable we should renounce calling upon means that are unworthy of mankind.

Consequently, in the case of bio-ethical research we should distinguish between the ends and means. There are ends which appear to be justified such as the curing of certain hereditary illnesses or of diseases linked with old age yet these ends do not justify the use of unworthy means. In the latter case, ethics does not justify the use of the easiest of the means available but only of those which do not raise grave moral and social questions.

Conclusion

We have, in this essay, focused solely on the ethical problems raised by bio-medical research since these are the most serious and the most topical. This does not mean that there are not plenty of problems in several other domains such as in the field of biotechnology in general. In both cases, the problems would be less acute if we had a better understanding of the mechanisms implemented within the framework of the manipulations that are carried out. From this point of view, the ethics of science would appear to be the prelude to the ethics of research. Yet as we have already observed, it should not be imagined that everything is clear in the field of scientific ethics. The fact that we need a code of ethics in the field of research demonstrates that we are confronted with a massive amount of ignorance, irrespective of the progress achieved, particularly within the field of genetics.

What is striking is that in face of this massive ignorance, research is being carried out so fast and furiously that the *caveat* lodged from an ethical point of view carry little weight in face of the thirst for results and the demands of the public. The fact cannot be concealed that throughout the world a line of conduct has been decided upon which makes it highly unlikely that such warnings will be heeded. How can this lack of ethical consideration in the field of research development be explained? We shall focus here on just two explanations. The first is undoubtedly the predominance of research personnel sitting on committees responsible for examining ethical questions raised within research itself. Even if we should not *a priori* doubt the sincerity of the ethical considerations of such personnel, it is impossible to imagine their total indifference with regard to the results they expect from their laboratories in this period of fierce international competition. It is moreover interesting to note that the first chairman of the French CCNE (National Advisory Committee on Ethics) set the reflections of his Committee under the aegis of two principles which he placed on the same level: respect of human beings and respect of science. What is outrageous is the idea of elevating science to the same level of dignity as human beings. We also know that science is more than capable of advancing its own interests whereas many human beings – be they real or potential – are unable to do so. A second explanation for the lack of ethical consideration is the legislation which over the last thirty years has encouraged both voluntary termination of pregnancy and medically assisted procreation. The effect of such legislation has been to devalue the traditional respect accorded to human embryos and foetuses. It has now become impossible to pass laws to protect them. Thus weakened by the principles expressed by its very own advocates, ethics finds itself doomed, in advance, to a state of legally enforced powerlessness.

What is thus to be done? Apparently, the philosopher Habermas, realising the hopelessness of the struggle against this looming eugenics, recently placed his hope in the intervention of the religious authorities. Indeed, we can only pray that the religious authorities make themselves loudly and clearly heard, as is the case in certain instances. Yet at a time when several factors are contributing towards limiting the influence of religion we cannot expect that any entreaties of a religious nature will be respectfully listened to and abided by. They would at the very least need to be seconded by public opinion. One method might be the creation of foundations that would only grant credit to research projects that are "ethically clean" in the same manner that certain banks only grant credit to "ethically clean" companies. Such institutional organisations could in time have a certain effect in so far as the public would become more aware of the consequences of research that is ethically delinquent in addition to the possibilities available for rectifying a situation that currently appears jeopardized. After the horrors that marked the 20th century – in which science and technology unfortunately played a part – the dawn of the 21st century should be accompanied by a widespread movement of ethical awakening. At a period where technology has taken on planetary proportions we are in need of an ethical policy of planetary proportions in order to make such technology more humane. Any endeavours that work towards this goal are naturally to be welcomed.

References

Agazzi, E., (1996), *Le bien, le mal et la science* ("The good, the bad and the scientific"), Paris, PUF.

Barreau, H., (1996), "Théorie générale de l'Évolution, le jugement réfléchissant et le principe anthropique" ("General theory of Evolution, reflective judgement and the anthropic principle"), *1ˢᵗ International Conference on Philosophy of Science*, Universidade de Vigo, p. 341-366.

Barreau, H., (2001), "La physique et la nature" ("Physics and nature"), *Annals of the Louis de Broglie Foundation*, Vol. 26, special edition 1/3, p. 43-53.

Schützenberger, M., (1992), "Le hasard peut-il produire la complexité du vivant?" ("Can fate produce the complexity of the living?"), *L'homme face à la science (Man in face of science)*, Paris, Critérion, p. 168-184.

Les valeurs éthiques
dans les sciences médicales

Peter KEMP

Professeur de philosophie, Copenhague
Président de la FISP

Mon propos est d'essayer de clarifier le statut des valeurs éthiques dans les sciences médicales, d'abord en montrant pourquoi elles sont inévitables et nécessaires, ensuite en réfléchissant sur le sens des valeurs, et finalement en dégageant de l'histoire de la médecine expérimentale les principes éthiques de base.

I. L'inévitable éthique

Il y a deux raisons pour repenser les valeurs éthiques dans les sciences médicales.

La première c'est le fait que la scientification de l'art médical soulève des questions sur les limites des interventions et les manières d'intervenir dans la vie du patient et celle du sujet d'expérimentations médicales. C'est ainsi que les médecins qui deviennent chercheurs ou simplement appliquent le savoir et les technologies qui sont à leur disposition doivent partager le dilemme où est mis aujourd'hui tout être humain dont le travail est devenu une science et une technologie. Il est tenu de s'interroger sur des questions que le travail scientifique soulève mais auxquelles il ne peut répondre. Ce sont les questions de savoir comment développer et appliquer le mieux possible les sciences et les technologies au service de toute la société et de toute l'humanité, et par conséquent aussi de savoir comment fixer les limites aux interventions des chercheurs et des experts dans la vie humaine. Ce sont là des questions éthiques, et on peut mettre en œuvre des études sur ce que les gens pensent et ont pensé pour répondre à ces questions, mais ces questions en elles-mêmes ne sont pas scientifiques. Elles expriment des attitudes humaines et des points de vue différents de ce qu'est l'être humain par rapport à la fois à lui-même et à la société et à la nature.

La deuxième raison pour reconsidérer les valeurs éthiques dans les sciences médicales est le fait que la scientification et la technologisation du travail des médecins soulèvent la question de savoir comment le rapport entre médecin et patient peut rester un rapport humain selon lequel le patient, aux yeux du médecin, n'est pas réduit aux organes, cellules et tissus qu'on peut traiter de manière scientifique, mais reste une personne entière dont le destin est influencé par le traitement du médecin et dont l'équilibre psychique et le courage d'être sont profondément affectés par la parole et l'attitude du médecin.

Certes, on peut se demander si le médecin dans le monde technologique d'aujourd'hui peut éviter d'observer le patient comme un pur objet scientifique ou simplement comme un système de fonctions dont le traitement doit rétablir la marche normale. N'est-ce pas même mieux pour le patient que le médecin reste un savant et un technicien aride ayant une capacité et une effectivité auxquelles nous pouvons faire confiance ?

Cependant, si nous ne pouvons pas accepter une telle attitude de la part du médecin, puisque nous ne souhaitons pas que les médecins nous traitent et traitent nos proches comme de simples appareils en panne à réparer, il s'ensuit que ni face aux patients ni dans le développement et l'application des sciences et des technologies les médecins ne peuvent éviter d'être jugés selon une dimension humaine de leur pratique. C'est une dimension qui en soi-même est préscientifique et qui soulève des questions qui concernent tout le monde et sur lesquelles d'autres ont réfléchi depuis des siècles, à savoir celle de la vie bonne.

II.   Les valeurs en général

On parle beaucoup de valeurs lorsqu'on parle de la vie bonne. Mais qu'est-ce qu'une valeur ?

Une valeur c'est ce que nous évaluons comme bon et juste dans une vie bonne. Une valeur est donc une évaluation. Espérons qu'il y a des valeurs universellement valables. C'est un espoir, non pas un savoir. Mais cela ne signifie pas que les valeurs sont subjectives au sens où il n'existerait pas de valeurs qui sont partagées par un grand nombre d'êtres humains. Dans une communauté culturelle il y a toujours des valeurs communes.

Les valeurs sont communautaires, même si elles ne sont pas universellement acceptées. Elles expriment des évaluations communes de ce qui est une vie bonne et un acte juste.

Mais qu'est-ce que le bon ? Disons que c'est la qualité de vie qui fait que la vie vaut d'être vécue. C'est une qualité de vie qu'on peut facilement détruire et qui par conséquent doit être considérée comme fragile et vulnérable. Mais c'est aussi une qualité qui est renforcée par la vie commune, par une amitié où l'autre n'est pas un simple moyen de ma satisfaction, mais est considéré pour lui-même en tant que membre de la communauté à laquelle nous appartenons tous les deux.

Ainsi la vie bonne est-elle fondamentale par rapport à l'action qui y contribue. Et l'action est juste dans la mesure où elle intensifie le bon.

On a cependant parlé du bon et du juste bien avant le concept de la valeur ne soit apparu dans notre culture européenne. Ce concept n'est pas connu, tel que nous l'utilisons aujourd'hui, dans la philosophie grecque classique. C'est un concept moderne dérivé de la théorie de l'économie politique. Ainsi Adam Smith, dans son traité sur *La richesse des nations* de 1776, développait la première théorie de la valeur économique portant sur les biens du marché ayant une valeur d'usage et une valeur d'échange. Mais aujourd'hui le concept de valeur inclut beaucoup plus que des valeurs économiques, et certains pensent même que la valeur purement économique n'est pas une vraie valeur, et en tout cas pas une valeur qui peut être première dans la vie sociale et culturelle.

C'est Émmanuel Kant qui, le premier, a transféré le concept de valeur de la théorie de l'économie politique à l'éthique, lorsque dans son petit livre sur les *Fondements de la Métaphysique des Mœurs* de 1785 il distinguait entre des valeurs relatives qu'utilise l'économie où tout peut être échangé avec tout, d'une part, et la valeur absolue de l'iné-changeable, d'autre part, que l'éthique présuppose, lorsqu'elle parle du respect pour « l'humain » ou « la loi morale » ou « la bonne volonté » dans chaque être humain qui possède la puissance de la raison.

Ainsi il n'y a qu'une seule valeur morale chez Kant – c'est l'être rai-sonnable comme être moral sans équivalent, c'est-à-dire irremplaçable. Certes, nous ne savons pas, selon Kant, s'il existe une seule personne concrète qui ne soit pas un hypocrite ou égoïste, mais nous ne savons pas non plus que des personnes de cette qualité n'existent pas. C'est pourquoi nous avons à nous respecter les uns les autres en tant qu'êtres moraux et à ne jamais traiter l'autre comme pur moyen, mais toujours aussi à le traiter comme une fin en soi. Et pour suivre Kant, nous devons admettre qu'il existe une valeur spécifiquement humaine et viser à créer une société où tous les êtres humains vivent comme une telle valeur. Il s'ensuit que la valeur est ici une capacité qui à la fois *est* et *doit être*.

Cette signification double de réalité et d'idéal est restée celle du concept de valeur après Kant quand progressivement on l'a élargie jusqu'à ce qu'elle devienne l'idée du « royaume des valeurs » (J. F. Fries en 1804) ou un « microcosme de valeurs » (H. Lotze dans son œuvre sur *Mikrokosmos* datant de 1856-1964). Plus tard, chez le philosophe danois Harald Høffding, dans son *Éthique* de 1887 et dans sa *Philosophie de la religion* de 1901, le concept de valeur est utilisé dans un sens très large couvrant tout ce qui peut nous satisfaire de même que les moyens de cette satisfaction. Tout ce qui est l'objet d'une évaluation et qui ne trouve aucune explication scientifique suffisante fut donc conçu comme valeur.

Aujourd'hui nous pouvons constater que l'élargissement du concept de valeur est poussé si loin que ce qui n'a pas de valeur n'a aucun intérêt. Le contenu du concept de valeur est devenu tellement flou que la distinction entre des valeurs essentielles et des valeurs moins importantes fait défaut dans le langage ordinaire et par conséquent les gens ne conçoivent aucun ordre de priorité des valeurs.

Tout ce qui plaît à quelqu'un est appelé valeur. Par-là le concept a aussi perdu son caractère spécifiquement éthique et nous sommes tombés dans un marais de valeurs où il est impossible de s'orienter. C'est sans doute la raison pour laquelle le concept de valeur n'est plus aujourd'hui un concept clé chez la plupart des grands moralistes comme Jürgen Habermas, Hans Jonas, Émmanuel Levinas, Paul Ricœur et autres.

S'il ne faut pas simplement renoncer à l'usage du concept de valeur, il faut au moins distinguer entre deux niveaux de valeurs :

1. Les valeurs de l'agréable. Cette conception des valeurs est certes la plus répandue, celle à laquelle les gens pensent immédiatement lorsqu'ils parlent de valeurs. Ici on suppose souvent que les gens adoptent des valeurs différentes et développent leur propre style de vie par leur valeurs personnelles. C'est à cette sorte de valeurs qu'on pense lorsqu'on prétend que les valeurs sont purement subjectives. Mais la limite de cette conception apparaît dans le fait que l'évaluation qui constitue les valeurs n'est qu'esthétique. Cette évaluation est un goût esthétique sans jugement de la validité communautaire d'une valeur, pour ne pas dire sa validité universelle. C'est pourquoi cette conception des valeurs ne peut pas être la seule.

2. La valeur absolue. Ici l'évaluation concerne la vie bonne elle-même qu'il faut juger comme une fin en soi et non pas seulement un moyen pour obtenir autre chose. Le fondement d'évaluation n'est pas le plaisir esthétique immédiat, mais une réflexion en vue d'un jugement de la manière dont on contribue le mieux à la vie bonne pour chacun. Par-là la valeur garde un caractère éthique. Et cette valeur éthique peut en certains cas entrer en conflit avec des valeurs de l'agréable et s'imposer comme supérieure à elles, quand par exemple je déteste une personne que néanmoins je dois respecter comme une fin en soi. Ou quand la société assure certains droits à un homme qui a commis un crime grave, par exemple le droit d'être défendu par un avocat et le droit de ne pas être considéré comme coupable avant d'avoir été jugé par un tribunal.

Le rapport entre les deux sortes de valeurs suppose une hiérarchie des valeurs selon laquelle il y a une valeur absolue supérieure à toutes les autres. Sans l'adoption d'une telle hiérarchie toutes les valeurs sont égales et une valeur ne peut pas être plus importante qu'une autre.

Cependant, ce n'est pas seulement l'absence d'une distinction claire entre deux niveaux de valeurs et l'absence d'une hiérarchie des valeurs qui demandent une critique si l'on veut justifier l'usage du concept de valeur dans l'éthique. Il faut aussi une critique de l'idée des faits purs qui se distinguent des valeurs.

Cette distinction est apparue dès qu'on a cru que les sciences exactes nous permettent d'avoir un accès direct à la réalité, sans interprétation, sans évaluation et sans jugement. Par cette distinction, tout ce qui concerne l'éthique et l'art serait réduit à une sorte de réalité secondaire et l'on considère que les phénomènes éthiques et esthétiques constituent un monde de valeurs indépendant. Or ce monde de valeurs était condamné à être dissous au fur et à mesure que les sciences découvriraient les faits dont elles sont des déguisements.

Mais tout change lorsqu'on découvre que c'est la distinction même entre purs faits et valeurs pures qui est erronée. Schopenhauer et Nietzsche nous apprennent qu'il n'y a pas de faits sans interprétation et pas d'interprétations sans évaluations.

Cela ne signifie pas que « tout est permis ». À l'encontre de Nietzsche, il faut dire que les faits ne sont pas n'importe quoi, mais sont constitués par l'intersubjectivité de l'expérience empirique.

III. Les valeurs dans les sciences médicales

Considérons maintenant les valeurs éthiques dans les sciences médicales. Ces valeurs se sont manifestées comme principes éthiques du souci pour le patient dans le traitement et pour le sujet dans l'expérimentation. Or je tiens ici à examiner comment ces principes sont en jeu dans l'évolution de la médecine expérimentale. Le problème de cette médecine est de savoir quelles sont les limites à respecter dans l'expérimentation pour protéger le sujet. Et les principes éthiques de protection indiquent ces limites en signalant en général ce que le médecin chercheur n'a pas le droit de faire.

Le premier principe de protection est *le respect de la dignité humaine* du fait que l'homme est irremplaçable. Nous retrouvons ce respect chez le premier grand théoricien de la médecine expérimentale sur l'homme, Claude Bernard, qui dans son *Introduction à l'étude de la médecine expérimentale*, datant de 1865 déclare qu'il « est immoral de faire sur un homme une expérience dès qu'elle est dangereuse pour lui, quoique le résultat puisse être utile aux autres » (Paris, édition Flammarion, 1984, p. 153). C'est l'idée kantienne d'être humain comme fin en soi qui est ici présupposée, mais non tant comme être rationnel que comme être vulnérable, car par rapport à l'homme il faut se soucier de ce qui « peut lui sauver la vie, le guérir ou lui procurer un avantage personnel » (*Ibid.*, p. 152). Il est vrai que ce souci de la vie corporelle vulnérable chez Bernard est lié à un paternalisme strict, convaincu comme il l'est que c'est le médecin et le médecin seul qui décide ce qu'il faut faire pour le patient ou ce qu'on peut se permettre sur un sujet d'expérimentation en bonne santé. Le médecin n'est responsable que devant ses collègues et devant sa conscience.

C'est l'insuffisance de ce paternalisme qui a fait entrer sur la scène médicale *la reconnaissance de l'autonomie* du patient et du sujet d'expérimentation comme l'autre principe de protection. Cela s'est produit à la suite d'une série de scandales en Allemagne liée aux expériences pratiquées sur des êtres humains qui n'avaient pas été informés et n'avait par conséquent pas eu la possibilité de refuser de participer à l'expérience qu'ils avaient subie. Plusieurs personnes, surtout des enfants, étaient mortes à la suite d'expérimentations faites essentiellement pour tester des vaccins.

Le dernier gouvernement de la République de Weimar a alors adressé une circulaire à tous les états sur les « directives concernant les recherches sur des sujets humains ». Cette circulaire stipulait qu'un traitement de type nouveau ne devait pas être entrepris sans « le consentement exprès et dûment éclairé de la personne concernée ou de son représentant légal ». On doit remarquer qu'il s'agit non seulement de la protection du sujet d'expérimentation, mais encore du patient dans le traitement. Et on ne permet pas que le traitement soit entrepris sans consentement éclairé, à moins qu'il ne s'agisse d'une mesure inajournable destinée à sauver la vie du patient ou à prévenir de graves risques. Lorsque plus tard, après la Seconde Guerre mondiale, certains médecins et savants seront jugés par le tribunal de Nurenberg parce qu'ils avaient pratiqué des expériences fatales sur des prisonniers, sans leur consentement, le code joint au jugement – et depuis lors connu comme le Code de Nuremberg – reprendra la demande de reconnaissance de l'autonomie des patients et des sujets d'expérimentation pour justifier les jugements.

Mais le respect de l'autonomie s'est avéré insuffisant aussi comme protection de l'être humain vulnérable, et c'est le monde médical lui-même par la voix de *l'Organisation Mondiale des Médecins* qui en 1975

faisait valoir dans la Déclaration d'Helsinki remaniée à Tokyo la nécessité d'établir des comités d'éthique pour veiller à ce qu'une personne
faisant l'objet d'une expérimentation médicale soit protégée, non seulement par le fait qu'elle a eu la possibilité de donner ou de refuser son
consentement éclairé mais aussi par le fait que l'expérimentation repose
sur un fondement scientifique solide, effectué par des personnes quali-
fiées qui par ailleurs ont évalué tous les risques et les avantages prévisi-
bles pour le sujet concerné. On peut dire que le principe de protection ici
présupposé est celui du *souci de l'intégrité vulnérable* de la personne. Et
je pense à l'intégrité parce qu'elle signifie la cohérence de vie dans le
temps et dans l'espace qui constitue l'identité de la personne qu'il faut
préserver dans l'expérimentation.

La dernière étape de l'histoire de la protection du sujet dans l'expérimentation médicale est celle de la transformation du comité d'éthique
professionnel composé de personnes du monde médical (médecins,
chercheurs, infirmières, psychologues, etc.) en un comité mixte des pro-
fessionnels et des non-professionnels représentant l'ensemble de la
société et de ses valeurs morales. Cette transformation témoigne du
besoin de maintenir ou de restaurer la confiance des citoyens en général
dans les experts médicaux et les médecins-chercheurs. Est présupposé
ici comme principe de protection *l'appel à la solidarité et à la justice*
dans les rapports entre le monde médical et le reste de la société. Les
médecins-chercheurs sont tenus d'être responsables devant la société
politique.

Les principes éthiques impliqués dans l'évolution de la médecine expérimentale sont donc ceux-ci :

1. le respect de la dignité humaine
2. la reconnaissance de l'autonomie
3. le souci de l'intégrité vulnérable
4. l'appel à la solidarité et à la justice

Or au fondement de ces principes de protection du sujet dans les
sciences médicales se trouve la valeur absolue de l'être humain irremplaçable qui en tant que tel a une dignité, exerce une autonomie et vit
une intégrité qui reçoit son sens plein dans une société solidaire et juste.

Proof as an Ethical Procedure

Valentin A. BAZHANOV

Department of Philosophy, Ulyanovsk State University

1. In the very core of rationally developing science the powerful system of argumentation lies. This system is versatile, dynamic and multi-dimensional; it influences the every cell of scientific knowledge to a degree this knowledge have been basing on the rational procedures of logical reasoning and soundness of the new knowledge. The crucial element here is the proof. In every type of argumentation we first of all deal with the proof.

The proof as a *logical* operation seems to be studied quite thoroughly. But nevertheless up to the date "the main disagreement is what may be called mathematical proof" (Kline, 1984, p. 359; see also: Epstein, Levy 1995, Weintraub, Gayer, 2001, p. 421). The new light might be shed on the nature of proof if social, ethical and psychological dimension of it are to be taken into account. What the nature of proof if it will be interpreted within the social context? Is the quest for truth the only goal of this procedure? What hidden reason may stand for the development of proof's techniques?

Perhaps, the first disciple where the above mentioned dimensions attracted attention was mathematics, although mathematical (and logical) proofs are only the special cases of universal process. In mathematics since the discovery of undecidability theorems nature and status of proof has been reconsidering (Thurston, 1994; Jaffe, 1997; Rota, 1997). Pre-Godelian paradigm of mathematics presupposed that the nature of mathematical truth manifests in its provability, as Dedekind put it: "Nothing, what provable couldn't be accepted in the science without proof" (Webb, 1980, p. IX).

Post-Godelian paradigm is basing on the account of much more complex and even discrepant nature of proof, tightly bound to social context (Bazhanov, 1991, p. 56-58). "The conception of proof didn't belong to mathematics (to mathematics belongs only its mathematical model – formal proof). It belongs to logic, linguistics and more of all to psychology" –, claims V.A. Uspensky (Uspensky, 1987, p. 139).

New philosophical norms which govern the foundation of mathematics caused important changes in the standards of logical and mathematical proofs. The new proof-norms appeared to some extent as "counter-directive" to the previous standards of mathematical rigor put upon sometimes the practical value and effectiveness. In the theory of catastrophes, for instance, proof qualification was some period surprisingly (in relation to traditional) low (Arnold, 1983, p. 10). Likely that proof qualification lowering is the result of vigorous development of some branches of mathematics where the problems are so interesting and easy to solve that rigorous considerations are put aside.

1.1. The fact that the notion of provable truth is narrower than the notion of informal truth spring out the revaluation of deductive method capabilities and resulted in the special informal logic (or often called theory of argumentation) construction.

1.2. Until recently proof was universally treated (and, by the way, continues to treat by many working mathematicians) as *impersonal* construction; meanwhile in the theory of argumentation the proof have been revealing the new dimensions, ingrained personal, subjective aspects of knowledge, the style of it presentation, the degree of belief of those, to whom the proof is addressed. To put it in another words, this theory makes emphasis on the proof not as a form of deductive knowledge, but as a form of convincing in the thesis truth, the correctness of it defender.

Although the concept of proof can't be rigorously and exhaustively defined, the nature and essence of this concept reveals in the general term within statement of persuasive intellectual construction, claim to be a proof, which can be viewed as a "persuasive reasoning, persuades us to a degree that we could persuade someone with it help" (Uspensky, 1987, p. 140). The persuasive side of the proof stressed even by those, who insist on understanding the proof as only a tool of gaining the new truths. Even scholars insisting on strictly impersonal nature of proof couldn't ignore (citing one of these scholars) that "the definite proof persuades the person and we assume it be completely valid (…) Mathematicians are engaged in self-persuasion and persuasion of others in perfectiveness of their proofs" (Perminov, 1986, p. 151).

Sharing the standpoint that the quest for new truths is an important goal of any proof, I'm prefer to claim that it belongs to another dimension of proof then those, which bounded to the reason, motive of the proof and its justification. Undoubtedly, the immediate goal, reason and justification of the proof can be distinguished with an amount of conventionality, but nevertheless the epistemological, social, axiological, teleonomical, communicational, etc. dimensions of proof are worthy to study and should came into the fore. The question of permissibility of definite arguments and means of argumentation are arises merely automatically and presuppose social and ethical aspects. We could argue even stronger: in the focus here we have to find socio-ethical content and status of the proof, sound the argumentation system and normative science space.

2. The development of more and more complex, subtle and refine methods of proof only to some extent may be explained by the desire to find more effective forms and tools of creative work in logic and mathematics: proof as a formal procedure – likely less the instrument of discovery, but much more an instrument of a sequent, consistent and justified reasoning. Proof is the disciplinary matrix of thought, its "grammar", the knowledge of which didn't make us closer to a success in reaching the outstanding scientific result. The question, hence, may be asked: what the ground and most powerful impetus for providing more and more rigorous, constructive and formalized methods of proofs?

2.1. The discovery of new statements, ideas, theorems etc. – usually is the result of a leap forward, great advance in the intellectual activity quality –, leap forward of truly being a sort of *insight*, the sudden dawn. The scholar in suchlike situation guided chiefly by its own intuitive representations, sensations, he relies on his informal, principally non-formalized experience. Perhaps, he acts under the guidance of what may be called heuristic "intuition principle".

As A. Weyl stated in "From metaphysics to mathematics": every mathematician is aware that there is nothing in the way of heuristic influence that is more fruitful than some vague similarities, dim glimmers of one theory to another, which are like "furtive endearments and inexplicable disagreements" (Weil, 1980, p. 408). Yu. I. Manin citing this thought reminds us of the metaphysics of infinitesimals – "the system of vague and hardly formulated analogies, which nevertheless played a the crucial role in the scientific discovery" (Manin, 1984, p. 47). Jeremy Gray expresses this idea in the following way: "(…) the proof is based on insights that have not yielded to expression in the form of definitions, lemmas, and proofs, but it seems clear to the author" (Gray, 1994, p. 7).

The theory, proposed by someone, could be readily accepted by person, who feels the same, to whom intuition prompted the same result, who, to put it in few words, rely on principles of co-sympathy (co-perceiveness) and co-intuition –, argues S.V. Meyen. If the insight of the idea creator immediately and always meet the co-sudden insight of contemporaries, then intuitively understandable at no time became co-intuitively understandable to anybody, then there have been no hurdles on the way of the "century-important" ideas…"However the interesting ideas from the starting point are judged by the fix claims of the full rigor and almost complete axiomatization" (Meyen, 1977, p. 418).

The proof and complex system of argumentation as a whole come into its own only after the thesis of proof gained as insight has been clarified for the ample degree.

The question arises whether the later claim contains the hidden contradiction: if the proof destined only for ordering and systematization of new knowledge, gained (at least in general terms) by another way –, the way of intellectual insight, then, perhaps, there is no vital need in the proof and argumentation, pretty complicated in its nature, at all? In this case what is the real aim and meaning of proof, what justify the stubborn efforts in improving the proof-tools, the subtle methods of argumentations, first of all in mathematics? What for instance has justified and gave impetus, creative inquiry for the proof of two Bernside hypothesis from the theory of finite groups (manifesting the existence of undecidable uneven groups), each of 500 pages – 500 journal pages! – long, and classification of finite groups 15,000 pages long?

2.2. It is not contingently novel methods of proofs have been discovering, no contingently that the knowledge, gained by insight, was never accepted by scientific community and was not estimated as *scientific* knowledge, reliable and true until it has passed the numerous "filters" of proofs, until it was reproduced by generation of scholars, until the ground of undisputable (at concrete historical context) argumentation was placed behind it. *Therefore the proof is the form of appeal to the scientific community.* It meaningful only within certain valuations, opinions, norms reasoning space, common in certain academic stratum; the proof is based on the paradigm elements. Outside this space the proof is empty, at best – is not convincing enough. We could recall the fates of numerous discoveries and ideas, being far ahead of their time, kept aloof of scientific thought flux and only later matured for the appraisal of such ideas and sometimes waiting for decades to be reinvented again. The imaginary, non-Aristotelian logic of N.A. Vasiliev is one of the examples (Bazhanov, 1990).

The definite scientific community is the carrier of concrete norms and standards of what is taken for granted, of argumentative means, ingrained in the worldview, methodological, axiological presuppositions, in the reasoning style. The comparison with the principle of relativity to the type of observation in quantum mechanics (V.A. Fock) is suitable here and gives us right to claim the suchlike principle of relativity for the argumentative (proof) means. The evaluation of perhaps any theoretical statement should include the evaluation of its proving and features of argumentation tightly bounded to the later and even capable to lose its meaning beyond the limits of argumentation.

2.3. To prove is to convince. Nevertheless the conviction not only the result but its starting point as well. The conviction is the predicate of both personal and above-personal. That's why certain reasoning might be estimated as proof only when social act of its acceptance happens, when it was approved by the leading experts in certain field.

Hence, the social and ethical nature of proof and argumentation is expressed in transfiguration of personal insight phenomenon to the phenomenon impersonal, reproduced and (at least principally) verified by any qualified member of scientific community. As V.A. Uspensky put it: "The proofs shifts from the category of individual experience to the category of collective experience. Even the notion of individual stringency (of proof. – *V.B.*) chuck away it individual tinge and gains the character of 'collective stringency'" (Uspensky, 1987, p. 147-148).

3. The logical and mathematical proof pretty often represents by itself only the concise schema of formal inference. The modern state of mathematical proof is distinct for the visible complexity of verifying its trustworthiness. Large amount of modern proofs are hardly reproduced (verified). In the cases when computers were used in the proving process, the situation even more complicated for the verifiable programs should be, as a rule, not less complex as original one. When one must verify the analytical proof she/he must reproduce the formal inference in it complete capacity. "The impression is created that in the development of mathematics the proofs loses its main feature – the feature of stringency for the proofs being longer and much more complicated. We wonder: what in such situation the proof could be as far as stringent implied by the very definition of the proof. Being longer and more complex the proof became more subjective (...). With the capacity of the proof increasing its image becomes fuzzy (...)" – claims V.A. Uspensky (Uspensky, 1987, p. 150-151).

3.1. When the scholar is proving something he takes the *responsibility* for the trustworthiness, reliability (in the limits of accepted abstractions and argumentative means) of new knowledge. The knowledge (reasoning) non-reproducible for some reasons, so to speak, unique, lies beyond the science, it immoral until proved within the scientific community standards, and thus becomes impersonal.

The process of bridging the gap between the pioneer achievements and gaining it the status of proof – is complicated and whimsical process. Dialogue is powerful tool of its ingraining to the scientific knowledge but only in the case of using by all sides of one-level (character) abstractions. But even the fulfillment of this requirement is not enough for understanding as Bohr-Einstein discussion reveals.

3.2. The sophistication of the proof implies the transition of verifying means to *indirect* considerations. Such considerations as, for example, the comparison with anybody expectations, assessment of the theory development trends, the criteria of succession, simplicity, the weight of certain scientific school or community, to which the scholar belongs, the authority of the scholar or the referee etc. In the other words the considerations of ethical and psychological character. That's why the author of the proof responsibility and his moral obligations becomes more and more important.

The external requirements, paused by scientific community, are enriched by internal and serve as a ground for internal motivation of person going something to prove. To the methodological, heuristic, paradigm regulatives added the regulative of scholar inward responsibility, his conscience. This is even more vital in the contemporary situation, marked for one is more interesting to prove own theorems rather then checking mistakes in the proof proposed by certain scientist.

The problem, described above, implies numerous social and ethical issues. One issue is well known as the *Simon syndrome*. If any analytical reasoning presupposes the text of some kind, the computer based proof often not provides the print and view of all details of computations. What the guarantee, for instance, when the 4 colors theorem was proved that the computer didn't made any fallacy (the computation lasted for 1200 hours). The computer proof in the case given is not (at least merely) reproducible, i.e. not fulfilling the vital condition for every proof.

The Simon syndrome is the instance of situation when the proof is not reproducible. Thus, the scholar who sometime have had shown good result, gained by traditional means, might turn – abandoning proof as, say, "evident" – on his previous authority. Suchlike situation – rather common in the former USSR and nowadays Russia and, likely, to some extent elsewhere – when referee gives his approval for the text he never read.

The case is that it is easier to push on with one's own research, ignore the reverse (or different) views. This leads to hampering the academic intercourse. The way for so called shadow science phenomenon is opened, the science which in fact is the imitation of science.

I hope that the present account of social and ethical aspects of proof has revealed at least some items of crucial role of moral responsibility, conscience and honesty in science.

References

Arnold, V.I., (1983), *Catastrophe Theory*. Moscow, Moscow University press, p. 80 (in Russian).

Bazhanov, V.A., (1984), *Mathematical Proof in Social Context*, in *Man, Philosophy, Culture*, Moscow, USSR Acad. of Sciences Institute of Philosophy press, p. 56-60 (in Russian).

Bazhanov, V.A., (1990), *The Fate of One Forgotten* Idea: N.A. Vasiliev and His Imaginary Logic, in "Studies in Soviet Thought", Vol. 39, No. 3-4, p. 333-341.

Bazhanov, V.A., (1991), *Science as a Self-Reflexive System*, Kazan, Kazan University press, p. 182 (in Russian).

Bazhanov, V.A., (1992), *Pre-, Post- and Non Godelian Philosophy of Mathematics*, in *First International Symposium on Godel's Theorem*, ed. Z. Wolkowski, Singapore, New Jersey, London, Hong Kong, World Scientific. p. 50-60.

Epstein, D., Levy, S., (1995), *Experimentation and Proof in Mathematics*, in "Notices of the American Mathematical Society", Vol. 42, No. 6, p. 670-674.

Gray, J. J., (1994), *Responses to "Theoretical Mathematics: Toward a Cultural Synthesis of Mathematics and Theoretical Physics"*, by A. Jaffe and F. Quinn, in Bulletin of the American Mathematical Society, Vol. 30, No. 4, p. 7-8.

Jaffe, A., (1997), *Proof and the Evolution of Mathematics*, in "Synthèse", Vol. 111, No. 2, p. 133-146.

Kline, M., (1984), *Mathematics. The Loss of Certainty*, Moscow, Mir., p. 446 (Russian translation).

Manin, Yu. I., (1984), *The new dimensions in geometry* in "Uspekhi matematicheskikh nauk [Advances of mathematical sciences]", Vol. 39, No. 6, p. 47-73 (in Russian).

Meyen, S.V., (1977), *The Principle of Co-Intuition*, in *Ways to Unknown*, Moscow, Sov. Writer, p. 402-430 (in Russian).

Perminov, V. Ya., (1986), *The Development of Proof Reliability Ideas*. Moscow, Moscow University Press, p. 240 (in Russian).

Rota, G.-C., (1997), *The Phenomenology of Mathematical Proof*, in "Synthèse", Vol. 111, No. 2, p. 183-196.

Thurston, W., (1994), *On Proof and Progress in Mathematics*, in "Notices of the American Mathematical Society", Vol. 30, p. 161-177.

Uspensky, V.A., (1987), *Seven Reflexions on the Subject of the Philosophy of Mathematics*, in *The Regularities in the Development of Mathematics*, Moscow, Nauka. p. 106-155 (in Russian).

Webb, J.C., (1980), *Mechanism, Mentalism and Metamathematics*, Dordrecht-Boston, Reidel, XII, p. 277.

Weil, A., (1980), *De la métaphysique aux mathématiques*, in Weil, A., *Œuvres scientifiques*. New York-Heidelberg-Berlin, Springer-Verlag, Vol. 2, p. 408-412.

Weintraub, E.R., Gayer, T., (2001), *Equilibrium Proofmaking*, in "Journal of the History of Economic Thought", Vol. 23 (4), p. 421-442.

The Vicious Circle Principle
and the Biological Basis of Morals

Craig DILWORTH

In discussions concerning *the vicious circle principle of human development* (the VCP),[1] the question has arisen as to its relation to human values, and to *morals* in particular. In this paper I shall consider this topic, beginning with successively more complex presentations of the vicious circle principle.

The Vicious Circle Principle

The VCP differs from the traditional Western view of human development, among other ways, in its seeing technological change as essentially a reaction to *need* rather than as a means of improving an already relatively acceptable situation.

The VCP is both easy to understand and in keeping with science and common sense. Briefly put, it says that in the case of humans *a situation of need, resulting e.g. from changed environmental conditions, sometimes leads to technological innovation, which becomes widely employed, allowing more to be taken from the environment, thereby not only alleviating that need but promoting population growth, which leads back to a situation of need.* Or, seeing as it is a matter of a *circle*, it could for example be expressed as: *population growth leads to technological innovation, which allows more to be taken from the environment, thereby promoting further population growth*; or as: *technological innovation allows more to be taken from the environment, the increase promoting population growth, which in turn creates a demand for further technological innovation.*

Thus we have a situation in which:

- Some humans experience a *need* for certain resources (paradigmatically, food);

---

[1] I present the VCP e.g. in my (2004), Appendix I, and, more thoroughly, in my book, *Too Smart for Our Own Good*, presently in preparation. One of its first presentations was in my (1994).

- a *new technology* capable of taking previously inaccessible resources from the environment is sometimes developed;
- this technology *alleviates* that *need*
- and moreover provides a *surplus*,
- which leads to *population growth*,
- the growing population eventually requiring more than the old and new technologies together can provide,
- which gives rise to *need* once again.

Here is the VCP in greater detail:

- a situation of *scarcity* leads to the experience of *need*
- which increases migration and the chance of *conflict* at the same time as it
- creates a demand for *new technology*
- which in certain cases is *developed* and then *widely employed*
- which allows previously *inaccessible resources* – renewable, non-renewable or both – to be drawn from the environment (or, in the case of war, to be taken from other people)
- *war* itself being an immediate cause of *migration due to conflict*
- the taking of resources *reducing* the quantity of *resources* remaining
- and in various ways leading to the *extinctions* of species of plants and animals
- while at the same time allowing the production of a *surplus* of goods and/or services normally or often of *lower quality* than those they are replacing
- the exploitation of new resources also underlying *migration for economic reasons*, first to areas where the new technology *is* being used, then to areas where it is *not*, taking it along
- the employment of the new technology increasing the *complexity of society*, and promoting *social stratification*
- and often increasing *work* for the lower strata, and worsening their *quality of life*
- while allowing an increase in *leisure* and/or the *consumption of luxury goods* on the part of the upper strata
- the surplus in the hands of the upper strata leading to *cultural development*: the arts, architecture, philosophy, science

- both the taking of more resources and the production of a surplus of goods and services increasing the use of *energy* (itself a re-source)
- while the existence of the surplus alters *morals, weakening internal population checks*
- and leading to *increased trade*, i.e. *economic growth*, amongst the upper strata
- which has the effect of reducing the *self-sufficiency* and thereby the *security* of the group or society
- while the increased quantity of goods and transformed energy gives rise to an increase in *polluting waste*
- at the same time as the consumption of the surplus gives rise to increased *resource consumption*
- which supports *population growth* (and *overshoot*)
- the increase in population relative to resources giving rise once again to *scarcity* and *need*.

1. Some Key Examples of Applications of the VCP

a. The Development of the Bow

Spear-technology relieved the need for food for the growing population of early *Homo Sapiens* hunter-gatherers. But hunting with spears eliminated many megafauna that served as prey. There thus arose a new need for food. Around 23,000 BP the bow was invented, perhaps in North Africa, its use gradually spreading over the world. The bow allowed smaller and more elusive fauna to be taken, which in turn allowed the total population of humans to continue to grow.

b. The Development of Horticulture and Agriculture

Overhunting together with population growth led to a situation of overpopulation and experienced need. The horticultural revolution (domestication of plants and animals) alleviated that need and provided a surplus. On the basis of that surplus the human population grew some tenfold (from about 5-10 million 10,000 BP, to ca. 80 million 5,000 BP), leading to a new situation of need. This situation was alleviated by agrarian agriculture, involving ploughing and the irrigation of monoculture crops. The world population grew about ninefold from the time of the introduction of agriculture up until the industrial revolution (i.e. from about 80 million in 5,000 BP, to 730 million in 1,750 AD).

c. The Industrial Revolution

There was an over-exploitation of wood in Britain which culminated in economic problems in the mid-18th century. Technological innovation (the steam engine) made coal available as a substitute for wood as an energy source. Between 1750 and 1860 the population of England and Wales tripled. Petroleum technology was developed (ca. 1850) meeting the needs of the larger population in Britain and elsewhere. World population continued and continues to grow, having now reached over 6 billion.

What is *vicious* about the vicious circle[2] is, most centrally, that it involves our exploiting our resource-base in a non-renewable way. Our extinguishing of prey species, and our extraction of finite resources of minerals and fossil fuels, are each irreversible. The problem of the disappearance of certain (prey) species, however, can be met by increasing the numbers of some still extant species (through animal domestication). But there is no replacement for the reserves of minerals and fossil fuels, the only remedy to their reduction being the discovery of a technology which would allow us to exploit them even more. Eventually, no matter what technology we have, the mineral resources simply won't be there. When our extraction of raw materials peaks (which in the case of oil will be in the very near future), we will find ourselves on the top of a mountain the other side of which looks bleak indeed. When resource availability begins to dwindle, a major portion of the world's inhabitants will experience even greater need than they do at present, and that need will constantly accelerate in its intensity.[3]

2. The VCP Perspective on Morals

The VCP as it has been presented above suggests that the presence of a surplus can lead to, and in fact has led to, a change in morals such that internal population checks have been weakened. Thus certain forms of behavior as may have been morally condoned in situations of scarcity, can become morally condemned in situations of surplus. If this line of reasoning is correct, it seems to imply that morals, from a biological point of view, might exist so as to keep the human population in a state of ecological equilibrium, i.e. from a systemic point of view be the manifestation of a biological homeostatic mechanism. Thus such morals as support population increase or decrease would have their roots not in

---

2 Which can also be seen as a *spiral*.

3 The circle has other vicious aspects as well, including e.g. its giving rise to constantly increasing pollution, and its weakening the human gene line as a result of the employment of modern medical techniques.

what in any sense is best for individuals, but what is best for the group or community, and thus indirectly for the species.

On the other hand, however, it may be possible to show that the same effects can be obtained by morals' stemming solely from the genetic arrangements of individuals. It is to this question of the nature of the biological basis of morals, given the vicious circle principle, that the rest of this paper is devoted.

3. Abstract vs. Concrete Biological Entities

In order to do justice to this question a number of clarifications must be made. In fact a good deal of what is to follow will consist in the making of such clarifications. First, then, a distinction should be made between abstract and concrete biological entities. Thus where genes and chromosomes, as well as cells, organs, organisms and populations, are *concrete*, such things as gene types, genotypes, karyotypes and phenotypes, as well as species, genera and orders etc., are *abstract*. More particularly, the latter are either *ordered sets* of entities, or *conceptual paradigms* of entities, the sets perhaps themselves functioning as paradigms. By a conceptual paradigm I mean the conception of a *unified* entity, the conception or the intended entity functioning as a *standard of comparison*.[4] Whether sets or paradigms, they constitute the *form* of the entities they represent, in the case of ordered sets the form being linear.

However, while such sets and paradigms are abstract, they are not *completely* abstract, as are e.g. mathematical sets. In that they are *of* real biological entities, they may at least to that extent be treated as concretely existing. Thus, for example, while noting that species are abstract, we can nevertheless say of them that they can *become extinct*, and that they constitute *biological systems*.

In the case of species this distinction between the abstract and the concrete is to be particularly noted (as many have failed to do): species are not the same things as the populations that constitute them.[5] This is supported by general intuition, manifest in our speaking, for example, of the population *of* a species.

---

[4] For more regarding the notion of conceptual paradigm, see Dilworth (2004), p. 160 & n.161 & n., 165 and 274.

[5] The conflation of species and their (total) populations – a conflation Darwin is not guilty of – has become widespread in theoretical biology. For instances of it in the context of the question of the nature of natural selection, see e.g. Hamilton (1975), Maynard Smith (1976), Ruse (1980), Hull (1981), and Dawkins (1989). For more on this point, see Dilworth (2004), p. 163-164.

4. Some Definitions

Other concepts of relevance here may also be clarified. Thus a *gene* is here understood to be an allele rather than an allele-pair; and a *gene type* a type of allele. A *phenotype* is a conceptual paradigm constituting an organism's *form* at one point in time; a *phenome* is a concrete, manifest organismic or group trait resulting from a combination of genetic, chromosomal and environmental influences on the organism or group. A *species* is a conceptual paradigm constituting the *form* of its members (organisms and groups of organisms), including their micro-states.

An organism's *genotype* is the ordered set of all of its gene types, as is determined by the genetic arrangements in its two parents' *genomes*. A genome is the set of an organism's genes as (linearly) ordered in its genotype. Thus while there may be billions of genes in an organism, the number in its genome is identical to the number of *gene loci* in its genotype – about 30-40,000 in the case of humans. And though there may be millions of entities with the characteristics of a genome in an organism, the genome itself is unique; and in this way it constitutes a conceptual paradigm as well as a set. Furthermore, each organism has its own particular genotype and genome (except in the case of identical twins). Nevertheless, parts of the genotypes of all organisms of the same species are identical, having the same gene types at the same loci in their respective genotypes. The gene types constituting these parts I shall call *constant*; other gene types, *variable*.

A genome's structure taken as a whole, however, such that it includes more than just its linear aspect, is also influenced by the organism's (and species') chromosomal structure or *karyotype*, which is here also conceived of as a conceptual paradigm.[6] This structure is determined by such things as the number of chromosomes in the species' DNA (e.g. 46 in the case of humans), the length of each type of chromosome, and the types of genes that can be incorporated at various loci in the chromosomes. The karyotypically structured groups of chromosomes common to a species, conceived of as but one such group (and thus as a paradigm), is what I shall term the species' *karyome*. Karyo-

---

[6] In being chromosomal structures, karyotypes can and do differ within a species; for example karyotypic differences exist between males and females, and are responsible for such syndromes as Down's, Turner's, and XYY in humans. The notion of karyotype intended here however is that referred to in speaking of the karyotype of the species as a whole, and might more particularly be termed the *species-specific* karyotype. Thus species are distinguished by their karyotypes. Here an advantage in conceiving of karyotypes as paradigms is that it allows us, for example, to consider people with Down's syndrome to be human, despite their karyotype diverging from the paradigm karyotype for the species.

mes are thus related to karyotypes as genomes are related to genotypes. Apart from environmental influences, the organism's phenotype is determined by the combined effects of its genome and karyome. Note that the karyome does not include the genome in that all members of a species have the same karyome while each has its own unique genome, and that the karyotype does not include the genotype, for the same reason.[7]

Note also that where genotypes and genomes may be conceived as ordered sets since they can be depicted linearly, the karyotype and the karyome, in involving e.g. the shapes of chromosomes, cannot be adequately characterized in this way. While both are abstract paradigms, neither is simply a set.

5. Biological Levels

In dealing with such entities as phenotypes, genotypes and karyotypes for example, we clearly have to do with at least two different biological levels. The level on which genes, gene types, genotypes, genomes, chromosomes and karyotypes exist is different from that on which organisms and groups of organisms exist. In fact we can see a number of such levels, such that atoms are on a lower level than genes (which themselves may be considered as molecules, being bits of the DNA molecule) and chromosomes, which are on a lower level than cells, which are on a lower level than organs, which in turn are on a lower level than organisms and groups of organisms, which may perhaps be thought of as being on a lower level that the biosphere as a whole.

This system of levels parallels the ontological hierarchy of modern science, which goes from the objects of physics to those of chemistry, to those of biology, and on to those of the social sciences.[8] The biological levels are much more complex, however, in that causal relations can go either upwards or downwards in the system, and the nature of the relations between levels may differ for different levels. For example, as regards the reciprocity of causal relations, gene types and karyotypes affect organisms, and organisms (through natural selection) affect whether gene types and karyotypes are instantiated; while as regards different kinds of relations for different levels, the influence of cells upon genes, for example, differs depending on whether the cells themselves are organisms. Not only this, but organisms affect their biophysical surroundings (the ecosphere), and at the same time are affected

---

[7]   Though this need not be the case if one were to take the terms "genome" and "genotype" in their species-specific senses, which we shall not do in the present paper.

[8]   Cf. Dilworth (2004), ch. 7.

by those surroundings, while we might say that gene types are affected "more" by the *organism's* immediate surroundings than by their own.

In what follows I shall mainly consider two of these levels: what I shall term the *micro* level, which will consist of such things as genes, chromosomes, genotypes and karyotypes; and the *macro* level, which will consist of phenomes, phenotypes, organisms and groups of organisms. The connections that exist between these levels include those between the concrete entities genes and phenomes, and the abstract entities genotypes and phenotypes on the one hand, and concrete karyomes and phenomes, and abstract karyotypes and phenotypes on the other.

The failure to clearly distinguish the micro and macro levels, such as when gene types are compared directly with groups of organisms, has resulted in a good deal of confusion in discussions concerning the nature of natural selection, a question of direct relevance to that of the biological basis of morals. There are theoretically at least five areas to be considered: the micro areas of the genetic and the chromosomal, the macro areas of the organismic and the group, and the combined area involving the species. To resolve the present issue, the relations amongst all five of these must be clarified. Thus genes should be compared with chromosomes, as well as with organisms and groups; groups should be distinguished from species, and considerations be applied to each of them separately; and the general nature of the relation between the micro and the macro should be made clear.

6. Survival of the Fittest and Natural Selection

Consideration should also be given to the notions of survival of the fittest and natural selection. As regards "natural selection", the everyday use of the term "selection" not only implies the existence of someone doing the selecting, but also that what is being selected plays a passive role in the process. While on the one hand it is clear that in nature there is no selector, making "natural selection" in this sense a metaphor, it is not immediately evident as to whether, or which, selected entities ought to be conceived of as being active (willing) or passive (merely behaving) in the selection process.

In the case of "survival of the fittest", we must consider both the notions of *survival* and *fitness*. As normally employed, the term "survival" is used with respect to organisms and groups of organisms – perhaps as well as species and such, and other uses must at least to some extent be metaphorical. As regards the term "fitness" we can say that it has the sense of *adaptability*. The fitness of those entities that survive consists in their being sufficiently well adapted to their environments.

Though on first consideration the term "survival of the fittest" may lead one to think of an active struggle between organisms, that which is closer to the expression's true meaning, viz. "survival of the better/best adapted", does not include such a connotation. Nevertheless, as in the case of "natural selection", we cannot say a priori whether what does or does not survive plays an active or passive role in the process; nor whether entities of all *types* that may be said to survive are active or passive. It goes without saying, however, that in all reasoning involving these concepts one should be awake to the possibility of the misleading influence of metaphor.

Darwin's notion of natural selection or fitness was intended by him to apply in the first hand on the macro level, such that we might possibly say that a particular organism, group of organisms, or species is *fit*, or has been *naturally selected*.[9] For Darwin, the fitness of an organism or group consisted in its ability to leave descendants; in the case of organisms, the more descendants (other things being equal), the more fit.[10] With the post-Darwinian discovery and specification of the micro level, however, the question arises as to whether the notion of natural selection should be applied to it as well, or perhaps to it exclusively. Thus we must ask just what is it that is selected in natural selection, and what it is that does the selecting.

Characterising organismic survival on the micro level, it consists of the organism's or group's leaving a gene line after itself, i.e. copies of its own genes in posterity. We can call this the organism's or group's *genetic* fitness. An organism's *individual* fitness is part of its genetic fitness and depends on the gene line it leaves after itself *through procreation and the rearing of offspring*, while its *inclusive* fitness is equivalent to its genetic fitness, and depends on those of its gene types whose continuing existence it supports in any way at all, including, for example, through its rearing siblings. (Normally the gene types in question are taken to be those which can distinguish individuals, i.e. to be variable gene types.) The gene line left by an organism through procreation and the nurturing of its offspring is the *direct* component of its genetic or inclusive fitness, while that which it leaves through such things as protecting kin that are not offspring constitutes the *indirect* component of its genetic fitness.

---

9   A number of modern writers, particularly kin-selectionists, want to see Darwin's view of natural selection as being limited to the selection of individuals. That Darwin also included groups and species is evident however from his (1859), p. 114, 126 and 127, and his (1874), e.g. p. 109, 137 and 633.

10   Cf. Darwin (1859), p. 116.

This is not all, however; organismic survival on the micro level also means the organism's or group's success in "seeing to it" that its and its species' karyotype is manifest in succeeding generations (*karyotypic fitness*). It would thus appear that while what is fit or unfit is the organism or group, what does or does not survive is *really* the organism's or group's gene types and karyotype.

Here, however, we must also answer our second question, namely what is it that "selects" in natural selection, or, in terms of fitness, what the entity in question is to be fit with respect to. I submit that in any instance of natural selection, it is the *environment* of what is being selected that does the selecting, and that to be fit is to fit into that environment. Thus, while the successful or unsuccessful replications on the micro level will influence the phenomes constituting organisms and groups on the macro level, *it is not the (intracellular) environment of the micro entities which selects*, or that a biological entity must fit, *but the (ecological) environment of the macro.*[11] Note that in the case of an organism this environment will include other members of its own species. This "selection" or adaptation in turn results in certain gene types and karyotypes either continuing to exist and to manifest themselves in certain numbers of phenomes, organisms and groups, or ceasing to exist altogether. So while the micro level influences the macro through determining its structure, the macro level influences the micro through the "selecting" of organisms or groups of organisms and thereby gene types and karyotypes. Thus with regard to selection and fitness, it is organisms (and perhaps also groups) that are selected *directly*, while gene types and karyotypes are selected only *indirectly*; and it seems to me that it just such directly-selected entities, and through them species, orders, etc., that we should say are fit or unfit. Similarly we should say that it is organisms and groups that survive or do not survive – though here we should keep in mind that it is gene types and karyotypes that have the potential to exist in unaltered form over time.

7. Replicators vs. Procreators; the "Unit of Selection"

In considerations of evolution by natural selection it is important to distinguish *perfect replicators*, which are *not actively*, but at most *behaviorally* involved in the production of *structurally identical copies* of themselves, from *procreators*, which *actively* produce *offspring* or *progeny* that are different from, though similar to, themselves (we can call both replicators and procreators *reproducers*). Replicators typically

---

[11] In this regard, see e.g. Brandon (1982), p. 136; and Villee & Dethier (1971), p. 266, 272, 275.

exist on the micro level, while procreators typically exist on the macro. In the case of sexually reproducing organisms, genes, chromosomes and karyomes are replicators; in the case of asexually reproducing organisms genomes are as well; while the organisms themselves (or, strictly speaking, *pairs* of them) are procreators.

In this way, the *forms* of genes, chromosomes and karyomes *continue to exist* through being manifest in a succession of different *concrete* (physical) materials. And we can say that *mutation* occurs when a replicator, whether it be a gene, genome or karyome, is not copied exactly. Thus mutation can either involve changes in gene type or changes in karyotype, the latter being necessary for evolution to take place. In the first case it is *intra*specific; and in the second, *inter*-specific. Natural selection or survival of the fittest *within* a species is the result of *genetic* advantages and disadvantages; natural selection or survival of the fittest *between* species is the result of *karyotypic* advantages and disadvantages.

In the case of perfect replication the copies are structurally and other than numerically identical with their templates; but less perfect ways of replicating are also possible, as in the case of sexual reproduction.[12] Thus genes normally replicate with 100 percent efficacy, while the variable parts of human genomes replicate with only 50 percent efficacy.

A word should be said here regarding Richard Dawkins' treatment of this issue.[13] First, Dawkins does not take up the notion of procreation at all, or say what he thinks organisms do given that they don't replicate; and furthermore, without argument, he takes only replicators to be potential "units of selection". On top of this, he quite misses the fact that chromosomes and karyomes also replicate.[14] And, unfortunately, he also fails to distinguish between behavior and action, taking only the latter to be potentially causal, and attributing it to genes.

As regards units of selection I would suggest that Dawkins is simply mistaken, since the units of selection are best understood as being macro entities, due to the importance of the role of the ecological environment in selection (and fitness). Thus just as we can say that individual organisms are more or less fit, we can say the same of groups of organisms, including total populations and thereby species (here we might note that when it comes to groups that constitute less than the total population of their species, relative group fitness is intra- and not inter-specific). Thus

---

[12] Cf. Dawkins (1982), p. 167.

[13] Cf. *Ibid.*, p. 162-163.

[14] A point missed by other contributors to the selection issue as well. In this regard see e.g. Hull (1981), p. 156.

a fit group or population is one that can maintain a habitat; and a fit species is one that does not become or tend to become extinct (independently of whether it evolves into one or more other fit species). As regards the replication of chromosomes etc., Dawkins might just as well have applied his reasoning concerning genes (actually, gene types) to e.g. karyotypes, in which case he would have ended up with species also being units of selection. And as regards behavior and action, by incorrectly taking only action and not mere behavior to be causal, he draws the erroneous conclusion that replicators act, when, at best, they only behave.[15]

8. Intra- vs. Inter-Specific Natural Selection and Survival of the Fittest

*Intra*species fitness involves rivalry between individuals or groups of the same species. Such rivalry in the case of adults is most often direct and involves aggression or display on the part of males in order to obtain females or territory or both.

Inter-species fitness, on the other hand, typically involves rivalry between organisms – often with similar phenotypes – of different species, and it primarily concerns the acquisition of food. Thus where *intra*species conflict between adults typically involves *procreation* and/or territory, *inter*-species conflict involves *food* (and indirectly territory). In inter-species rivalry there is normally no open conflict or even contact between the members of the respective species. Rather, in the case where one species survives and the other does not, the surviving species gradually shoulders the other out.

With regard to the relation between these two kinds of fitness it should be noted that intraspecific fitness *presupposes* inter-specific fitness: if a species becomes extinct, its members can leave no progeny.

9. Karyotype vs. Gene Type

Where on the macro level selection involves organisms and groups of organisms, on the micro level it concerns gene types and karyotypes. Thus where on the macro level the fitness of an organism consists in its ability to leave progeny, on the micro level the same phenomenon consists in the organism's ability to leave its gene types. And where on the macro level the fitness of a species consists in its continuing to be

---

[15] In this regard, cf. Lewontin (1991), p. 48: "Nor are genes self-replicating. They cannot make themselves any more than they can make a protein. Genes are made by a complex machinery of proteins that uses the genes as models for more genes".

manifest in populations, on the micro level it consists in the continuing instantiation of the species' karyotype.

To this we may add that where on the macro level an organism's leaving of progeny presupposes a population in which the progeny are left, on the micro level *the replication of a gene presupposes the existence of the karyotype in which the replication occurs*. Should the karyotype disappear, the gene types would have lost a vehicle for their continued existence – though of course the same gene types normally exist elsewhere in the gene pool of the biosphere as well, and would continue to do so. Furthermore, *the continued existence of a karyotype means the continued existence of (the vast majority of) the gene types that occupy it*. Note also the primacy of the karyotype as relative to individual gene types – if a particular gene type detracts sufficiently from the fitness of the organisms possessing it, it will disappear from the species' pool of gene types through the demise of those organisms, while the karyotype itself continues to exist through the procreation of other organisms lacking that gene type.

From this synthetic-plus-atomistic or synthetic-plus-analytic point of view,[16] we should say that the species' *karyotype* has "seen to it" that the genes for which it provides the structure are instantiated (it "reaps a harvest" of genes). The karyome is just as important as the genes that partially constitute it. The karyotype accepts or discards gene types depending on whether they see to its continued existence (if it didn't, it wouldn't exist); and genes occupy karyomes depending on whether the karyotype continues to be instantiated. Though from the point of view of genes, karyomes are only means by which gene types can continue to exist, nevertheless they are *necessary* means once adopted.

A rather important implication of the above is that, were we to advocate only the gene as the "unit of selection", we could only account for *intra*specific, genetic, mutations, and subsequent evolution *within* a species. On such a view the question of karyotypic change does not arise, and the whole side of evolution having to do with species change is left untouched.[17]

This prerequisite of the existence of the karyotype is of great importance to the issue of selection. Among other things, it means that no "preferred" genetic arrangements as would undermine the existence of the species can be admitted by the karyome/karyotype, and that the more

---

[16] Cf. the distinction between analytic and synthetic simplicity in Dilworth (2001).

[17] Cf. the kin selectionist Dawkins, who believes that "Darwinian selection does not choose among species". (1981, p. 559). One is inclined to ask: if Darwinian selection doesn't choose among species, what does? For something clearly does, otherwise some species would not survive while others become extinct.

fit organisms are naturally those whose existence supports the karyo-type's continued existence.[18]

The karyotypic's being more fundamental than the genotypic is also manifest phenotypically. Thus e.g. humans' having four limbs, five digits, particular organs, etc.; and our having a particular ontogenic development such that in the uterus we first resemble a fish embryo, then an amphibian embryo, then a reptilian embryo, and so on; and our territoriality and other basic instincts – all these are determined by our karyotype. In fact you could say that all the phenotypic traits shared by the members of a species are the result of its karyotype.[19]

Thus, contrary to everything's being explicable in terms of gene se-lection, I would suggest that virtually everything is explicable in terms of species/karyotype selection: mother's tending their infants, all forms of altruism, in fact every phenotypic trait is more strongly influenced by the organism's karyotype than by the variable part of its genotype. Even as regards the variable part, that one organism is fitter than another in the sense of being able to leave a strong gene line presupposes its being fit in the sense of being well adapted to its group, and ultimately to its species. And this is because of the existence of the species' sub-populations is necessary for it, and for its and its populations' karyotype, to persist. But being well adapted to the group does not necessarily mean, on the other hand, leaving a strong gene line. Well-adapted mother's don't benefit their own gene lines by killing the infants of other mothers. They do disservice to their own gene lines by killing their own infants, as this is best for the group and thus indirectly for the species; and mothers who did not behave in this way would be selected against. Lemmings don't commit suicide to benefit their siblings (who are also committing suicide), but in reaction to the problem of over-population for their community. And guppies don't eat their own off-spring in situations of overcrowding in order to spread their own genes, but because it supports the continuing existence of their karyotype.

Where the karyotypic determines what is basic, the variable part of the genotypic determines what is more a matter of outward appearance – what distinguishes different members of a species, such as individual organisms' specific coloring, relative size and shape, learning ability, and so on. Note at the same time however that it is less than 1 percent of the genes in the genome that are responsible for such differences; the

---

[18] Note however that in the case of speciation and the extinction of the original species, the majority of the gene types "outlive" the karyotype in continuing to be manifest in the new species.

[19] In keeping with what I have suggested in my (2004), Ch. 7, the karyotype may be considered to constitute the *real essence* of the species.

other 99 percent are of the same types and have the same loci in the genotypes of all members of the species, and thus give rise to the same phenome types in all organisms. *That* these 99 percent remain the same can be seen as a result of the operation of the karyotype. Both the genotypes and the karyotype we have are the result of our successive evolutionary ancestors' relations to the ecosphere that existed when they did with the genotypes and karyotypes that they had. It is this state of affairs that has led up to the last of their line of karyotypes mutating so as to give rise to *Homo Sapiens*.

The role played by the karyotype in evolution is also important with respect to the question of species selection. Since the karyotype essentially defines a species, and natural selection can work on the macro level such that extant karyotypes can disappear and new ones become instantiated, we obtain a further clarification of the nature of species selection: it is the ecological determination of the continuing instantiation of a karyotype.

10. The Unity of the Karyome

The considerations of the previous section suggest that the karyome constitutes a homeostatic system (and the karyotype an abstract such system) – one whose homeostasis is at least partly a result of interaction between its phenotypic manifestation (and its predecessors' phenotypic manifestations) and the environment (ecosphere). Within the karyome this homeostasis is the result of the operation of the karyotype such that, as just mentioned, variable genes for example occupy less than 1 percent of the genome. As expressed by Ernst Mayr in this context: "Most genes are tied together into balanced complexes that resist change. The fitness of genes tied up in these complexes is determined far more by the fitness of the complex as a whole than by any functional qualities of individual genes. [...] [G]enes are tied together into balanced adaptive complexes, the integrity of which is favored by natural selection".[20] Mayr refers to this state of affairs as *the unity of the genotype*. As far as unity is concerned, however, the concept of the genotype *per se*, or of the genome for that matter, includes only the idea of a linear ordering. Thus in order to employ a concept in which the unity referred to by Mayr is represented, we should suggest here that what is at issue is the unity (or integrity) of what we have termed the *karyome*.

---

[20]   Mayr (1975), p. 71 and 82.

11. Species With and Species Without Internal Population Checks

I would suggest that the unity of the karyome may be expressed in different species in different ways. In this regard it may be of interest to consider the difference between what are termed r-selected and K-selected species. r-selected species are those which in some sense ensure their continued survival through having a high rate of reproduction (whence the "r"), where the existence of K-selected ('Krowding toler-ant') species is ensured through the production of individual offspring with a relatively high likelihood of survival. Here we have evidence of karyotypic influences operating in clearly divergent ways.

All "healthy" species exist in a state of equilibrium with their environments. Among other things, this means that the total population of the species cannot at any one time be so great that it eradicates the species' food source. In the case of r-selected species this eventuality is avoided by a number of factors, one of which is that during one part of the year the populations of the species do not consume food, thereby allowing their source to recover. In the case of such species the check to population growth is completely *external*; a homeostasis is maintained between the species seen as a system and its environment seen as a system.

In the case of K-selected species, on the other hand, the situation is more complex. Members of most K-selected species consume food year round, and if their populations were to grow too large – say, due to a periodic diminution in the number of their predators – in certain cases they might well eliminate their food source, whereby the species would become extinct. Avoiding such an eventuality, K-selected species have themselves evolved so as to maintain, via their respective karyotypes, their own numbers at or below what their environment can support. Of course presumptive species of the K-selected sort which have *not* evolved in this way would become extinct. Here then we have the idea of *internal* population checks. The karyotypes of certain species have developed in such a way that they "see to it" that in situations of over-crowding members of the species e.g. cull their own numbers. This is a homeostatic mechanism existing *within* the species itself, a mechanism stemming from the species' karyome/karyotype, the existence of which is a prerequisite for the existence of the species.

12. The Biological Categorical Imperative

The manifestation of the karyotype in the form of internal population checks is also evident in the case of humans. Thus, for example, the practice of infanticide can be seen as being such a check. It is a karyotypically induced form of behavior the existence of which is supportive of the survival of the species. More than this however, as is in keeping with the vicious circle principle, in many contexts it can be seen as a *moral* act.[21] And morality more generally can itself be seen as stemming from the karyotype.[22]

From the point of view of the vicious circle principle, *morality*, or *human altruism*, might perhaps have been explicable solely in terms of variable gene types. But recognition of the important role played by karyotypes in evolution makes it natural on the VCP to say that morality is more a result of karyotypic influences. That moral behavior amongst humans should be the result of the presence of some particular "altruistic" gene type or types in the less than 1 percent of individuals' genomes that contain variable genes is not only highly doubtful against this background, but that it should be the case is also difficult to account for on the gene-selectionist view due to the high rates of population extinction it would require.[23] Much more reasonable is the view that morality is a cultural manifestation of the functioning of our common karyotype in its replication of itself, including its influence on individual genes such that e.g. 99 percent of each genotype is the same for all humans.

Our behavior, like that of the members of any species, has to be such as sufficiently to promote the survival of our species over that of individuals when the behavior of individuals is of a sort that can be detrimental to the species. Of course there is room in the population of any species for some truly species-unfriendly behavior – but such behavior can never dominate. The greater the extent of such disturbing behavior,

---

21 "[A]nthropologists have seen babies put to death, usually because the culture being studied considered it immoral or unethical to let certain kinds of infants survive. […] Among the Tapirapé Indians of Brazil, couples could raise two children of one sex, three in all. Tapirapé culture banned parents from raising more, because additional mouths would siphon resources needed by other families. The Tapirapé considered it selfish and immoral to try to keep a surplus baby. The death of the infant, who was not defined as human, was considered morally necessary for other members of the group to survive". Kottak (1994), p. 250. Cf. also Darwin (1874), p. 121: "The murder of infants has prevailed on the largest scale throughout the world, and has met with no reproach; but infanticide, especially of females, has been thought to be good for the tribe, or at least not injurious".

22 Cf. *Ibid.*, p. 123: "We have now seen that actions are regarded by savages, and were probably so regarded by primeval man, as good or bad, solely as they obviously affect the welfare of the tribe […] This conclusion agrees well with the belief that the so-called moral sense is aboriginally derived from the social instincts, for both relate at first exclusively to the community".

23 Concerning which see, e.g., Wilson (1975), p. 103, 106, 109, 113; and Hull (1981), p. 156.

and the longer it lasts, the greater the likelihood of its resulting in the species' ceasing to exist. This situation is of course very complex, raising such questions as, for example, under what circumstances rebellious behavior in a human population is or is not to the benefit of the species.

As a consequence of this then, we can say that *no long-term moral rule which might have worked against the survival of the human species would tend to persist*. This does not mean that such a rule would be impossible; but it could never be of such significance as actually to lead to the end of the species, or it would have done so or be on the way to doing so.

Given the viability of the above reasoning with regard to karyotypes, we may say that from the point of view of the vicious circle principle, *the existence of human values in general, and morality in particular, stems from the biological requirement for the species to survive*. Thus, on this view, what we *ultimately* value is, or ought to be, what maintains the existence of the species; and we may say that in the case of humans there exists a *biological categorical imperative*, namely *to behave in that way as best supports the survival of our species*.

Like Kant's categorical imperative, the biological categorical imperative is an ideal which is not always met, and the conception of which is not always correct. Thus, as regards the first point, there may exist a good deal of species-unfriendly behavior in the human population; and, as regards the second, what is thought to be species-friendly behavior, or experienced as moral behavior, may not in fact be so. In this latter regard, behavior which for example in certain conditions supports the continued existence of the species may, under different conditions, no longer provide such support: e.g. having many children when the population density is particularly low may benefit the species, while the same behavior would not be species-friendly when the population density is high.

Thus we see as a result of the considerations of this paper that the line taken on the vicious circle principle, that morality is essentially a question of what is good for the human species, can be accepted without having to be reinterpreted in terms of the propagation of individual variable gene lines. What the vicious circle principle further suggests, however, is that our conception of what is good for humankind is faulty: it is a conception that, with its belief in expansionism, *might* be correct under circumstances involving, say, the colonising of a newly discovered continent. But in the world in which we live, which is already more than filled with human beings, its effects can be nothing other than evil.

References

Brandon, R. N., (1982), "The Levels of Selection", p. 133-141 of Brandon & Burian.

Brandon, R. N. and Burian, R. M. (eds.), (1984), *Genes, Organisms, Populations: Controversies over the Units of Selection*, Cambridge and London: MIT Press, 1984.

Darwin, C., (1859), *The Origin of Species by Means of Natural Selection*, Harmondsworth, Penguin Books, 1968.

Darwin, C., (1874), *The Descent of Man*, 2nd ed. (1st ed. 1871), NY, Prometheus Books, 1998.

Dawkins, R., (1979), "Twelve Misunderstandings of Kin Selection", *Zeitschrift für Tierpsychologie* 51, 1979, p. 184-200.

Dawkins, R., (1981), "In Defense of Selfish Genes", *Philosophy* 56, 1981, p. 556-573.

Dawkins, R., (1982), "Replicators and Vehicles", p. 161-180 of Brandon & Burian.

Dawkins, R., (1989), *The Selfish Gene*, 2nd ed. (1st ed. 1976), Oxford, Oxford University Press, 1989.

Dilworth, C., (1994), "Two Perspectives on Sustainable Development", *Population and Environment* 15, 1994, p. 441-467.

Dilworth, C., (2001), "Simplicity", *Epistemologia* 24, 2001, p. 173-201.

Dilworth, C., (2004), *The Metaphysics of Science*, 2nd ed. (1st ed. 1996), Dordrecht, Kluwer, 2004.

Fisher, R. A., (1930), *The Genetical Theory of Natural Selection*, Oxford, Oxford University Press, 1999.

Hamilton, W. D., (1964), "The Genetical Evolution of Social Behavior. I and II", *Journal of Theoretical Biology* 7, 1964, p. 1-52.

Hamilton, W. D., (1975), "Innate Social Aptitudes of Man: An Approach from Evolutionary Genetics", p. 193-202 of Brandon & Burian.

Hull, D. L., (1981), "Units of Evolution: A Metaphysical Essay", p. 142-160 of Brandon & Burian.

Kottak, C. P., (1994), *Anthropology: The Exploration of Human Diversity*, 6th ed., NY, McGraw-Hill, 1994.

Lack, D., (1954), *The Natural Regulation of Animal Numbers*, Oxford, Clarendon Press, 1954.

Lewontin, R. C., (1991), *Biology as Ideology*, NY, Harper, 1991.

Lorenz, K., (1963), *On Aggression*, London, Routledge, 1966.

Mahner, M. and Kary, M., (1997), "What Exactly Are Genomes, Genotypes and Phenotypes? And What About Phenomes?" *Journal of Theoretical Biology* 186, 1997, p. 55-63.

Maynard Smith, R., (1964), "Group Selection and Kin Selection", in *Nature* 201, p. 1145-1147.

Maynard Smith, R., (1976), "Group Selection", p. 238-249 of Brandon & Burian.

Mayr, E., (1975), "The Unity of the Genotype", p. 69-84 of Brandon & Burian.

Mayr, E., (1988), *Toward a New Philosophy of Biology*, Cambridge, Mass. and London, Belknap Press, 1988.

Ruse, M., (1980), "Charles Darwin and Group Selection", p. 9-28 of Brandon & Burian.

Villee, C. A. and Dethier, V. G., (1971), *Biological Principles and Processes*, Philadelphia, W. B. Saunders Company, 1971.

Wilson, E. O., (1975), *Sociobiology: The New Synthesis*, Cambridge, Mass. & London, Belknap Press, 1975.

Wynne-Edwards, V. C., (1963), "Intergroup Selection in the Evolution of Social Systems", p. 42-51 of Brandon & Burian.

Wynne-Edwards, V. C., (1965), "Self-Regulating Systems in Populations of Animals", *Science* 147, 1965, p. 1543-1548.

Wynne-Edwards, V. C., (1986), *Evolution through Group Selection*, Oxford, Blackwell Scientific Publications, 1986.

Creation Belief and Natural Science

A Systematic Theological Approach[*]

Otto Hermann PESCH

University of Hamburg

I. The End of Contact Anxiety

"No God has made us but evolution [...]" This is the conclusion of the German journalist and expert in recent scientific developments, Dieter E. Zimmer, at the end of his 1978 report about the present state of socio-biology.[1]

The doctrine of evolution is no longer a theological problem – but belongs only to the realm of inorganic reality and that of non-human life. Christian theology, however, must insist on an immediate creation of the human rational soul through God himself, and that in the case of every individual human being. This is, at the same time, the statement of the old German Catholic dogmatist Michael Schmaus (1994) in his extensive work *The Faith of the Church* (*Der Glaube der Kirche*).[2]

Two judgments, two types of mistakes, one is inclined to say. Zimmer is still totally determined by that old type of struggle between faith and the natural sciences according to which "God" is an *alternative* paradigm to explain the origin of the universe and of human beings. At

---

[*] The following deliberations present a summary of some modest attempts, partly not yet published, to find a path through the jungle of the problem indicated in the title. I amvery grateful to my colleague and friend Eric W. Gritsch, Baltimore/USA, Emeritus Professor of Church History at Gettysburg Lutheran Seminary, and his wife Bonnie for their very helpful linguistic and stylistic revision of the manuscript; and in addition to my colleague Stuart G. Hall, Elie, Fife/UK, Vice-President of the AISR, for his assistance in the final wording.

[1] See Dieter E. Zimmer, "Die Lehre der Soziobiologen", in *Die Zeit* Nr. 40, Sept. 29, 1978, p. 33-35; Nr. 41, Oct. 6, 1978, p. 33-35. In the following footnotes, I quote only bythe name of the author, eventually by an abbreviated title. See all bibliographical information in the Appendix.

[2] See Schmaus, p. 194-216.

the other end of the extremes Schmaus wants to reorganize the front-line after one lost the running fight: evolution of the whole material, indeed living reality, is all right except the specific human reality which is inexplicable without a new specific and immediate intervention by God the Creator.

It is characteristic for both positions that they presuppose no relationship between the assertions of either the natural sciences or faith and/or theology. A divine reality is beyond discussion for the one, an atheistic interpretation of human existence is beyond discussion for the other. There is no question of any points where theological and scientific assertions may encounter one another even from different methodological ways, of course, but referring to the same reality.

This seems to be the state of late 1970s, a quarter of a century ago. On the other hand, the contact anxiety seems to have melted down in the meantime – notwithstanding certain long-distance effects in the form of the actual discussions about the reality value of "religious experience".[3] In recent years, an astonishing amount of publications have appeared about the relationship between faith and the natural sciences in general, and between theological and scientific anthropology in particular.[4] An increasing number of scholars have studied both disciplines and take the floor. The time has come for an intermediate balance and an ascertainment of the questions which should be raised. Therefore it is useful first to look back to the way we have gone.

II. A Retrospective View of Patterns and Arguments

1. From the Viewpoint of Theology

In the modern times, Christian creation-faith and theology were confronted with the famous three humiliations of the modern mind, also the religious mind: the earth is not the center of the universe (Copernicus); human beings evolved from the realm of the animals (Darwin); and he/she is no longer master in his/her own house between the "Super-Ego" and the "Id" (Freud). Faith and theology have doggedly and unsuccessfully struggled against these scientific insights. At the end they were forced to capitulate, not withstanding that final breaking of

---

[3]   See the extensive report and the evaluation in Loichinger, *Glaube*, p. 671-832.

[4]   See the bibliography in the Appendix.

the waves in the form of US-American (and occasionally also German) "creationism".[5]

This capitulation, however, needed time – basically until the middle of the 20th century. Still in the 1930s and 1940s theologians thought of faith and theology as "negative norm" for philosophy and all other sciences. It means that a scientific result is proven to be false if it is in conflict with assertions of faith and theology.[6] Example: since the age of the world is a "secondary object of the Revelation", the biblical chronology as interpreted by Thomas Aquinas must be defended against the evolution theories.[7] Another example: the official doctrine of transubstantiation guarantees that bread and wine are uniform substances no matter what the natural sciences may say. For, this doctrine forces to apply the distinction between "substance" and "accidents" with regard to bread and wine. In this sense, theologians have to develop a "dogmatic physics".[8] Later on one seriously tried to reconcile the doctrine of transubstantiation with quantum mechanics.[9]

Those attempts of a "dogmatic physics" and of corresponding philosophical statements have become obsolete, not least because of better insights into the history of dogma and its hermeneutics. Of course, theologians and faithful Christians in general presuppose their faith as being certain and raise their questions on the basis of this certainty. But the time is over when they in the name of their creation-faith felt obliged to reject radically all kinds of evolution theories. Instead of this, theologians dealing with questions of the relationship between faith and the natural sciences presuppose a fundamental compatibility with their

---

[5] With regard to Germany, see the report by Urs Willmann, "Entwürfe in Gottes Namen: Darf ein Biologe die Evolutionstheorie infrage stellen?", in *Die Zeit*, 19 (April 2003), p. 29.

[6] See the final breaking of the waves in the *Encyclical Letter Fides et Ratio*, especially Nr. 73, 76, 80-82, 86-90 (*Acta Apostolicae Sedis* 90, 1998, German translation: *Verlautbarungen des Apostolischen Stuhls* 135, ed. by Sekretariat der Deutschen Bischofskonferenz, Bonn, 1998); and in the *Motu proprio Ad tuendam fidem* (*Acta Apostolicae Sedis* 90, 1998, 457-461; German translation: *Verlautbarungen [see above]* 144, Bonn, 1998, p. 11-15) which obliges *all the faithful* to maintain even secondary assertions, including philosophical ones, which are so intimately linked with a magisterial doctrine that one could not be held without the others. This position is in tension to the surprising openminded plea for the "autonomy" of philosophical thinking in the same *Encyclical Letter* which has been justly admired by public reactions. See on this Seckler, "Vernunft und Glaube".

[7] See the article by Jakob M. Schneider.

[8] See the article by Josef Ternus; and already in advance the philosophical support in the article by Petrus Sedlmayr.

[9] See the article by Wolfgang Büchel.

assertions. In the case of an apparent conflict they first conclude that they misunderstood the *real* doctrine of their faith.

The first step to opt for such a compatibility was that theologians realized the illegitimate marriage between the conceptual and verbal expression of creation-faith and its details on the one hand and certain scientific (or better: pre-scientific) assumptions in the realm of world knowledge. It was always a painful task to dissolve this marriage because it was linked with specific attitudes of concrete spiritual and pious existence. The most famous case of such a divorce is that of Galileo who forced the Christians to give up a specific view of creation-faith and creation-spirituality which were centered in the idea of a closed picture of the world within which an almighty and loving God determined personally the course of natural events and of human history, thus guaranteeing security under the providence of a heavenly Father.[10] Mindful of this and many other capitulations in the face of scientific results which they had attacked for a long time, theologians are now extremely afraid of so called "mixed assertions" implying scientific theses because they can quickly lose their validity.

The consequence and the next step was always to distinguish the divergent ways of consideration and therefore to underline the different methods of objectifying the same reality. Thus, theologians tend basically towards a strict separation of both disciplines. They have nothing to do with one another, it is said, and this for methodological reasons. We must renounce the attempt of a synthesis because it is theoretically and practically impossible in view of the tremendous extension of knowledge both in the natural sciences and in theology. Let us create an "armistice" instead of a "synthesis", contended Karl Rahner,[11] and then look further what can be done together in the field of detailed questions, particularly where ethical consequences are at stake. But the armistice of the methods implies a description of the difference. Generally, one prefers to speak of divergent "dimensions" or "different levels". Where

---

[10]   See now the article by Francesco Beretta, who offers an exact presentation and a theological evaluation of the proceedings against Galileo. With some amusement one reads the old article by Paul Wyser: Galileo was right, but the Thomist philosophy of nature was not decisively responsable – followed by the demand to the adress of the Thomists to dissolve the wrong mixture of faith and science. This rehabilitation of Galileo, confirmed in the meantime also by the Magisterium; see Bergold, p. 246-251 – does not touch the hidden philosophical implications of Galileo's theories, particularly with regard to their reception by the scientists and philosophers in the modern times up to our days; on this viewpoint of the problem see Hattrup, p. 128-161; and, summarizing the historical conflicts and their consequences for a future dialogue, Seckler, "Schöpfung", p. 161-173; p. 182-188.

[11]   See Rawer/Rahner, p. 44 f.

these "dimensions" are named theologians consent to a statement like this: science deals with a limited part of reality, faith and theological reflection deal with reality as a whole. This is the most frequent definition of the difference.[12] Variations of this viewpoint are the function of things in relation to each other over against the meaning of things in themselves;[13] or one escapes to the contrast of "explaining" and "understanding", or of "analysis" and "interpretation", even of "science" and "thinking".[14] It is clear that such ways of contrasting do not convince natural scientists, not least because of the hidden arrogance implied in them. The attempt to overcome those simplistic confrontations is part of recent new encounters. We have to return to that.

2. From the Viewpoint of The Natural Sciences

Just as theological fundamentalism, which rejects every dialogue with evolution theories, has disappeared today, so also a kind of "scientific fundamentalism" seems to have been overcome with its judgement that theological and religious perspectives in view of the world are obsolete and replaced by scientific insights such as: "No God has made us but evolution". To be sure, sometimes it could happen that the state of the question within the natural sciences, the "consensus of research", is such that theologians can only deny it. A scientific anthropology, for instance, which had been dominated by behaviorism at the beginning of the 20th century, was not prepared to enter into dialogue with Christian theology.[15] And, another example, also can one only say No, where as philosophical result of scientific research a universal determinism of all natural proceedings, consequently an identity of nature and reality and finally the pantheistic identity of the nature and God is established, according to Spinoza's famous formula *Deus sive natura*.[16] But this time seems more and more over. It is striking that from the 1920s the ice is slowly melting. Famous scientists, beginning with Max Planck risked

---

[12] The most prominent representative: Karl Rahner; see id., in Rawer/Rahner, p. 34-45; see also, for example, Bergold, p. 107-113; Bosshard, p. 121f.; Hattrup, p. 37-42; 199.

[13] See for example Traugott Koch, p. 33-51.

[14] See for example Bergold, p. 236-240.

[15] See Pannenberg, *Anthropologie*, p. 25-32.

[16] It is well known that this was the hope of Albert Einstein. Its collapse in the consequence of the quantum mechanics appeared to Einstein as the "tragedy" of physics, and for a series of decades the admirers of Einstein expressed the big regret that they were unable to refute Bohr and Heisenberg, despite all new endeavours and new experiments. See the whole monograph by Hattrup for whom the non-identity of nature and the whole of reality, proved by the natural sciences themselves, is the red line of his entire argumentation.

the first steps towards the question of religion.[17] We may today consider these first steps as insufficient, but we have to appreciate the courage of these scientists against the background of a Christian theology which was generally dominated by distrust and was, above all, inclined to reject the results of empirical sciences altogether.[18] Moreover, it is quite important that these first steps were undertaken in a critical discussion of the statements and positions of the so-called "Logical Positivism" which had claimed to develop a universal theory of natural science.[19]

Today, it is a matter of fact that scientists – even those who "regret" the "tragedy of physics" and try to establish new forms of determinism – are strongly aware of the methodological restrictions which do not allow assertions beyond the field on which their methods of research are effective. Starting with this evidence, one can look for those points at the very end of research where the questions of science move to a philosophical and finally religious question. The natural sciences are, of course, not in a position to verify the religious answers or to falsify them. But they can opt for "compatibilities"[20] and they can help to exclude obsolete religious ideas such as the idea of a God who personally creates thunderstorms and/or friendly weather. The methodological restrictions raise rather seldom the question of an "integration" of religious convictions and/or theological theories in the framework of scientific work, be it with a positive result,[21] be it with a negative one.[22] In particular, the question, indeed the project of a compatibility, arises not so much in the field of research but rather on the level of concrete personal existence of the researcher who cannot agree to a way of life

---

[17] See the presentation of this development, not withstanding divergent nuances and evaluations, in the works of Barbour, Ganoczy, Gisel, Hattrup, Heisenberg, Hüttenbügel (ed.), p. 295-471 (articles by Udo Becker, Johannes Haas, Paul Overhage, Adolf Haas, Heimo Dolch), Jordan (Religiöse Frage), Traugott Koch, Sprockhoff, Weizsäker, Wuketits; especially significant is the collection of articles by Dürr (ed., Physik), where the famous scientists themselves formulate their options for a relationship between religion and science; see also the autobiographical excursus in Hattrup, p. 38-42.

[18] At least in continental theology. In Anglosaxon theology one showed a greater openness. See the article by Stephen Sykes in this volume.

[19] See the retrospect in Heisenberg, p. 116-130; p. 279-195. What concerns "Logical Positivism", see Pannenberg, *Wissenschaftstheorie*, p. 31-37; and Küng, *Existiert Gott?*, p. 119-128; and most recently Loichinger, *Glaube*, p. 19-43.

[20] See for example Rawer, in Rawer/Pesch, p. 71-73; Ditfurth, p. 143-150; Eigen, in Eigen/Winkler, p. 197f; Heisenberg, p. 116-131; Meurers, p. 104-115; Bernhard Philberth, *passim*; Weizsäcker, Sterne, p. 100-141.

[21] For example in Ditfurth, l.c.

[22] Extremely radically in Monod; and in all those who are not willing to say goodbye to a deterministic view of the nature; see Hattrup, p. 149-247.

which pushes him/ her into some kind of schizophrenia. To realize here the fact of a compatibility or at least non-contradiction creates a good conscience for scientists who want simultaneously stay faithful Christians.

3. Can We Go One Step Further?

In a word, the relationship between the natural sciences and creation-faith seems to be relaxed and peaceful. Nevertheless, this state of affairs cannot be the last word. Different methodological approaches and divergent interests of questioning – Yes! But renunciation of any kind of synthesis, self-limitation to a mere compatibility and/or non-contradiction – No! It is the same reality about which both the natural sciences and faith/ theology make their assertions, present their evaluations and draw their conclusions. For a theologian, the idea of a basic incompatibility is unacceptable, the statement of a mere compatibility is not sufficient. Both ways to "solve" the problem do not set faith and theology free from the suspicion of irrationality and/or poetic subjectivism. They shatter the faith in God's creation. We must go one step further and have the courage to relate scientific and theological assertions at individual points. Certainly, we must be careful in the case of the "mixed assertions" already mentioned. But that must not prevent us from the attempt to relate, even under the reservation of a later correction of the theory.[23]

To clarify what we must do I will first sketch that on which both the natural sciences and creation-theology have to insist.

III.   Essentials in the Natural Sciences and in Theology

1. What Must the Natural Sciences Insist On?

a) *The claim for unrestrained questioning.* To stress this may no longer be necessary for the natural sciences as such, but perhaps for some Christian scientists who sometimes may feel some anxiety when they could reach results which apparently cannot be integrated into their faithful convictions. But it is especially necessary to bring this emphasis

---

[23] See the powerful approach in Pannenberg, *Systematic Theology*, II, p. 77-161. Pannenberg summarizes here his deliberations since decades. See also Seckler, "Wissenschaft"; *id.*, "Schöpfung"; Loichinger, "Theologie"; *id.*, "Bewußtseins-Hirn-Problematik"; and recently in Barbour, especially p. 113-229; p. 294-348; Bergold, p. 4-26; p. 110-113; Bernhard Philberth: they all underline the necessity of a dialogue in favor of mutual enrichment of both the natural sciences and theology, particularly under the viewpoint of ethics.

to the attention of the theologians. Remember the famous "dogmatic physics" already mentioned.

b) *The claim for a theological disinterest.* Scientists do not need to synthesize their insights with theological assumptions. I am speaking of the discipline as such, not of the faithful scientists! It is the concern of theologians to raise the question of something like a "synthesis", not for the sake of the truth of their faith but for the point of reference when they – as they need do – develop theological theories. Natural scientists *can* be interested in what theologians say. But in the name of their methods – all controversies included – they are not obliged to get involved in the interdisciplinary debate. Scientific research is methodologically "a-theistic", that means – and this is *theologically* important: God does not count as a worldly factor within their experiments, patterns and statistical rules.[24]

c) *The claim for both an internal and an interdisciplinary synthesis.* For instance: a synthesis between molecular biology, biochemistry, zoology, paleontology, geology, cultural anthropology, ethology, sociology and historical research in view of the questions of the evolution of life, of the mind and of ethics. To be sure, there are few attempts to create such a synthesis. Regularly they are undertaken only by the elite of the discipline at the end of their career, and then they restrict themselves to a synthesis of only a few sciences. It is the philosopher and the theologian who mostly risks such an attempt, and as a non-expert, he/she depends totally on what they have learned by understandable presentations of scientific results beyond the scientific terms.[25] Thus, they may develop a general view of the whole, but it is always endangered by one simple detail which can arise and falsify the theological theory because it had falsified the scientific presuppositions before. Anyway, it cannot be justified that theologians too quickly limit the sciences only to a particular value of their research work whereas the theologian alone is considered competent for assertions covering the totality of the material world and human beings in it. Sometimes that may be necessary, when scientists move too quickly from particular to

---

[24] This is a criterion for all attempts to relate scientific results *immediately* to assertions concerning creation-faith. There is no possibility of a scientific demonstration of a divine Creator. See Heisenberg, p. 128; Dürr, Gott, p. 29f.; Hawkins, p. 179; most recently the two articles by Mittelstaedt from the viewpoint of science, and the two articles by Fischer and by Seckler from the viewpoint of theology.

[25] In this respect, for me as a non-expert were very helpful the publications by Barbour, Dürr, Eigen/Winkler, Hattrup, Heisenberg, Jordan, Müller, Polkinghorne; Rawer; Rees, Weckwerth, Weizsäcker, Wuketits; and the impressive analysis of the problems by Loichinger, "Bewußtseins-Hirn-Problematik".

total assertions about human beings and the universe.[26] On the other hand, it belongs to the innermost ethos of each science to reach a synthesis as far as possible. Theologians are not authorized to minimize the natural and human sciences as suppliers of special knowledge nor to take away their scientific ethos.

d) *Finally, the claim for scientific controversy within their own discipline without a theological ombudsman.* Theologians may be irritated by an ideal image of the "exact empirical sciences". But it is a matter of fact: scientists have their internal struggles. Theologians may not yield to the temptation to play the umpires and to consider the nearness or distance of a scientific hypothesis to certain theological assertions as a criterium of truth. Who guarantees protection against another change of scientific paradigm? Once as before, theologians should be prepared for the "worst" scientific results, compared with the traditional assumptions, even at the price to be forced to say only "No" for the moment.[27]

2. What Must Theology Insist On?

I forgo here to present abstract methodological principles and I explain them at once concretely in the form of a summary of Jewish-Christian creation-faith. Only one general remark is necessary. Faith, and consequently theology, deal essentially with what is strange for scientific methods such as experiments, mathematics, patterns and tests. Theology deals basically with history, a peculiar history which in various ways determines our understanding of ourselves and of the world, even the experience of rejection.[28] Already from this perspective, creation-faith and creation-theology are neither a meta-theory of natural sciences and thus dependent on the actual state of their results and paradigms nor a critical reconstruction of the Jewish-Christian tradition in the context of religious history. Faith and theology imply a specific assent to that history, theologically speaking to the Word of God heard in and out of this history. This is an understanding which permits one to question the natural sciences whether or not their knowledge and meaning reach the level of those answers which faith and theology can give with regard to human beings in the world. What should faith and theol-

---

[26] See the "atheistic confession" in Monod, p. 151; p. 156f; Knapp on the Sociobiologists; Neuner (ed.) on the contemporary US-American life sciences; or the fantastic transformation of theology into physics and *vice versa* in Tipler; see Hattrup, p. 204-209.

[27] See above II.2. with No. 5 and 16.

[28] This is precisely seen for example in Barbour, p. 195-204; and thoroughly reflected in Müller, p. 353-404. See also Schmitz-Moormann (ed.), p. 33-57; p. 76-95; and Seckler, "Schöpfung", p. 174-177.

ogy do, concerning the essentials of creation-faith beyond any biblical fundamentalism?[29]

3. The Essentials of Jewish-Christian Creation-Faith

a) *Created by God.* The world, human beings are created by God. That is, as it were, the "hardware"-assertion of Jewish-Christian faith (and not of Jewish-Christian faith alone!) about all worldly reality and human life. This assertion may need endless interpretations. Nevertheless, theological reflection cannot renounce this assertion because it focuses on the decisive propriety of a Christian appreciation of being and human life: the basic difference and thus the fundamental "overagainst", the confrontation between God and what is not God, between God and world, God and human being, God's eternity and human space and time, in a word: *God's transcendence*. God is nor the nature, and the universe is not God. The divine reality is the reality which as such is inaccessible by the "atheistic" methods of the natural sciences. There has not been found a more appropriate expression for this view of the world than "creation".

Contrary to an initial and widely spread impression the biblical expressions of creation-faith ("Thus the heavens and the earth were finished, and all their multitude", Gen 2:1; "And so man became a living being", Gen 2:7b), have nothing to do with the question of the "origin" of world and of life. This faith enters the world in a certain way. It is not a cosmogonic assertion. Biblical experts teach us that according to the Israelite way of thinking, the biblical writer expresses his understanding of the *present* situation of human beings under God in the *form* of a statement about its *beginning*. One defines the *nature* of human beings by describing their *origin*. If one wants to characterize the Canaanites as degenerate underdogs one could say that Ham, the father of Canaan, already did very obscene things (Gen 9:20-27). If one wants to state that it is good that human beings exist one could say that God himself has created them, or more exactly: has *prepared* them (*bara*). "Adam and Eve" are not a (historical) first couple but human beings in general. Theologians no longer understood this when the biblical tradition had transgressed the borderline of Semitic way of thinking and speaking. Nevertheless, already Augustine realized, without any idea of evolution-theory, that the real course of things was not in harmony with the bibli-

---

[29] For more extensive information to the following summary, both under biblical and under systematic viewpoint, see the dogmatic monographs in the Appendix: Ebeling, Gisel, Joest, Moltmann, Pannenberg, Sattler/Schneider, Schmaus – and others; but also Ganoczy and Bergold. With regard to the biblical topics I refer among others to Arenhoevel, Westermann, Berger and Steck.

cal narrative of the six days of creation. He could already develop a theory of the *rationes seminales* ("germinating principles") which God has laid into the original matter and out of which then developed the individual species of things in the empirical world.[30] Thomas Aquinas, moreover, does not contest, based on the biblical word, the temporal beginning of the world. But he states that the notion of creation would also be valid if the world had no beginning in time. In a word, Thomas distinguishes thoroughly between creation faith as an essential statement on the contingent reality and as an assertion of its beginning.[31]

"Created by God" means that the whole of reality without any exception is to be understood as to be indebted. In this sense, that being which under the perspective of the evolution-theory is an accident, human life, is in the view of faith really the "accident", that what happens by chance, unexpected, a gift. Human beings did not develop on their own. It is no longer an open question whether or not it is a good idea that human beings intervene in their own evolution. But humans have not been asked whether or not they wish to live as humans – neither individually nor in view of the whole of humankind. Being a creature means to be radically contingent, not necessary, not conditioned by the creature itself but thoroughly dependent on the source of its being. This contingency is once again enhanced through the extreme variety within the same basic structure. All human beings are able to learn every other language. And they do so under the irrefutable presupposition of a possible polygenetic development of humankind, despite the recent hypotheses of a first primitive Eve in East Africa.

b) *Under Salutary Dominion.* To be contingent does not only mean to be dependent on a non-worldly source of being and not on oneself. It also means that to be under this source of being is salutary. As the German Protestant theologian Gerhard Ebeling formulates it: to be created means to be together with God.[32] This is already the sense of the biblical creation-narratives. They do not address themselves to modern natural scientists but to mythologies in the cultures surrounding Israel. In contrast to them, the biblical God does not work as a power *within* the reality of heaven and earth but is sovereign above them. The stars, for instance, far away from being gods, become lamps which God attaches at the firmament. The monster of the ocean obeys the dividing word of

---

[30] See Augustin, *De genesi ad litteram* IX, 17,32: ed. *Corpus Scriptorum Ecclesiasticorum Latinorum* [CSEL] Vol. 28/2, Prag-Wien-Leipzig 1984; cf. Pannenberg, *Systematische Theologie*, p. 166.
[31] See Thomas Aquinas, *Summa Theologiae*, I 46-42; cf. Pesch, "Schöpfungslehre", p. 7f.; Seckler, "Schöpfung", p. 179-181.
[32] See Gerhard Ebeling, *Dogmatik*, p. 222f.; p. 226.

God. The biblical narratives are already, so to speak, a step towards "demythologization" within a mythological narrative.

But what is more important is that according to the creation myths in the world around Israel human beings are *not* well taken care of by the gods. They have to suffer on earth for their heavenly conflicts. The God of biblical faith, however, is Lord over the gods and as such is the one who grants homeland for human beings. He creates nature for human beings (creation-narrative 1), he works even as a gardener for them (creation-narrative 2: "And God planted a garden in Eden"). The creation-psalms (Ps. 8, Ps. 104!) vary the topic. Jesus underlines God's care for human beings by referring to the lilies and sparrows (Math. 6:26-30), and the Apostle Paul brings the idea of the salutary importance of the creation to the culmination by making it parallel with the awaking of the dead: "God who gives life to the dead and calls into existence that things which not exist" (Rom. 4:17). The full echo of this is the fundamental thesis which spans the whole of history of theology: God has created the world and human beings *for love*. In the earlier times, this assertion opposed all ideas about necessary "emanations" from the "one", or whatever one may call the original ground of all things. Today, this assertion is to be verified in view of the "immeasurable indifference of the universe" (Jacques Monod) as the evolution theory brings it to light to us. For the judgment of Christian faith it is clear: to exist means to be dependent. But for human beings this dependence means being gifted, being liberated, being in good care, valued and loved.

c) *"Crown of Creation"*. For the Bible and the history of Christian thought it is self-evident and beyond any doubt that human beings are at the top of all creatures, the "crown of creation". They alone – man and woman together! – are the "image of God" (Gen. 1:27). As such, they have power on the earth (Gen. 1:28), "made little lower than God" (Ps. 8:5). Adam has the world at his disposal by giving names to all beings (Gen. 2:19f.), and they resist him first when he forgets that he uses granted and indebted power instead of the power of temptation "[to] be like God" (Gen. 3:5). It must be emphasized against later influences which adulterate the original idea that being in the divine image consists, according to the biblical witness, in the fact that human beings have God-like power. This assertion, once again, does not address to modern scientists nor to modern ecologists but again to the myths of the gods. The gods cannot stand a powerful human being. The action of Prometheus is a catastrophe and must be punished with the greatest severity. The God of the Bible, however, is not afraid of human beings as competitors. Power and creative acting of human beings are to his honor. They are, as the end product, "very good".

Sometimes in the course of the history of Christian thought, one was anxious to emphasize too much the power and the activity of human beings. One was afraid that this happened at the cost of God's sovereignty. With regard to those anxieties one should state that those interpretations do the best justice to the high-spirited attitude of the biblical creation-witness which keep the perfect interrelationship of divine and human power. Accordingly, whatever human beings do comes simultaneously from God and from themselves. God's power, Thomas Aquinas declares, does not become smaller when he shares power with human beings but greater. Human beings are the "crown of creation" precisely by the fact that God communicates to them, in the language of medieval Aristotelianism, the "dignity of causality" (*dignitatem causalitatis*) [33]

d) *Bound to be in Nature*. Notwithstanding their power over the non-human creation, human beings are bound to it. Nature is the space of their lives, illuminated by the lamps at the firmament. Its rhythm of life impresses theirs. They find their nourishment in it, and they have no possibility at all to escape its conditioning necessities. Human beings hear the same mandate as the animals: be fertile, multiply (nothing was worse than this for an classical Greek mind, the enemy of his body!). They will end like the animals ("return to dust"). For, it is not yet said in Gen. 3, that death as such is the punishment of sin. In fact, Gen. 2 provides us a kind of pre-evolutionary theory. The author determines the material from which human beings take their origin: the earth!

How difficult it was sometimes to accept this "naive" biblical tension between "dust of the earth" and "crown of the creation"! This difficulty spans from gnostic spiritualism, the platonic-neoplatonic devaluation of all bodily (sexual!) reality, the partial acknowledgement in 13th-century Aristotelianism, the Renaissance and the Reformation up to German Idealism, terminating with Feuerbach and Nietzsche. Theologically judging, one must consider this ongoing tendency to deny the integration of human beings in the natural world as a way not to accept one's being as a creature, to speak frankly: as a subtle form of sin and unbelief. For human beings to be dependent on nature, is not as such a consequence of sin, according to the biblical witness. The fact that the integration into the material creation becomes a burden, is due to human self-glorification and self-dominion. Could one say that the technological overwhelming power and finally the destruction of creation is in a certain way a double sin by which human beings revenge themselves for the fact that the creation has become a burden? Anyway, it is certain that the famous phrase "Subdue the earth" (Gen. 1:28) is, according the biblical experts, totally misunderstood when it is considered as a blank

---

[33] Thomas Aquinas, *Summa Theologiae*, I 22,3 in corp.

check for an unrestrained exploitation of creation.[34] The bad term "graceless consequences" of Christianity[35] has its truth, but in a totally different sense, namely, that the Jewish-Christian creation-faith reminds the conscience how literally "graceless" the consequences are when and where human beings do not accept their existence as creatures bound to be in nature.

e) *Called to Responsibility.* The tension between the dominion over the creation and the integration in the natural world means to be called to responsibility. Human beings shall not only function according to powerful programs or according to accidental chance. They shall understand what they are doing – they shall offer names! Simultaneously, they shall cultivate their garden, as fellow creatures, among other creatures. In a word, they shall be free. This freedom, according to Christian convictions, is never a freedom of decision over against *God. Vis-à-vis* to him there is only grateful obedience and consensus, or the apparent freedom of self-dominion which is in fact slavery by egoism. Big words, of course! But they can be realized in daily spontaneous actions and reactions. Freedom of choice is granted to human beings only in those things and realities which are not God and thus cannot fulfill the unlimited human desire. Thus freedom and responsibility happen always within a given framework. With eyes sharpened by this conviction, the theologian sometimes is amused when he listens to contemporary discussions of "autonomous" ethics. They may be far away from theology – for, "theology", one thinks, means "heteronomy". Nevertheless they offer a wonderful test for the theological insight that freedom is either dependent on a given framework within which it takes its space and obeys its mandates, or freedom is a condemnation going into a vacuum of perfect indifference. In other words, freedom is either responsibility over against its transcendent source and its creatures and thus is "answer", or it abolishes itself.

f) *Held Above "Nothing".* The core of Jewish-Christian creation-faith, according to the common sense, is the assertion: God has created the universe "out of nothing" (*creatio ex nihilo*). It is evident that this assertion appears rather late in the Bible. *Both* creation-narratives presuppose an original chaos. God does not "make" creatures and human beings, he "prepares" them. From whence the original chaos comes, is no question for the Bible, also not – a strange parallel! – for the evolution-theories which do not ask what was before the Big Bang. The Second Book of Maccabees (later than 160 B.C.) formulates this idea (7:28). But the youngest Book of the Old Testament and the Apocrypha,

---

[34] See especially the articles by Klaus Koch and by Lohfink.

[35] See Carl Amery, *Das Ende der Vorsehung*; cf. Pannenberg, *Anthropologie*, p. 71-76.

the Book of Wisdom (between 80 and 30 B.C.) only suggests this idea (11:25) but can also formulate along the lines of the ancient imagination (11:17; 19:6). In any case, the idea of a creation out of nothing is offered only in the Greek parts of the Old Testament.

But in earliest Christianity the idea is self-evident, already in the sense of 2 Maccabees. We quoted already Rom. 4:17. In John 1:3 and Col. 1:15-7 the idea is combined with the confession of Christ as Mediator of creation. To sum up: creation means total reduction of all being to God, the result of a kind of "transcendental reduction" from the reality of the covenant.

The idea of a creation out of nothing must not be misunderstood as if the "nothing" was also a kind of material. It does not only hint at the temporal beginning of the universe either. The idea of a creation out of nothing will not transform the creation-faith into an assertion of the origin of the cosmos. Just like the evolution-theories, faith has no knowledge about what was "before"; it cannot be reconstructed.

The idea of a creation out of nothing only makes sense when it, just by its paradox, expresses the existence of creatures together with God. It is similar to what we have said about the contingency of the "accidental" existence of human beings in theological perspective. Or, to use risky words: faith sees the accidental character of life as an empirical sign, an empirical hint of the character of life as divine gift.

Moreover, the idea of a creation out of nothing makes a very special point today: outside of God, things and humans are literally nothing. Seen from the side of human beings, God is literally the absolute necessity for human beings. Of course, the need not to be able to be is a logical impossibility. But this logical impossibility becomes a daily experience in the fatal or willingly produced phenomena of annihilation and of a "being unto death". The talk about being "held above nothing" has a tremendous reference to reality, be it answered by faith or not. Above all, the logical contradiction just mentioned is once again the assertion of that faithful conviction that it really would be a *need* not to be, namely of the conviction that God *loves* human beings and is willing to be together with them in a creative way. In a word, that human life, despite all bad experiences, is "very good".

IV. A New Problem Between Creation Faith and the Natural Sciences?

1. The Decisive Point

No alternative cosmogony, trustworthiness of being, power in cooperation with God, interdependence between human beings and natural world, responsibility for the world inasmuch it is at their disposal, "creation out of nothing" as "creation against nothing" – all that had brought peace between creation-faith and the natural sciences, be it by simple non-contradiction between faith and scientific research, or by the divorce of the illegitimate marriage between faith and a specific astronomic or physical notion which has become out of date. The question of how the universe has begun, be it answered or not, belongs to the field of scientific research, not to theology. The natural sciences are and must be free from any theological prejudice. Surely, this freedom was attained with blood and tears in the struggle against Christian theology and the Church authorities. But the results are to be welcomed: the de-deification and de-demonization of the world. Christian theology today can accept this exit from the old controversies without embarrassment, as it simultaneously guards against the permanent danger that creation faith may not be linked with specific scientific theories of the process of the universe, as well as with some mythological ideas which serve as expression of faith still in the Bible. On the other hand, it is only by the natural sciences that theology can learn to make the distinction between creation-faith and creation myth or creation-idea.

But why a *new* problem? If "creation" means reality as a whole existing together with God and is therefore trustworthy, then this position stays and falls with the uniqueness of human beings in the world, a uniqueness which is more than the singularity of an accident or a mistake which evolution will not repeat.[36] If this uniqueness falls then the reality as a whole can no longer be trustworthy. In other words, if human beings were indeed nothing but an unhappy accident of evolution, what confidence does evolution as such earn when it produces such an accident? Thus the notion of creation moves once again to the question: when did human beings begin as human beings? Or in the old language, when did God create human beings? The importance of this question becomes clear when we reflect on the question *how* the uniqueness of human being has become a problem.

---

[36] This remains valid also under the presupposition of multiverses, a presupposition which actually appears not very probable; see Rees, p. 168-191.

The problem was first put on the agenda by Pierre Teilhard de Chardin who, based on his paleontological research, in the field of theology took seriously the insights of the sciences and the evolution-theory, that the human spirit is also a result of evolution. More exactly, it is a result of that fundamental tendency of the evolution to increase interiorization and complexity, that is: to increase consciousness into self-consciousness of humans who therefore (and that is the all decisive turning point of evolution) put them into a position to "criticize" evolution and to determine partly its future direction. In Teilhard de Chardin this idea is still integrated in a general faith in God's plan for evolution. God has communicated this tendency to self-transcendence the culmination of which is human existence and acting.

This position is radicalized – as far as I can see without being an expert – by Jacques Monod's book "Le hasard et la nécessité".[37] This book is explicitly written against Teilhard de Chardin's theological vision of a "plan" as an inner law of evolution. The atheist Monod argues that evolution is fortuitous, and he proves that by bio-chemical arguments. Thus even the human race is a product of chance, a rather risky product of accident. Not only have theologians such as André Dumas, Helmut Thielicke, Hans Küng and, as former physicist, Dieter Hattrup, reacted against Monod, but also natural scientists like Paul Lüth and particularly Manfred Eigen have written against Monod. We cannot deal here with the details. But all objections, which I share, do not change anything with regard to the presuppositions, namely principally two insights which are partly proved by experiments:

a. The transition from "dead" chemical processes to the first "living" single cell took intermediate steps. There was no new beginning of a higher creative quality as vitalism declared which Michael Schmaus still referred to.[38]

b. Within this transition and within the evolution in general, the "chance" plays an important (Eigen) if not decisive (Monod) role. But this "chance" or "accident" is steered by statistical rules; Eigen calls them "natural laws". But statistics are a matter of subjective observation. The "rules of the game" according to Eigen cannot imply assertions about how these processes present themselves from a higher perspective than that of a human observer, for instance from that of a divine creator. But anyway, it remains true that human beings are from their own point of view a product of chance, an episode, even a mistake of evolution. "Big bang" and "Big Soup"["*Ur-Suppe*"] presupposed,

---

[37] See this and the following titles in the Appendix.

[38] See No. 2.

that the cosmic evolution and, at least on our earth, the evolution of life to that of the "intellectual" and "rational" human being takes place without any external intervention, so to speak by itself, open to description only according to these "rules of the game" mentioned above. Seen from a traditional philosophical and theological standpoint, it seems that present-day natural sciences are inclined to think or better: are convinced, "that according to them the old ontological principle is no longer acceptable, following which a cause must contain at least as much of reality and power of being as its effect, in order to be really and adequately the cause of its effect" (Karl Rahner).[39] It does not help to go back to the old idea of a "virtual" implication of the effect in the power of the cause and to transfer this idea to the "rules of the game" of evolution.[40] "Chance" and "rules of the game" are no ontological "causes" but descriptive patterns in relation to certain scientific procedures to gain knowledge. Then scientists may have no problems with the idea of a "spiritual background" of evolution which may lie "in the steering of the process or within the ingenious structural design of the atoms" (Karl Rawer).[41] But this is already the statement of the scientist as a believer. The scientist as scientist must give up all hope to make evident such a "spiritual background" since the quantum mechanics have brought to light for us the total indeterminism of the subatomic processes.[42]

2. The Question of Freedom

All this is valid both for the non-human creation and for human beings. Theology could be satisfied if one could agree with the idea, perhaps not of a "plan", but of an ability to self-organisation and self-transcendence towards the next step of evolution – an ability invested by God in the nature of matter. The specific problem of the creation of human beings comes to light first when we ask what human freedom means. How is it to be understood in the framework of evolution, and does at least this freedom require a *specific* activity of God, such as an "intervention"?

Indeed, the natural sciences have brightened all material presuppositions of human free acting. Human actions happen on the basis of a biochemical information-system. Specific chemical micro-elements arouse specific actions. As far as I can see, the scientist by his/her own

---

[39] See Rawer/Rahner, p. 58f.

[40] It seems that Küng, p. 712f., is inclined to think so.

[41] See Rawer/Rahner, p. 32.

[42] See Mittelstaedt from the scientific standpoint, and Hattrup, *passim*, from the theological standpoint, but based on the same radical evaluation of the quantum mechanics; see also Loichinger, "Bewußtseins-Hirn-Problematik", p. 136-144.

methods cannot decide whether or not within this system these micro-elements are determined or not determined and thus determine themselves or grant freedom. For, as already said, the "rules" are only statistical, not causal. Thus human freedom is not excluded but reintegrated into the biological information-system and bound to its conditions.

Thus the question arises – and not only for theologians! – whether or not human freedom in principle can be explained by arguments from the natural sciences. Is freedom *identical* with that indeterminacy of the micro elements? Here the spirits separate.[43] Some scientists are convinced that this field of indeterminacy breaks up the chain of causes in such a way that we are in a position to accept an intervention of a God without a *sacrificium intellectus*, without an intellectual dishonesty.[44] Other scientists reject those ideas. A third group pleads for a modification of those rules which are established for non-living systems. For, the natural sciences ignore, due to their methods, all specialities which are characteristic for intelligent beings. Therefore a regress to scientific deliberations to explain the free will and its physical consequences is neither necessary nor helpful and also not threatening. Only if, with Max Planck or Bernulf Kanitscheider and recent American neo-naturalism, we stick to a strong deterministic causal coherence of all processes, freedom would be not only not explained by science but unmasked as illusion.[45]

What have theologians to say to all this? Surely, they are not the ombudsmen between the scientific theories and/or hypotheses.[46] But they also have to insist on the clarified essentials of their creation-faith. This probably opens the eyes for certain dilemmas within the scientific theories and evaluations. First, the idea of a causal chain which not even God can break up must be unacceptable for theologians; the possibility of a "miracle" is unavoidable as a borderline-assertion of God's deity, even if we do not really look for a "miracle".[47] On the other hand, the idea of a direct divine intervention within this "broken" chain is problematic for the theologian, because God would then be a wordy and natural factor among all others. In addition, the theologian has to take into consideration the analogy between divine and human freedom.

---

[43] See the summarizing report and references in Rawer/Pesch, p. 90f.

[44] See for example Pascual Jordan, also Karl Rawer himself, in Rawer/Pesch, p. 71f.

[45] See the titles in the Appendix.

[46] See above, III. 1. d).

[47] By the way, the *biblical* notion of "miracle" does not mean a breaking up of a natural causal chain but an unexpected surprising event which a faithful conviction "reads" as a hint to and an expression of God's power and love. See Weissmahr/Knoch and Pannenberg, "Miracle".

Thus the question over-against the theories of the natural sciences runs like this: *either* human freedom is *nothing more* than what the micro biological facts leave open. In this case, there is *no freedom in God*. Consequently there is no free and even controlling encounter between God and the free human being. God's "free acting" would be not more than a metaphor, just as when we call God a "lion".[48] *Or* freedom is *more and something else* than micro biological indeterminacy. In this case, freedom is compatible with scientific data, but not explicable by scientific means. It would be a misunderstanding to consider scientific results as explication or even as evidence of freedom.

The decision is evident for a theologian. And this with regard to God and with regard to human beings. Not to think of God as free is not to think of him as God. And to imagine God as a hidden secret within the phenomena of indeterminacy in natural processes is to imagine him as a factor of the world and thus as part of the world. And with regard to human beings, the indeterminate micro-processes in the brain cannot be all of freedom because human beings *know* these micro-biological controlling elements, and they *know* once more *that* they know them. In a word, human beings are *subjects* over against the scientific self-objectivations. They can keep distance from them, they can willingly inaugurate them, can stop them, can keep distance also from their results. In a word, they remain subjects in all scientific procedures because they are the "beings of transcendence" (*"Wesen der Transzendenz"*, Karl Rahner). If the sciences would be in a position to explain human freedom, they ought to explain this subjectivity and self-transcendence by scientific retracing within the micro-biological processes in the brain. And even then the human subject would at once be aware of that.

Thus it must be concluded that human freedom is a fundamentally other reality than only a property of those natural and material presuppositions with their indeterminacy, not withstanding that without these material presuppositions no free action of humans can happen.

We have now reached the point where the systematic theological approach to the relationship between creation-faith and the natural sciences is at stake.

3. God Has Created Freedom for Religious Experience

The problem of freedom is placed at the same point where in former times the question of the transition from "dead" to "living" matter was situated as point of reference, and in very ancient times the question of

---

[48] Cf. Thomas Aquinas, *Summa Theologiae*, I 13,3.

the temporal beginning of the universe. In one way or another, the natural sciences are faced with the problem and simultaneously with the limits on their ability to solve it by scientific means. Theology, on the other hand, on the basis of the presupposition that faith seizes reality, is faced to the problem of how to interpret freedom in harmony with the irrefutable results of the natural sciences. Scientists are not obliged to take further steps in order to integrate theological assertions into their own research work. Theology however, is not obliged to develop an alternative theory in competition to the natural sciences. At least one can agree from both sides, that there is non-contradiction, even an open compatibility in which both sides may have their advantages, particularly under the viewpoint of practical consequences.

But is this the end of the story? Is it not possible to take another step forward – a step together? It is a matter of fact, that evolution has produced a being which is subject over-against its producer; keeping distance from it; even able to intervene in it, probably with disastrous consequences; in a word, a *free* being. Thus we have to conclude that evolution has the potential to join such a free being who transcends all evolutionary determinism. That is not a philosophical or theological but already a scientific statement, be it explicable by scientific means or not. One can describe the astronomic, physical, chemical and finally biological presuppositions which must be granted at least on this speck of dust – "earth" –, so that such a being can arise. I have learned that this inner potential of evolution is called the "anthropic principle" of evolution.[49] Obviously, this principle is only helpful in its so-called "weak" version, focussing upon the *potential*, not in its "strong" version, asserting a *teleology* of the evolution towards human beings, which is speculation beyond scientific methods. But in its "weak" version it is true and valid also under the presupposition of Monod's and Eigen's theses of humans as an accidental result of evolution and of Mittelstadt's thesis of the universal validity of the quantum mechanics. Even if objectively non-determined and only "controlled" by to statistical "rules", the evolution must contain the inner potential of such a crazy accident called *Homo Sapiens*.

What is highly important in the context of our topic, is the fact that this free being raises the *religious* question, the question of *God the Creator*. Human beings id and do this frequently in insufficient and inadequate, even superstitious ways. But they do it from time immemorial, whereas a consistent atheistic interpretation of the world is not older than 250 years.

---

[49] See Barbour, p. 286-289; Weckwerth; Berger, p. 49f. ; Pannenberg, *Systematic Theology*, p. 93ff.

Where else, if not here, is the common point of reference, the place of encounter of creation-faith and the natural sciences, at least in a common *question?* The religious *answer*, faith in God the Creator cannot be forced, if, as it is said, the act of human freedom cannot be totally explained by scientific means. But *when* performed, this faith creates tasks for theological reflection. Before we move from here to concluding deliberations, we should briefly interrupt our reflection and insert a short remark on the notion of that faith, more exactly: on the specific peculiarity ob the act of believing.

4. A Short Excursus on the Notion of Faith

According to the "worst case law", the theologian will indeed appreciate all sympathetic attempts of his/her colleagues to open up the God question at the end of their research work, be it on the line of the idea of a divine intervention within the micro-cosmic structures of the material world, be it by questions beyond the "Big Bang", or be it in the framework of the theory of the "anthropic principle" in a teleological sense. Nevertheless he/she will agree to those scientists who underline that this type of a God question is not a meaningful scientific question, not only because it cannot be answered by scientific means, but rather because all these "indeterminisms" are an *objective* reality and not the distinctive mark of a subjective incapability which could be solved by reduction to a higher transcendent power. In fact, it is the "worst case" scenario.

The important point, however, is that a Jewish-Christian theology cannot be interested at all in those "places" reserved for "God" within the structures of the physical world. Strictly speaking, scientists should not ask for the relationship between the natural sciences and (Jewish-Christian) theology but between the sciences and the God idea. For, supposing that the scientists of the first group come successfully to a positive answer to the God question at the end of their research, at least in the sense that the God question is a legitimate but unanswerable question, even then "God" comes on the stage as a factor of physical processes and thus himself as a worldly reality. The theologian however, as already mentioned, has to insist on the absolute transcendence of the God in whom he/she believes. This transcendent reality of Godf of which the theologian is speaking and which nevertheless is related to the whole of the physical reality without being touchable in it, cannot be seized except by faith. What is frequently expressed in unconsidered formulations seems to be obvious: namely that to believe is a subjective decision and as such irrational, not accessible to arguments. To be sure, faith is an act of the subject and in this sense obviously subjective. However, faith claims that it is not its own work to constitute its "object", God, but to perceive him. If this is really knowledge, then a knowledge of a totally different kind compared with the sciences. All authors dealing with the relationship between faith and sciences underline this difference, what consequences they may ever draw from this fact. Thus the question focuses as follows: is there a kind of knowledge of reality beyond all scientific procedures and methods and nevertheless explicable by arguments, even demonstrated as plausible?

The fundamental difficulty results from the fact that faith is an act without any analogy. It is not intuitive knowledge of a person as it is typical for personal love, for, the loved person does not encounter to me in an empirical way. Nor it is knowledge by representation, since the act by which I perceive the trustworthiness of the person through whom I am represented in knowing does not precede the act of faith, it coincides with it. Faith is the total act of the self-commitment of the person to confidence concerning life and death against the suspicion of absurdity. This happens, however, not by trusting in a personal or *supra*-personal divine reality which empirically encounters me but trusting in a word which becomes audible for me, in thousands of refractions and adulterations, out of history, a very peculiar history. I can allege many good arguments in favor of trusting in this word. But never can I commute these arguments into an intellectual constraint. It is only insofar that one can call faith a "decision". In fact, this "decision" happens rather seldom in the form of a sudden "jerk" in one moment. Mostly it will take place unfolded into countless single occurrences at the end of which I may say, alluding to a wonderful word of the famous German poetess Gertud von Le Fort: "I did not decide, I found myself decided". Nevertheless, it is legitimated, abstracting and summarizing, to call this process of faith a "free decision". It is precisely therefore that I feel: here is the point of contact with the natural sciences. The sciences are not in a position to explain this strange possibility of that fortuitous and accidental human being because this possibility is no longer a meaningful scientific question. But they must acknowledge that this question is really in the world and one moves to another field of questioning by dealing with it. And moreover, one has to realize that a theology reflecting on the act of faith is concerned just with it, and the same is already the case with a philosophy which asks for the reason why such a question is possible.

That means in view of the continuation of our deliberations: all I have to say right now is said from the perspective of faith searching the point of contact with the assured results of the natural and human sciences. Since the question is of two different types of knowledge, all I have to say must be said in the form of analogy, that is to say: using the same words, but in another sense and nevertheless claiming to seize reality which as such can only perceived in this analogous way.[50] It is a matter of the sciences whether or not this does help them to win a further perspective for evaluating precisely at the end of their research work. Theological reflection, on the other hand, is preserved from any arrogant claim of a "higher" insight by the tradition of "negative" or "apophatic" theology to which I come back at the end of my deliberations. From here we can enter concluding systematic reflections, which argue now on the basis of cognitive power of faith as described.

V. Creation Faith and the Natural Sciences

1. *Being Human Together with God*

The first task which theology has to undertake is to give an account of what "creation" of human beings means after the end of any "vitalism" and "creationism". Under the risk of being misunderstood I summarize it in some theses which cannot be explained here in detail.[51]

a) *Creation of human beings – of the human race – is identical with the creation of human freedom and its capability of raising the religious question.* One could also say, that it is identical with the creation of the ability to believe – no less! In the literal sense of the word: God is the freedom of human beings.

b) *Creation of human freedom is identical with the beginning of communication between God's own subjectivity and personality and that of humans,* or in other words, *the human "spirit" is granted participation in God's Spirit so that God creates the free human spirit precisely through granting this participation.* This double thesis shares ground with the natural and human sciences. On the other hand it joins the oldest biblical tradition of the God who has made human beings "in his image" (Gen. 1:27) and "participants of the divine nature" (2 Peter 1:4).

c) *The beginning of the communication between God and human beings and thus the creation of the human spirit must indeed be understood as an independent and irreducible act from the side of divine freedom.* Not in the sense of the old (and new) creationism following which God "infuses" the rational soul when the body is prepared for it.

---

50 Is it a misunderstanding when I am afraid that in Pannenberg, *Systematic theology*, p. 96-138; and in Hattrup, p. 248-270, this law of analogy is underexposed?

51 More extensive in Rawer/Pesch, p. 90-104; Pesch, "Gott – die Freiheit", p. 104-114. See also Ganoczy, *Suche*, p. 271-288; Karl Philberth, who argues on a similar line. I also enjoy to join without a previous discussion the partly converging, partly parallel argumentation in Loichinger, "Bewußtseins-Hirn-Problematik".

But one must not be afraid of a final *appearance* of "creationism" inasmuch as this communication is not possible on *every* stage of evolution but only in that stage where the hominid is prepared, whenever that may be. And it is no contradiction that in this process the spirit as well as the religious conscience continues under the conditions of evolution. From the human side, this divine communication appears as the process of humanization. Human sciences merge here with research into religious history and finally into biblical history and the history of Jewish-Christian theology.

d) *This is a first approach to understanding the mutual relationship between divine and human free acting.* The "spirit" as participation in God's own Spirit is essentially linked to the body and its evolution, and simultaneously, as "spirit", it is unlimitedly opened up towards God as the unique fulfilling and perfect goal of human existence. Since no particular limited worldly thing can fulfill this ontological openness of the human mind, human beings have free choice. In this sense, as already said,[52] all human acting is simultaneously totally from God and totally from the human performer. Divine and human acting do not take place in competition, as crucial controversies in the history of Christian theology have suggested. However, Jewish-Christian creation-faith insists that faith, on the one hand, *judges* human freedom, namely that it is *granted* freedom through communication with God. On the other hand, creation-faith *guides* human freedom towards its essential goal in God – and turns it back to it when and where it was or is diverted towards an ungodly "autonomy".

e) *Human spirit as participation of the divine Spirit is inextinguishable.* Its extinction would mean that God revokes his vocation which He has literally promised through communicating with the accidental result of evolution. Thus creation-faith joins human eschatological hope. Far away from old theological struggles whether or not immortality is an essential claim of human beings or an unmerited new creation, far away also from old controversies about nature and grace, in the context of an encounter between faith and sciences one can only affirm that God's promise of community with humans is irrevocable. And if it is grace, then it is the grace of beginning. When God awakes the dead, he finishes his work of creation. And that human beings will be raised from the dead, does not happen on the line of evolution, not more than the abro-

---

[52] See above III. 2. c).

gation of the law of the "survival of the fittest" and the mandate of love.[53]

We could and should now extend these theses further into the field of systematic theology and into that of practical, that is to say, ethical consequences, not to forget the consequences in the field of what one can call a "creation spirituality"! It cannot be done here.[54] Instead I conclude with some general remarks about future requests within the relationship between theology and natural sciences.

2. Creation-Faith and the Natural Sciences in Dialogue

To emphasize again: the time of an "alternative", of competition, of mutual exclusion between faith and science is over. Just imagine that theology – the theologians! – no longer evaluate their assertions as immediate scientific arguments, and that scientists keep in mind the proprieties and limits of their methods. Nevertheless, the unhappy historical legacy of old inadequate controversies has long-distance effects which still frequently appear in some mutual embarrassments. Theologians are inclined to suppose and to reject encroachments. Scientists have difficulties in taking seriously theological statements at the end of their research.[55]

a) It is not superfluous to request from both sides a greater amount of unaffectedness. The more theologians leave behind all hidden arrogance of yesterday and demonstrate their basic openness to all new results of scientific research, the more this dialogue can be demanded also from the side of the natural scientists. This openness is rather easy for theologians since they themselves apply certain scientific methods in their own research fields: the historical disciplines, for example, use physical and chemical procedures to secure the written and/or non-written sources; systematic and practical disciplines use methods of verification and falsification, statistics, even demoscopic (population) polls, etc. There is place for partnership and solidarity in the incorruptible search for truth.

---

53   About coherence and difference of creation-faith and eschatological hope see Pannenberg, *Systematic Theology*, p. 163-202; Ganoczy, *Suche*, p. 283-288; and Seckler, "Schöpfung", p. 175f.

54   See my attempts mentioned in No. 51. On the ethical consequences see especially Ganoczy, Moltmann, Müller, Ratz, and under biblical viewpoint Klaus Koch and Lohfink.

55   Sometimes only old scientists at the end of their career can have the courage to enter into a dialogue with theologians. Younger scientists have no fear to make statements about theological matters without talking to any theologian. As an example of the necessity and fruitfullness of the dialogue see especially the monographs by Bergold, Ganoczy, Gisel, Müller, Polkinghouse and Weizsäcker.

b) The natural sciences within their own methods have their own ideal of making totality-assertions. Faith and theology unavoidably *interpret* realities which are first of all known by other approaches. Consequently, the faithful interpretation, the "theological theory", *cannot* be true where it contradicts scientific results which are irrefutably proved in their own field. Remember the unsuccessful struggle against the three "humiliations" of the modern mind. Such a capitulation should not happen again. After all, theologians are also in a position to compete about an interpretation of reality as a whole and to raise questions, as: how certain is a new scientific theory? What interest propels the research? What is the scientific state of a theory? What is its "if-then"-structure?[56] Above all, where do scientific notions come from? From where, for example, does science take the notion of "life"? Obviously out of daily experience. The code words are always a second order business. When natural scientists consider the single cell a "living substance" in opposition to a simple molecule of DNA, and not only as a new variation of a chemical process, then the notion of life obviously comes from former theories of what "living" means, theories which the new theory is just going to refute! Thus the question of the origin of the ideas is quite justified.

And this in general! What strikes a novice is the "anthropomorphic language" within some disciplines dealing with the micro- or macro-cosmic problems. One benefits from some analogies. It is better understandable for novices, when, for example, molecules and cells communicate information, differentiate, make projects and execute them, translate, test, accept or reject, read galley proofs and behave themselves like the members of a Max-Planck-Institute![57] Nevertheless, these "analogies" come from general pre-scientific human experiences which, properly speaking, are inadequate.

c) Under those circumstances, it is not a sign of arrogance but the unrenounceable perspective of faith and theology when we must declare, that creation-faith is principally not dependent on the sciences for its self-expression. For, creation-faith existed long before the rise of the natural sciences, and it needs for its self-expression nothing more than the daily experience of reality and language which also scientists use outside their scientific research and its code words.[58]

---

[56] A competent example of such penetrating questions is the book by Hattrup, especially p. 179-247.

[57] See the consequent parallelism between moleculs and games resp. players in Eigen/Winkler!

[58] See the energetic vote in Traugott Koch, p. 44-49.

d) The most important service of the natural sciences for creation-faith consists in their *comment* on what creation-faith confesses as God's "very good" work. Evolution-theories teach us what a world it is which in daily language is described in Gen. 1 as a world in progress. Astronomic research shows us what a universe it is within which our planetary system is (until now) not yet devoured by "black holes" but preserved for perhaps accidental but privileged beings in order to grant them a chance to live and to come to know God. In view of the dark enigmas of this work, such as catastrophes, violence and suffering, the sciences can listen to an answer which transcend their comment inasmuch the sciences by their very nature have no answer to the question of theodicy and to the question of the future at all.[59] Methodological borderlines become unimportant over against this commenting function. In this regard, Christian believers and theologians cannot desire and promote enough such commentaries on their faith provided by the natural sciences. The borderline is only reached where the methods of their research or its application threaten what they want to research. Thus the natural sciences can stimulate admiration and appreciation for that reality which creation-faith confesses to be "very good". Faithful scientists find frequently more fervent words about this reality than theologians.

e) In the context of this commenting function it is not an illegitimate "theologization of scientific facts" when God's presence is also linked with concrete details of a scientific explication of the world. We have to resist both to the misunderstanding of God and his acting as a factor on the level of natural processes, and to attempts to de-realize God through a too radical separation from the worldly reality. Surely, pantheistic tendencies are a permanent danger at the borderline between faith and the natural sciences. The "over-against" between Creator and creature must remain clear. But even the fear of pantheism has its limits. The transcendence of God must not under-expose his immanence. If the potential of the religious question is an inner potential of evolution, then the transcendent God, who shares his spirit with human beings making them spirited subjects and partners in dialogue by faith, must be seen as the inner mystery of all reality, notwithstanding the unique "overgainst" which he keeps with the "crown of creation".[60]

The sum it all up: the best relationship between creation-faith/ creation-theology and natural sciences is: *a great mutual curiosity.*

---

[59] See Bayer, p. 387-389; Hattrup p. 184-188; p. 275-283.

[60] In this respect, after all the attempts mentioned in No. 50 are stimulating, not withstanding the law of analogy.

The summary of the summary is well formulated by two statements made over a distance of 2,500 years. The first is biblical: "What is man that you are mindful of him, and the son of man that you care for him?" (Ps. 8:5). This question hints not only at the *way* of creation-faith which *asks* for God's thought about human beings. In the form of a rhetoric question it implies the answer. Viewed in this way, we must vary the question and ask: "What is the hominid, this accident of evolution, that you are mindful of him, look upon him, talk to him and call him 'very good' and make him thus a 'living being'?" (Gen. 2:7)?

The other statement is a quotation of Simone Weil which I discovered by chance and which follows so adequately the line of "apophatic (negative) theology": "I am totally certain that there is a God, inasmuch I am totally certain that my love [I add: my freedom] is no illusion. I am totally certain that there is no God inasmuch I am totally certain that nothing real resembles that which I can imagine when I pronounce this word, for I cannot form an idea of God [...] This God that we can neither imagine nor define is for us an emptiness. But this emptiness is more for us than every abundance".[61]

References

(only publications quoted or mentioned above)

Carl Amery, *Das Ende der Vorsehung: Die gnadenlosen Folgen des Christentums*, Reinbek near Hamburg, 1972.

Evandro Agazzi/Jan Faye (eds.), *The Problem of the Unity of Science: Proceedings of the Annual Meeting of the International Academy of the Philosophy of Science*, Copenhagen-Aarhus, Denmark, 31 May-3 June 2000, New Jersey-London, 2001.

Diego Arenhoevel, *Die Ur-Geschiehte: Genesis 1-11*, Stuttgart, 1970.

Ian G. Barbour, *Wissenschaft und Glaube: Historische und zeitgenössische Aspekte*, Göttingen, 2003 (American: Religion and Science, San Francisco, 1998).

Oswald Bayer, "Unangepaßte Wissenschaft: Zum Verhältnis von Glauben und Wissen", in *Evangelische Kommentare*, 20 (1987), p. 384-389.

Francesco Beretta, "Katholische Kirche und moderne Naturwissenschaft von Galilei bis Darwin: Die Voraussetzungen einer konfliktbeladenen Begegnung", in Mariano Delgado/Guido Vergauwen (eds.), *Glaube und Vernunft-Theologie und Philosophie: Aspekte ihrer Wechselbeziehung in Geschichte und Gegenwart*, Fribourg, 2004.

Klaus Berger, *Wer bestimmt unser Leben? Schicksal – Zufall – Fügung*, Gütersloh, 2002.

---

[61] Simone Weil, Vol. I of *Schwerkraft und Gnade*, München, 1952, p. 332, quoted according to Karl-Dieter Ulke, "Das Wirkliche und die Imagination", in *Orientierung*, Nr.13/14, 15./31 Juli 2003, p. 155.

Ralph Bergold, *Der Glaube vor dem Anspruch der Wissenschaft: Der Dialog zwischen Naturwissenschaft und Theologie am Beispiel von Schöpfungsglaube und Evolutionstheorie*, Frankfurt am Main-Bern, 1991.

Stefan Niklaus Bosshard, "Evolution und Schöpfung", in *Christlicher Glaube in moderner Gesellschaft: Enzyklopädische Bibliothek in 30 Teilbänden*, Franz Böckle, Franz-Xaver Kaufmann, Karl Rahner, Bernhard Welte (eds.), Vol. 3. Freiburg im Breisgau, 1981, p. 90-127.

Wolfgang Büchel, "Quantenphysik und naturphilosophischer Substanzbegriff", in *Scholastik 33* (1958), p. 161-185.

Hoimar von Ditfurth, *Wir sind nicht nur von dieser Welt: Naturwissenschaft, Religion und die Zukunft des Menschen*. Hamburg, [3]1982, München, 1984.

André Dumas, "Geschichte und Kosmos", in *Neues Glaubensbuch: Der gemeinsame christliche Glaube*, Johannes Feiner and Lukas Vischer (eds.), Freiburg i. Br., 1973, [19]1994, p. 423-445 (English Translation: The Common Catechism, London-New York N.Y., 1975, p. 408-433; Italian Translation: *Nuovo libro della fede: La fede comune dei cristiani*, Brescia, [2]1990, p. 377-396).

Hans-Peter Dürr (ed.), *Physik und Transzendenz: Die großen Physiker unseres Jahrhunderts und ihre Begegnung mit dem Wunderbaren*. Bern-München-Wien [4]1987 (Pocket-Book 1990) [quoted: Physik], *Id.* (ed.) *Gott, der Mensch und die Wissenschaft* [documented discussion], Augsburg, 1997 [Gott].

Gerhard Ebeling, *Dogmatik des christlichen Glaubens*, (Vol. I) Tübingen, 1979, p. 262-333.

Manfred Eigen, Ruthild Winkler, *Das Spiel: Naturgesetze steuern den Zufall*, München, [3]1979.

Johannes Fischer, "Ungeklärte Fragen im Dialog zwischen Glaube und Naturwissenschaft", in *Freiburger Zeitschrift für Philosophie und Theologie*, 37 (1990), p. 441-464 [Fragen].

Id., "Kann die Theologie der naturwissenschaftlichen Vernunft die Welt als Schöpfung verständlich machen?", in *Freiburger Zeitschrift* (see above), 41 (1994), p. 491-514 [Theologie].

Alexandre Ganoczy, *Suche nach Gott auf den Wegen der Natur: Theologie, Mystik, Naturwissenschaften – ein kritischer Versuch*, Düsseldorf, 1992, [Suche].

Id., *Chaos – Zufall – Schöpfungsglaube: Die Chaostheorie als Herausforderung der Theologie*, Mainz, 1995, [Chaos].

Pierre Gisel, *La Création*, Genève, 1987, p. 177-210.

Id., *La création du monde: Discours religieux, discours scientifiques, discours de foi*, Genève, 1999.

Id., "La vision du monde comme création. Quelle pertinence aujourd'hui", in *Revue Connaître: Association foi et culture scientifique*, No. 18, juillet 2003.

Dieter Hattrup, *Einstein und der würfelnde Gott: An den Grenzen des Wissens in Naturwissenschaft und Theologie*, Freiburg im Breisgau, [3]2001.

Stephan W. Hawking, *Eine kurze Geschichte der Zeit: Die Suche nach der Urkraft des Universums*, Reinbek near Hamburg, 1988 (English: *A Brief History of Time*, 1988).

Werner Heisenberg, *Der Teil und das Ganze: Gespräche im Umkreis der Atomphysik,* München, 1969, [5]1981.

Johannes Hüttenbügel (ed.), *Gott – Mensch – Universum: Der Christ vor den Fragen der Zeit,* Graz-Wien-Köln, 1974, p. 295-471.

Wilfried Joest, *Dogmatik,* (Vol. I), Göttingen, [3]1989, p. 169-178.

Pascual Jordan, *Der Naturwissenschaftler vor der religiösen Frage,* Oldenburg, Hamburg, [6]1972.

Id., *Schöpfung und Geheimnis: Antworten aus naturwissenschaftlicher Sicht,* Oldenburg-Hamburg, 1970.

Andreas Knapp, "Soziobiologie und christliche Moral", in *Internationale Katholische Zeitschrift* 17 (1988), p. 227-241.

Klaus Koch, "Gestaltet die Erde, doch heget das Leben: Einige Klarstellungen zum dominium terrae in Genesis 1", in *Wenn nicht jetzt, wann dann?* Festschrift für Hans-Joachim Kraus, Göttingen, 1984, p. 23-36.

Traugott Koch, *Das göttliche Gesetz der Natur. Zur Geschichte des neuzeitlichen Naturverständnisses und zu einer gegenwärtigen Lehre von der Schöpfung,* Zürich, 1991.

Hans Küng, *Existiert Gott? Antwort auf die Gottesfrage der Neuzeit,* München, 1978, Pocket-Book, 1981.

Norbert Lohfink, "Wachstum: Die Priesterschrift und die Grenzen des Wachstums", in *Id., Unsere großen Wörter: Das Alte Testament zu Themen dieser Jahre,* Freiburg im Breisgau, 1977, p. 156-171.

Alexander Loichinger, *Ist der Glaube vernünftig?: Zur Frage nach der Rationalität in Philosophie und Theologie,* Neuried near Munich, 1999, [Glaube].

Id., "Theologie und Naturwissenschaft: Eine Grundbestimmung", in *Theologie und Glaube* 92 (2002), p. 195-208, [Theologie].

Id., "Bewußtseins-Hirn-Problematik und Theologie", in Wolfgang Winhard (ed.), *Froh in gemeinsamer Hoffnung: Festschrift für Abt Gregor Zasche,* St. Ottilien near Munich, 2002, p. 111-152 [Bewußtseins-Hirn-Problematik].

Paul Lüth, *Der Mensch ist kein Zufall: Umrisse einer modernen Anthropologie,* Stuttgart, 1981.

Joseph Meurers, *Metaphysik und Naturwissenschaft: Eine philosophische Studie über naturwissenschaftliche Problemkreise der Gegenwart,* Darmstadt, 1976.

Peter Mittelstaedt, "What if Quantum Mechanics is Universally Valid?", in Agazzi/Faye (eds.), *The Problem of the Unity of Science* (see above), p. 177-188.

Id., "On possible relations between physics and theology", in Winfried Löffler/Paul Weingartner (eds.), *Proceedings of the 26th Wittgenstein-Symposium* (2003), Wien, 2004.

Jürgen Moltmann, *Gott in der Schöpfung: Ökologische Schöpfungslehre,* München, [4]1993.

Jacques Monod, *Le hasard et la nécessité.* Paris, 1970 (German translation: *Zufall und Notwendigkeit. Philosophische Fragen der modernen Biologie,* München, 1971, Pocket-Book, [4]1979).

Simon Conway Morris, "The Paradoxes of Evolution: Inevitable Humans in a lonely Universe?", in *Borderlands. A Journal of Theology and Education*, Issue 2, Summer 2003, p. 6-9.

A.M. Klaus Müller, *Die präparierte Zeit. Der Mensch in der Kriese seiner eigenen Zielsetzungen*, Stuttgart, [2]1973.

Peter Neuner (ed.), *Naturalisierung des Geistes-Sprachlosigkeit der Theologie? Die Mind-Brain-Debatte und das christliche Menschenbild*, Freiburg i. Br., 2003.

Wolfhart Pannenberg, *Wissenschaftstheorie und Theologie*, Frankfurt am Main, 1973 (English translation: *Theology and Philosophy of Science*, Philadelphia, 1975) [Wissenschaftstheorie].

Id., *Anthropologie in theologischer Perspektive*, Göttingen, 1983 [Anthropologie].

Id., "Gott und die Natur", *Theologie und Philosophie*, 58 (1983), p. 481-500.

Id., *Systematische Theologie*, (Vol. II). Göttingen, 1991, p. 96-188 [Systematische Theologie].

Id., "The Concept of 'Miracle'", in *Zygon* 37 (2002), p. 759-762 [Miracle].

Otto Hermann Pesch, *Frei sein aus Gnade: Theologische Anthropologie. Freiburg im Breisgau*, 1983 (Italian translation: *Liberi per gracia: Antropologia teologica*, Brescia, 1988).

Id., "Gott – die Freiheit des Menschen: Theologische Anthropologie zwischen Seelenlehre und Evolutionstheorien", in *Id.*, *Dogmatik im Fragment: Gesammelte Studien*, Mainz, 1987, p. 89-114 [Gott – die Freiheit].

Id., "Schöpfungslehre und Schöpfungsperspektive in der Theologie des Thomas von Aquin", in *Kerygma und Dogma*, 49 (2003), p. 2-23 [Schöpfungslehre].

Id., "Glaube – Erfahrung – Theologie: Einblick in einen ökumenischen Diskussionsstand – Eckdaten einer Klärung", in *Freiburger Zeitschrift für Philosophie und Theologie* 50 (2003), p. 5-49 [Glaube].

Bernhard Philberth, *Offenbarung*, Plumpton NSW/BAC, Australia, 1994.

Karl Philberth, *Geschaffen zur Freiheit*, Plumpton NSW/BAC, Australia, [2]1998.

John Polkinghorne, *An Gott glauben im Zeitalter der Naturwissenschaften: Die Theologie eines Physikers*, Gütersloh, 2000.

Erhard Ratz, *Der interdisziplinäre Dialog: Die gemeinsame Verantwortung von Theologie und Naturwissenschaften*, München, 1997.

Karl Rawer/Karl Rahner, "Weltall – Erde – Mensch". In *Christlicher Glaube in moderner Gesellschaft* (see above), Vol. 3, Freiburg im Breisgau, 1981, p. 9-33 (Rawer); p. 34-82 (Rahner); p. 82-85 (Bibliography).

Karl Rawer/Otto Hermann Pesch, "Kausalität – Zufall – Vorsehung", in *Christlicher Glaube in moderner Gesellschaft* (see above), Vol. 4, Freiburg im Breisgau, 1982, p. 50-73 (Rawer); p. 74-113 (Pesch); p. 113-119 (Bibliography).

Martin Rees, *Das Rätsel unseres Universums: Hatte Gott eine Wahl?*, München, 2003.

Dorothea Sattler/Theodor Schneider, "Schöpfungslehre", in Theodor Schneider (ed.), *Handbuch der Dogmatik*, (Vol. I), Düsseldorf, 1992, p. 120-238.

Michael Schmaus, *Der Glaube der Kirche*, (Vol. III), St. Ottilien near Munich, 1979, p. 194-216.

Karl Schmitz-Moormann (ed.), *Schöpfung und Evolution: Neue Ansätze zum Dialog zwischen Naturwissenschften und Theologie*, Düsseldorf, 1992.

Jakob M. Schneider, "Theologisches und Geologisches zur Lehre über das Alter der Menschheit", in *Divus Thomas* 5 (1927), p. 295-326.

Max Seckler, "Der christliche Glaube und die Wissenschaft: Überlegungen zu den Dimensionen eines keineswegs sinnlosen Konflikts", in *Theologische Quartalschrift* 170 (1990), p. 1-9 [Wissenschaft].

Id., "Was heißt eigentlich 'Schöpfung'? Zugleich ein Beitrag zum Dialog zwischen Theologie und Naturwissenschaft", in *Theologische Quartalschrift* 177 (1997), p. 161-188 [Schöpfung].

Id., "Vernunft und Glaube, Philosophie und Theologie. Der innovative Beitrag der Enzyklika 'Fides et ratio'" vom 14. September 1998 zur Theologischen Erkenntnislehre, in *Theologische Quartalschrift* 184 (2004).

Petrus Sedlmayer, "Die Lehre des hl. Thomas von den accidentia sine subiecto remanentia – untersucht auf ihren Einklang mit der aristotelischen Philosophie", in *Dibvus Thomas* 12 (1934), p. 315-326.

Harald von Sprockhoff, *Naturwissenschaft und christlicher Glaube – ein Widerspruch?*, Darmstadt, 1992.

Odil Hannes Steck, *Die Herkunft des Menschen*, Zürich, 1983.

Pierre Teilhard de Chardin, *Die Zukunft des Menschen*, Olten-Freiburg im Breisgau, 1963.

Id., *Das Auftreten des Menschen*, Olten-Freiburg im Breisgau, 1964.

Josef Ternus, "'Dogmatische Physik' in der Lehre vom Altarssakrament", in *Stimmen der Zeit* 132 (1937), p. 220-230.

Helmut Thielicke, *Mensch sein – Mensch werden: Entwurf einer christlichen Anthropologie*, München, 1976.

Frank J. Tipler, *Die Physik der Unsterblichkeit: Moderne Kosmologie, Gott und die Auferstehung der Toten.* München, 1994.

Joachim Track, "Naturwissenschaften und Theologie", *Kerygma und Dogma*, 21 (1975), p. 99-119.

Gerd Weckwerth, "Religionsprinzip des Kosmos: Die Evolutionstheorie und das Handeln Gottes", in *Herder Korrespondenz* 57 (2003), p. 207-212.

Bela Weissmar/Otto Knoch, "Natürliche Phänomene und Wunder", in *Christlicher Glaube* (see above, Rawer/Rahner), Vol. 4, Freiburg im Breisgau, 1982, p. 121-148.

Carl Friedrich von Weizsäcker, *Schöpfung und Weltentstehung: Die Geschichte zweier Begriffe* (*Die Tragweite der Wissenschaft* I), Stuttgart, 1964 [Schöpfung].

Id., *Die Sterne sind glühende Gaskugeln und Gott ist gegenwärtig: Über Religion und Naturwissenschaft*, Freiburg im Breisgau, 1992.

Claus Westermann, *Genesis*, (Vol. I), Neukirchen-Vluyn, 1974.

Id., *Genesis* 1-11. Darmstadt, [5]1993.

Franz M. Wuketits, *Evolutionstheorien. Historische Voraussetzungen, Positionen, Kritik*, Darmstadt, 1988.

Religion and Psychology of Values
"Universals" and Changes

Vassilis SAROGLOU

Université catholique de Louvain
Faculty of psychology and educational sciences
Center for psychology of religion

Introduction

The idea that values hold a privileged place within religious and spiritual life is a traditional conception. Nevertheless, this common general idea may be examined through a variety of disciplinary approaches. What is meant exactly by "privileged place"? The fact that religion is supposed to promote values in general? Or some values more than others and some even not at all? Or that it mainly promotes values that are in correspondence with what is considered important and socially desirable because it is assumed to contribute to individual well-being and social cohesion? In this text, an effort will be made to integrate this question into the psychology of values by reviewing the psychological studies that have investigated how individual religiosity in general and some religious dimensions in particular are associated with the importance attributed to a series of values as they are structured within Schwartz's (1992) model of values. This theoretical model, dominating today's psychology of values, has been empirically validated in more than 60 countries from the five continents.

Religion and Values: Which Direction of Causality?

If a link exists between religiosity and values, nothing can be automatically assumed with regard to the direction of the causality. A common theoretical hypothesis is that religions – as large sets combining cognitions and beliefs, ethics and specific rules, ritual and practices, communities and specific experiences – have an impact on the importance attributed to various types of values by some people as a consequence of their religious affiliation or identity, internalization of religious discourse, emotional religious experiences, or identification with specific religious and spiritual models.

The other hypothesis of a reverse (possibly complementary) causality is not to be excluded. In terms of individual differences, it is likely that some people (more than others, controlling for all other elements), by their individual characteristics, i.e. personality, education, socialization, show specific tendencies for some values, and consequently are more inclined to look for socio-ideological frameworks (beliefs, world views, sets of traditions, communities, spiritualities, moral codes) that are in resonance with, provide support to, or amplify these values. Some studies indicate that the second hypothesis of an individual predisposition for some values has an empirical foundation. On the one hand, individual differences in the degree of importance attributed to values reflect differences in personality traits to an important extent (Bilsky & Schwartz, 1994; Roccas *et al.*, 2002), the latter being known to partially originate in genetics (Plomin & Caspi, 1999). On the other hand, genetic differences seem to some extent to predict individual differences in religiosity, both in religious affiliation and specific religious dimensions (D'Onofrio *et al.*, 1999). This effect could be understood as a translation of genetics into individual differences in personality dispositions.

Another theoretical hypothesis is that if something specific characterizes the link between religiousness and values, this could be the willingness for coherence and integration across values. Such a perspective is inspired by the integrative character of religion in general, whose main characteristic may be the fact that it encompasses many components, i.e. emotions, ritual, moral rules, beliefs, and community, into a coherent and harmonious whole (Hinde, 1999). We will treat this question in an indirect way: are there values that share some similarities and can constitute a subgroup when examining the associations between individual religiosity and values? Similarly, are there conflicts or strong oppositions between some values? Another question will also be treated, at least indirectly: if privileged links exist between religion and certain values, are the latter also the ones that have priority in social valorizetion or, in more technical terms, in social desirability? Moreover, we will pay careful attention to an additional question. Is there some constancy in the pattern of values that are privileged or discredited within a religious context, when we compare different countries, religions, and religious denominations? Or do we come across strong differentiation as a function of underlying theological and anthropological differences? Finally, could this pattern of the religion-values associations vary as a function of other variables such as the socio-economic development or historical context of the groups involved?

Other hypotheses could be advanced. For example, through its integrative character and its concern for an ultimate finality in human actions, religion could be suspected of favoring the promotion of terminal values (values relative to the ends and goals of individual existence) and leaving instrumental values (values relative to means, ways of behaving) in the background. However, this hypothesis cannot be verified here because in Schwartz's (1992) model we do not find the distinction between these two types of values which were present in the previous model of values by Rokeach (1973). In addition, sociologists of values have criticized this distinction between means and ends: whereas the two types of values can be distinguished in the present moment, the distinction loses its pertinence when applied to a process that continues over the time (the means may become ends at a later stage).

I. Psychology of Values in the 1990s: Schwartz's Model

Since the 1990s, psychology of values has been dominated, not without reason, by the model of Schwartz, which has replaced the previous operationalization of values by Rokeach (1973). According to Schwartz (1992), values are desirable, transsituational goals, varying in importance, that serve as guiding principles in people's lives. The hierarchy of values is progressively formed during childhood, is stabilized during adolescence, and can be remodeled during adulthood.

Several series of studies from almost 60 countries have allowed for the validation of Schwartz's theoretical model. The model suggests that a large number of values (indeed, more than 50 single values) can be structured into 10 meta-values or value types. This hierarchical structure is found to be stable across these countries representing different cultures from the five continents. Attempts to find other values beyond these 10 types have failed, a finding suggesting that the model of Schwartz is rather exhaustive of the different values essential to human beings. Another pan-cultural universal, beyond minor cross-cultural differences, seems to be the values hierarchy, i.e. the order of importance people attribute to each of the 10 value types (Schwartz & Bardi, 2001). Within each society, however, interesting individual differences can be observed in the importance attributed to values. This is also the case when groups are compared between each other (e.g., Schwartz & Sagiv, 1995). Finally, several series of empirical studies demonstrated that importance attributed to specific values is predictive of number of specific behaviors related, for instance, to study and professional choices, prosocial (cooperation) and antisocial (delinquency) behaviors, political preferences, intergroup relations, and environmental attitudes.

Values	Definitions and corresponding *single items*
Power	Social status and prestige, control or dominance over people and resources (*authority, social power, wealth, preserving my public image, social recognition*)
Achievement	Personal success through demonstrating competence according to social standards (*ambitious, successful, capable, influential, intelligent*)
Hedonism	Pleasure or sensuous gratification for oneself (*pleasure, enjoying life, self-indulgent*)
Stimulation	Excitement, novelty, and challenge in life (*daring, a varied life, an exciting life*)
Self-Direction	Independent thought and action – choosing, creating, exploring (*creativity, freedom, independent, choosing own goals, curious*)
Universalism	Understanding, appreciation, tolerance, and protection of the welfare of all people and for nature (*equality, social justice, a world at peace, wisdom, broad-minded, protecting the environment, unity with nature, a world of beauty*)
Benevolence	Preservation and enhancement of the welfare of people with whom one is in frequent personal contact (*helpful, forgiving, honest, responsible, loyal, true friendship, mature love*)
Tradition	Respect, commitment, and acceptance of the customs and ideas that traditional culture or religion provide (*respect for tradition, devout, humble, moderate, accepting my portion in life*)
Conformity	Restraint of actions, inclinations, and impulses likely to upset or harm others and violate social expectations or norms (*self-discipline, politeness, honoring parents and elders, obedience*)
Security	Safety, harmony, and stability of society, of relationships, and of self (*family security, national security, social order, clean, reciprocation of favors, sense of belonging, health*)

**Table 1. Types of Values, their Definition,
and Corresponding Single Values (adapted from Schwartz, 1992)**

The 10 (types of) values, their definition, and the corresponding single values that are included in each of the 10 (types of) values are provided in Table 1 (for more theoretical issues, see Schwartz, 1992). These values are measured by a corresponding instrument, the Schwartz Value Survey, that allows for empirical investigations. In addition, theory and consecutive research have demonstrated that these values are structured into a set (circumplex model) where both conflicts-oppositions and similarities-congruencies between values can be observed (see Figure 1).

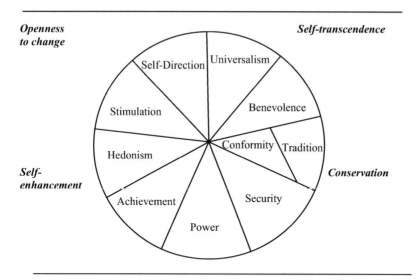

**Figure 1. Theoretical Model of the Relations between Values
(following Schwartz, 1992)**

As far as similarities-congruencies are concerned, a first observation (Figure 1) is that each of the 10 values shares a common motivational goal with the value that is next to it in the circumplex model. For instance, Hedonism and Stimulation have in common the goal of provoking an emotionally pleasant sensation, whereas the motivation shared by Hedonism and its other "neighbor" value (Achievement) is to put an emphasis on personal, individual satisfaction. A second way to consider similarities and oppositions between values is to realize that some values taken together constitute larger sets of values, and these sets are in opposition with each other following two almost orthogonal axes (see also Figure 1). A first conflict exists between *Conservation-Continuity* values (Tradition, Conformity, Security) that refer to stability, certainty, and social order, and *Openness to change* values (Stimulation and Self-Direction) that refer to novelty and personal autonomy. A second conflict opposes values reflecting *Self-transcendence*, i.e. the promotion of the well-being of others, close ones (Benevolence) or others in a broad sense (Universalism), to values reflecting *Self-enhancement* and the pursuit of personal interests (Achievement, Power). A 10th value (Hedonism) is located between Openness to change and Self-enhancement.

II. Values and Religion in Empirical Studies: a Universal Pattern?

II.1. A Meta-analysis of 21 Samples from 15 Countries

In the last fifteen years that the Schwartz's model has dominated psychology of values, 21 studies have been published with data from 15 countries providing results on the associations between religiosity and values. All the studies used the same methodology, i.e. a questionnaire including, first, Schwartz's validated instrument, and second, measures or indexes of religiosity. Most samples were constituted by students but adult samples were also included. We carried out a quantitative meta-analysis of these 21 studies, a statistical method that allows for measuring the "mean effect size", i.e. the average importance of the association weighted by the number of participants in each study. Ten mean effect sizes were thus provided, for the associations between religiosity and the 10 values, respectively (Saroglou *et al.*, 2004).

The increasing use of meta-analytic research strategies is the consequence of a serious methodological debate in social and psychological sciences originating from the assumption that it is the accumulation of results from many similar studies that can produce solid and coherent scientific knowledge, rather than interesting but fragile information collected from isolated studies that also often give the impression of having inconsistent results. A quantitative meta-analysis disputes the arbitrary character of previous strategies in reviews of empirical studies where scholars drew conclusions after having counted the percentage of studies that confirmed the hypothesis (on the basis of a magical but arbitrary significance level) against the total number of (published) studies that tried to test it. The meta-analysis attempts to estimate the (mean) size (power) of the effect across the whole spectrum of the studies concerned. It also attempts to demonstrate either a relative homogeneity of the effect – if the results from all studies go in a similar direction – or the conditions (e.g., moderators) that can explain the opposite, i.e. heterogeneity of the effect – if some studies indicate a bigger, lower or absent effect or even one in an opposite direction than in other studies.

The studies we found and reviewed in our meta-analysis mainly included samples from European and Mediterranean countries (Belgium, Czech Republic, Germany, Greece, Hungary, Israel, Italy, the Netherlands, Poland, Portugal, Spain, Switzerland, Turkey) but also from the USA and Mexico. They can thus be considered as representative of populations with a Christian background (mostly Catholics, but also Protestants and Greek Orthodox) as well as populations from Jewish and

Muslim traditions (see Saroglou *et al.*, 2004, for more details). Finally, the meta-analysis was based on a total of 8,851 participants.

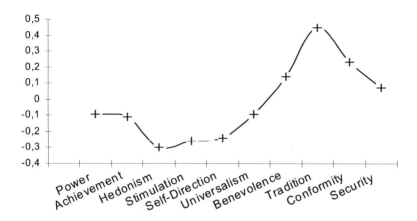

**Figure 2. Mean Effect Sizes of the Associations
between Religiosity and Values (n = 21 Studies; N = 8551)**
Based on results from Saroglou *et al.*, 2004.

Figure 2 allows for a visual inspection of the results (in terms of average correlations weighted by the number of participants per study) for all the studies taken together. Based also on what the ranges of correlations indicated across the different studies (see Saroglou *et al.*, 2004), it turned out that in all 21 samples religiosity corresponds to high importance attributed to *Conservation-Continuity* values. This is clearly the case for the values *Tradition* (correlations varied from .10 to .64, mean correlation = .45) and *Conformity* (*rs* varied from .11 to .45, mean $r = .23$). Notice that the link of religiosity with Tradition decreases when the item "devout" is dropped from the Tradition subscale but remains important ($r = .25$; Saroglou & Galand, 2004; Schwartz & Huismans, 1995). Similarly across all samples, high religiosity is a sign of small importance attributed to values typical of *Openness to change* and *hedonism*, i.e. *Self-Direction* (*rs* varied from .01 to -.37, mean $r = -.24$), *Stimulation* (*rs* varied from -.08 to -.44, mean $r = -.26$), and *Hedonism* (*rs* varied from -.19 to -.49, mean $r = -.30$).

In a weaker way, but still meaningful and almost systematic across studies, religiosity tended to be negatively associated with *Self-enhancement* values, i.e. *Power* (*rs* varied from .03 to -.29, mean $r = -.09$) and *Achievement* (*rs* varied from -.01 to -.32, mean $r = -.11$). As far as the *Self-transcendence* values are concerned, people high in religiosity are inclined towards a limited openness to others and the world. Except in three studies, religiosity was generally positively associated with *Benevolence* (*rs* varied from -.11 to .43, mean *r* = .14) but negatively related to *Universalism* (mean *r* = -.09). Interestingly, the latter negative effect was mainly due to the Mediterranean countries (Greece, Israel, Italy, Portugal, Spain, and Turkey) that, comparatively to the other countries represented in the meta-analysis (mean *r* = -.01), provide the image of a religiosity not open to the ideals of Universalism, as defined in Schwartz's model (*rs* varied from -.08 to -.55, mean *r* = -.26). Finally, with regard to the value of *Security*, an interesting contrast comes out between countries depending on the status of the Church and its relations with the State: in ex-communist countries from Eastern and Central Europe (notice that data were collected in the early 1990s) religious people do not seem to be preoccupied by Security values (Roccas & Schwartz, 1997), whereas in the other countries, a weak but positive association exists between religiosity and Security.

Social Desirability Bias?

One could object that that the above findings should be considered with suspicion because of possible contamination by a social desirability bias. Not only do previous studies suggest some association between religiosity and social desirability, especially with its component of impression management (Gillings & Joseph, 1996; Saroglou & Galand, 2004; Trimble, 1997), but there is also evidence that some of Schwartz's values are in correspondence with social desirability while others may be contrary to it. In two studies, in Israel and Finland, Schwartz *et al.* (1997) found that social desirability was positively related to values emphasizing social harmony (Tradition, Conformity, Security, Benevolence) and negatively related to values defying conventions and social harmony (Hedonism, Stimulation, Self-Direction, Achievement, Power). The similarity between this pattern of associations and that of the associations between religion and values is striking. However, two elements allow for dismissing the hypothesis of a social desirability bias. First, the same study by Schwartz *et al.* (1997) suggests that, besides the links of values with social desirability, one has to see a substantial personality trait rather than a self-presentation bias. Religious participants would attribute a strong or a weak importance to this or that value, not to make a good impression on the researcher or out of social conformity, but because they really value the social harmony embodied by these values, a harmony that makes these values socially desirable. Second, in a recent study in Belgium, it turned out that, when the effect of social desirability was neutralized, the associations between religiosity and values still remained significant in most cases (Saroglou & Galand, 2004).

II.2. Values and Specific Religious Dimensions

Obviously, speaking about "religiosity" in general, as has been the case in this text up till now, may appear as too simplistic given the apparent plurality and diversity of specific religious dimensions and pathways. However, such a global variable as "religiosity" allows for grouping together a large number of studies and for carrying out comparisons necessary for the investigation of cross-cultural similarities, what would be impossible if we based ourselves on indicators of specific multiple religious dimensions such as fundamentalism, faith maturity, quest religious orientation, etc. A more important problem is that there are only two or three studies focused on how values relate to such specific religious dimensions.

Two American studies have used the classic distinction in psychology of religion between intrinsic (in motivation) religiosity, extrinsic (in motivation) religiosity, and "quest" religious orientation (valuing doubts and openness to possible changes) (Burris & Tarpley, 1998; Faiola, 2002). The second study is an unpublished doctoral dissertation; we are thus limited to the first one. It seems that "quest" religiosity contrasts with the pattern presented above because of its discomfort with conservation values and its openness to change values, whereas extrinsic religion differs from intrinsic religion by the absence of valorization of Benevolence and by the valorization of Power (Burris & Tarpley, 1998). Such a finding can be considered as is in line with Allport's (1950) theorization of the intrinsic dimension as implying internalization of religious values contrary to the extrinsic dimension.

In another study in Belgium with 1,695 Dutch-speaking participants (Fontaine *et al.*, 2005), researchers made a distinction between two dimensions-axes: Inclusion vs. Exclusion of Transcendence (a distinction close to the one between believers and non-believers) and Symbolic vs. Literal Thinking (applicable to both believers and non-believers). Crossing out the two axes allows for distinguishing between rigid believers or non-believers and flexible believers or non-believers who leave an important place to the symbolic interpretation of religious texts. This study suggested that, as far as values are concerned, the first axis (which is closer to the essence of religion) mainly reflects the conflict between Conservation and Openness to change: it is positively related to Tradition and Conformity and negatively related to the hedonistic values and Self-Direction. According to the authors, this dimension is concerned with the conflict between dependence and autonomy, but not with the one between Self-enhancement (see Power and Achievement) and Self-transcendence (Benevolence and Universalism). It is the second dimension, the symbolic vs. literal thinking, that is related positively to Benevolence and Universalism and negatively to Power, Achievement, and Security. The authors advanced the argument that the prosocial character of religion seems to be less a consequence of theological considerations and more likely a function of cognitive structures, perhaps the capacity for perspective taking and for understanding the perspective of others (see the construct of empathy).

II.3. Differences between Religions?

In the meta-analysis of the 21 studies (Saroglou *et al.*, 2004) whose findings were presented above, the associations between religiosity and values seemed to be stable across all studies (for some values) or almost all studies (for the other values). Such a cross-cultural consistency implies that the pattern of the associations found expresses a deep psychological reality that seems stable across different religious environments, in this case, samples from different Christian religious denominations, i.e. Catholics, Protestants, and Greek Orthodox, but also samples of Jews (three samples from Israel) and Muslims (one sample from Turkey and a second one from Belgium). The similarity between Catholics, Muslims, and Jews with regard to the order of associations between religiosity and values (see Figure 3) was statistically tested and confirmed.

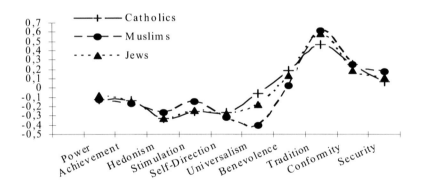

**Figure 3. Correlations between Religiosity and Values,
distinctly for Jew (*n* = 3, *N* = 1075), Catholic (*n* = 11, *N* = 5113),
and Muslim (*n* = 2, *N* = 255) Samples**

Figure published in Saroglou *et al.*, 2004 © Elsevier Science Ltd.

A more subtle question could be to examine whether there are cross-religious differences in the size of the associations themselves. For instance, one could hypothesize – always as a function of the degree of religiosity – that Self-Direction is perceived less negatively in Protestants than in Catholics or the Orthodox, or that traditionalism is stronger in a Muslim or Jewish *milieu* compared to countries with a Christian background in "secularized" Europe. However, in our meta-analysis, this type of analysis was statistically impossible to carry out. First, the non-Christian participants were highly underrepresented. Second, studying the impact of religion or denomination on the links between religiosity and values without controlling for the role of other factors, i.e. socio-cultural or socio-economic differences between countries or samples, could lead to a confounding of the effects. For instance, in Protestant countries, would a hypothetically lower discomfort of religiosity with autonomy in comparison with Catholic countries be due to strictly denominational differences (e.g., theological, anthropological differences) or to differences on the socio-economic and cultural level? Would a hypothetically higher traditionalism of religiosity in Muslim countries comparatively to Christian ones really be an effect of respective theological differences or would it be due to differences in social, economic, and cultural structures?

One way of studying the effect of religion or denomination without confounding it with the effect of other variables is to focus on studies that have included samples from different denominational groups coming from the same country. Interestingly, when comparing Protestants and Catholics living in Germany, there is no difference in the links between their religiousness and the importance they attribute to values (Schwartz & Huismans, 1995). Similar results tend to characterize Protestants and Catholics living in Switzerland (Devos *et al.*, 2002). Moreover, when comparing native Belgians and second generation immigrant Muslims living in Belgium, both groups receiving the same education at the same school, it turned out that beyond a difference in the mean importance attributed to Tradition (the second group scoring higher), there were no significant differences in the links that religiosity maintains with the system of values (Saroglou & Galand, 2004) (notice however that the size of the two samples was small and that some differences came out when focusing on values predicted by spirituality).

Within another research tradition, i.e. The European Values Survey, Bréchon (2003) has found that despite some differences (on the individual and/or the national level) between Catholics and Protestants in individual and collective ethical values that concern family and sexuality, civic attitudes, economics, participation in political life and political orientation, xenophobia and attitudes toward nationalism, Protestants and Catholics are more similar to each other than different when compared to their non-religious peers. In addition, the same survey indicated that, similarly to studies from the Schwartz's perspective, the differences between Catholics and Protestants tend to disappear when focusing on groups living in the same country, for instance in Germany or the Netherlands (for similar conclusions by other researchers, see Halman & Riis, 2003). This last finding reminds us of the possible role of economic and socio-cultural factors as well as factors linked to the historical context of each country. (It has been classically documented, for instance, that Protestant countries tend to be more economically developed than Catholic countries). Notice also that, within a country, the minority vs. majority status of a specific religious denominational group may have an impact on values. For instance, Procter and Hornsby-Smith (2003) found that Catholics living in countries with a Protestant tradition tend to accentuate a restrictive sexual morality or the importance of collectivistic values; the authors interpret these findings as confirming the hypothesis of a "cultural defense".

II.4. Socio-economic Impact or Cross-religious Differences?

The meta-analysis of 21 studies (Saroglou *et al.*, 2004), whose main findings were presented above, also demonstrated that the socio-economic level of countries has an impact on the size of the religiosity-values associations. Indeed, the more a country is socio-economically developed, the less religiosity reflects conservation-continuity values (Tradition, Conformity, Security) and discomfort with openness to change (Self-Direction), and the more it seems to become intrinsic since its associations with Benevolence and Universalism tend to increase. Similar results were obtained (see Figure 4) when we contrasted two sets of countries, all of them with a Christian background, i.e. Mediterranean countries (Greece, Italy, Portugal, Spain) and Western European countries (Belgium, Germany, the Netherlands). This comparison allows us to introduce an additional factor in our interpretation: the fact that the first set of countries is characterized by a uni- or mono-religious culture, whereas in the second set of countries there is a tradition of bi-confessionalism (Germany, the Netherlands) or co-existence of two opposite ideologies with established subcultures and social networks (Catholics and atheists "free-thinkers" in Belgium).

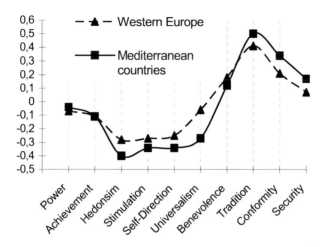

**Figure 4. Correlations between Religiosity and Values, distinctly
for Mediterranean Countries (Greece, Italy, Portugal, Spain;
N total = 1641) and Countries of Western Europe
(Belgium, Germany, the Netherlands; *N* total = 3964)**

Based on results from Saroglou *et al.*, 2004.

How can we understand these results? The impact of socio-economic
development on the size of the religiosity-values associations is unlikely
to be direct. A first possible interpretation consists in the assumption
that such a development is followed by great cultural changes that can
lead, in the end, to transformations in faith, religious experience, and
religious institutions, in a way that conforms with these cultural
changes. Thus, in so-called developed societies, minimization of the
importance of conservative values, promotion of individual autonomy,
and openness or tolerance of differences (see the value of Universalism),
as well as a relaxation of traditional anti-hedonistic norms (for a review,
see Boudon, 2002), could lead religious individuals and groups to a re-
adjustment of their values such that they will no lag behind societal
changes.

A second possible interpretation can be based on the fact that socio-
economic development is generally synonymous with secularization. It
could thus simply be that a decrease in indicators of religiosity is followed by a weakening (both in real life and statistics) of the underlying
psychological realities, in this case, the decrease of the associations
between religiosity and values (either positive or negative associations).

However, even if this hypothesis were legitimate (one could in fact object that religion becomes more intrinsic, less extrinsic, and thus that the underlying psychological realities should appear in a clearer way), it does not seem to explain all the above-mentioned findings. Contrary to many associations that decrease as a function of socio-economic development, the importance of Benevolence associated with religiousness seems to increase.

Can we envisage that the socio-economic differences, both on an individual and country level, are so determinative for the religiosity-values relations that the theological and anthropological differences between religions or between religious denominations (at least as transmitted within specific cultures) have no effect? Researchers who have analyzed data from the 1990 European Values Survey seem to come to this conclusion (Halman & Riis, 2003). However, Inglehart and Baker (2000) have analyzed data from 60 countries representing 75% of the global population and came to two main conclusions. First, socio-economic development of a country leads to a move from traditional to secular and rational values, and to a move from values emphasizing survival to "post-materialist" values emphasizing self-expression, such as values accentuating participation, confidence, tolerance, subjective well-being, and concern for the quality of life. Second, beyond the effect of socio-economic level, when comparing sets of countries that are historically and culturally distinct, it turns out that differences in values are still observable depending on whether a country has been historically Catholic, Protestant, Orthodox, communist, Islamic, or Confucian. For instance, after controlling for the impact of socio-economic differences, the Protestant cultural heritage is still associated with a high appreciation of post-materialist self-expression values whereas the Orthodox or communist heritage has a negative impact on these values.

II.5. Modern Spirituality

A few recent studies using a measure of modern spirituality, not necessarily linked to religious traditions and institutions, suggest both convergences and divergences with (classic) religiosity in the importance attributed to values (see Saroglou, 2003a, for a review). Beyond some minor discrepancies between studies, a fairly clear pattern emerges. First, modern spirituality shares with religion (a) the concern for, respect of, and self-limitation in front of the other (positive correlations with Benevolence and negative ones with Power and Achievement), and (b) the lack of valuing hedonistic values (Hedonism and Stimulation). Notice however that the negative association with the hedonistic values seems less strong and systematic in spirituality than in classic religiosity. It is not to be excluded that spirituality does not necessarily imply (or not to the same degree) the continuity of the religious discomfort with sexuality and enjoyment ("*jouissance*"), but it may continue to reflect a critical attitude towards materialism in general.

Second, modern spirituality differs from classic religiosity through (a) the lack of a high importance attributed to conservation values (Tradition, Conformity) and even the low importance attributed to Security, and (b) the widening of the benevolent attitude to universality and to the world considered as a whole (Universalism). With regard to these values, modern spirituality appears to be taking part in the changes that the socio-economic and socio-cultural development provoke in values traditionally supported by religion.

II.6. The Case of Buddhism in the West

The case of Buddhism, at least as it is experienced and practiced in the West by people often educated in Christian environments, is exemplary of this move from classic religiosity to modern spirituality because it is located at the halfway point between the two. In a recent study of one hundred Belgians converted to or invested in Buddhism (Saroglou & Dupuis, 2006) it was found that, similarly to studies on modern spirituality and in contrast with the ones on classic religiosity, practice of or investment in Buddhism are not negatively related to Achievement, Universalism, and Stimulation, and are not positively related to Tradition and Conformity; in addition, the link with Security becomes negative. Nevertheless, it remains that, similarly to classic religiosity, pro-Buddhist attitudes-practices are followed by low valorization of Hedonism and Power and by high valorization of Benevolence. Interestingly, in this study, another dimension measured, i.e. interest in the emotional-relational-esthetic aspect of Buddhism, although predictive of openness to Universalism and Stimulation, was found to resemble the traditional religious quest by a valorization of the three conservation values.

III. Discussion

III.1. Universality, Globalization, and Religious Specificity

A first conclusion is the fascinating universality of the pattern of values that seem to be privileged or neglected as a function of religiousness across a large variety of countries and many different religious denominations. Contrary to an excessively culture-oriented approach in psychology of religion, which assumes the only way of understanding a religious phenomenon consists in the discovery of all the historical and cultural factors that can explained this phenomenon as unique, an approach that is rather nomothetic also brings out the psychological or psychosocial constants ("universals") that explain a religious phenomenon across a variety of contexts. Since the question of the direction of causality between religion and values remains open (see the Introduction), these "constants" can be understood either as contributing to the psychological explanation of religiousness on the basis of individual differences in personality dispositions (see Saroglou, in press), or as indicating a possibly universal impact of religion on psychological dimensions of life, for instance, in terms of associated goals and motivational values. Nevertheless, the studies reviewed here only represent the three great monotheistic traditions (and countries with a Christian tradition were over-represented), and nothing can exclude *a priori* certain divergences when one moves to the context of Eastern religions.

The pattern of the results provided empirical evidence that can be considered as contesting the sociological theory that assumes postmodernism and globalization will lead to an accentuation of religious differences between different religious groups (see Halman & Pettersson, 2003). These results are rather in favor of an opposite sociological theory asserting that globalization will lead to the leveling of religious particularities and to the emergence of a global religious culture (see also Halman & Petterson, 2003), or at least – notice that longitudinal data are missing – they are in favor of the existence of psychological "universals" in religion and different religious expressions (see also Saroglou, 2003b). The studies reviewed here demonstrate that, in a systematic way across various countries and contexts, religious people are similar with regard to the values they consider important in their life beyond any minor particularities, whose reasons for existing remain complex and multiple (economic development, history and geography, social and cultural development, theological and anthropological differences).

At the same time, with regard to another theoretical argument, that within modern society we increasingly witness the emergence today of a general cultural convergence within which the ethical specificity of religion tends to fade, the studies reviewed here suggest that religious people are still characterized by their specificity in comparison with their non-believer or atheist peers. This is particularly interesting when taking into consideration the fact that these studies were carried out during the last decade and that most of the participants were young adults. Notice also that the specificity of religiousness with regard to value priorities-importance may be strong, since in Schwartz's questionnaire values are not measured by specific behaviors but by abstract concepts-values expressed by substantives and adjectives, the latter favoring high convergence among participants.

III.2. Values as Orienting Attitudes and Behaviors

This pattern of the religion-values links does not reflect purely ideal goals devoid of any practical implication for people's lives. This is not only because values in Schwartz's model are theoretically supposed to be motivational goals orienting action; neither it is because the pattern of the associations does not seem to be an artifact of social desirability. The main argument is that the religious disposition towards specific values seems to be translated into specific relevant attitudes and behaviors.

For instance, the attachment to *conservation-continuity* values and a low interest in *openness to change* values is reflected in a certain conservatism of religious people regarding political attitudes and attitudes towards institutions guaranteeing order, authority, and continuity, such as the Church, the nation or the family (there are, however, no differences between believers and atheists in Europe regarding attitudes towards participatory democratic institutions; Bréchon, 2003). Notice also the resistance to sociocultural changes relative to the conception of the place (and, in our view, autonomy vs. subordination) of the individual within the social group (see for example the issues of euthanasia, divorce, abortion, homosexuality), resistance that is now well documented (Bréchon, 2003; Campiche, 1997; Lambert, 2002).

In addition, the systematic character of the negative association between religiosity and *Self-Direction* opens the thorny question of whether the reference to a corpus of texts, a tradition, or an institutionalized community possessing a legitimate authority, reference supposed to constitute a source for inspiration and creativity, can be held responsible for the low valuing of autonomy in the lives of believers. Another hypothesis of an opposite but perhaps complementary causal direction (which can be found for instance in Dostoevsky's *The Brothers Karamazov*) is also legitimate: people with high personal dispositions towards dependence on and submission to authority need to refer to religious traditions and authorities as necessary sources legitimizing their thoughts, emotions, and behaviors (see the definition of religious orthodoxy by Deconchy, 1980). The Freudian perspective goes even further. In *The Future of an Illusion*, a work that clearly posits the supremacy of reason and science over all forms of infantile dependence, including religion, Freud (1927) argues that it is by lack of autonomy that people continue to believe because they are lacking the necessary strength to abandon religion, possibly because the interdictions are strong and the historical weight of the associated tradition heavy (see Freud's parallelism between paternal and ancestral figures). Besides, according to Freud, it is these kinds of people who usually renounce religion when they feel they are allowed to do so.

As a function of religiousness, the limited attachment to values underlying *Self-transcendence* (Benevolence but not Universalism) and the low attachment to values reflecting *Self-enhancement* (Power, Achievement) put an emphasis on the valorization of prosociality in interpersonal relationships. There is a concern for preserving and improving the welfare of the people with whom religious people are in contact (Benevolence), for avoiding expressing dominance over people and resources (Power), and for remaining in one's proper place and not taking advantage of others (Achievement). Consequently, it is not surprising that religious people prove to be morally rigorous with regard to civic issues. Compared to non-believers, they have a higher tendency to evaluate as immoral behaviors such as fraud, cheating, lying in order to get personal benefits, or simply declaring that the goal of life is to take the best for oneself (Bréchon, 2003; Campiche, 1997; Lambert, 2002). They also show a higher tendency to report solicitude towards vulnerable targets such as the ill and the disabled, the old-aged, the unemployed, and immigrants (Lambert, 2002). They are also known to devote more time and effort to volunteer work (Spilka *et al.*, 2003) and to be ready to help, at least under some conditions (Batson *et al.*, 1993).

However, this prosociality seems limited here to the context of rather close interpersonal relations and is not extended to a universal ethical perspective. Overall, the association between religiosity and *Universalism* is inexistent and even becomes clearly negative when focusing, for instance, on Mediterranean countries with a mono-religious tradition. This limitation, or even this conflict between openness to close ones and closing oneself off to the world as a whole, has been interpreted (Schwartz & Huismans, 1995) as resulting from a problem inherent to religious groups and to the religious identities that characterize their members. These groups do not escape from well-known mechanisms in social psychology typical of the distinction between ingroups (to which favoritism is usually applied) and outgroups (to which discrimination is usually applied). As presented by Batson (1983), although religion promotes the extension of natural altruism from the limits of natural kinship to the broader frontiers of a cultural kinship (for instance, a large community of believers), at the same time it possesses mechanisms that accentuate the barriers with what is located beyond the extended cultural kinship. It is thus not surprising that in Europe (taken as a global entity without distinguishing between countries), when moving in a continuum from atheists to practicing believers, an increase is observed in xenophobia, measured for instance in terms of national preferences in job attribution or refusal of some types of neighbors such as alcoholics, drug-addicts, homosexuals, immigrants, and gypsies (Bréchon, 2003; Lambert, 2002). Finally, as the value of Universalism includes environmental attitudes, it is interesting to report that, at least according to one study in the USA, religiosity does not seem to correspond to pro-environmental attitudes and that religious fundamentalism is rather negatively related to these attitudes (Tarakeshwar *et al.*, 2002).

Finally, the tendency to attribute low importance to hedonistic values (Hedonism, Stimulation) seems to be clear and systematic across all studies. This way of perceiving these values is predictive of relevant attitudes and behaviors, in other words, conservative and restrictive ones concerning sexuality (Bréchon, 2003; Procter & Hornsby-Smith, 2003; Rowatt & Schmitt, 2003), excitement seeking (Saroglou & Fiasse, 2003), risk-taking (Miller & Hoffmann, 1995), openness to new and complex experiences (Saroglou, 2002b; Saroglou, in press), as well as behaviors that imply loss of self-control or a frivolous, playful consideration of things such as alcohol and drug use (Koenig *et al.*, 2001), spontaneous humor creation (Saroglou, 2002c; Saroglou & Jaspard, 2001), impulsive shopping or gambling (Pichon & Saroglou, 2003; see also Saroglou & Fiasse, 2003). Besides a mistrust of novelty (that could be a consequence of the religious attitude towards the "conservation-continuity vs. change" axis values), what seems here to be essential is the ethical attitude, and its consequences in case of excessive behavior, that values self-mastery as a spiritual ideal (enjoyment, desire, humor, passions and strong emotions in general escape from this ideal) and is colored by an emphasis on the finality, and thus seriousness, of existence (see also, Saroglou, 2002a). In addition, the low propensity towards the hedonistic values within a religious perspective may result from an ethical attitude that consists in questioning materialism. Notice that besides a disdain for materialism, another attitude may be hidden, i.e. sensitivity to disgust and to anything that recalls human animality and death (for the links between disgust, animality, and religion, see Rozin *et al.*, 1999a, 1999b; Saroglou & Anciaux, 2004).

Taken together, the results of the meta-analysis of the studies on religiosity and values suggest that the size of the negative association with hedonistic values is almost twice as great as the one with the prosocial values (Benevolence), without even taking into account the absence of a positive association with Universalism. Such a finding is even more striking given that the studies reviewed here were carried out recently (during the last 10-15 years); that most of the samples were constituted by young adult participants; and that theological discourse today tends to value the role in spiritual life played by realities such as body and bodily expressions, affectivity and sexuality, pleasure and enjoyment (even humor) and to correct the so-called misperception of the Church by the media, which emphasize an excessive focus of the Church on questions of sexual ethics rather than on issues of social ethics. It seems as if a Freudian explanation of religion that attributes great importance to the repressive dimension of religion with regard to sexuality and natural animality (Freud, 1927) still has a strong, at least partial, explanatory power with regard to religion as a psychological reality. The classic theoretical perspective emphasizing the role of religion in promoting altruism and prosocial attitudes and behaviors, on the other hand, seems to have less explanatory power.

III.3. Understanding Changes

The studies reviewed here suggest both some invariance and some changes in the religion-values relations. As a function of socio-economic development, and probably of its correlate, secularization, religion tends to imply to a lesser degree values of order and conservation, dependence and lack of autonomy, as well as discomfort with hedonistic values. Religiosity may even be becoming more intrinsic, judging from an increase of the religiosity-Benevolence association. We can even expect that, in a secularized world where religion is not a substantial part of social norms people have to conform to or transmit, an intrinsically motivated faith becomes an increasingly dominant reality compared to an extrinsically motivated religion that is likely to lose its reasons for existing.

These changes, however, remain modest and do not yet lead to a reversal of some tendencies, for instance, towards a positive link between religiosity and Self-Direction or Universalism. A reversal of tendencies seems rather to be characteristic of modern spirituality, a reality independent of traditional and institutional religion. From some points of view, modern spirituality appears to correspond to the Allport's (1950) ideal of an intrinsic, mature faith: people who find spirituality important in their life tend to value autonomy and to be open to universalistic values; not only do they not tend to value order and tradition but they move on the opposite side of the spectrum, by neglecting quest for social and personal security. Elsewhere, we have examined the implications that modern spirituality could have for the classic psychological theories of religion (Saroglou, 2003a).

III.4. Limitations

One limitation of the studies reviewed here is that most samples consisted of students. Generability thus of the results can not be guaranteed, although there is no reason to suspect important differences in the religion-values associations between different ages or cohorts; indeed, some of the studies included here provide results in favor of generabil-ity. Another limitation of the studies is the fact that they provide results on the global 10 types of values level and not on the lower, more de-tailed level of the 50-55 single values that constitute the 10 types. Despite some (but still not very high) reliability between the single values that compose each global type, it remains theoretically question-able whether the associations between religiosity and the different single values within a type of value would always follow the same direction. We point out three examples that may be intriguing. The value of Achievement is composed by items reflecting success, but also by items referring to the ways one adopts, i.e. intelligence, influence, and ambi-tion, in order to reach it. The value Benevolence is a mixture of items clearly indicating a quality in interpersonal relations (helpful, forgiving), but also items linked to rigorousness in maintaining engagements (hon-est, loyal). Finally, Universalism combines environmental values with values of universalistic social ethics; indeed, a factor analysis of data from our own studies in Belgium confirms the distinctiveness of these two facets within the global value of Universalism.

Interestingly, a finer analysis on the single values level of our data in Belgium indicates that the positive association of religiosity with Tradi-tion is mainly due (in addition to the item "devout") to the item "respect for tradition", but less or not at all to the item "humble". The same positive link of religiosity with Conformity is mainly due to the values of "self-discipline" and "honoring parents and elders", and less or not at all to the values of "politeness" or "obedience". Among old participants, the link of religiosity with "healthy" and "clean" (two Security items) is negative, but its link with "sense of belonging" (also a Security item) is positive. Similarly, as far as Achievement is concerned, whereas religi-osity predicts valorization of "intelligence" in young people, it predicts no valorization of being "influential" and "ambitious" in either young or old participants. Finally, with regard to Universalism, older religious people tend not to value items corresponding to the subfactor "univer-salistic social ethics" (r = -.18) whereas young religious people do (r =.11); interestingly in both groups, young and old, spirituality (but not religiosity) predicts openness to environmental values (rs = .22 and .19).

Conclusion

Dozens of recently published studies provide important empirical evidence that allows us to capture the complexity of the ways in which religion seems to relate to a variety of pan-cultural values. Not only does religiosity imply specific attitudes (positive or negative) towards each value, thus providing an argument in favor of the religious specificity of ethics in the modern globalized world, but it is also related to these values in a way that seems to overcome religious and denominational frontiers, thus providing an argument in favor of some universality (still limited to Western cultures) in the psychological dimensions of religion. Moreover, related attitudes and behaviors of religious people seem to validate the theoretical assumption that values are motivational goals orienting actions. However, beyond stability, some changes can be observed in the religion-values associations either as a function of socio-economic development or of the recent shift from classic religiosity to modern spirituality. The two important needs or ideals that seem to be particularly emphasized within a religious perspective, need for order, both in the internal and the external world, and need for connectedness with others and self-transcendence, seem to constitute essential universals of religious attitudes although social and cultural transformations may lead to changes in the degree, extension, and domains of applicability of these needs and ideals.

References

Allport, G.W., (1950), *The individual and his religion*, New York, McMillan.

Batson, C.D., (1983), Sociobiology and the role of religion in promoting prosocial behavior: An alternative view, *Journal of Personality and Social Psychology, 45*, p. 1380-1385.

Batson, C.D., Schoenrade, P. & Ventis, W. L., (1993), *Religion and the individual: A social-psychological perspective*, New York, Oxford University Press.

Bilsky, W. & Schwartz, S. H., (1994), Values and personality, *European Journal of Personality, 8*, p. 163-181.

Boudon, R., (2002), *Déclin de la morale? Déclin des valeurs?*, Paris, Presses Universitaires de France.

Bréchon, P., (2003), Integration into Catholicism and Protestantism in Europe: The impact on moral and political values, in L. Halman & O. Riis (eds.), *Religion and secularizing society: The Europeans' religion at the end of the 20th century* (p. 114-161), Leiden, Brill.

Burris, C. T. & Tarpley, W. R., (1998), Religion as being: Preliminary validation of the Immanence scale, *Journal of Research in Personality, 32*, p. 55-79.

Campiche, R. (ed.), (1997), *Cultures jeunes et religions en Europe,* Paris, Cerf.

Deconchy, J.-P., (1980), *Orthodoxie religieuse et sciences humaines,* The Hague, The Netherlands, Mouton.

Devos, T., Spini, D. & Schwartz, S. H., (2002), Conflicts among human values and trust in institutions, *British Journal of Social Psychology, 41*, p. 481-494.

D'Onofrio, B.M., Eaves, L. J., Murrelle, L., Maes, H.H. & Spilka, B., (1999), Understanding biological and social influences on religious affiliation, attitudes, and behaviors: A behavior genetic perspective, *Journal of Personality, 67*, p. 953-984.

Faiola, T.J., (2002), The relationships among religious orientation, conceptual systems, and values, (unpublished doctoral dissertation, University of Fordham), *Dissertation Abstracts International, 63*, p. 585.

Fontaine, J.R.J., Duriez, B., Luyten, P., Corveleyn, J. & Hutsebaut, D., (2005), Consequences of a multi-dimensional approach to religion for the relationship between religiosity and value priorities, *International Journal for the Psychology of Religion*, 15, p. 123-143.

Freud, S., (1961), *The future of an illusion* (J. Strachey, Trans.), New York, Norton (Origan work published in 1927).

Gillings, V. & Joseph, S., (1996), Religiosity and social desirability: Impression management and self-deceptive positivity, *Personality and Individual Differences, 21*, p. 1047-1050.

Halman, L. & Pettersson, T., (2003), Globalization and patterns of religious belief systems, in L. Halman & O. Riis (eds.), *Religion and secularizing society: The Europeans' religion at the end of the 20th century* (p. 185-222), Leiden, Brill.

Halman, L. & Riis, O., (eds.), (2003), *Religion and secularizing society: The Europeans' religion at the end of the 20th century*, Leiden, Brill.

Hinde, R., (1999), *Why Gods persist? A scientific approach to religion*, London, Routledge.

Inglehart, R. & Baker, W.E., (2000), Modernization, cultural change, and the persistence of traditional values, *American Sociological Review, 65*, p. 19-51.

Koenig, H.G., McCullough, M.E. & Larson, D.B., (2001), *Handbook of religion and health*, New York, Oxford University Press.

Lambert, Y., (2002), Religion: L'Europe à un tournant, in *Les valeurs des Européens: Les tendances à long terme* [special issue], *Futuribles: Analyse et prospective*, 277, p. 129-159.

Miller, A.S. & Hoffmann, J.P., (1995), Risk and religion: An explanation of gender differences in religiosity, *Journal for the Scientific Study of Religion, 34*, p. 63-75.

Pichon, I. & Saroglou, V., (2003, May), *Are there religion stereotypes?,* paper presented at the 100 years of Psychology and Religion Conference, Amsterdam, The Netherlands.

Plomin, R. & Caspi, A., (1999), Behavioral genetics and personality, in L. A. Pervin & O. P. John (eds.), *Handbook of personality: Theory and research* (p. 251-276), New York, Guilford.

Procter, M. & Hornsby-Smith, P., (2003), Individual context religiosity, religious and values in Europe and North America, in L. Halman & O. Riis (eds.), *Religion and secularizing society: The Europeans' religion at the end of the 20th century* (p. 92-113), Leiden, Brill.

Roccas, S., Sagiv, L., Schwartz, S. H. & Knafo, A., (2002), The Big Five personality factors and personal values, *Personality and Social Psychology Bulletin, 28*, p. 789-801.

Roccas, S. & Schwartz, S.H., (1997), Church-state relations and the association of religiosity with values: A study of Catholics in six countries, *Cross-Cultural Research, 31*, p. 356-375.

Rokeach, M., (1973), *The nature of human values,* New York, Free Press.

Rowatt, W.C. & Schmitt, D.P., (2003), Associations between religious orientation and varieties of sexual experience, *Journal for the Scientific Study of Religion, 42,* p. 455-465.

Rozin, P., Haidt, J. & McCauley, C.R., (1999a), Disgust: The body and soul emotion, in T. Dalgleish & M. Power (eds.), *Handbook of cognition and emotion* (p. 429-445), New York, Wiley.

Rozin, P., Lowery, L., Imada, S. & Haidt, J., (1999b), The CAD triad hypothesis: A mapping between three moral emotions (contempt, anger, disgust) and three moral codes (community, autonomy, divinity), *Journal of Personality and Social Psychology, 76,* p. 574-586.

Saroglou, V., (2002a), Religion and sense of humor: An a priori incompatibility? Theoretical considerations from a psychological perspective, *Humor: International Journal of Humor Research, 15,* p. 191-214.

Saroglou, V., (2002b), Religion and the five factors of personality: A meta-analytic review, *Personality and Individual Differences, 32,* p. 15-25.

Saroglou, V., (2002c), Religiousness, religious fundamentalism, and quest as predictors of humor creation, *International Journal for the Psychology of Religion, 12,* p. 177-188.

Saroglou, V., (2003a), Spiritualité moderne: Un regard de psychologie de la religion, *Revue Théologique de Louvain, 34,* p. 473-504.

Saroglou, V., (2003b), Trans-cultural/religious constants vs. cross-cultural/religious differences in psychological aspects of religion, *Archiv für Religionspsychologie, 25,* p. 71-87.

Saroglou, V., (in press), "Religion and personality: A Big Five Factor perspective" in D. Wulff (ed.), *Handbook of psychology of religion,* Oxford, Oxford University Press.

Saroglou, V. & Anciaux, L., (2004), Liking sick humor? Coping styles and religion as predictors, *Humor: International Journal of Humor Research, 17,* p. 257-277.

Saroglou, V., Delpierre, V. & Dernelle, R., (2004), Values and religiosity: A meta-analysis of studies using Schwartz's model, *Personality and Individual Differences, 37,* p. 721-734.

Saroglou, V. & Fiasse, L., (2003), Birth order, personality, and religion: A study among young adults from a three-sibling family, *Personality and Individual Differences, 35,* p. 19-29.

Saroglou, V. & Dupuis, J. (2006), Being Buddhist in Western Europe: Cognitive needs, prosocial character, and values, *International Journal for the Psychology of Religion,* 16, p. 163-179.

Saroglou, V. & Galand, P., (2004), Identities, values, and religion: A study among Muslim, other immigrant, and native Belgian young adults after the 9/11 attacks, *Identity: An International Journal of Theory and Research,* 4, p. 97-132.

Saroglou, V. & Jaspard, J.-M., (2001), Does religion affect humour creation? An experimental study, *Mental Health, Religion, and Culture, 4,* p. 33-46.

Schwartz, S.H., (1992), Universals in the content and structure of values: Theoretical advances and empirical tests in 20 countries, in M. Zanna (ed.), *Advances in experimental social psychology* (Vol. 25, p. 1-65), Orlando, FL, Academic Press.

Schwartz, S.H. & Bardi, A., (2001), Value hierarchies across cultures: Taking a similarities perspective, *Journal of Cross-Cultural Psychology, 32*, p. 268-290.

Schwartz, S.H. & Huismans, S., (1995), Value priorities and religiosity in four western religions, *Social Psychology Quarterly, 58*, p. 88-107.

Schwartz, S.H. & Sagiv, L., (2000), Identifying culture-specific in the content and structure of values, *Journal of Cross-Cultural Psychology, 26*, p. 92-116.

Schwartz, S.H., Verkasalo, M., Antonovsky, A. & Sagiv, L., (1997), Value priorities and social desirability: Much substance, some style, *British Journal of Social Psychology, 36*, p. 3-18.

Spilka, B., Hood, R.W., Jr., Hunsberger, B. & Gorsuch, R., (2003), *The psychology of religion: An empirical approach* (3rd ed.), New York, Guilford.

Tarakeshwar, N., Swank, A.B., Pargament, K.I. & Mahoney, A., (2001), The sanctification of nature and theological conservatism: A study of opposing religious correlates of environmentalism, *Review of Religious Research, 42*, p. 387-404.

Trimble, D.E., (1997), The Religious Orientation scale: Review and meta-analysis of social desirability effects, *Educational and Psychological Measurement, 57*, p. 970-986.

·

Evangelical Values
and the Foundations of Science

Jean-Marie VAN CANGH

Louvain-la-Neuve, Belgium

A preliminary remark is called for. There is no attempt here to found science on religion or any religious value whatever, just as there is no question of founding science on ethics or morality. But it is rather a matter of showing that there is an inevitable relationship between the man of science and the values of an ethical and religious order he necessarily uses in scientific work. Just as the man of science cannot suppress life or kill another human being impudently, similarly, he cannot ignore the central value founding all religions: respect for human life and his relationship to his fellow man and to the transcendent. This truth was announced in Christianity in the form of a dual commandment that is unique: "You shall love the Lord your God with all your heart, and with all your soul, and with all your mind. This is the great and first commandment. And a second is like it, You shall love your neighbor as yourself". (Mt 22, 34-40 and parallel references). This theme of the relationship between science and love in the person of the scientist, who is one and same being, will be the object of the second part, dealing with the beatitudes.

The first part will study the Bible creation narratives and their prompting in favor of science. We might go a bit further: these biblical creation narratives have favored the autonomy of science by the power and influence of their command: "Dominate the earth and transform it" (Gen 1, 27 writes literally: "fill the earth and subdue it").

This subject was already taken up at our colloquium in Lima in 1989 on the theme: "Philosophy and the Origin and Evolution of the Universe", Dordercht, Boston, London, Kluwer Academic Publishers, Vol. 217, 1991. Our text bore the title "Creation and Origin of the World in the Bible".[1] I shall also rely on the fine work by Jacques

---

[1]   J.-M. Van Cangh, text published in the review of Prof. Evandro Agazzi in *Epistemologia*, XIV (1991), p. 139-152.

273

Vermeylen, *La création. Un parcours à travers la Bible*[2] and on André Wénin, *L'homme biblique. Anthropologie et éthique dans le Premier Testament*, and also, by the same author, *Actualité des Mythes. Relire les récits mythiques de Genèse 1-11*[3].

1. The Biblical Creation Narratives

A. The Creation of Man and Woman (Gen 2 and 3)

The biblical creation narratives of Genesis have certain points in common with the Babylonian myths of Gilgamesh (the search for immortality), of Atrahasis and Enuma Elish. In these last two epopees, man is always presented as being created from the earth and a divine element. But their differences from the biblical narrative are numerous. Two principal ones concern the origin of man. For the Mesopotamian texts, man comes from the blood of a vanquished and fallen god who marks the species with an original taint. For the Bible, it's the unique, essentially good God who breathes his own divine breath into him (Gen 2, 7). In the Babylonian texts, man is created in order to free the gods from arduous work, whereas in Genesis the goal of creation is to associate man with divine mastery of nature and make him master and possessor of the world.

Genesis contains two creation narratives (Gen 1, 1-2, 4a and 2, 4b-25). The second is considered more ancient and is attributed to the Yahwist tradition (= J). It presents a cosmology extending out along two axes. The first axis is that of the *general and the particular*. The author begins with the generic (the sky and earth) to distinguish the rainless wasteland from the arable earth (*adamah*) whence comes man (*Adam*). Then comes the garden, a veritable storehouse for man, irrigated by a river with four branches. Finally, in the middle of the garden, are two privileged trees, one the tree of life and the other of the knowledge of good and evil. Unlike the cosmology of the Genesis 1 narrative, which is "aquatic" and where the earth appears as an islet in the midst of the waters, one might describe the cosmology of Genesis 2 as "terrestrial", in which the earth is a well irrigated and fruitful oasis of life in the middle of an impressive desert.

The second axis is *vertical and horizontal*. At the center of the world, the garden is presented as a cosmic mountain where four rivers

---

[2] J. Vermeylen, *Cahiers du Centre d'Études Théologiques et Pastorales*, Bruxelles, 1993.

[3] A. Wénin, *Collection Théologie Biblique*, Paris, Le Cerf, 1995 ; *Id.*, *Cahiers du CEFOC*, Namur, 2ᵉ éd., 2001.

rise, irrigating the whole universe (Gen 2, 10-14). The garden's center is a double tree: the tree of life in the more archaic narrative (Gen 2, 9; 3, 22.24) and the tree of the knowledge of good and evil in the Yahwist narrative (2, 9; 3. 3). The trees represent the cosmic tree whose roots sink into the earth and whose top reaches the skies. The man, placed in an internal, sacred space, cannot take possession of the center (2, 16-17). Wanting to become the sole master of life and the knowledge of good and evil leads to his banishment to an external, profane space (3, 23-24: the Angel of Yahweh chases the man out of the garden of Eden).

We should avoid interpreting the divine restriction as to the tree of knowledge of good and evil negatively. "You may eat freely of every tree of the garden, but of the tree of the knowledge of good and evil you shall not eat" (Gen 2, 16-17). This is not a God jealous about his privileges, wanting to reserve knowledge and moral autonomy for himself. It is first of all a gift: "You can eat of every tree of the garden". God sets only one limit on this gift. And the limit is positive. If man wants to be the whole of the universe and seize all the divine gift, he will remain alone and die. Man should assume his limits and make room for others. Man should begin sharing and recognizing others. That is why the text continues with the creation of the woman, as a helper (*'ezer*) for the man and as his true partner (Gen 2, 18 "It is not good that the man should be alone. I will make him a helper fit for him", *kenegdô*). There is always something about God and others that escapes us. This element of non-knowledge is essential to relationships. Confidence in others structures relationships[4]. The serpent appears as a liar, as transforming the order of God, which is a gift, into a simple interdict: "You shall not eat of any tree of the garden [...] for God knows that when you eat of it your eyes will be opened and you will be like God, knowing good and evil" (3, 1.5). The serpent's lie is deforming the meaning of the divine words. He presents God as someone who is afraid that the man will become like him through knowledge. That knowledge is presented by the serpent as a privilege God wants to keep jealously for himself. The sentiment of limit or finitude leads men to covetousness and rivalry with other men. Instead of considering the gift of life as the essential gift of God, man dwells on the limit imposed on his knowledge of good and evil and on his autonomy in relation to others. God protects man from death by imposing a limit. Wanting to grasp everything for oneself is refusing relationships with others, "And the man and his wife were both naked and they were not ashamed" (Gen 2, 25). The man and his wife naked before one another, observe the limit; they accept their difference and

---

[4] A. Wénin, *Actualité des Mythes*, p. 27-29.

understand that they are not everything. In love, the partners are not afraid of showing their limits and vulnerability.

Covetousness leads to violence and death. As Paul Beauchamp writes: "Envy makes us suffer from a good if it's someone else's, enjoy a good if we deprive others of it. That's why envy leads to both desiring a good and destroying it, because the true good is always shared. Envy behaves towards good with the same violence as towards love"[5]. The biblical message is to rejoice at the happiness of others, unlike Cain who kills Abel quite simply because he cannot bear his happiness.

Man's envy perturbs not only his relationship to God but also:

– the relation of man to nature, marked by barren soil ("thorns and thistles", Gen 3, 18 a) and man's arduous work ("In the sweat of your face you will eat bread" 3, 19 a)

– the woman's relation to her specific function, maternity ("In pain you shall bring forth children" 3, 16 a)

– the man's relation to the woman marked by the double intrusion of the woman's desire and the man's domination ("Yet your desire shall be for your husband and he shall rule over you" 3, 16 b)

– man's relation to life and death: "You are dust, and to dust you shall return" (3, 19 b).

On our part, that presupposes recognition of God as the God of life and free giving, who wants man's happiness and our recognition of the other, consenting to our own finitude and lack of total mastery, making room for confidence. As to the tree of life and the tree of knowledge, A. Wénin suggests that they are one and the same or, in any case, that they symbolize the same reality. "Maybe there is one sole tree, the middle one, in between 'you' and the other, to make the relationship possible. That tree is the source of life for those accepting the limit of ignorance it represents, thus making room for others and giving credit to the Lord and his will to life"[6].

In the beginning, there were harmonious relations between man and nature and between man and animals. Like them, man is drawn from the dust of the earth (*'adamah*), whence the name *Adam*, the man, the human in general. Animals do not, however, receive the breath of life (*nishmat ḥayyim*) representing the divine part of man (*rûaḥ*). Man is to name the animals, thus learning language. He is to exercise a mild

---

[5]   Paul Beauchamp, *Psaumes. Nuit et Jour*, Paris, Le Seuil, 1980, p. 72 ; A. Wénin, *L'Homme biblique*, p. 51-52.

[6]   A. Wénin, *Pas seulement de pain… Violence et alliance dans la Bible*, Lectio Divina 171, Paris, Le Cerf, 1998, p. 47.

mastery over them, without violence, which is signified in Gen 1, 29 by the gift of food to man exclusively in vegetable form. But to dialogue with him, God decides to accord man a specific helper (*'ezer*) who will be "a helper fit for him" (*kenegdô*). The imagery of Adam's rib is there to stress the equality and intimacy he shares with the woman (Gen 2, 23: "This at last is bone of my bones, and flesh of my flesh").

The author changes the man's name (Adam) so that he might share it with his companion. Adam becomes *ish* (the male, the husband) and gives his partner the name *ishshah* (the woman, the wife). The man only accedes to self-knowledge in the reciprocity of his relationship with the woman. As the Bible d'Osty writes, "man is endlessly seeking something that has been torn from him, whereas women live in yearning for the quarry of flesh they were extracted from".[7]

The narrative's anthropology is founded on the symbolism of the potter who models a form from clay: the Lord God formed man from dust from the ground (*'adamâh*), and breathed into his nostrils the breath of life (*nishmat ḥayyim*) and man became a living being (*nephesh ḥayyah*) (Gen 2, 7). The day God withdraws his breath from man, he will return to his original dust (3, 19 or Qoh 12, 7 "The dust returns to the earth from whence it came and the breath returns to God who gave it"). The object of the narrative is not the creation of the world in general, where man arrives last as the summit of a pyramid (as in Gen 1), but rather the creation of the man and the woman, as a unique work, placed at the center of a secondary environment (the cereals and fruit trees are only there as storehouses).

B. Creation of the Independent Cosmos (Gen 1-2, 4)

The narrative is attributed to the priestly author (P). This is the narrative of creation in 6 days, which concludes with the rest of the Lord, the *Shabbat*, the seventh day. The final author has taken a traditional text and transformed it by the interdict of Shabbat, the seventh day, and the introduction of the fourth day, which occupies the central place: the creation of the stars which will be "signs" for both liturgical feasts and the days and years (Gen 1, 14). Day 3 and day 6 each contain the creation of 2 works. There are 8 works spread over 7 days, that are fruits of 10 words of God.

The first part of the narrative (works 1 to 3) insists on the separation (opus separationis) of the forces of death to permit life: separation of light from darkness (Gen 1, 3-5), separating the waters that were under

---

[7] *La Bible, translated by E. Osty and J. Trinquet*, Paris, Le Seuil, 1973, p. 40 (note on Gen 2, 22).

the firmament (the sea) from the waters that were above the firmament (1, 6-8) and, finally, separating the dry land from the sea (1, 9-10). The negative elements are not abolished but mastered by the mild power of the word of God[8]. The second part (opus ornatus) insists on the arrangement of the earth: the plants and the trees (1, 11-13); the sun, the moon and stars (1, 14-19), the fish and birds (20-23); and the land animals (1, 24-25).

Man comes in the third part "in the image and likeness of God" (1, 26-27). God tells man to subdue the earth, having dominion over the animals: "Fill the earth and subdue it" (1, 28).

But this domination is a mild domination, without violence. As food man receives not the flesh of animals, but cereals and fruits (1, 29: "Behold, I have given you every plant yielding seed which is upon the face of all the earth, and every tree with seed in its fruit; you shall have them for food").

Only after the flood does man receive permission to eat meat, yet with a stipulation, the forbidding of blood (which symbolizes life) and belongs to God (Gen 9, 2-4).

The seventh day, God finished creation by resting (Gen 2, 2). He leaves room for man to finish his work. God refuses to fill everything and direct the universe puppet style. He withdraws (the *tsimtsûm*); he leaves room for the autonomy of nature and man. Creation is not an emanation from God (pantheism) nor the fruit of divine generation, but is placed in front of the creator and is radically distinct from him. This distinction will allow us to break with a sacral conception of nature and so form the basis of the scientific and technical project of transformation of nature and the world.

2. A Revolutionary Ethical Project: the Beatitudes

A recent book, written by a non-believing geneticist, obliges us to reflect on the foundations of a universal ethic, which might serve as a basis for the scientific practice of scholars of any religion, as well as for agnostics and non-believers. Albert Jacquard passionately refuses the Christian Credo, but propose Jesus' Sermon on the mount as a model. He writes: "Love your enemies; do good to those who hate you. Bless those who make imprecations against you, and pray for those who calumniate you"[9]. A. Jacquard cites here freely from the text of Matthew

---

[8]   A. Wénin, *L'Homme biblique*, p. 39-40.
[9]   A. Jacquard, *Dieu ?*, Paris, Stock-Bayard, 2003, p. 87.

5, 44 and the parallel, Luke 6, 27-28, which develop the preceding beatitudes. He continues:

> This programme is properly revolutionary; it is the opposite of what society proposed at that time, marked by a total absence of respect for the lives of most humans [...]. It is almost as opposed to what western society proposes today, it being always a question of domination, competition and elimination. It should thus provoke a similar scandal; but we are particularly skilled, undoubtedly more than Jesus' contemporaries, in not dealing with overly troublesome ideas.[10]

Hence, we are going to propose a brief study of the beatitudes of Jesus, principally the first three, which are considered authentic by exegetes, and then bring out their significance in the mouth of Jesus and in the versions of Matthew 5, 3-12 and Luke 6, 20-26.

An initial observation is called for. Matthew has nine beatitudes and no maledictions, whereas Luke has four beatitudes and four maledictions. The contents are also different. Luke describes concrete, painful situations (the poor, the hungry, the afflicted), whereas Matthew above all speaks of spiritual states of mind (the poor in spirit, those who hunger and thirst for justice).

It is generally admitted that the authentic beatitudes, meaning those that were spoken by Jesus, are nearer to the four beatitudes of Luke, who represents the lesser common denominator between the two versions. Yet we notice that the fourth beatitude is quite different from the three first and must have been pronounced at another moment in the life of Jesus (probably at the moment when Jesus envisaged his Passion and death) or else it could be the work of the primitive community undergoing persecution. Personally, we lean more towards the first hypothesis, feeling that there are two quite distinct parts to the ministry of Jesus: a first period that we might call "the Galilean spring", when everything succeeded and when sizeable crowds came to Jesus, and a second period, that of the increasing hostility of the Pharisees and the Saducees, when Jesus envisaged his Passion and death, is principally dedicated to training the Twelve in view of their pursuing his work. This vision of things facilitates our explaining that, during the first period, Jesus should have announced the coming of the Kingdom of God soon (Mk 9, 1 and 13, 30) and that, in the second period, he should have refused any evaluation of time (Mk 13, 32), that he should have considered himself the initiator of that Kingdom and expected its coming "in power" later (cf. the announcement of table fellowship in the Kingdom (Mk 14, 25 par.), and also the arrival of the Son of man in glory of Mk 13, 24-27

---

[10] *Ibid.*, p. 88.

and confessing the earthly Jesus as the condition for recognition by the celestial Son of man, Lk 12, 8.

We might attempt the following reconstitution of the primitive text of the beatitudes, following Dom Jacques Dupont[11]:

Blessed are the poor, for theirs is the Kingdom of heaven.

Blessed are the afflicted, for they will be consoled.

Blessed are the hungry, for they will be satisfied.

Blessed are you when men hate you and when they exclude you and revile you and cast out your name as evil, on account of the Son of man. Rejoice and be glad, for your reward is great in the heavens, for so the prophets were persecuted before you.

To understand the sense that Jesus gave the first three beatitudes, they have to be placed in a dual context: the prophetic announcements of Isaiah and the signs accomplished by Jesus during his public ministry. Whereas John the Baptist announced a wrathful judge, whose "axe is laid to the roots of the trees (Lk 3, 9) and whose winnowing fork is in his hand, to clear his threshing floor, and to gather the wheat into his granary, but the chaff he will burn with unquenchable fire" (Lk 3,17), Jesus, on the contrary, delivered a message of joy and salvation. To the disciples of John who asked him: "Are you the one who is to come or must we await another?", Jesus answered by enumerating the miracles mentioned by the prophet Isaiah (Is 26, 19; 29, 18; 35, 5-6; 61, 1-4): "Go and tell John what you hear and see: the blind receive their sight and the lame walk, lepers are cleansed and the deaf hear, and the dead are raised up, and the poor have the Good News preached to them" (Mt 11, 4-6 and Lk 7, 22-23). Jesus realizes in words and acts the salvation announced to the poor by Isaiah in favor of the poor. The Good News announced to the poor appears at the end of a *crescendo*, as the most important of the messianic signs accomplished by Jesus, the one that precisely fulfills the prophecy of Is 61, 1-4:

The Spirit of the Lord God is upon me, because the Lord has anointed me to bring good tidings to the poor, he has sent me to bind up the broken hearted, to proclaim liberty to the captives, and the opening of the prison to those who are bound,[...] to comfort all who mourn,[...] to give them a garland instead of ashes, the oil of gladness instead of mourning, the mantle of praise instead of a faint spirit.

In the same way, Jesus announces the imminent coming of God and gives signs (healing the sick and happiness for the poor). The coming of

---

[11] J. Dupont, *Le message des Béatitudes*, in Cahiers Evangile 24, Paris, Le Cerf, 1978, p. 33.

the Reign of God leads to the end of suffering for the poor. When God comes, there will be no more poors. It is precisely this extraordinary promise that Jesus expresses in announcing the Kingdom of God. The Reign of God is what happens when God comes as a good and just King. What is the role of such a King? His principal role is to ensure justice is done. In a world where exploitation of the weak by the strong appears as taken for granted, the King's concern is to redress the balance in favor of the poor, ensuring a justice in which the weak have nothing to fear from the powerful. This role of God-King is described in Psalm 146, 7-9: "He executes justice for the oppressed; he gives food to the hungry. The Lord sets the prisoners free; the Lord opens the eyes of the blind. The Lord lifts up those who are bowed down; the Lord loves the righteous. The Lord watches over the sojourners. He upholds the widow and the fatherless; but the way of the wicked he brings to ruin". The *Magnificat* proclaims the same reversal of human values, at Lk 1, 52-53: "He has put down the mighty from their thrones, and exalted those of low degree; he has filled the hungry with good things, and the rich he has sent empty away".

This is the function of King Jesus proclaims and accomplishes. The affirmation of Jesus does not first rely on the psychology of the poor but on the psychology of God, on his idea of God, who, as just King, owes it to Himself, quite simply because He is God, to re-establish justice in favor of the weak and oppressed. The beatitudes are not first of all a morals lesson, but the proclamation of the Good News: God has taken sides with the poor. God has had enough of seeing the poor suffer. When God comes to establish his Reign, and that indeed is what he has decided to do in Jesus, the poor are happy. Hence, the viewpoint of Jesus is first of all *theological*. The advent of the Reign of God signifies, as an immediate consequence, the poors' happiness.

In this sense, one might say that Jesus is a "realistic utopian". But one should add right away that posing the problem of the permanence of poverty is posing the problem of the efficacity of Christians, according the principle of Mt 25, 40: "As you did it to one of these the least of my brethren, you did it to me". Jesus promises the poor happiness and works at it by healing them and the audacious positions he adopts in their favor, but entrusts his disciples with pursuing his work, the coming of the Kingdom of God on earth.

For his part, Luke is going to up-date the beatitudes by employing the second person plural ("Yours is the Kingdom of God; you shall be satisfied; you shall laugh"). He addresses them to Christians living in concrete situations of poverty or affliction. On the other hand, Luke introduces a "now" into the first part of the second and third beatitudes

("Blessed are you who hunger now […] Blessed are you that weep now […]"), which has the effect of hinting at a "later" in the second part of the phrase and deferring the reward promised. Luke is a realist who lives in the times of his Church and is aware of the situation of lasting poverty in the community. He thus puts the happiness announced by Jesus off to "later", which for him corresponds to the individual death of each Christian. We need not await the Parousia, it is at the very instant of his death that the disciple of Jesus will find his salvation (Lk 23, 43: "Today you will be with me in Paradise", Jesus tells the good thief).

Yet there is a real danger in the fact of magnifying present poverty and promising happiness later, for the great beyond. Luke did not fall into that; we see his concrete concern to improve the life of the primitive community, just as his master, the apostle Paul, did. But we cannot say as much for certain Christians, who have all too easily taken advantage of the suffering poor, satisfied with promising them happiness, later, in the "sky". That position unconsciously leads to making Christianity the opium of the people!

For his part, we can say that Luke situated the problem of communitarian poverty in the summaries of the Acts of the Apostles quite accurately (2, 42-47; 4, 32-35; 5, 12-16). Luke is inspired by the Greek ideal of friendship. Friends do not renounce what they possess, but place their goods at one another's disposal. Poverty is not a good in itself; it is rather a situation God revolts against, for it contradicts his role as a just and good King, as appears in the thought of the great prophets and of Jesus. But the ideal of charity can sometimes lead to the need of impoverishing oneself in order to share with those who are in need, so as to alleviate their poverty. Luke begins with the ideal of fraternal communion (Acts 4, 32: "Now the company of those who believed were of one heart and soul, and no one said that any of the things which he possessed was his own, but they had everything in common") to show the inevitable consequence of sharing (Acts 4, 34: "There was not a needy person among them; for as many as were possessors of lands or houses sold them, and brought the proceeds of what was sold and laid it at the apostles' feet; and distribution was made to each as any had need"). For Luke, the question to be asked is not; "What do I still own?", but rather: "What do I have that I refuse to share?".

For his part, Matthew is going to develop the beatitudes (he counts nine instead of four) in a spiritualistic and moralizing sense. He no longer talks about those who are simply poor, but about the poor in spirit. He no longer talks about those who are simply hungry, but about those who hunger and thirst for justice. The beatitudes which, in Jesus' mouth, first and foremost described God's royal and sovereign dispositions and justice, in Matthew describe the conditions that will facilitate our entering the Kingdom, the "how to" for taking part in the happiness promised. From kerygmatic affirmations to instructions on the Reign of God's actualization, they become exhortations to possessing the qualities required for enjoying the happiness of the Kingdom, meaning they become a practical programme for Christian life. The viewpoint is no longer first theological (proclaiming the divine will), but *anthropological*. They shed light on the human aptitudes necessary for obtaining salvation. Yet it would be mistaken to reduce Matthew's viewpoint to an anthropological one. His viewpoint is first of all *christological*. Matthew begins with the concrete condition of the heart of Jesus, a model for all Christian life. The beatitudes are a reflection of what Jesus himself lived. Mt 11, 28-30 is the only evangelist to provide us these important words of Jesus about himself: "Come to me all who labor and are heavy laden, and I will give you rest. Take my yoke upon you, and learn from me; for I am gentle and lowly in heart, and you will find rest for your souls. For my yoke is easy and my burden is light". This text follows a refusal to reveal divine truths to the sages and scholars, meaning to the doctors of the Law, but divulging them to the least among the brethren, meaning to disciples lacking learned religious instruction. The beatitudes of the mild and the merciful added by Matthew are in perfect harmony with Jesus' behavior; for the disciple, they are the logical consequence of the life and behavior of their Master "gentle and lowly in heart".

Father Emile Puech has revolutionized this research by bringing to light a text of the Dead Sea scrolls (1QH VI 13-16) which is parallel to the nine beatitudes of Mt 5, 3-12. This Qumrân text contains at least three of Matthew's beatitudes: the poor in spirit, the merciful and the peacemakers.[12]

Here is the text:

1. Happy the men of truth and the elected of justice
2. the seekers after wisdom and the seekers of intelligence
3. builders of peace (bôney shalôm) and the...of...
4. those who love mercy ('ôhabey rahamim) and the poor in spirit ('anwey rûah)
5. those cleansed by poverty and those purified by trials
6. the merciful of pardons... and those of perfect behaviour

---

[12] E. Puech, "Un hymne essénien en partie retrouvé et les Béatitudes", in *Revue de Qumrân*, 13, (1988), p. 59-88 et *Id.*, "4Q525 et les périscopes des Béatitudes en Ben Sira et Matthieu", in *Revue Biblique*, 98, (1991), p. 80-106.

7. moderate until the end of your judgements and those awaiting your salvation.

We agree with E. Puech that this Qumrân text may have influenced the composition of Matthew's beatitudes. But, unlike E. Puech, we think that Jesus intended the word "poor" (ptôchos) in the general sense of all the poor of the earth, all the miserable men he heals and with whom he deals concretely in his ministry (see the explicit texts of Mt 11, 5 and Lk 4, 18). Jesus is not Matthew, he does not promise the Kingdom only to those "poor in spirit", but to all the needy of the earth, whatever the misfortune they are afflicted with. Jesus is thus closer to Luke's meaning.[13]

We should also note the general differences between the Qumrân beatitudes and those of Jesus. For the latter, the Kingdom of God is already present in his person and is accessible to all men of good will. In Qumrân, the Son of light impatiently awaits the day of Yahweh for a future that is near and desired, yet indeterminate. If Qumrân's eschatology is future orientated, Jesus' is already being realized.

The second difference is the general tone of the Qumrân beatitudes, which declare: "Blessed are those who search after wisdom and the seekers of intelligence [...] and those perfectly behaved", whereas Jesus is constantly uplifting marginals and sinners. In Qumrân, we would have a hard time imagining a phrase of the type: "Truly, I say to you, the tax collectors and harlots go into the Kingdom of God before you" (Mt 21, 31). In Qumrân, there is a minute, almost scrupulous, search for an exact comprehension of the Scriptures and internal and external purity. Whereas Jesus addresses himself, first of all, to sinners of all sorts, as the envoy of the Father of mercies, who sends rain on the just and on the unjust (Mt 5, 45) and who hugs the prodigal son and covers him with kisses (Lk 15, 20).

The novelty of the message of Jesus' beatitudes, is precisely surpassing the Jewish law of retribution. What is at stake here are not the merits or virtues of the poor, nor even their favorable spiritual aptitudes. What is in question here are the royal dispositions of God. God, quite simply because he is God, has decided to re-establish justice in favor of the small and weak, those who are exploited and oppressed. God has taken

---

[13] J.-M. Van Cangh, "Nouveaux horizons en exégèse grâce aux études juives", in F. Bousquet, H. J. Gagey, G. Médevielle, J. L. Souletie (eds.), *Mélanges Joseph Doré. La responsabilité des théologiens*, Paris, Desclée, 2002, p. 139-156 ; *Id.*, "Béatitudes de Qumrân et béatitudes évangéliques", in F. Garcia Martinez (ed.), *Wisdom and Apocalycticism in the Dead Sea Scrolls and in the Biblical Traditions*, BETL 168, Leuven, Peeters, 2003, p. 413-426.

sides with the poor! Here are the Good News: God has had enough of seeing the poor suffer and has decided to make them happy!

Conclusion

These few reflections on the creation narratives in the book of Genesis and on the importance of the beatitudes of Jesus as a basis of social life do not answer the question of how God intervenes in our world and, particularly, about the origin of the human soul and self-consciousness. On this subject, we simply recall the thoughts of one of our eminent members, Sir John C. Eccles, Nobel prize in medicine:

> Because materialistic solutions are unable to explain our experience of unicity, I feel myself constrained to attribute the unicity of my self (or the soul) to a spiritual creation of a supernatural order. To express myself in theological terms: each soul is new divine creation implanted in the fœtus at some moment between conception and birth. It is the certainty of an interior core of unique individuality that makes the idea of this divine creation necessary […] Thus there exists not only a transcendent God, creator of the universe, the God of Einstein, but also a loving God to whom we owe our being.

For our part, we feel we have shown that the biblical creation narratives represent a considerable progress in relation to the mythologies then current because they liberate the created world from all pantheism and liberate man to transform nature.

We also agree with Albert Jacquard that the Gospel beatitudes present a revolutionary ethical project able to serve as a basis of practice for agnostics as well as believing men of science.

Value and Truth in the Fathers

Is there a Patristic Axiology?

Stuart George HALL

1. The Fathers and Philosophy

This is an attempt to explore what the Fathers of the Church might make of a discussion of axiology, which means a philosophical discussion of values, their basis and function. The Fathers were not philosophers, according to Christopher Stead.[1] He makes a major exception of Augustine, and a partial one for Origen. Boethius, John Philoponus, and Dionysius the Areopagite already belong to the dawning medieval scholasticism, when there was undoubtedly a Christian philosophy. We are chiefly concerned with the first four centuries, when Church writers knew and used the great philosophy of the past and the lively developments of the present. But they were often at pains to deny their own philosophical sources, and to impute them to their enemies.[2] The Fathers worked from Scripture and Tradition as their sources for Truth and Ethics. Philosophy, historic and contemporary, provides the unexpressed and often unconscious background, the definitions and presuppositions which they brought to interpreting their material. Furthermore, while not engaged in philosophy as such, they make fruitful contributions, at least in two of its recognized fields: "logic" and "ethics", less clearly the third field, "physics". In the first, while serious logic awaits Marius Victorinus and Augustine, earlier writers like Clement of Alexandria explored the theory of knowledge. Clement also reflects on ethics in a context of psychology and epistemology, as we shall see.[3]

---

[1] Stead, p. 69-83; references are to books and articles listed at the end of the chapter.

[2] For example, Tertullian's famous denunciation in *Praescr.* 7, *Quid Jerusalem Athenis* "What has Jerusalem to do with Athens? What has the Academy to do with the Church?", sits ill with his heavily Stoic physics, ontology and ethics; and for the emininently well-educated Gregory of Nyssa the imputation of Platonism and Aristotelianism is abusive: Gregory of Nyssa, *Contra Eunomium* II 404 (Jaeger 344); *Ibid.*, p. 411 (Jaeger 346). Conversely, Basil does not distinguish contemporary Neoplatonism from received tradition: *De sancto spiritu* 9,22f. See also Stead, p. 83.

[3] Stead p. 83-5.

The engagement with philosophy begins early.[4] An interesting case-study might be Marcion of Pontus. Before AD 140 he reformed the Scripture and tried to reform the Church. Harnack reckoned that unlike his gnostic contemporaries Marcion had no system, and his Christianity was "nothing but 'biblical theology'".[5] But when his teachings are considered, even allowing for the distorting glass of Tertullian and other hostile sources, there are striking comparisons to be made.

1. Marcion sets a Good God above the Just God of Moses' Law. No Platonist would object to the supremacy of the Good. In fact it is central to Plato, notably in the Republic, that supreme among the forms, that which holds all knowledge together, is the Good, τὸ ἀγαθόν. The fact that elsewhere the same highest reality is called τὸ ὄν, "Being" or "That which Is", merely confirms the fundamentally axiological character of Platonic epistemology: reality is value-laden.

2. In Marcion's account, the work of Creation is attributed to the Just God, an inferior Demiurge as in Plato's most popular work, the Timaeus. The Demiurge works according to Logos, rational principle, but is unable to cope with the evil arising from the recalcitrant material he must work with. Marcion speaks in terms of Paul's teaching on the failure of the Law to cope with the sinful Flesh: the Law of Moses is for Marcion given by the Creator, but too feeble to deal with the sin inherent in the flesh, which corrupts and imprisons the souls of men.

3. Marcion's stranger-God, the Good who saves, is unknown as Paul teaches, because "the world by its wisdom knows not God", "the world" being understood as "the God of this world". His creatures are imprisoned in the material of ignorance, condemnation and death, and come to know the Good God through an act of sheer revelation: Christ appears suddenly with the Good News from on high. Similarly, though not suddenly, in Plato the knowledge of the ultimate reality, as distinct from the shadowy acquaintance with contingent things, is open only to those who can rise up the ladder of realities and values to the contemplation of the highest Good, and such men are few and far between.

This comparison of Marcion with Plato is made solely to illustrate how one who, so far as we know, never discusses philosophers and philosophy except perhaps to disparage the "wise of this world", still works in a framework parallel to, or derived from, contemporary philosophy.

---

[4]   I exclude the New Testament itself from consideration, though the same principles may apply there.

[5]   "nichts anders [...] als 'biblische Theologie'", Adolf von Harnack, *Marcion. Das Evangelium der fremden Gott*, Leipzig, 1924 (*TU* 45), p. 93.

This does not mean that the Fathers have nothing more. Quite the contrary. Stead, having denied that they are philosophers, still adds a number of pages summarizing, and a number of chapters expounding, the way the Fathers develop and contribute to philosophical discussion.[6] Osborn argues that Christianity goes beyond Judaism and Greece by developing four patterns of ethical thought: righteousness, discipleship, faith, love.[7]

The great majority of early Christian writers relate to Platonism differently from Marcion. They may, like Justin Martyr, find his philosophy the way towards hearing and receiving the scriptures;[8] or they may, like Augustine, find the way illumined by the study of Platonic (actually Plotinian) books, for in the Platonists "God and his Word are everywhere implied".[9] Almost universal among them is the idea of an ineffable, infinite God, in principle One, who relates to the multiplicity, contingency and limitations of this world by an intermediary, his Son, often called Logos. This pattern is probably derived by Justin from the Middle Platonism of his contemporary Albinus, who attributed the created order to a "second mind", and later writers are influenced by the Neoplatonism in its various guises.

We shall illustrate this relationship through Clement of Alexandria, Augustine of Hippo, and the dogmatic Creeds of the 4th century.

2. Faith in Clement of Alexandria

Clement, writing at the end of the 2nd century and the beginning of the third, is not a clear writer. He moves between scripture, pagan literature and philosophy with more facility than discipline, so much so that some writers have despaired of finding any underlying system. Others find it possible to perceive, under his meandering discussions, some clear and useful ideas. Among the latter, Raoul Mortley is particularly helpful. We report here some ways in which Clement adapts elements of philosophical logic to his Christian sources in the matter of Faith, especially in Stromata II.

Faith (πίστις), the virtue of the faithful person (πιστός), is not a promising word where Platonism prevails. Epistemologically it operates in the area of opinion (δόξα) and speculation (εἰκασία), of contingent and uncertain knowledge. Not surprisingly Christians find themselves criticized for encouraging people to believe uncritically, by such writers

---

[6] Stead, especially p. 83-93.

[7] Osborn 11.

[8] Justin, *Dialogue* 2-7.

[9] Augustine, *Confessions* VIII 2,3.

as Lucian, Galen and Celsus.[10] Yet it is central to Christian thought and practice, which we usually call, "Christian faith". One can find some virtue in its passive sense as fidelity (πιστότης, *fides/fidelitas*).[11] Clement explores various epistemological avenues to demonstrate the centrality of faith. He acknowledges the fundamental status of faith in biblical tradition, as the means to knowing God, especially the famous verse of Isaiah, "If you do not believe, you will not understand".[12] Then he uses some interesting words: "Faith, which the Greeks disparage, deeming it empty and barbarous, is a voluntary preconception, an assent of devotion to God",[13] Strom. II,8,4. He sees this as corresponding to the Scripture: " [...] the substance of things hoped for, the proof of realities not seen".[14] The idea of a voluntary preconception (πρόληψις ἑκουσιός) is on his own testimony derived from Epicuros:[15] faith is therefore the apprehension appropriate to fundamental axioms or truths, to what in Aristotelian logic are the first principles (ἀρχαί), without which no argument can proceed. It is furthermore "an assent of devotion to God" (θεοσεβείας συγκατάθεσις). Here he uses a well-worn term of Stoic science and ethics, "assent", which is precisely the correct response to the divine Logos infusing the world. This is not merely the proper response to epistemological fundamentals; it is also the assent properly given to correct logical deductions. Far from being a slight and contemptible form of apprehension of the contingent, it is both fundamental and necessary. Furthermore, being itself the true and right response to the world, God and the facts of the case, it is also virtuous. So far is that true that Clement can invoke Plato in evidence that faith is "the mother of the virtues". Without the stability of purpose it entails, one may not become wise; certainly one cannot proceed to that *knowledge* (γνῶσις) which is the goal of Christian, and indeed of Platonic, devotion.

Clement of course regards the proper object of such faith to be God as revealed by his Word, which means Jesus Christ. He is in turn mediated by the Scriptures and by the Tradition of holy teachers in the Church. So there is an enrichment of the epistemology and axiology of the philosophers with the content of the Gospel. Much of what Clement writes is concerned with the kind of behavior instilled by the Word as the divine Schoolmaster, Paedagogos; his works are addressed to the

---

10   References in Mortley p. 109. Origen, *c. Cels.* I,9 is particularly illuminating.
11   Even Plato, *Laws* 630 b.c.; Mortley p. 111.
12   Isaiah 7,9, in the LXX ἐὰν μὴ πιστεύσητε, οὐδέ μὴ συνῆτε.
13   πίστις δέ, ἣν διαβάλλουσι κενήν καὶ βάρβαρον νομίζοντες Ἕλληνες, πρόληψις ἑκουσιός ἐστι, θεοσεβείας συγκατάθεσις
14   ἐλπιζομένων ὑπόστασις, πραγμάτων ἔλεγχος οὐ βλεπομένων, Hebrews 11,1.
15   Clement, *Strom.* II,16,3.

less sophisticated convert learning the foundations of faith and life. But in his later books, especially the Stromata, he is dealing with ways in which faith develops into knowledge (γνῶσις) in those who understand the parables or symbols which the Word provides. There is no direct apprehension of God, and the true gnostic is raised by divinely suggested mysteries to the apprehension of the supreme Reality.

3. Spiritual Reality and Divine Grace in Augustine

Augustine of Hippo records in *Confessions* VIII his famous surrender to the voice of God, his "conversion". Less well known is his earlier "conversion", recorded in *Confessions* VII. The relation between the two illustrates our theme well.

In the course of his autobiographical work, Augustine confesses from time to time the development of his ideas about God. Starting from the biblical literalism of rural African Catholics like his mother, he was swept along in his youth by the beautiful, dramatic and demanding mythology of the Manichees. This was failing him by the time he went to Rome, where he was still unable to escape the idea of God as a corporeal being, a view not uncommon in Christianity, and held in different forms by Stoics and Manichees. For a time he was with the Sceptics, whose Platonism led them to deny that knowledge was possible of anything beyond contingent acquaintance with the physical world (a true agnosticism). Then at Milan he came upon the "Platonic books", probably works of Plotinus, which were known in educated Christian circles in the Latin version of Marius Victorinus, or possibly Porphyry.[16] He read in these books, rationally argued, God and his Word, spiritually existing as true Light, and man's fall by turning from that true Light to physical things.

> Admonished by these books to return to myself, I entered into my inward soul, guided by thee. This I could do because thou wast my helper. And I entered, and with the eye of my soul – such as it was – saw above the same eye of my soul and above my mind the Immutable Light [...]. When I first knew thee, thou didst lift me up, that I might see that there was something to be seen, though I was not yet fit to see it. And thou didst beat back the weakness of my sight, shining forth upon me thy dazzling beams of light, and I trembled with love and fear. I realized that I was far away from thee in the land of unlikeness,[17] as if I heard thy voice from on high: 'I am the food of strong men; grow and you shall feed on me; nor shall you change me, like

---

[16] See O'Donnell II, p. 421-323.

[17] *in regione dissimilitudinis*; for this phrase from Plotinus and ultimately Plato himself, see O'Donnell II, p. 443-444.

the food of your flesh into yourself, but you shall be changed into my likeness.'[18]

Augustine was disappointed that he failed to sustain this vision,
which critics discuss in terms of "Plotinian ecstasy",[19] but which I
regard as a moment of intellectual vision: he became aware of, assented
by an act of συγκατάθεσις to, a great truth:

> I marveled that I now loved thee, and no fantasm in thy stead, and yet I was
> not stable enough to enjoy my God steadily. Instead I was transported to
> thee by thy beauty, and then presently torn away from thee by my own
> weight, sinking with grief into these lower things. This weight was carnal
> habit.[20]

The instability was due to the pressure to make a good marriage, and
his fleshly need for a mistress. It was at this point, probably, that the
priest Simplicianus directed him to compare the highly regarded Platonic books with the sacred scriptures, especially St John and St Paul.
The substance of this comparison is already in *Confessions* VII. There
he professes to find much of John's first chapter in the Platonic books

> [...] not indeed in the same words, but to the selfsame effect, enforced by
> many and various reasons that "in the beginning was the word, and the
> Word was with God, and the Word was God. All things were made by him,
> and without him was not anything made that was made". That which was
> made by him is "life, and the life was the light of men. And the light shined
> in darkness; and the darkness comprehended it not".

He found furthermore that the soul of man bears witness to this light,
and that he was in the world and the world knew him not.

> But that "he came unto his own, and his own received him not. And as many
> as received him, to them gave he the power to become the sons of God, even
> to them that believed on his name" – this I did not find.

Similarly he found the heavenly generation of the Son in John 1,13
and Philippians 2,6, but not the incarnation of John 1,14 or the conde-
scension to human form and death of Phil. 2,7-11.[21] He found in Paul
what the Platonists lacked:

> Whatever truth I had found [in the Platonists] was here [in Paul] combined
> with the exaltation of thy grace. Thus, he who sees must not glory as if he
> had not received, not only the things that he sees, but the very power of
> sight – for what does he have that he has not received as a gift? By this he is

---

[18] *Conf.* VII 10,16 (tr. Outler p. 146-147).
[19] O'Donnell II, p. 434-435.
[20] *Conf.* VII 17,23 (tr. Outler p. 150-151).
[21] *Conf.* VII, 9,13-14 (tr. Outler p. 144-145).

not only exhorted to see, but also to be cleansed, that he may grasp thee, who art ever the same.[22]

Here is the human side of the need for the Gospel history of the incarnation and death of Christ. The Platonic books say nothing of "the tears of confession, thy sacrifice, a troubled spirit, a broken and a contrite heart, the salvation of thy people, the espoused City, the earnest of the Holy Spirit, the cup of our redemption".[23] It is from here that Augustine goes on in *Confessions* VIII to tell of his interviews with Simplicianus, the stories of the conversion of Marius Victorinus to Christianity and of Pontitianus and his companion to monastic life, and to his own call from God through the words of St Paul.

This may seem remote from axiology, but it is not. The Neoplatonist sought, and experienced, illumination by the One, that which truly is. That is philosophical argument, though infused with religious tone. It is not exactly value-free: it is beautiful, and it requires, as Augustine felt acutely, an exacting morality. But it lacks the power, in the reflecting mind of the mature Augustine, of the Gospel of redemption to meet human needs. God is not just there to be seen if we are pure or clever enough. His ultimate reality reaches out to us in love, and invites us to respond likewise in love, faith and hope.

4. The Dogmatic Creeds of the 4th Century

To some the arguments about Christ's godhead and manhood, partly expressed in the official Creeds of the Church, represent a surrender of the original Gospel to arid formulations. Of the Chalcedonian Formula it has been written, "Jesus Christ disappears in the smokescreen of the two-nature philosophy. Formalism triumphs, and the living figure of the evangelical Redeemer is desiccated to a logical mummy".[24] In my view this is a mistake. It is true that the language and ideas are those of a philosophy often difficult and obscure to us. But it is not those ideas themselves which we should consider, but what the Fathers did with them.

First, there is the notion of one God the Father, maker of heaven and earth: in the final version of the Nicene/Constantinopolitan Creed, "and of all things visible and invisible". A Father of all must be the ungenerated First Cause, the Absolute One, who is the source of all besides. At this point we are not at variance with the kind of philosophy which

---

[22] *Conf.* VII, 21,27 (tr. Outler p. 155).

[23] *Conf.* VII, 21,27 (tr. Outler p. 155-156).

[24] G.L. Prestige, p. 146.

prevails: there is an ultimate Being, whose goodness admits no variation. Such a thought may penetrate the second clause too, inasmuch as between the contingent world and the Father there is One Lord, the Son, through whom all things were made; and that he is God from God, Light from Light, is within the possibility of a Neoplatonic Confession: we are still in Augustine's *Confessions* VII. But already, quoting 1 Corinthians 8,6, that is glossed with a name: "One Lord Jesus Christ". That, and the account which follows, moves the Nicene Creed into another kind of confession.

Having stated the glories and status of the Only Son, consubstantial with the Father, co-eternal with him ("Begotten of the Father before all worlds"), through whom all things were made, a fundamental move is made. "For us men and for our salvation he came down from heaven". This attributes to the Consubstantial Word a motive which is not always apparent in the philosophical sources of theological science: love of humanity, φιλανθρωπία. It is unthinkable to Aristotle that God should love the world or the people in it: he has better things to think about. The Fathers insist that God reaches out to mankind in love.[25] It is typical that Athanasius, arguing that the universe is made by the divine Word which proceeds from the Father, writes:

> The God of all is good and excellent (ἀγαθὸς καὶ ὑπέρκαλος) by nature. Therefore he is also kind (φιλάνθρωπός ἐστιν). For a good being would be envious of no one, so he envies nobody existence but rather wishes everyone to exist, in order to exercise his kindness (πάντας εἶναι βούλεται, ἵνα καὶ φιλανθρωπεύεσθαι δύνηται).[26]

The reference to envy (φθόνος) takes us back to the Fathers' favorite Platonic book, *Timaeus*:

> [The reason for creation is that the creator] was good, and in him that is good no envy arises ever concerning anything; and being devoid of envy he desired that all should be, so far as possible, like himself.[27]

Not surprisingly, when Athanasius moves on from creation to restoring the likeness of God in man through the Word's coming in the flesh, we find the word again:

> Our case (αἰτία) was the reason for him to come down, and our offence called forth the filanqrwpiva of the Word, so that the Lord came to us and appeared among men. We became the reason for his embodiment: he was

---

[25] See Lampe 1478, s.v. φιλανθρωπία B.

[26] *C. gentes* 41 (Thomson p. 112-115).

[27] Plato, *Timaeus* 29e.

generous (ἐφιλανθρωπεύσατο), so as both to be born and to appear in a human body.[28]

Thus the fundamental presuppositions are Platonic: God is good, envy-free, and invariable. But the relation to the world and men in the embodiment in Jesus Christ adds a necessary development: God cannot be perfect in goodness without the active φιλανθρωπία which human need, salvation and glory call for: "for us men and for our salvation he came down from heaven".

Thus the fundamental axiological principle of the philosophical tradition from Plato is accepted. The truly real, τὸ ὄντως ὄν, is to be identified as the absolute Good, with the converse implication that to be is better than not to be. But for the absolute Being to be perfectly good, concrete gestures or actions are needed, first for the creation of that which is not God, and then for its salvation, correction, restoration or glorification. There may be implications about the status of the *Logos* who mediates these good things, but however the status of the Son is resolved, the motivation is perfect goodness, expressed as love or *philanthropia*, in all the historic actions of God towards mankind, but supremely in his identification with needy man in Jesus Christ. It is not that God becomes less than perfectly good, and changeable in that sense, but that his permanency is identified as Love, active in grace.

The final section of the Nicene-Constantinopolitan Creed involves another reworking of classical philosophy. The classic statement of the deity of the Holy Spirit in the 4th Century is Basil of Caesarea's *De spiritu sancto*. We cannot examine it here, but it notoriously exploits a few biblical texts to make available all the Stoic ideas of a creative universe shot through with the immanent divine Spirit. But the Spirit is not of course the same as the *Stoic Logos/Pneuma*, since it is the Spirit who, as the Creed says, comes forth from the Father, is worshipped together with the Father and the Son, inspires the historic scriptures, and meets believers in the sacraments of the one holy catholic and apostolic Church. The Spirit is not merely a wisdom to which the wise conform, but the place of communion where, personally and historically, the individual believer comes into contact with the actions of the Father through the Son, and is caught up himself into that divine life, adoring the Father in the Son by inspiration of the Spirit.

A final axiological note might be in order. The moral implications of value were worked out in the Platonists and Stoics with the four Cardinal Virtues of prudence, fortitude, temperance and justice. These remain cardinal for the Fathers, but with shifts of emphasis and content (as

---

[28] *De inc.* 4 (Thomson 143; my own translation).

Osborn's treatment of the ethical pattern of righteousness/justice shews). But they are reshaped by the theological virtues: faith, a massively important virtue in the face of God's call and command, as Clement perceived; hope, which relates our personal destiny and the shape of cosmic existence as a totality to the same generous *philanthropia* of God's purpose; and love, which is the heart of God's own goodness, the proper object of human aspiration and the consummation of our hope.

References

Athanasius, (1971), *Contra Gentes and De Incarnatione*, edited and translated by Robert W. Thomson, Oxford (Oxford Early Christian Texts).

Augustine, (1992), *Confessions I, Introduction and text; II-III Commentary*, by James J. O'Donnell, Oxford.

Augustine, (1955), *Confessions and Enchiridion*, translated and edited by Albert C. Outler, London (*The Library of Christian Classics VII*).

Basile de Césarée, (1968), *Traité du Saint-Esprit*, Benoît Pruche (ed.), Paris, (Sources chrétiennes 17bis).

Clément d'Alexandrie, (1954), *Les stromates: Stromate II*. Intro. et notes de P. Th. Camelot/Texte grec et trad. de Cl. Mondésert, Paris (Sources chrétiennes 38).

A. Dihle, "Ethik": *RAC* 6, p. 646-796.

Adolf von Harnack, Marcion, (1924), *Das Evangelium der fremden Gott*, Leipzig (TU 45).

Raoul Mortley, (1973), *Connaissance religieuse et herméneutique chez Clément d'Alexandrie*, Leiden.

Iris Murdoch, (1970), *The sovereignty of the Good*, London.

Enrico Norelli, (2002), "Marcion: ein christliche Philsoph oder ein Christ gegen die Philosophie?": *Marcion und seine kirchengeschichtliche Wirkung. Marcion and his Impact on Church History. Vorträge der Internationales Fachkonferenz zu Marcion, gehalten vom 15.-18. August 2001 in Mainz.* Herausgegeben von Gerhard May und Katharina Greschat in Gemeinschaft mit Martin Meiser (*Texte und Untersuchungen zur Geschichte der altchristlichen Literatur 150*), Berlin/New York, p. 113-130.

Geoffrey W. H. Lampe (ed.), (1961), *A patristic Greek lexicon*, Oxford.

James J. O'Donnell: see Augustine, *Confessions I.*

Eric Osborn, (1976), *Ethical patterns in early Christian thought*, Cambridge.

G. L. Prestige, (1948), *Fathers and Heretics. Six studies in dogmatic faith with prologue and epilogue*, London (Bampton Lectures for 1940).

(George) Christopher Stead, (1990), *Philosophy in Christian Antiquity*, Cambridge 1994; based on: Theologie und Philosophie 1. Die Zeit der Alten Kirche, Stuttgart (Theologische Wissenshaft 14/4).

Robert W. Thomson: see Athanasius.

"Philosophy & Politics"

Open to thinkers from all countries and cultures who are not limiting their efforts to understand the processes of social institutions, but are raising questions about their goals and meaning, this series hopes to contribute to a renewal of political philosophy. Beyond the different disciplines of social sciences, ideological commitments and the limits of "national schools," philosophy is bound to pursue its universal enquiry on human wisdom in a world chaotically pushed towards greater unity.

Series directed by **Gabriel FRAGNIÈRE** *and* **Hendrik OPDEBEECK**

Series Titles

Robert Schuman. Neo Scholastic Humanism and the Re-Unification of Europe, Alan FIMISTER, No. 15, 2008, ISBN 978-90-5201-439-5

Science and Ethics. The Axiological Contexts of Science, Evandro AGAZZI & Fabio MINAZZI (eds.), No. 14, 2008, ISBN 978-90-5201-426-5

Rôles, action sociale et vie subjective. Recherches à partir de la phénoménologie de Michel Henry, Raphaël GÉLY, n° 13, 2007, 205 p., ISBN 978-90-5201-347-3

Identités et monde commun. Psychologie sociale, philosophie, société, Raphaël GÉLY, n° 12, 2006 (3e tirage 2008), 206 p., ISBN 978-90-5201-416-6

Feminists Contest Politics and Philosophy, Lisa N. GURLEY, Claudia LEEB, Anna Aloisia MOSER (eds.), No. 11, 2005, 272 p., ISBN 978-90-5201-252-0

The Importance of Ideals. Debating Their Relevance in Law, Morality, and Politics, Wibren VAN DER BURG & Sanne TAEKEMA (eds.), No. 10, 2004, 274 p., ISBN 978-90-5201-226-1

Social Sciences and Political Change. Promoting Innovative Research in Post-Socialist Countries, Robin CASSLING & Gabriel FRAGNIÈRE (eds.), No. 9, 2003, 297 p., ISBN 978-90-5201-168-4

Working-Class Women in Elite Academia. A Philosophical Inquiry, Claudia LEEB, No. 8, 2004, 220 p., ISBN 978-90-5201-979-6

L'autonomie éthique. Débat démocratique et vérité, Giuseppe G. NASTRI, n° 7, 2002, 200 p., ISBN 978-90-5201-972-7

Plus est en l'homme. Le personnalisme vécu comme humanisme radical, Vincent TRIEST, n° 6, 2000 (4ᵉ tirage 2004), 214 p., ISBN 978-90-5201-922-2

Enlightenment and Genocide, the Contradictions of Modernity, James KAYE & Bo STRÅTH (eds.), No. 5, 2000, 278 p., ISBN 978-90-5201-919-2

Les défis du nationalisme moderne. Québec, Catalogne, Écosse, Michael KEATING, n° 4, 1997, 298 p., ISBN 978-90-5201-705-1

Pour une philosophie de l'opinion et de la citoyenneté. Essai européen de mémoire et de stratégie sophistiques, Henri WIBAULT, n° 3, 1996, 389 p., ISBN 978-90-5201-514-9

L'obligation morale et l'éthique de la prospérité, Gabriel FRAGNIÈRE, n° 2, 1993, 270 p., ISBN 978-90-5201-304-6

L'État-providence. Un débat philosophique / The Welfare State. A Philosophical Debate, Guus (A.) J.M. VAN WEERS (ed.), No. 1, 1986, 164 p., ISBN 978-90-7077-612-1

Peter Lang – The website

Discover the general website of the Peter Lang publishing group:

www.peterlang.com